FAITHFUL NARRATIVES

FAITHFUL NARRATIVES

HISTORIANS, RELIGION, AND THE CHALLENGE OF OBJECTIVITY

EDITED BY ANDREA STERK
AND NINA CAPUTO

CORNELL UNIVERSITY PRESS
Ithaca and London

First published 2014 by Cornell University Press

First printing, Cornell Paperbacks, 2014

Printed in the United States of America

Library of Congress Cataloging-in-Publication Data

    Faithful narratives : historians, religion, and the challenge of objectivity / Andrea Sterk and Nina Caputo, editors.
       pages cm
    Includes bibliographical references and index.
    ISBN 978-0-8014-5182-9 (cloth : alk. paper)
    ISBN 978-0-8014-7857-4 (pbk. : alk. paper)
    1. History—Religious aspects. 2. Religion—History. 3. Religion—Historiography. I. Sterk, Andrea, editor of compilation. II. Caputo, Nina, editor of compilation. III. Elm, Susanna. Pagan challenge, Christian response. Contains (work):
    BL65.H5F35   2014
    200.9—dc23   2013032205

Cloth printing   10 9 8 7 6 5 4 3 2 1
Paperback printing   10 9 8 7 6 5 4 3 2 1

CONTENTS

ACKNOWLEDGMENTS

The present volume is the result of a three-semester series at the University of Florida in 2008–9, followed by a session on the same topic cosponsored by the American Historical Society and the American Society of Church History in Boston in 2011. The idea to organize this series on religion in history was spurred partly by the personal interest of the organizers and our students, partly by the professional challenges that we face on a daily basis in our teaching and research. Our goal was to foster a sustained cross-disciplinary discussion that would include undergraduate and graduate students, faculty, and members of the general community. Toward this end, each of the twelve visiting scholars addressed the broader community in a public lecture and led a seminar for graduate students and faculty that engaged pedagogical challenges as well as research. We were pleased that this multilayered series fostered an ongoing conversation that finds its most concrete expression in this book.

Because this project has developed over the course of several years, we are indebted to a large number of institutions and individuals to whom we would like to express our gratitude. The initial funding for this project was provided by the Wabash Center for Teaching and Learning in Theology and Religion and the Gladys Krieble Delmas Foundation. Grants from both these institutions helped subsidize expenses associated with the graduate seminar that ran in tandem with the lecture series.

While we could not have put together this series without these external sources of funding, the series and resulting volume would have also been impossible without the cooperation and support of numerous departments and centers at the University of Florida. At a time in which the humanities are under siege—both financially and intellectually—it was particularly gratifying that the lecture series received significant support from more than a dozen units on campus: the Department of History, the Bob Graham Center for Public Service, the Center for the Humanities and the Public Sphere, the College of Liberal Arts and Sciences, the Center for Jewish Studies, the UF Office for Research, the Alexander Grass Chair in Jewish Studies, the Rothman

Distinguished Lecture in Classics, the Richard J. Milbauer Chair in History, the Department of Classics, the Department of Religion, the Center for African Studies, the Center for Latin American Studies, the Center for Women's Studies and Gender Research, and the Center for Medieval and Early Modern Studies. The Christian Study Center of Gainesville also provided financial as well as institutional support for the project as a whole.

Alongside institutional sponsors we would be remiss to omit a few specific individuals who contributed to the success of the series and its legacy in this volume: Jack Kugelmass, Richard Horner, Bonnie Effros, and Joseph Spillane, and our graduate assistants Anna Lankina and Valentina Istrate. Anna has been involved in the project from beginning to end, and we are especially grateful for her work on the index. We would also like to thank Peter Potter, our editor at Cornell University Press, and the anonymous readers who reviewed the manuscript. We are perhaps most grateful to Mitch Hart and Howard Louthan, who endured the planning and execution of this project, from the first day to the very last, with excellent humor. (We would also like to thank them for taking Anthony Grafton to a local nature reserve to see the alligators, and even more, for bringing him back in one piece.)

Finally, we are deeply indebted and grateful to the contributors themselves. All of them were intellectually generous and gracious during their campus visits—even as they endured the difficulties of interminable airport layovers and breakneck schedules once they arrived. They were also encouraging and supportive of our students, patient with the editors as the volume made its way through the long publication process, and unflaggingly enthusiastic about the project as a whole. We hope that this book will be as engaging for the reader as it has been for the editors and contributors.

FAITHFUL NARRATIVES

Introduction

The Challenge of Religion in History

ANDREA STERK AND NINA CAPUTO

Contemporary Western society presents a baffling array of religious options, opinions, and extremes, from militant secularism to radical fundamentalism. The success of antireligious writers like Richard Dawkins and Christopher Hitchens suggests that atheism is not simply on the rise but an increasingly potent force to be contended with in public discourse. Churchgoing may be on the decline in Europe, but there is no shortage of devotion in other parts of the world, especially in Africa, Asia, and Latin America, where religious fervor has kept pace with processes of secular democratic reform.[1] On the local level, within our own town of Gainesville, Florida, site of a major public research university, diverse religious groups are thriving on campus. And in the town itself, the inflammatory anti-Islamic rhetoric of fundamentalist pastor Terry Jones has garnered national and international media attention. His threatened Qur'an burnings in fall 2010, his trial of the Qur'an and its subsequent "execution by fire" in spring 2011 and again in spring 2012, inevitably bring to mind the practices of the medieval Inquisition.[2] Most recently his promotion of a provocative anti-Islamic video helped spark fatal protests in the Middle East.[3] Vigorously denounced by almost all the churches and synagogues in Gainesville and around the world, such incidents expose the intensity of religious feeling that still motivates large segments of our population both in and beyond the West.

1

While by no means new to the twenty-first century, these conflicting religious impulses pose an ongoing challenge to scholars, who must grapple with the role of religion and the interpretation of religious developments in history. Some historians exclude religious phenomena entirely, leaving only economy, society, and politics as valid subjects of historical inquiry.[4] On the other end of the spectrum is the notion that particular moments in history are themselves sacred, for example, the parting of the Red Sea and conquest of the promised land, the Virgin birth, Muhammad's Hajj, or even the signing of the U.S. Constitution.[5] Such critical or defining events are deemed by the faithful to be beyond the purview of secular history or best left beyond the probe of skeptical historians. To be sure, few scholars today would argue that only religious insiders can adequately understand a tradition's practices and ideals, and on the other side, few would exclude religious phenomena from the study of history altogether or relegate it to the domain of seminaries and divinity schools. Yet recent scholarly trends and approaches have raised fresh dilemmas. Teleological or triumphalist narratives of religious history, which marked the scholarship of an earlier age, have given way to a reductionism that may equally distort the meaning of religion for the communities being studied. And increased attention to methodological issues as well as postmodern concerns have posed new challenges for historians: the complex role of memory, the ambiguity of evidence and its interpretation, the function of narrative, and the tension between text and representation, to name only a few.

It is fair to say that many of today's historians of religion find the task of writing as well as teaching religious history an increasingly precarious endeavor.[6] On the one side, seeking to be sensitive to religious experience and conviction while, on the other, maintaining intellectual and scholarly integrity, historians of religion require almost supernatural navigational skill. The religiously committed historian may have to negotiate particularly tricky currents.[7] An emphasis on the personal combined with the call for methodological transparency has encouraged openness about one's own religious convictions or orientation. Some offer such admissions as an expression of intellectual transparency or honesty, recognizing the elusive nature of objectivity; others meanwhile advocate outright partisanship on the grounds that all knowledge is radically subjective, that objectivity is not merely elusive but illusory.[8] Moreover, in an age when public figures are expected to wear their religious beliefs and commitments on their sleeves, and the failure to do so is viewed with increasing suspicion and hostility, historians who are agnostic or nonbelievers, even those who treat religious belief sympathetically, may face distinctive pressures of their own. The task of teaching religious history in a critical, analytical vein—whether in public, nondenominational, or religiously affiliated institutions—can be fraught with tension when students bristle at any challenge to a traditional religious narrative that many have come to accept as beyond dispute. And all historians of religion—those who work on their own tradition as well as those who cross confessional boundaries—are subject to false assumptions about their identity or suspicions about their motives for pursuing such research.

Yet despite such tensions, it has become increasingly important to address the subject of religion in our own day. Whatever the impact of secularism and postmodernism, religious concepts and language lie at the foundation of political, scientific, and cultural life, as well as many of the conflicts that plague the modern world. In recent years world events have brought religion into the center of history in ways unanticipated even a generation ago. A variety of fundamentalisms have pushed religious faith from the private to the public sphere, provoking "fundamentalist-like" agnostic or atheistic reactions against religion.[9] Amid renewed concern about the role of religion in society and global politics, historians of religion have faced new questions and occasionally assumed new roles in attempts to understand or explain the complexities of world events. While religion has come to occupy a central place in the public arena, many historians in the past fifty years have shifted their focus to the personal, the private, and the role of non-elites in history, examining different kinds of sources and emphasizing bottom-up rather than top-down processes in religious history.[10] Attention to the private sphere of religious practice and experience has also raised new questions for historians regarding the nature and forms of religious evidence, the interpretation of religious phenomena, and the meaning of religion itself for particular communities in specific eras and social contexts. And recent developments remind us that we must take religious ideas and practices as seriously as political, economic, or social ones—forces with which they are often intertwined—in the making of human history and therefore in our analyses and accounts of the human past.

Motivated in part by the widespread public ignorance of religious traditions and communities that so influence contemporary realities and discourse, the contributors to this volume address perennial scholarly debates as well as newer methodological questions. The book presents the work of twelve scholars whose research and teaching have exemplified compelling strategies for negotiating the difficulties inherent in this increasingly important subfield of historical study. In essays ranging chronologically from Late Antiquity to the twenty-first century, historians engage with particular religious issues and a range of methodological questions in a theoretically critical yet sensitive manner. The title *Faithful Narratives* functions on at least two levels. First, encompassing widely varied case studies and approaches, it nonetheless captures the unifying focus on faith as a historical force that had consequences in the lives of individuals and the development of communities. Second, the essays themselves are narratives that attempt to be faithful to the demands of critical analysis and sensitive to the beliefs, ideals, and struggles of their religious subjects. As suggested by the subtitle, then, these studies address the challenges of integrating a responsible scholarly engagement with religious texts, practices, people, and power into historical analysis and narrative.

We do not intend for this volume to be comprehensive in scope. Most of the essays grapple with issues generated in a specifically "Western" Christian context and are refracted through a double Christian lens. The treatment of Judaism and Islam, for example, is shaped by the dominant Christian culture of the period and region under investigation. Moreover, the essays inevitably reflect the scholarly discourse of a largely secular Protestant North American intellectual environment in which the authors teach and pursue their research. Despite these limitations, we have attempted to strike a balance in our focus on Judaism, Christianity, and Islam that mirrors particular religious landscapes in their historical contexts.

The essays are organized chronologically around central themes for the study of religion in history: textual traditions and authority, interreligious discourse, practices of piety, and notions of community and identity. Part I probes the ways in which religious texts and ideas have shaped premodern cultures and subcultures and how they continue to reverberate in the modern world. Authors in this section examine disputed sites of textual authority (Elm and Nirenberg) or notions of poverty and labor (Brown and Van Engen), reflecting on the enduring influence of these premodern debates in contemporary scholarly discourse or in modern perspectives on religion, economy, and society. Part II focuses on the reading, writing, redaction, and proliferation of religious texts in the early modern period. Although distinctive interpretations contributed to the construction of confessional boundaries (Eire), the use and assimilation of textual traditions across religious boundaries also come to the fore (Ruderman, Grafton, Mills). The essays in this section explore not only the construction and crossing of religious boundaries but also the permeability of those boundaries and the interpenetration of religious values and ideas in what have most often been regarded as distinct traditions. Revealing the subtle shift from the premodern to the modern era, part III continues the emphasis on sacred texts, specifically examining their role in promoting individual agency, communal identity, or public piety (Mack, Heschel, Sanneh, Noll). Particularly evident in this section is both the legacy and the resonance of premodern religion in diverse contexts of the modern world, a thread that runs through the volume as a whole.

Despite the diversity of topics covered, several significant points of convergence link the individual chapters. All of the studies included in this volume deal with either sacred texts and their interpretation or religious practice and experience. Authors in each section examine how texts gained authoritative or canonical status within particular communities, conflicts over interpretation, or the role of texts in interreligious discourse. Others, meanwhile, investigate the rituals, practices, and spiritual experiences that marked the religious life of particular communities from antiquity to modernity. Moreover, some of the groups or individuals considered—holy wanderers, apocalyptic figures, female prophets—were located on the peripheries of what is considered mainstream if not orthodox religious traditions and hence bring the spirituality and experiences of those on the margins into historical focus. Such thematic overlap between sections illustrates the recurrence or persistence of central themes and common analytical challenges for historians working in all eras and geographical regions.

Indeed, despite our decision to organize the essays along chronological lines, the actual content of many of these essays challenges typical divisions between the premodern and the modern and even the very notion of modernization as it relates to the study of religion. Whether we consider sources of moral, intellectual, or political authority; notions of work and leisure; conceptions of the rich and the poor and obligations of the one toward the other; questions of ethnic and national identity; beliefs about gender, agency, and the self; or the meaning of magic, superstition, or miracles, we find deep religious layers still at work in modern assumptions about the nature of reality and the nature of human involvement in society. Historians dare not ignore these formative religious attitudes, practices, and teachings, which remain deeply ingrained in the contemporary world. Indeed, as David Nirenberg has noted, historians of religion in recent years have recognized that pressing questions about the interrelationship of the three Abrahamic religions have created distinctive opportunities for the study of the past to intervene in the present.[11]

Closely connected to the premodern/modern divide that this volume attempts to mitigate is the barrier between the religious and the secular. Indeed, the vast majority of intellectuals equate modernity with secularization, de facto removing serious engagement with religion or religious ideas as such from the realm of modern historical study and absolving themselves of the obligation to interrogate the contours and parameters of secularism as a practice and ideology—in other words, to historicize secularism. Similarly, the secular-religious dichotomy has affected the very shape of the historical discipline. For example, as Susanna Elm shows with regard to the study of late antiquity, we find "secular" historians studying the life and writings of the pagan Roman emperor Julian while "confessional" or "church" historians focus on the leading Christian theologians of the same period, rarely bringing such figures into dialogue even though they were direct contemporaries who knew and interacted with each other.[12] Further difficulties arise when scholars adopt *either* a religious history frame, which expands evidence of religion or religious communities in shaping social and cultural norms to undue proportions, *or* a secular frame, which assigns religion a separate, secondary, and often insignificant role. This artificial barrier, then, has tended to distort or limit our understanding of historical developments in all periods.[13] Closely connected with an overly simple divide between the secular and the religious is the fact that we have promoted a master narrative of secularization that no longer seems tenable.[14] The story is familiar: thanks to the philosophical interventions of Enlightenment thinkers and the political consequences of the French and American revolutions, church and state were disaggregated. As a result, the church was stripped of its powers of coercion, and expression of religious faith was relegated to the private sphere.

To be sure, some historians have resisted the urge to perpetuate this narrative, endeavoring instead to uncover the deeply religious convictions and practices underlying many of the notions we consider "secular."[15] Most recently Brad Gregory's revisionist study of the Reformation and its legacy has undercut long dominant notions about the roots of secularism and pluralism in the contemporary Western world. He not only exposes the religious roots of these developments but also shows that secularism has been no more successful in living up to the ideals commonly associated with it than were the medieval church or the Protestant Reformation.[16] In a similar vein, several studies in this volume challenge reigning notions of secularization and its history. Analyzing medieval representations of labor and modern scholars' efforts to understand the meaning of work in the Middle Ages, John Van Engen finds notions of the worldly or the secular within medieval as much as modern culture and medieval religious ideals underlying modern secular attitudes toward labor. Tracking changing boundaries between the natural and "supernatural" worlds, Carlos Eire explores the very definition of religion, examining the evidence and significance of shifting conceptual structures we label secularization. Incorporating perspectives from the global south, Lamin Sanneh shows how religious developments in Africa have forced a reappraisal of the received wisdom about secularization.

Phyllis Mack analyzes the spiritual authority and ideals of two female religious leaders in late eighteenth-century England. Their religious consciousness alongside their challenge to contemporary gender roles, she argues, reflects the complex processes that scholars have too easily equated with secularization and modernization. All of these studies approach religion and religious expression as integral to the very framework of social organization from late antiquity to the modern period.

While these essays challenge still largely dominant notions of modernity and secularization, they also build on significant developments in historical scholarship on religion. The crumbling of traditional binaries—center/periphery, on the one hand, and orthodoxy/heresy, on the other, comes to the fore in essays examining those on the margins of their respective religious communities. We learn, for example, of certain Jewish scholars' fascination with Islam, radically different notions of the holy among eastern ascetics, and the religious agency and moral authority of Quaker and Methodist women. Traditional geographic as much as theological markers are also reassessed. As Ken Mills and Lamin Sanneh remind us, Christian expansion in early modern Latin America and late modern Africa can no longer be considered peripheral to the history of a dominant European Christianity; indeed recent developments in non-Western Christianity suggests a hemispheric shift in the religion's center of gravity.[17] And while religious institutions and elites receive their due, these essays also bring into focus religious practices and ideas we associate with popular piety. Local context, developments from below, and beliefs of those on the presumed fringes of society must be taken seriously in any historical study of religion that aims at a responsible representation of its role in a given cultural, intellectual, or political climate.

Assumptions about clear-cut boundaries, like traditional binaries, have shaped and occasionally distorted modern views of particular religions or interreligious relations; yet in different ways scholars have begun to challenge those imagined boundaries demonstrating that they were more often negotiated than fixed. In keeping with these new perspectives, authors in this volume examine the interaction between Jewish-Christian, Christian-pagan, Muslim-Christian, and Jewish-Muslim communities and individuals. For example, Susannah Heschel shows that Jewish scholars who immersed themselves in the study of Islam—some to the point of conversion—tested the boundaries between religious, political, and cultural modes of public expression. She argues that this engagement with Muslim literature and culture, which persisted until the Second World War, enabled some Jewish scholars to fashion themselves as intermediaries between eastern and Western aesthetics and theology. By forging a middle ground, they helped to relieve the social and political pressures Jews experienced in late-nineteenth- and early twentieth-century Europe.

Several authors employ another common methodological strategy: reading the sacred text as a site of contact, conflict, or disputed authority between established religious communities and their outsiders or among members of the same religious community. David Nirenberg examines contested readings of the Bible and the Qur'an both between and within religious traditions. He ultimately affirms the potential of Jewish, Christian, and Muslim scriptural hermeneutics to be self-critical without requiring relativism or negating revelation. Reassessing perceived boundaries between Christian and pagan culture in late antiquity, Susanna Elm traces a protracted struggle by members of a relatively homogeneous elite—consisting of theologians and Greco-Roman philosophers—for control over normative and canonical texts. In a similar register, Anthony Grafton and David Ruderman address Christian scholars' pursuit of the skills and resources necessary to produce and study Jewish books with the birth of the printing press, which played a significant role in relocating the boundaries between Judaism and Christianity. Jewish scholars had to negotiate carefully in sharing skills and knowledge that had been strictly guarded by Jewish elites who were protective of theological and political autonomy and who used their specialized knowledge as a means of exerting some control over the version of Judaism that emerged from European publishing houses and universities. Turning to the identity-forming role of the Bible, Lamin Sanneh shows how vernacular translation of the sacred text shaped the nations of modern Africa, challenging widely accepted postcolonial assumptions about the colonial project. In a similar vein, Mark Noll explores the construction of a powerful common discourse based on biblical language and motifs, both Jewish and Christian, that undergird American public and political culture.

Approaching religious texts and traditions in a way that is neither totalizing nor reductionist, the essays collected here reflect the seemingly obvious yet no less challenging objective that John Van Engen stated a generation ago: "Any study of religious culture must take religion seriously."[18] A reflection on interpretations of the Christian Middle Ages, often distorted by the failure to do justice to faith or belief as a dynamic motivating force, Van Engen's thoughtful reminder could well be applied to the study of religious developments in any historical period. In this volume, then, authors devote significant attention to the ways in which psychological, political, sociological, and economic factors interact with and shape religious ideals and religious communities in diverse settings and periods. Yet at the same time, historians express concern about the limitations of social scientific tools and models in the study of religion. Phyllis Mack, for example, describes the inadequacy of psychology, specifically current theories of agency, to adequately account for the reality of religious women's behavior, experiences, and choices.[19] Common conceptual formulations or theoretical frameworks used to analyze religious beliefs or practices may have explanatory force today that would have been completely lost on the individuals and communities we study and may significantly misrepresent the meaning of religious rituals or convictions for those believers. And despite the tendency of many historians to interpret religious beliefs primarily as symptoms of a particular sociopolitical or cultural climate or to view religion as a component of another more tangible matrix of power or identity, religion can be a cause as much as an effect of social, economic, or political change. For example, Peter Brown's analysis of a religious struggle over the meaning of work and the definition of "the poor" in late antiquity shows how theological principles and their institutional application affected the economy and society of entire regions for centuries. Moreover, the victory in this struggle of one religious ideal over the other has shaped even modern models of an economically divided society and our modern conscience concerning the duties of the rich toward the poor. Similarly, challenges to traditional beliefs about death and purgatory in the Protestant Reformation had significant material consequences, engendering what Carlos Eire has described as no less than an "economic revolution." In short, these essays treat religion as an entity sui generis, a causative force in history rather than merely a symptom of social or political change.

Indeed, the study of religious beliefs and practices in particular historical settings not only reveals their socioeconomic implications but also illumines ongoing debates on the human condition, the dignity of humanity, or the very notion of humanness. Perhaps nowhere is the issue of the human more explicit in this volume than in Ken Mills's treatment of an early modern missionary's chronicle of his outward and inward journey across the desert of Pariacaca in Peru. Drawing from a rich apostolic narrative tradition, the friar's chronicle, sensitively and empathetically analyzed by Mills, not only reveals the lessons he has learned "about little known peoples and new corners of the exterior world" but also draws readers into his own interior spiritual journey of suffering and deliverance, an intentionally emulative narrative that exposes both the frailty of human existence and the meaning of human experience. As they explore the value and meaning of work, miraculous phenomena, notions of the sacred, questions of agency and authority, or emotions and the religious self, other studies grapple with fundamental human issues that have long posed points of tension for believers and their communities. What often comes to light are the ways in which connections with other religious traditions shaped individual or communal identity. Exchanges of religious texts and ideas involved complex human interactions that might reveal the transcendence of human relationships as much as the fragility of human understanding. The fundamental connection between religion and notions of the human that permeates this volume helps to explain the dilemma and yet the importance of the personal that often arises in academic discussions of religion. Though historians rarely reflect directly on this dimension of their work, it is implicit in the questions they raise, the approaches they take, and the meanings they ascribe to the evidence they study. However open to critique, correction, and argument a given historian may be, any interpretation of religious events or experiences inevitably passes through the prism of the personal.

Finally, although these essays focus on historiographical and methodological issues in historical scholarship on religion, the challenges scholars face in research often carry over into the classroom setting. A recent treatment of pedagogy in the journal of the American Historical Association described the temptation to avoid discomfiting questions or conflicts by presenting religion in functional terms: "Whatever it might mean to the believer, religion is 'really' a form of community building, or an ideology that supports the status quo, or the pre-reflective source of normative impulses. Reduced to its function in society in this way, religion is better thought of as being 'about something else' rather than in terms that attempt, at least, to plumb its perhaps ineffable meaning for adherents."[20] Thus words like *sacrifice, redemption, conversion, repentance,* or *ecstasy* are not understood in terms of their stated meaning or their meaning for historical actors, but as pointers to other, allegedly more profound meanings: poverty, social marginality, sexual desire, political ambition. Just as in historical research and writing on religion, the tendency in the classroom has been to reduce religion to its lowest common denominator or to attribute religious sentiments or experience to something else. In religiously affiliated as well as secular colleges and universities, historians have tended to avoid or talk around religious beliefs rather than attempt to understand or explain them. That these concerns are paramount is reflected in our commitment to make pedagogy alongside scholarship an important consideration in this volume. Scholars need to take stock of religion in the history classroom as well as the historical monograph. Whether explicitly or implicitly, several essays address the pedagogical challenges posed by the critical study of religion and religious themes in history.[21]

Indeed this volume is intended to help pave the way forward in the study, analysis, and teaching of religion in history. It is our hope that these essays will serve scholars and students as models of serious engagement with the social, intellectual, and experiential dimensions of religion in the lives of individuals and communities. We also hope that the approaches taken and the questions raised will stimulate further research and conversation that contributes to our understanding of both the challenge of religion in history and the challenge of history to religion. To the extent that we succeed in these modest aims we will have not only provided models for historical scholarship but will help prepare students and future citizens for sensitive reflection on and meaningful engagement with our pluralistic, postmodern, yet no less deeply religious world.

PART ONE

Late Antique and Medieval Religious Debates and Their Modern Implications

CHAPTER 1

Pagan Challenge, Christian Response

*Emperor Julian and Gregory of Nazianzus
as Paradigms of Interreligious Discourse*

SUSANNA ELM

On December 11, 361, a man called Julian
arrived in Constantinople, a city at the time also known as the New Rome.[1]
Julian entered this city as the sole ruler of the Roman Empire and as the
legitimate successor of his recently deceased cousin Constantius. Later, the
Emperor Julian became famous, known as the Apostate, because he had
reverted from his Christian religion back to the religion of the gods of the
Greeks and the Romans. As such, he has been a subject of plays, romance
novels, poems, and literary works by authors such as Henrik Ibsen, Vladimir
Majakovskij, Gore Vidal, and Constantine Cavafy. In addition, hardly a year
goes by without the publication of a scholarly monograph on the emperor.

Scholars who write about Julian are, as a rule, historians of the Roman
Empire, "secular" historians who look at the later Roman Empire from the
perspective of social, imperial, and political history. Here the Emperor Julian
stands out among his peers, that is, other Roman emperors, because together
with Marcus Aurelius, he is the only Roman emperor whose personal writings we possess. Indeed, Julian wrote a great deal, far more than Marcus Aurelius, whom he considered a model, because he wished to explain himself and
his actions to persons that mattered to him: members of the Greek-speaking
elite of the Roman Empire, also known as the *oikoumenē*. Julian's reasons for
writing were, on the face of it, straightforward. As Caesar, the second most
important person in the empire, Julian had challenged the supremacy of the

15

reigning Augustus, his cousin Constantius. Julian had, in fact, been a usurper, and he was the first to acknowledge this. While marching to engage the ruling emperor in battle, he also engaged in a veritable letter writing campaign. He composed letters to the Senate in Constantinople and to cities in the Western part of the empire he already controlled—Rome, Corinth, Sparta, Athens, in sum, cities with a great degree of cultural cachet—to persuade his audience of the legitimacy, indeed divinely preordained inevitability, of his actions.

Writing about the divine in relation to his imperial mandate was to become one of Julian's central preoccupations. Thus, immediately after his arrival in Constantinople, he invited a wide circle of persons to his court and engaged them (and through them all his subjects) in philosophical debates, in which he proclaimed his own perspectives and positions regarding the correct way to rule the empire as a person chosen to rule by the gods. These ideas were preserved and subsequently published. No Roman emperor wrote more and no Roman emperor is therefore better known to modern historians than Julian.[2]

Surprisingly, however, few of the modern historians writing about the Emperor Julian are actually interested in much of what he wrote. In part, this may be explained by the content of these writings, treatises about gods such as the Great Mother of the Gods, also known as Cybele, or about Zeus, whom Julian equated with the Sun or Helios, phrased in the highly abstract language of Neoplatonism. Julian's abstract philosophical treatises, for example on the relation between the transcendent One, or Zeus-Helios, and the sublunar sphere of the material world, are rarely of interest even to those historians who are concerned with his religious views, because Julian also expressed these views in the more concrete forms of imperial edicts and laws, the stuff true histories are made of. Moreover, Julian had been fairly straightforward about his political as well as religious decisions. The reason he had offered for his attacks against the ruling emperor, certain to result in civil war, was in fact that Constantius had murdered Julian's entire family, and that he had done so as a Christian. Thus Julian hated Constantius and the Christianity he represented, converted back to the gods of the Greeks and Romans, and became known as the Apostate or deserter.

Modern historians of Julian are even less interested in another set of writings with religious overtones, those composed by Christians, better known as Fathers of the Church, who made the emperor into the infamous Apostate. Methodologically speaking, this is deplorable, because these Christian men belonged nearly without exception to the very elite whose opinion Julian sought to sway. Further, it was they who through their writings determined the emperor's long future as the Apostate and Anti-Christ, a characterization he only escaped as a consequence of the Enlightenment and the works of Montesquieu and his successors. These Christian elite men included Basil of Caesarea, Ambrose of Milan, Jerome, Augustine of Hippo, and most prominently, Gregory of Nazianzus, the protagonist of the remainder of this paper. These men were fully aware of Julian's proffered reasons for reverting to the gods of the Greeks and the Romans, as he called them, because of his murderous cousin, whom these authors often praised as a model Christian emperor. Not only were they aware of Julian's philosophical treatises on the nature of the gods, which to them were not so abstract because they wrote in the same register, but they were also directly affected by the emperor's laws regarding religion. Julian, his actions and his writings, thus elicited a phenomenal response on the part of the Christian members of the elite, terrified by the specter that this emperor could find an imperial imitator at any moment.[3]

Historiographical Impasse: Pagan versus Christian

The Emperor Julian and Gregory of Nazianzus, the most important of his Christian adversaries, are, in effect, representative for two different yet related matters. First, Gregory of Nazianzus's entire literary oeuvre, which remains foundational for Christian orthodoxy to this day, is paradigmatic for the response of Julian's Christian subjects. Second, the engagement of modern scholars with Emperor Julian and his Christian opponents is indicative of the ways in which modern scholars address religion, here Christianity, and what is commonly known as paganism. Scholars engaged with Julian, that is, historians, pay scant attention to Gregory of Nazianzus's ample writings, in which he made Julian into the Apostate. Conversely, scholars who traditionally deal with men such as Gregory, Basil of Caesarea, and Augustine, that is, scholars of early Christianity, patristics, and theology, do not deal with the Emperor Julian. The reasons for such mutual disinterest are not difficult to parse. Julian the Emperor, the "Apostate," and Gregory of Nazianzus, "the Theologian," are emblematic for the relationship between Christianity and the later Roman Empire and its scholarly conceptualization. This relationship between Rome and Christianity continues to be cast in the familiar binary mode of the grand narrative. According to this narrative, the Roman Empire declined and fell soon after Christianity had triumphed and thus forced Romans to become pagans, destined to fade away, at the very latest when Christianized barbarians arrived at its gates. We are all familiar with the many variations of this theme. Such narratives assume, of course, that the Roman Empire and Christianity acted as distinct entities, oil and water, preserving their essential nature even when thrown together. Here the Roman Empire of the pagan gods and there Christianity, catapulted into the Greco-Roman world fully formed. Of course, recent scholarship has modified and nuanced such binary narratives to a considerable degree.

Yet old dichotomies are hard to shake, and the division of the late Roman world into pagans and Christians has proven particularly resilient. Because of the manner in which our modern scholarly disciplines are arranged, scholars of history still pay insufficient attention to phenomena that are, broadly speaking, religious, and scholars who specialize in theology—even though they may pursue "historical theology"—rarely acknowledge the historical context in which "their" authors wrote. "Historical theology" differs from systematic theology in that it deals with theological issues formulated in the past, for example, by these Fathers of the Church, but not as a set of intellectual responses to a defined historical context. There is very little history involved in historical theology. Conversely, historians of a period that arguably witnessed the rise of Christianity, including its theology, to the preeminent religion of the Roman Empire, often write as though this fact were of little consequence to the history of this period. If one wanted to be polemical, one could say that this is akin to studying the history of the French Revolution from the perspective of its leading men and on the basis of taxation, administration, and bridge building, but without paying any attention to topics such as liberty, equality, and brotherhood, since the latter topics fall under the purview of theologians, or cultural theorists. One can certainly write the history of the French Revolution quite profitably by focusing on the roads and bridges then built, but I hope to have made my point (and will make it again a bit more subtly below). In-depth study of the interactions of Julian and Gregory, two men supposedly on either side of the secular historian versus church historian and theologian (that is, the pagan-Christian) divide, shows how arbitrary these scholarly dividing lines really are, and how much they obscure rather than illuminate the history of the later Roman Empire.

Both Julian and Gregory belonged to the first generation of Romans born after Constantine had made Christianity legal and hence a real career option for elite men. These elite men were without exception deeply imprinted by their formation in *paideia*. Every Christian writer who mattered had undergone training on the basis of the writings of Homer, Hesiod, Thucydides, Herodotus, Plato, Aristotle (or in the case of the Latins, Cicero, Varro, Livy, Sallust, Vergil, Ovid, Seneca, and so forth). These Christian writers were forensic rhetoricians, physicians, teachers, including teachers of the imperial family (regardless of its religious affiliation), high imperial administrators, including leaders, advisors, and administrators of their fellow Christians, as well as the emperor and his court. For them, in sum, as for all other members of the elite, classical learning was *the* status marker as well as the *conditio* sine qua non for any leadership position. Christian members of the elite were thus very similar to their non-Christian elite contemporaries.[4]

As far as Julian's Christian contemporaries are concerned, men such as Gregory emphasized in their writings the deep gulf separating them from those "on the outside," that is, their pagan relatives, friends, and neighbors. At the same time Julian's hostility vis-à-vis his Christian cousin Constantius and all those similarly deluded fairly leaps off the pages of his writings. But what does this really mean? What lies behind these codes? Modern scholarly disciplines, as noted, are not conducive to bridging that gulf constructed (nota bene) by our sources.[5] Scholars of ancient history usually end their studies with Constantine's precursor Diocletian, often appending a short last chapter gesturing toward a Roman Empire ruled by a Christian and hence no longer part of their intellectual domain. Those who venture further into that Christian Roman realm tend to remain on the safe side of individual emperors and their rule, dealing with questions of imperial legislation, administration, and the army, with occasional forays into Christian councils, especially those where imperial involvement is palatable. Here the Emperor Julian provides welcome relief as a "pagan" emperor and thus "normal" material for real ancient historians. The strangeness of his paganism (potentially tainted by his Christian upbringing) can be further tempered by ceding his philosophical writings, such as his *Hymn to the Mother of the Gods* or that to *King Helios,* to the professional philosophers, better equipped to deal with such obtuse musings than ancient historians concerned with the *realia* of governance. Alas, most philosophers interested in classical philosophy are just that. Hence, for most of them Julian's philosophical writings have little to offer, since Julian (as emperor) was no "professional" philosopher and his writings thus lack originality or system; he was undoubtedly no Iamblichus or Proclus.

As far as Julian's impact on the writings of his most prominent Christian contemporaries is concerned, we enter the realm of social historians (who are very interested in the writings of these men, but not so much in their theology, that is, in the "philosophical" dimension of these men's writings where Julian's impact might be located), theologians, and church historians.[6] The latter two groups in particular have their own concerns and scholarly traditions, which do not necessarily privilege dedicated searches for the pagan roots of the foundations of Christian thought and action, that is, orthodoxy. Julian, therefore, makes cameo appearances in many historical studies of Gregory, while most strictly theological studies devoted to Gregory of Nazianzus, Basil of Caesarea, and other contemporaries directly affected by Julian's rule pay no attention to the emperor's writings and thus do not investigate their potential impact.[7] Of course, all involved in the study of late antiquity, whether from a secular or theological vantage point, labor hard to cross disciplinary boundaries, disrupt and complicate narratives of triumph and decline, and to soften the divide between non-Christian and Christian, both orthodox and heretical. To speak of transformation has therefore been one of the hallmarks of recent scholarship, and despite welcome and necessary caveats, that admittedly somewhat vague term continues to be of heuristic value.[8] Transformation implies a small but significant point: the Roman Empire became a Christian Roman Empire over time and through numerous incremental steps, in a dynamic process of challenge and response, trial, error, dialogue, and fierce debate. Very little was set in stone. Many of the developments we now take for granted need not have turned out the way they did, were it not, for example, for the short reign of Julian and for the long and stable reigns of Emperor Theodosius I, who ruled from 379 to 395, and especially Theodosius II, emperor from 408 to 450. But to posit transformation (in our context the transformation of late Roman elites from pagan to Christian) is one thing; to prove and demonstrate such a process of small but significant adjustments is quite another. The *adventus* of Julian into Constantinople as sole Augustus, his actions, laws, and especially his writings and the response they elicited from his audience as captured by the young man who purposely embraced the "true philosophical life" only a few months later was just such a moment of adjustment.

Julian the Pagan and Gregory the Christian

Emperor Julian's reign lasted a mere twenty months. He died during the night of June 26, 363, fatally wounded on the battlefield while on retreat from Ctesiphon—the ignominious end of his glorious Persian campaign.[9] Yet these twenty months reverberate until today. As mentioned earlier, Julian rejected the Christianity into which he had been born and which he associated with his cousin's criminal deeds. Inspired instead by Plato's definition of the ideal ruler as philosopher king, Julian understood and presented himself as philosopher, priest, and emperor, divinely inspired and called to rule by the gods who had created Greece's greatness, Zeus-Helios, the Sun, Athena, and Hermes.[10] Therefore, immediately upon his accession, Julian began to publish imperial letters and edicts aimed at strengthening and invigorating the triad he considered the basis of Greece's greatness: *logoi, hiera,* and the *polis,* Greek language and culture, its gods and all things sacred, and the city as the physical locus of Greek culture, government, and religion. These three he also considered the wellspring of Rome's supremacy and hence guarantor of its *imperium,* without which the *oikoumenē* of the Romans could not be safeguarded and far less prosper. For Julian, Rome and its empire was the divinely appointed heir to Greece. In his words, "The Greek colonies civilized the greater part of the *oikoumenē* thus preparing it to more easily submit to the Romans. For the Romans are not only Greek by origin, but also the sacred laws and the pious belief in the gods, which they have instituted and preserve, are from beginning to end Greek."[11] Greek language, culture and learning, worship of the gods that had inspired them all, and the invigoration of the municipalities were, therefore, Julian's political program. In addition, the war against Persia was central. Victory where his Christian cousin had failed was to be the ultimate sign that his imperial power had indeed been bestowed *nutu caelesti,* by divine grace.[12]

Part and parcel of that political program was an attempt at reeducation. According to Julian, the Christians had foolishly deserted—"apostate" is the Greek term for deserter—the community of educated, civilized men, namely the community of the Greeks and Romans, and the universality they represented because they had succumbed to childish myths about a so-called god. That god, if he was one, was at best responsible for a tiny corner of the vast empire, Galilee, and by adopting him his followers had in fact deserted their Greek and Roman roots to become "Galilean." How this myth had fogged their minds Julian could not fathom. It was as if they not only suddenly declared the governor of an insignificant region more powerful than the emperor of the entire known world (following the mistake of the followers of Moses), but had then deserted even that minor lord "to worship the corpse of the Jews."[13] Yet Julian considered it an important part of his imperial philanthropy to "teach, but not to punish, the insane," that is, to reintegrate the demented Christians into the universal community of the civilized.[14]

One way to achieve that aim was to point out, by imperial letter with the force of law, that those who did not believe in the gods who had laid the foundation of Greek and Roman civilization, especially its philosophy, could not then use that philosophy to elucidate the simplistic assumption of their myth (for example, how *one* God could be Father, a Son born of a human woman, and a Divine Spirit, elucidations which forced them "to gnaw at the learning of the Greeks").[15] Further, such persons could not publicly engage in teaching and living the true philosophical life, though they were welcome to expound Matthew and Luke in the churches of the Galileans.[16]

Julian's entire program, but especially the imperial letter 36 of late June or early July 362, sent shockwaves through the Christian elites. Among those directly affected was Gregory of Nazianzus. He was Christian, he had just returned from advanced study of philosophy at Athens, he had been teaching as a public rhetorician, and he had decided to embark precisely on the kind of philosophical life now declared unfit for Christians by the new emperor. Julian had grown up not far from Nazianzus, Gregory had met him at Athens, where both had studied philosophy, and Gregory's younger brother Caesarius was one of Julian's personal physicians.[17] In sum, Gregory had a fair idea of what Julian proposed. He had means to gain access to the emperor's writings and pronouncements beyond imperial letters, and he was personally affected by them. The affront Julian's actions, thoughts, and writings represented for Gregory galvanized him into a response with far-reaching consequences. Spurred by Julian's laws, edicts, writings, and above all by his self-presentation as Platonic emperor and philosopher-priest, devoted to lead his *oikoumenē,* the empire, to salvation as a servant (really slave) of the true gods of the Greeks and the Romans, Gregory developed his own concept of the Christian leader as philosopher and priest, now in the form of the bishop as servant (really slave) of the God *Logos.* Both followed Plato in considering the philosophical life *the* condition for leadership. Since Julian had proclaimed that those who did not believe in the Gods who had founded Greek philosophy could not use its techniques, for example, to define the nature of the Trinity as three in one, Gregory set out to do just that in a manner that took Julian's writings on the relationship between the Supreme Divine Father and his Sons (Helios, Apollo, Asclepius, and so on) into account. Where Julian had denied that Christianity could be the foundation of Rome's world rule as proven by Constantius's amorality and his corresponding losses in Persia, Gregory sought to show the opposite, especially after the emperor's disastrous death on the Persian battlefields. It is Gregory who created the image of Julian as *the Apostate* still dominant today.

Because Julian sought to force Christians to do without pagan learning, Gregory and other Christians had to acknowledge and grapple with the pagan elements in their ways of thinking as never before. One result was Gregory's entire oeuvre of forty-five orations in all classical genres and nineteen thousand verses in all meters, in which he rewrote the key concepts of the pagans from Plato's notions of leadership as laid down in the *Republic* and the *Laws,* via Aristotle's use of logic. Using Homeric themes and the language of Demosthenes, Gregory demonstrated in his writings how Christians should be honored through funeral orations, how to praise Christian emperors, how to compose letters and write poetry as a Christian. In so doing he laid the foundations of Byzantine and much Western thought.[18]

Gregory did so by incorporating Christian elements into the classical matrix. As a result, he became one of the leading intellectuals of his day and one of the most widely read authors of Byzantium. Only the Scriptures have a wider manuscript distribution. In addition, Gregory had significant impact on Westerners such as Jerome, Ambrose, Augustine, and Gregory the Great. He became Saint Gregory of Nazianzus, *the Theologian,* whose signal contributions to the formulation of the Trinity—"the God who is one must be preserved and three hypostases professed, each with its own specific properties"[19]—informed Christian doctrine for generations and made him one of the three Hierarchs of the Orthodox Church (and one of Pope Benedict XVI's favorites). And the Emperor Julian, for his part, was henceforth dubbed Julian *the Apostate.*[20]

Historiography Redux—More Pagan versus Christian

Paradoxically, however, Gregory's very success as "the Theologian" and one of the leading Fathers of the Christian Church as a whole turned him, historiographically speaking, into a somewhat marginal figure. Scholars consider him so Christian, so passionately devoted to philosophical retreat and pure thought, as to be constitutionally incapable of functioning in the real world of the church and of politics. In fact, if one considers normative the bishop as an institutional figurehead, wedded to one see and characterized by his sacramental functions (influenced, for example, by Max Weber or Hans von Campenhausen), then Gregory was indeed an abject ecclesiastical failure.[21] He was a reluctant priest and a lackluster adjunct bishop. After his ordination as bishop of Sasima he refused to assume his duties and never even went there, though the place was close by. Instead he disappeared for three years of retreat, from whence he emerged, somewhat inexplicably for modern scholars, as the leader of the Neo-Nicene Christian congregation in Constantinople in 379. Less than a year later, the new emperor Theodosius I made him bishop of the capital, but a mere nine months after that, while presiding at the first ecumenical council of 381, Gregory resigned, left Constantinople, and retired to his estate near Nazianzus.[22]

Such fits and starts have garnered him scholarly characterizations as a sensitive soul and a *romantique avant la lettre,* or as an indecisive, pusillanimous, and labile man.[23] These near canonical scholarly characterizations of Gregory as gifted theologian but absentminded man and disastrous bishop were also what piqued my own curiosity. Could a manmade bishop of Constantinople at a highly tension-filled time by the mandate of the very emperor

Theodosius who made catholic Christianity the religion of the entire empire really have been such a loser?

My answer to this question is no, but to arrive at that conclusion required first an opening of the Christian bubble in which scholars have sealed Gregory so hermetically. What if Gregory had not just contemplated the Christian Scriptures in solitary splendor, but had actually read Julian's writings and responded to them? This would mean that he had shaped his concept of the bishop as philosopher alternating periods of active political involvement with those of retreat and writing in direct response to Julian's claim to embody just such a philosopher as leader. Such a possibility, I should point out, has been categorically excluded by nearly all scholars who have ever published on Gregory, with the exception of Leonardo Lugaresi and Ugo Criscuolo.[24] And yet, that was the case. This was the model of the orthodox Christian bishop Gregory had first delineated in his famous *Oration 2,* entitled by the manuscript editors *Apology for his Flight* or *On the Priesthood.* This was the model he propagated time and again in his subsequent orations, a model that became normative for Ambrose, Augustine, and Gregory the Great. Julian, the man and his writings, had been the explicit catalyst.

To puncture Gregory's Christian bubble required a similar operation on behalf of Julian, firmly encased in the historiographical bubble of the pagan Apostate intent on persecuting Christians, albeit more subtly than by throwing them to the lions.[25] Julian had been brought up Christian. He was, in fact, the first Roman emperor who had been baptized before ascending the throne. Among Julian's teachers had been George of Cappadocia, who later became bishop of Alexandria. However, for Klaus Rosen "there is no trace of his Christianity to be found in his rather obtuse philosophical speculations."[26] As a consequence of this assessment, one Rosen shares with other scholars, there is little reason to mention a single work of Gregory in connection with the emperor with the exception of two invectives against Julian I will address below. Thus Julian's knowledge of, and engagement with, contemporary Christian debates has remained largely unexamined. Nor, as a consequence, have scholars investigated how much Christian writers responded to Julian's pagan challenge. In sum, despite the enormous scholarly attention lavished on Julian, scholarship has not truly considered *all* of his writings and has only scratched the surface of the actual impact of Julian's writings on his Christian contemporaries, also known as the Fathers of the Church, who were then formulating the tenets of orthodoxy.[27] In sum, historians with "an active interest in secular aspects of the end of the Roman world, such as its political, economic and military history," are understandably reluctant to probe Julian's philosophy for Christian influences and have thus failed to explore Julian's impact on Christian orthodoxy.[28] Theologians and most church historians, equally reluctant to concede that Gregory may have read a single piece of writing by the pagan Apostate, even when he cites its titles, also have not explored this impact and have not probed whether Gregory's oeuvre does, in fact, respond to Julian's writings.[29]

Gregory's Response to Julian: Creating the Apostate

To make my remarks more plastic, I will briefly discuss *Orations* 4 and 5, the two orations by Gregory evoked by everyone, the historians concerned with Julian and the church historians concerned with Gregory.[30] These are the famous invectives in which Gregory "created" Julian as *the Apostate*. For many historians they are symptomatic of Gregory and his value as a historical source. Considered "simultaneously hysterical and pedantic, fiercely caustic and pompously ponderous," these orations are often read as exhibit A demonstrating their author's utter lack of historical sensibility.[31] Church historians also dislike these orations since to witness "this happy dance, [in which Gregory gleefully] swings the scalp of his barely deceased enemy, is somewhat embarrassing."[32] Indeed, it is a challenge to integrate the picture of the happily dancing Gregory, swinging Julian's bloody scalp, with that of the "sweet and gentle man," paragon of a "spirit of high culture, brilliant and gracious, a sweet and tender soul... badly armed to sustain the battles into which the hazards of life have thrown him": the historiographic Gregory in a nutshell.[33]

In fact, the metaphor of the dance is apt. Gregory's orations against Julian are performance. First, Gregory explicitly and emphatically did not wish to write history (*Or.* 4.20) but to perform a sacred ritual. His orations were a *panegyric,* a celebratory hymn (4.7, 4.8, 5.35) and a "bloodless sacrifice of words to the Word," Christ, the *Logos* (4.3). As such, his performance stood in sharp contrast to that of the emperor. While Gregory's orations performed a sacred ritual, Julian's entire reign had been theater, a "fiction without any roots in reality" (4.113 and 114), "making one laugh rather than cry" (4.78). Gregory wanted Julian to lose face. For him, Julian the man and his rule were nothing but histrionics. Through his performance of Julian's reign as theater, Gregory formed his future. His picture of Julian has shaped historiography more than anything the emperor himself had done or written in the short twenty months of his reign.

Though usually treated as one piece, Gregory wrote the two orations against Julian more than one year apart and for different, albeit overlapping audiences. *Oration* 4, prepared while Julian was still alive but completed after his death, addressed an (intended) audience concerned with the theological controversies that so predominated the early 360s. *Oration* 5, in contrast, was written during the usurpation of Procopius and uses the specter of Julian and the glorification of his memory—after all, Julian was and remained a duly divinized legitimate Roman ruler—to argue against Procopius and in favor of Emperor Valens. It thus entered a fierce debate about the legitimacy of Julian's successors. Both orations address members of the new service elite then becoming an empirewide aristocracy. These men, many of whom sat in the new Constantinopolitan senate, were scions of the municipal elites such as Gregory and his brother Caesarius.[34] Most were Christian, and it was for their benefit that Gregory formulated how, as Christian public men, they should conduct themselves and the affairs of the *oikoumenē*.

As his two orations against Julian reveal, Gregory shared the emperor's assessment of the centrality of *logoi, hiera,* and the *polis,* that is, Greek culture, the sacred, and the city. He also saw them as intrinsically linked and foundational for the well-being of the Roman Empire. Gregory differed sharply, of course, with regard to the divinity that had created all three (four, if we count the empire). Those whom Julian had considered gods, Gregory considered demons, and Julian's pseudodivinity of a marginal people was Gregory's universal *pantokrator.* A small but significant difference: because Julian had, according to Gregory, misconstrued the sacred, his understanding of *logoi* and the *polis* was equally faulty. In a private person such a mistake might be merely reprehensible, but in an emperor, "such comportment alone suffices to pillory the moral character of a ruler," because a ruler's comportment affects the fundaments of the state (4.81). And these are the central issues at stake in Gregory's allegedly ahistoric orations: the Roman Empire (*archē*), the roots of its power, and the manner in which the community of the Romans ought to be governed (4.74). To clarify his views, Gregory focused on the central places where the emperor performed imperial rule: the theater and the marketplace.

The theater was crucial for the representation and constitution of any city. Here the city's elites were seated in hierarchical order, enjoying the fruits of their financial munificence, and here they were observed doing so by the non-elites (4.113). In addition, in the theater mimes and pantomimes performed tragedies and comedies about the myths of the gods of the Greeks and Romans, that is, the essence of *logoi* and the *hiera*.[35] These very same *logoi* and the *hiera* were what Julian had sought to reinvigorate, albeit not their theatrical performance. That interpretation was Gregory's obvious defamation. Like many intellectuals, Julian and Gregory shared the ambivalence the theater evoked.[36] It was powerful and attractive, it transmitted Greek culture, but in a popular, mocking, and often sexually explicit fashion. To be a mime and pantomime was considered shameful, and the theater was by nature dissimulation, fiction, and lie.[37] To call Julian's entire reign nothing but theater said it all (4.113).[38] Julian had erected "a polis constructed of words" that could not be sustained by deeds, because it lacked "the force of a system that is derived from divine inspiration" (4.44; 4.113; Pl. *Rep.* 369c). All of Julian's imperial acts were simulations of reality destined to be fleeting.[39]

Gregory's argument works on several levels. First, if Julian's acts and deeds, including his laws and edicts, were "theater," demonically inspired dissimulations destined to be transitory, then Gregory's words were "reality" rooted in deeds and lasting because they expressed a divinely inspired system. Thus, his words overwrote Julian's (legislative) acts and deeds. Second, in a long disquisition about the nature of the myths portrayed in the theater, myths so dear to Julian, Gregory dismantled the religious and thus ethical foundations on which Julian's transient *polis*—that is, his rule—rested. Like their theatrical performances, the myths of Julian's gods were devoid of the ethical prerequisites of appropriate rule, such as restraint, justice, prudence, philanthropy, and above all, piety. No wonder that Julian's disastrous performance as ruler showed such deficiencies (4.113–123). Third, Gregory's attack aimed not only at Julian's deeds and works but also at his person. Gregory knew that Julian personally disdained the theater because he, too, considered the mockery of the Gods and the licentious displays of their myths shameful. The emperor had made his feelings known, for example, in his treatise chastising the inhabitants of Antioch for, among other things, their love of the theater. Gregory had cited this treatise by its title, *Antiochikos* or *Misopogon*, in *Oration* 5.41.

For Gregory, Julian's actual attitude toward the theater was of no consequence. At every stage he sought to portray the emperor as a bad actor who did not comport himself as a real emperor. Already when Gregory had first laid eyes on Julian in Athens he had seen a man who twittered and twitched. Already then Gregory knew what the future had in store: "What more can I say? I looked at the man prior to his deeds and recognized him…and I said to [my companions]: "what disaster is the Roman state nurturing here!" (5.32).[40]

The theater was a place where the emperor interacted directly with his subjects, where he performed imperial rule and was seen doing so. It was also one of the places where imperial letters and decrees were received and read aloud in a highly ritualized manner as if the emperor was present.[41] A second site where the same interaction occurred was the *agora,* the marketplace, and it is here, too, that Gregory engaged Julian. Gregory declared that his *Orations* 4 and 5 against Julian were not invectives (though he follows the genre's structure), because it was impossible to do full justice to Julian's misdeeds as an invective would have required (4.79). For the same reason, Gregory did not want to write a history. His insistence on this is relevant. By explicitly forgoing these two genres Gregory chose to forgo the role of the prosecutor arguing his case to elicit a conviction, the generic conceit characteristic of the invective.[42] Instead, he called his orations a "stelographia," a "writing-on-a-stele" or pillar (4.20). As Alois Kurmann has pointed out, this term is a neologism deriving from the verb *steliteuein,* to inscribe the name of convicted criminals after their execution onto a pillar in the marketplace. Persons thus inscribed or pilloried were shamed forever and for all to see.[43]

In Gregory's eyes, Julian had already received his sentence and had been condemned to execution in the theater of war by divine decree. God had been prosecutor, judge, and executioner. Gregory merely proclaimed the sentence and explicated it to all present and to those in the future. Gregory's oration merely explained God's providential plan to let Julian rule and die, an enormous calamity for all Romans. God had permitted Julian to rise so that he could chastise the Christians, who had not used their new power to rule wisely, but in his mercy he had let Julian perish after a brief rule that was as transient as a theater performance. Gregory's explication, his sentence, was a "writing-on-a-stele," a public proclamation of Julian's shame. Such public proclamations were the domain of those who ruled. On such pillars in the public places Julian's edict and imperial letters had been posted, including his famous edict excluding Christians from *logoi,* but also the *Misopogon,* in which Julian had presented himself as the embodiment of the just Platonic philosopher-king outlined in Plato's *Laws.* Gregory's *Oration 4,* consequently, showcases Julian as the embodiment of the unjust ruler, whose legislation cannot be allowed to stand since it is driven by mistaken assumptions of justice, lack of ethical fiber, and above all, mistaken ideas about the divine. In his metaphorical counterstele, Gregory, in a performative act of his own, overwrote all of Julian's acts and most of his concepts, one by one. And while Julian's words, written on stone, would pass like dried grass, Gregory's words, though written on flimsy linen, would last: "Here our *stele* for you, higher and more visible than those of Hercules, because those are merely planted in one place and are visible only to those who go there. This *stele* instead cannot but move about and make itself known to all. It will even be received in the future, of that I am certain, to pillory you and your works and to teach everyone not to attempt such a rebellion, 'apostasy' against God, so that they may not be punished in like manner for having committed similar crimes" (5.42).

Emperors and Priests—Ruling Rome,
Whether Pagan or Christian

Julian was a deserter (*apostate*) whom God had judged and condemned to execution in war. Julian and his fate was, therefore, God's stern warning to Christian rulers to conduct imperial rule of the *oikoumenē* of the Romans properly. This included the appropriate relation between Christian God, emperor, and priest. By calling his discourse a "writing on a stele," Gregory signaled that he was posting a divine decree that overwrote imperial ones. By attacking Julian as lacking imperial *gravitas* and, more important, the crucial ability to act as just imperial legislator, Gregory defined what being a true and just Christian emperor entailed. To further highlight his point, Gregory juxtaposed Julian's negative image with a positive portrayal of his cousin Constantius, who had killed Julian's parents, as the paragon of an ideal Christian ruler. Constantius's sole fault had been his overabundance of philanthropy out of which he had spared Julian's life (4.3). Constantius, however, "knew very well, because he reflected upon such things in a manner more elevated and imperial than most, that the Roman power had grown together with Christianity and that the imperium arrived together with Christ" (4.37). To assure the greatness of the empire required the appropriate nurturing of all things Christian, the unity of Christian teaching (or *orthodoxa*), the appropriate protection of Christian *hiera,* and, of course, creation of the Christian *polis* through tax exemptions, removal of "pagan" symbols, and similar policies. Julian, this "best of all governors of the commonwealth" (4.74), had failed to realize that to eradicate Christianity "now that it ruled sovereign" was "to rip out the roots of Roman rule and to place the entire commonwealth into grave danger."

Gregory wrote these two orations during the reign of Julian's successors, who were all Christian. But much remained uncertain: How would these new emperors comport themselves as Christian emperors? Julian's edicts needed to be rescinded, but would they do that given that he had been a legitimate and duly divinized emperor? How would *they* treat Christian *logoi?* After all, Julian had been the first baptized Roman emperor, but he had deserted. Instead of adhering to what his priests and bishops had taught him, he had gone off to invent his own *logoi*—a stern warning to Christian emperors not to deviate from the words of their bishops such as Gregory. And what about the theater and the marketplace? How was a Christian emperor to comport himself there? For example, as Neil McLynn has so persuasively pointed out, the manner in which a Christian emperor should perform imperially in the new theater, the church, was then still in flux.

No one knew how to integrate the emperor into the liturgy.[44] When Gregory wrote *Oration* 5 such issues had become even more pressing. Procopius, after all, had justified his usurpation against Valens on the basis of his shared dynastic lineage with Julian and Constantine the Great, whereas Valens was a mere Pannonian upstart. Gregory's call to support Valens against Procopius, and that is one point of *Oration* 5, had to be very convincing indeed.[45]

To conclude, characterizing Julian as a bad actor performing the part of a ruler badly allowed Gregory to achieve a number of aims. It permitted him to define what he considered appropriate Christian rule by opposing Julian and Constantius, tyrannical and just legislation, disastrous and justified conduct of war, appropriate behavior in the *agora* and its opposite. However, it allowed him to do more. Gregory also used the theatre to attack Julian's understanding of myth and to undermine his concept of divinely authorized rule based on myths, as the emperor had defined it in his writings against the Cynic Heraclius and in his two hymns, to the Mother of the Gods and to King Helios. At the same time and with the same arguments Gregory engaged inner Christian debates then raging about the literal or allegorical exegesis of the "mythical" elements of Scripture.[46] Further, Gregory used arguments he had sharpened in *Oration* 4 against Julian to define what would soon become the standard definition of pagan, for which the Greek term is precisely "being Greek," *hellen*. Everything for which Julian stood became associated with "being Greek," now considered pagan, whereas the positive inheritance of things Greek, including the *agora* and the polis, and Homer, Plato, and Aristotle, Gregory claimed as Christian, as "ours." After all, as Gregory stressed, the *imperium* of the Romans had begun with Christ.[47]

Point by point, argument by argument, Gregory's orations counter Julian and his notions. What is true for *Orations* 4 and 5 also applies to the rest of Gregory's phenomenally influential oeuvre. Julian's rule, then, may have been a transient theater performance, but the effect of his writings on his Christian audience proved to be of a magnitude that has yet to be fully appreciated. Bringing Julian's and Gregory's writings into dialogue shows that both men had far more in common than divided them: merely the definition of the divinity that had created Greek and Roman supremacy. Integral for all and to everything these men thought and wrote was the pagan learning they shared. Phrased differently, without paganism no Christianity; without Julian's writings, no Gregory the Theologian. And what is true for Gregory's writings also applies to a number of his important contemporaries and successors. Thus, paradoxical though it may sound, through the Christian (and especially Gregory's) response to the pagan Apostate's writings, Julian became in effect another Father of the Church.

Abandoning preconceived notions about the binary divide separating pagan from Christian thus realigns the landscape of the later Roman Empire. Politics and religion are not separate entities, and secular historians and church historians deal with the same historic persons, whose interests overlap. Indeed, the interplay between Julian and his Christian elite subjects, and the reaction his actions caused, reveals that the boundary between pagan and Christians is so porous that it renders these two categories almost meaningless for modern analytical purposes. This is not to say that faithful narratives such as those offered by Gregory who denigrated pagans and those by Julian who similarly disparaged Christians are not binary. But it is the historian's duty, I think, to go beyond the easy oppositions such narratives offer on the surface. Digging deeper reveals far more complex interactions, as behooves persons who had far more in common, namely, a deeply cherished shared culture, than divided them—even if their gods were not entirely the same.

CHAPTER 2

Between Syria and Egypt

Alms, Work, and the "Holy Poor"

PETER BROWN

I have been led to write this paper by one fact, which struck me as I worked, in recent years, on the issues of wealth and the care of the poor in the Christian churches of late antiquity. I found myself asking who, actually, were "the poor"? And I realized, somewhat to my surprise, that, in the eastern Christian world of the later third and fourth centuries, there was, as yet, no simple answer to that question.

My surprise deserves to be emphasized. We now tend to take for granted that the principal duty of good Christians in the disposal of their wealth has always been to show mercy to the "real" poor. We assume that this view already went without saying among the majority of Christians in around 300 AD. It was from this definition of "the poor" that the charitable ventures associated with late antique and Byzantine Christianity derived.[1] But, in reality, this notion of alms to the poor had to be defended in Christian circles against strong and persistent alternatives. As a result, our accustomed way of seeing society as divided between rich and poor, and the Christian church as an institution that provided for the poor through encouraging and organizing the charitable distribution of alms, was not a given. It was, itself, the outcome of a silent struggle in which the religion and economy of entire Christian regions had been involved.

This brief study will expose some of the challenges we face in attempting to historicize notions of poverty, charity, and labor that emerged in diverse religious communities in late antiquity, forcing us to reevaluate our assumptions about issues still much debated in our own day. Specifically it will show that the monks of Syria and Egypt in the last centuries of the Roman Empire were far from being the weird and wonderful drop-outs that we often imagine them to have been. Rather, the monks acted as a catalyst for the social imagination of an entire society. Like many other extremist movements in other ages, early Christian monasticism was a sort of social seismograph. We can trace, often in exaggerated forms (like the abrupt up and down movements of the needle on a seismograph) the more silent earth tremors of the normal Roman society from which the monks broke loose. Furthermore, we can see how those who supported the monks did so because they saw their own social dilemmas writ large (again, as in the dramatic high lines of a seismograph) in the persons of the monks. What happened at this time was like what happened in the Middle Ages, when the extremist poverty of Saint Francis and his followers arose as a comment on the boom and bust economy of the Italian cities of the thirteenth century, or when, nowadays, the mission of Mother Theresa in the slums of Calcutta focuses, in dramatic, personal form, the anxieties of privileged nations in the face of the seemingly limitless poverty of much of the rest of the world.

Standing as they did for extreme positions that cast a vivid oblique light on the society in which they moved, the attitudes of monks to work, food, and the care of the poor were taken seriously by contemporaries. How monks (and nuns) supported themselves plainly had an immediate effect on the regions in which they were settled. But the imaginative effects of these options were even more significant. Each option cast light on the way in which normal society was organized, on the position of labor, on the nature of the human person and on the relation between the individual and society. When we study the monks of Syria and Egypt, we are not only looking at how small groups of radical religious figures managed to support themselves. We are listening in to a serious debate on issues which still concern us—what it is to be human, what it is to work, what it means to care for the poor—even if this debate is conducted in a religious language that is deeply unfamiliar to us.

In order to do this listening in, we must go back to around the year 300 to Christian regions where a very different constellation of ideas from the ideas to which we are now accustomed was equally vibrant. This constellation privileged, above all, giving to the "holy" poor—to religious virtuosos, who claimed to give the ethereal benefits of "spiritual" blessing, advice, and prayer, in return for the "earthly" offering of daily sustenance. For this strong current of opinion, almsgiving was, above all, a religious action directed "upward," as it were. "True" almsgiving took the form of gifts to religious leaders who were deemed capable of securing the salvation of the donors because they themselves were so totally detached from the normal rhythms of society (which included the necessity of working for a living) that they had to be supported by alms as if they were beggars. Only by holding this current in check were the churches of late antiquity able to establish what we might call a more "downward" flow of alms into society itself, in the form of alms to the "real" poor, such as we now associate with the "mainline" traditions of Christianity. Hence the last part of my title: "Alms and Work . . . "

In the late third and early fourth centuries, this division of opinion was particularly acute throughout a distinctive geographical area—hence my title, "Between Syria and Egypt." We are studying two distinctive landscapes. On one side we have the mountains, the open plains and the partially inhabited steppe lands of northern Mesopotamia, Syria, and the eastern Mediterranean— a world conducive to movement and to various forms of charismatic vagrancy. On the other, we have an Egypt squeezed into the single, miraculously fertile valley of the Nile. The Fertile Crescent joined Mesopotamia to the Mediterra- nean in a great, northern arc that stretched from southern Iraq to Antioch, and southward as far as the Delta of the Nile. In the words of John Ward-Perkins: "The frontier territory between Rome and Parthia [the Persian Empire] was neither a cultural barrier nor mere gateway and point of passage between East and West. It was a vital creative center in its own right, and it was this fact above all which enabled it to serve as an effective intermediary between two great civilizations which flourished on its borders."[2]

Already in the 270s this crucial area was crisscrossed by extreme religious groups of Christian origin. These groups were distinguished by an "apos- tolic" mobility that combined the missionary universalism of Saint Paul with the ideal of wandering poverty associated with the disciples of Jesus in the Gospels. They expected to be supported entirely by the alms of those to whom they ministered.

They were a sight to be seen. The author of a letter written to direct the behavior of one such group warned them that, when they passed through pagan villages, they should not burst out into singing the Psalms (which they usually did, so as to hearten the local Christians), lest they be mistaken for a troupe of traveling musicians![3] These "Spirit-filled" wanderers were local products. They had a long history before them in the Syriac-speaking piety of the Christian Middle East.

Others came from further to the East, from central Mesopotamia. They were the messengers of a new prophet, Mani, who had died as a martyr at the hands of the Sasanian king of kings in 277.[4] Mani saw himself as the

Paul of his age. He sent his emissaries as "Apostles" to establish his "Holy Church" in all regions of the earth—from the Roman Empire in the West to the Kushan kingdom of Central Asia in the East.[5] Mani's missionaries soon established themselves as the "Elect" of his Church, ministering to local Manichaean communities. The Manichaean Elect claimed to model their behavior on exactly the same pattern of extreme poverty combined with ceaseless mobility that the radical Christians of Syria had come to see as the distinctive mark of all true disciples of Jesus. In the words of the Manichaean Coptic *Psalms of the Wanderers:*

> they went from village to village.
> [They] went into the roads hungry, with no bread in their hands.
> They walked in the heat, thirsting, they took no water to drink.
> No gold, no silver, no money, did they take with them on their way.
> They went into the villages, not knowing anybody.
> They were welcomed for His sake, they were loved for his name's sake.[6]

Dramatic though these forms of wandering and mendicant asceticism might be, as they spread throughout the Syriac-speaking world, they were met by an alternative constellation of expectations, primarily associated with Egypt. Egypt lay at the extreme southwestern end of the Fertile Crescent. It was far from being a world locked into itself. At the end of the third century, the entire length of the Nile valley was more open to the religious life of the Fertile Crescent than at any other time in its long history. Manichaean missionaries soon reached Alexandria. Major Manichaean texts were found, in 1930, in the Fayum—an oasis on the edge of the Nile Delta, with close links to Alexandria—and, in 1990, yet more were discovered far to the south, at Ismant al-Kharab (ancient Kellis) in the Dakhleh Oasis of the Western Desert of Egypt.[7]

It was in the Fayum around 270—less than a decade before the death of Mani in 277 and well over a generation before the conversion of Constantine in 312—that Anthony, a young man and a comfortable farmer (the owner of an estate of some two hundred acres)—decided to move out of his village. He had been converted by hearing, in the village church, the crucial passage from the Gospel of Saint Matthew: "Just then it happened that the Gospel was being read and he heard the Lord saying to the Rich Young Man: If you would be perfect, go, sell what you possess and give to the poor, and you will have treasure in heaven" (Matthew 19:21).[8]

Anthony grew up in a religious world where alternative forms of Christian asceticism were already clearly visible within Egypt itself. The steps that Anthony took at the time of his renunciation differed significantly from the pattern established by his contemporaries, the holy wanderers of Syria and their *Doppelgänger,* the missionaries of the "Holy Church" of Mani. Anthony did not take to the roads. He took to the desert and stayed there. His renunciation was accompanied by a dramatic act of almsgiving to the poor of his own village: "Selling all the rest of his portable wealth [his house, furniture, silverware, and clothes], when he had collected all the cash realized by this sale, he gave it to the poor."[9] Furthermore, once he had divested himself of this wealth, he refused to receive alms himself. Although established in the desert, Anthony was believed to have maintained himself by the work of his own hands.[10] His followers imitated him with studied intensity. The words of Paul's Letter to the Thessalonians, which show the Apostle at his most anxious to avoid the accusation of being, himself, a charismatic free-loader, became the mantra of the monks of Egypt: "For even when we were with you, we gave you this command: If any one will not work, let him not eat" (2 Thessalonians 3:10). They were literally a mantra. The influential late-fourth-century monastic writer Evagrius of Pontus advised reciting Paul's words "against the thought that hinders us from working with our hands and persuades us to receive what we need from others."[11]

We should always remember that the only account of the conversion of Anthony that has come down to us was written eighty years after the event. It is the *Life of Saint Anthony,* written by Athanasius, patriarch of Alexandria.[12] The book rapidly became a classic throughout the Christian Mediterranean. This was because Athanasius presented Anthony very much as what has been acutely termed a "Verbal Icon."[13] It was a "Verbal Icon" painted with great care. The story of Anthony was the patriarch's considered answer to patterns of ascetic behavior of which he did not approve. Behind its crisp lines, we can catch the hint of a debate between Syria and Egypt that had already rumbled since the late third century. In Egypt, the act of renunciation itself and the subsequent relations between monks and the society around them were presented in the *Life of Anthony* (and in subsequent Egyptian sources) as sharply contrasted to forms of ascetic behavior that were taken for granted in Syria and in other parts of the Fertile Crescent.

To most of us, Mani, the Mesopotamian prophet, the holy wanderers of Syria, and Anthony of Egypt appear to belong to very different worlds. But this was not so. They each shared, if in different ways, in the currents of ascetic experimentation that flowed, unhindered, across the Fertile Crescent and deep into Egypt. The alternatives represented by each group were clearly visible to all the others. If they seem to us to be very different from each other, it is because we tend to separate each group from the other according to theological principles. We deem the Manichees to be total outsiders to "normal" Christianity, and we also tend to regard the monasticism of Egypt as, somehow, more "normal" than the wild and woolly men of Syria.

As is well known, recent scholarship on the history of the Christian church has cast doubt on these rigid distinctions. They are often based on projections backward from later times. It has proved more fruitful to think of late antique Christianity itself as a set of movements, each of which was in lively dialogue with all the others. The problems they debated were often problems they all shared. It was only in the solutions that they varied. This means that it is wiser for the historian to look, first, at the issues over which these groups argued, rather than at the differences that eventually emerged from their different solutions.

The time has come to pay more attention to the essential things that these seemingly disparate groups had in common. They brought to the surface, in Christian form, millennial arguments on the nature of man and society. Among the Manichees, the manner in which sustenance was given to the Elect raised the question of the relation of human society as a whole to the material world. The wanderers of Syria posed a less drastic but no less urgent issue. The support given to them, as members of the "holy poor," revived (by implication) the ancient sadness associated with the fact of work. The freedom of the happy few—represented by the Syrian wanderers—cast a dark shadow on the *ponos* (to use the Greek word, heavily charged since ancient times) and the *'amla'* (its Syriac equivalent), the "drudgery" to which the vast mass of humankind remained condemned as if by some ancestral curse.[14] By contrast, among their exact contemporaries and neighbors, the monks of Egypt, work itself was raised to the status of a privileged denotator of the human condition. Work was what was thought to bind the monks to the society around them. It is in the light of these fundamental issues, confronted, in different ways, by each group, that I would like to interpret the various ascetic currents available in Egypt and Syria in the late third and early fourth centuries.

Let us begin among the Manichees. Kellis lay more than six hundred miles to the south of the Fayum. In around 340—in exactly the same years as Anthony was reaching the zenith of his fame in northern Egypt—the Lady Eirene, a "Hearer," that is, a lay disciple of the Manichaean Elect, was putting "treasure in Heaven" in the manner distinctive to her sect. She was praised by the local Elect for offering them material support:

she whose deeds resemble her name [Peace], our [spiritual] daughter. [She was] The daughter of the holy church, the catechumen of the faith: the good tree whose fruit never withers, which is your love which emits radiance every day. She who has acquired for herself her riches and stored them away in the *treasuries that are in the heights, where moths shall not find a way nor shall thieves dig through to them to steal.* (Matthew 6:19–20, my emphasis)

The Elect then adds an explanation: "which [treasuries] are the Sun and the Moon."[15] It was only this last, telltale reference to the Sun and the Moon as active agents in a cosmic drama of salvation, which identified the writer of the letter as a Manichee.

This newly discovered exchange of Manichaean letters shows, with the crispness of an X-ray photograph, one path by which (in circles adjacent to mainline Christianity) "treasure on earth" was thought to flow directly upwards so as to become "treasure in heaven." The Elect needed Eirene and her fellow "catechumens":

You being for us helpers and worthy *patrons* and firm unbending pillars [of the church cf. Galatians 2:9]; while we ourselves rely upon you ... I was very grateful to you, ten million times! [Whether] we are far or [we are near]; indeed, we have found remembrance among [you]. Now, therefore, may it stay with you: this Knowledge and this Faith [which you have] known and believed in. Therefore, [I] beg you, [my] blessed [daughters], that you will [send] me two *choes* of oil. For [you] know yourselves that we are [in need] here; since we are afflicted.[16]

But what did Eirene gain from this exchange, and what views of the world were implied in it?

Among the Manichees, it was the nature of the material world itself that was at stake. It was their view of the material world that gave a sharp flavor to their notion of almsgiving to the Elect as members of the true, the "holy" poor.

Manichaean attitudes to the circulation of wealth contrasted markedly with the consensus that had begun to emerge in many Christian communities. Following a tradition shared by Judaism, in these Christian communities wealth was thought to circulate within the Christian church because it was deemed, in itself, to be a good thing. By giving to the church and to the poor, the pious Christian gave back to God a little of the abundance of a created world shot through with His blessing. This attitude was vividly condensed through the central Christian ritual of the Eucharist. The first fruits brought to the altar at the time of the Eucharist were seen as a return to God by those who gave them of God's gift of a fertile and beneficent material world.[17]

Such prayers of offering were a condensed statement about nature itself. They assumed that human society rested unproblematically in the bosom of a natural world created by God and bathed in His blessing. But no Manichee could possibly harbor such comfortable illusions. They knew, for instance, that the wine offered at the Christian Eucharist was no gift of God. It was not even a creature of God. It was the "bile of the Princes of Darkness." It was one of the many toxic substances of demonic origin with which the earth was saturated.[18] The best that could be said of the material universe was that it was (in the words of a later, Chinese catechism of the Manichaean faith) an immense distillery. It was like one of the magical laboratories in which alchemists had sought, through a prolonged process of refinement, to wrench from base matter, in minute, ethereal fragments, the unalloyed essence of gold and of similar time-defying substances. For the Manichaeans, what would be extracted from a natural world poisoned by demonic elements was the ethereal, luminous essence of pure soul.[19]

It is against this cosmic backdrop that we should place the ritual support offered by the Manichaean Catechumens to their Elect. The "wealth" they offered to the Elect was not a representative portion *of* the goodness of a material world, created by God and gladly offered back to Him by the faithful. It was a last, thin vestige of matter, painstakingly prized loose *from* an inherently evil world and sent on its way (in the form of a solemn gift of sustenance to the Elect) toward some final transmutation in "the treasuries in the heights." Such wealth, offered in this way, somehow carried with it the very souls of its donors.[20] These were the "alms" that lay persons in the Manichaean church gave to their Elect, and to the Elect only. For these alms were "saving" alms. They were offered to persons whose entire life had come to a stop. The Elect were "sealed" on their mouths, their hands, and their genitals.[21] They were thus sealed off from process. They did not join themselves to fully "living" matter through unregulated eating. They did not contribute to the headlong pullulation of human flesh through intercourse and the begetting of children. Above all, they did not lend their hands to manual labor in the fields. For by stooping to work, they would have involved themselves in the most bloody process of all—the tearing of the earth through ploughing and the slashing of living vegetation.[22] With pale faces and soft, white hands, the Elect—men and women alike, for, in this, they were indistinguishable—had left "the world." They already lived on the threshold of the mighty "cessation" that would eventually fall on the cosmos as a whole. They were what their lay supporters might yet be.

Such a view had palpable social implications. For Mani and his disciples, the social world was somehow transparent. The distribution within it of wealth and poverty lacked any providential purpose. What happened in society—above all, the division between rich and poor—was merely a baneful reflection, on earth, of a universe stirred at random by the distant influence of demonic planetary "lords."[23]

Labor, the world of drudgery, was a peculiarly charged aspect of the demonic whir that characterized the world of matter. To hold oneself back from labor was to draw a clear line between oneself and the perpetual turning of a cosmic machine. As a young man, Mani had annoyed his fellow villagers by refusing to feed himself through tilling the ground and through plucking vegetables from the lush gardens that surrounded their settlement in southern Mesopotamia. Instead, he would stand outside the gardens and ask to receive his food as an act of almsgiving, as though he were a beggar.[24] For the only relation to the world of which a "chosen" soul such as his own was capable was one of being as totally outside its sinister processes as a beggar was outside the normal processes of the economy.

Altogether, deep thought on the drudgery of labor was central to the radical tradition that became so prominent in Syria. This is perhaps not altogether surprising. We are dealing with a region of dense agrarian settlement, sufficiently wealthy to be able to support a certain number of wanderers, and flanked, to north and south, by regions of mountain and steppes that enabled the lucky few—the nomad, the brigand, and the holy man—to slip into an environment free from the harsh discipline of the plough. The same surge of population that, in the fourth and fifth centuries, covered the highlands of Syria with villages of unparalleled density, also cast loose on the roads an impressive number of charismatic wanderers.[25]

Furthermore, this was the same geographical region that had produced the Atrahasis myth in ancient Sumer and the opening chapters of the book of Genesis, and that had decisively influenced the *Works and Days* of Hesiod.[26] Its inhabitants had long wondered why it was that human beings had come "to bear the drudgery [passed on to them] by the [toil-less] gods."[27] Seen against a truly millennia-long background, the exegesis of the fall of Adam and Eve into toil (as this became current in a vocal stream of Syriac Christianity) was the last of a long series of sad ruminations, by means of which the settled populations of the Fertile Crescent had attempted to make sense (since at least the second millennium BC) of the social trauma created by the agrarian revolution of the Later Stone Age.[28]

Like all narratives of the loss of a golden age, where human beings had once enjoyed freedom from toil, radical Christian accounts of the Fall of Adam and Eve presented human society as caught in the dull creak of ponos, of drudgery. Unlike the Manichees, Syrian writers in this tradition did not believe that the entire material world had been corrupted. But they did believe, in no uncertain terms, that human society as a whole had fallen. Adam and Eve and their descendants had lost a first moment of sublime leisure. They had declined into the present careworn state of society, by which human beings were dominated by the need to work so as to eat. Unlike the Augustinian tradition, with which we are better acquainted in the Latin West, the fall of Adam and Eve had not brought about a profound inner weakening of the will, which was shown in its most subtle and enduring form in unregulated sexual desire. Rather, the true fall—the fall that blotted out all others in the imagination of many Syrians—had been a fall from the work-free abundance of Eden into the present world of toil.

As the Syriac author of the *Liber Graduum* (*The Book of Degrees*) explained, in the early fifth century, Adam and Eve had not known drudgery in Eden. Wrapped in contemplation, their "labor" had consisted only in the "labor of angels"—the *pôlhana' de mala'kê*.[29] They had been *fellahin*, "workers," all right. But they had been workers of the spirit: their backs had not been broken, their hands had not been hardened by "earthly" toil. Their toil, instead, had been the weightless, ethereal toil of prayer, joining their voices with the angels in ceaseless praise of God, their bodies swaying gently, but without violent effort, as they bowed before Him.[30]

Christ had brought back, in Himself, the "unbearable lightness" of Adam, and had extended it to His true followers. A few elect souls might free themselves from the world of labor, to wander freely along the roads of the Middle East. In so doing, they would fulfill the saying of Jesus to his disciples: "Therefore, do not take care for tomorrow, for tomorrow will take care for itself" (Matthew 6:34).

This was yet another opaque and potentially dangerous saying of the Lord that seems to have taken on a new, more urgent, and more concrete social meaning in the later years of the third century. Quite as much as His command to place one's "treasure in Heaven" by giving one's fortune to the poor, it set the Christian Middle East on fire.[31]

Recent excellent work by Philippe Escolan, *Monachisme et Église. Le monachisme syrien du Ive au Viie siècle. Un ministère charismatique,*[32] combined with the vivid survey of Daniel Caner, *Wandering, Begging Monks: Spiritual Authority and the Promotion of Monasticism,*[33] have pointed clearly, in their very titles, to the existence of an entire "Third World" of monastic practice, whose extent and vigor we had not formerly appreciated.

Thus, throughout Syria and other eastern provinces, the spread of Manichaeism coincided with a wave of "wandering, begging monks" who considered (like the Manichaean Elect) that they were fully entitled to the support of the faithful because, being freed from the shame of physical labor, they were engaged in the "weightless" labor of prayer on behalf of all persons. No matter how deeply they might differ in their beliefs, the structures of the groups crystallized by these two movements were startlingly similar: a core of "perfect" religious virtuosos lived in a symbiotic relationship with lay disciples in whose economic activities they shared in no way, and on whose generosity they depended entirely.[34]

It is against the background of these presuppositions that we should place the answer offered by the monks of Egypt to the Christian piety that had prevailed in Syria and that threatened also to make its way far up the valley of the Nile. In the mid-fourth century, the Christian regions of the East as a whole (Egypt and Syria alike) were poised between two great and evenly balanced alternatives, represented by two conflicting wings of the ascetic movement. One wing, as we have seen, claimed to have risen above labor, and to be entitled to support through the alms of the laity. The other wing (of which we know more, because it came to be more fully represented in the monastic traditions of Western Europe) projected an image of ferocious self-sufficiency, in which sedentary monks were expected to feed themselves by the work of their own hands. More than that: the monks were supposed to do so with such zeal and efficiency that they could send food to the poor of distant regions.[35]

It was because of this wider debate that manual work came to enjoy pride of place in Egyptian monastic folklore. Precisely because it formed part of a counterimage to Syrian practice, the issue of work in the self-image of Egyptian monasticism was peculiarly charged—and charged in a manner diametrically opposite from that presented in the Syrian world. Work was embraced because it summed up the stance of the "true" monk to society and to the world around him. It was a denotator of his abiding humanity. The monk had to eat. Therefore the monk had to work. Therefore the monk was human. Visitors to the notoriously austere Apa Sisoes noticed the little pile of newly made baskets stacked against the wall of his cell. They asked what this meant. "Sisoes has to eat from time to time" was the old man's answer.[36] Unlike the ethereal Manichaean Elect and the "angelic" wandering holy man of Syria, who seemed to float above the human condition because they were linked to society only by the thin thread of "alms" offered by the pious, the Egyptian monk put himself forward as a normal human being. And this was plain for all to see, in the most blunt manner possible. The monk was still linked to his fellows by the crude fact of work and by the need to sell the products of the labor of his hands—and even (on occasions) of the labor of his own body, as a seasonal harvester in the fields of local landowners—in order to live.

It is important to point out that what was at stake were not social and economic issues, as modern persons might conceive them. Modern scholars of Egyptian monasticism (and especially of the great monasteries founded in the 340s by Pachomius) have often hailed the monks of Egypt for having discovered the dignity of labor.[37] But concern for "the dignity of labor" was alien to the monks of the fourth century. They were exercised by a far more serious matter. Could any human being hope to recover the dignity of Adam? Or was that dignity so far removed from humankind that it could be recovered only through long decades of labor on the self, through penance and self-mortification, sheltered from human society by the charged, if largely notional, frontier of the desert? That is: Did the monk remain human? The answer was firm. Monks could not become angels, and the most unambiguous sign of their continued humanity was the fact that they had to work in order to feed themselves.

As a result, the illusions of work-free "angels" in the Syrian tradition were the stuff of humor in the hermitages of Egypt. There was to be no room, in Egypt, for "angelic" Wannabees:

It was said of John the Dwarf, that one day he said to his elder brother, "I would like to be free of all care, like the angels, who do not work, but ceaselessly offer worship to God." So he took off his cloak and went away into the desert. After a week he came back to his brother. When he knocked on the door, he heard his brother say... "Who are you?" He said, "I am John, your brother." But he replied, "But John has become an angel, and henceforth he is no longer among men."... His brother did not let him in, but left him there in distress until morning. Then, opening the door, he said to him: "You are a human being and you must work again in order to eat." Then John made a prostration before him and said, "Forgive me."[38]

We must be extremely careful not to draw premature economic conclusions from such anecdotes. We are dealing, rather, with a vigorous war of self-images. In many ways, this war of self-images was as insubstantial as a dramatic shadow play. It bore very little relation to the real life of real monks. But behind this play of shadows lay real divergences of outlook. The monks of Egypt liked to present themselves to outsiders as holy stakhanovites. They claimed to live in fully autarkic communities, capable of generating large surpluses to be dispensed in the form of alms to the poor. Latin and Greek observers passed on this industrious and eminently charitable self-image of the monks of Egypt with evident approval to later generations.[39] When Augustine contrasted the otiose life of the Manichaean Elect with the industrious monks of Egypt and the Christian East, his confident picture showed how little Augustine and his Western contemporaries knew (or wished to know) about the real East.[40] They had listened to one side only of the battle that had raged, between Syria and Egypt, for almost a century.

Alas, the patient work of papyrologists, those merciless destroyers of pious representations (I think especially of the studies of Ewa Wipszycka and Roger Bagnall), has shown that the monks of Egypt did not live up to the image that they projected to the outside world. We should not exaggerate the economic potential of the monks. In the fourth and fifth centuries, the great monasteries of Egypt never became the economic powerhouses they claimed to be. Only too often they lay like great beached whales on the social landscape of the Nile. Even if they were not as totally dependent on their laity as the Manichaean Elect and the "angelic" wanderers of Syria claimed to be, the monastic settlements of Egypt remained in constant need of gifts from pious lay persons in order to stay afloat.

Altogether, we are faced with a situation that is similar to that experienced by students of early Buddhist monasticism, where (as in Egypt) legal texts tell a very different story from that passed on to modern scholars through monastic self-presentations. In the words of Geoffrey Schopen, writing on the Buddhist monasteries of northwestern India: "The monks that the redactors [of the legal texts relative to monks and monasteries] envisioned, and the monks that modern scholarship has imagined, are . . . radically different."[41]

But that is another story. What matters is that, by the year 400, a battle of the social imagination had been fought and won in Egypt and in other parts of the Christian world. Let me end by sketching the consequences of the victory, in much of Byzantine Christianity and in the Latin West, of the particular imaginative model of society implied by the labor of the monks. Put in a nutshell, human society, and the human suffering associated with real divisions between rich and poor, took on a density that was lacking in the "cosmic" option of the Manichees and even in the "angelic" option of the Syrian wanderers. For both these religious groups, human society somehow lacked substance. Dwarfed by the majesty of a fallen cosmos, as with the Manichees, or overshadowed by the great sadness of Adam's fall into a world of labor, as with the wandering monks of Syria, the present-day organization of society itself, and its all-too-palpable divisions between rich and poor, represented but a thin sliver of the human condition. The division of rich and poor seemed trivial compared with the stark division between the freedom of a spirit-filled few and the dull servitude to material things in which the majority of humanity, rich and poor alike, found itself caught.

By claiming to live from the labor of their hands, the monks of Egypt did little to improve the economy of their region or to alleviate the misery of the poor. But they did assert, through working, that they were fully paid up human members of a human society characterized by sharp contours. The division between rich and poor was fundamental to the human condition. It was associated with the perpetual burden of work. It was a division that demanded to be bridged through alms to the real poor. Products of real work by monks, who did not only offer the ethereal benefits of prayer and teaching, were distributed—by these monks quite as much as by every other pious Christian—to those who stood at the very bottom of the sinister slag heap, piled up through the ages, by perpetual labor. For it was the real poor, and not a spiritual elite raised above human care, who were to receive the fruit of the real labor of others. This "downward" flow of alms, into society, was the only way in which treasure moved "upward" from earth to heaven. As a result, the dogged insistence of the monks that manual labor should be combined with almsgiving to the poor (largely symbolic though it might have been, in many cases) contributed to an imaginative victory that has placed at the very heart of our modern conscience a model of society divided between rich and poor, in which the rich have a religious duty to support the poor. We must remember that this victory was by no means a foregone conclusion. In this matter, modern persons are the heirs of the monks of Egypt. Our sense of responsibility for the poor, based on the sense of a shared human nature, expressed through shared involvement in the world of labor, is based on their victory over a powerful, cogent, and widespread alternative. We should remember this distant but decisive victory when we discuss issues of social responsibility in our own times.

If we look out at the great Third World of Christianity in Africa and the Middle East, we find a very different social and religious landscape. We need to appreciate the power and the sheer geographical extent of the alternative model represented by the Manichees and by the begging monks of Syria. For, when seen against the spacious background of Eurasia as a whole, the Manichees and the monks of Syria were the norm, and the self-supporting communities of Egypt and the West were the exception. Looking at the world from Mesopotamia rather than from Rome, it is quite possible to imagine the emergence of a Christian monastic landscape that closely resembled the spread of the *sangha* of Buddhist countries—communities of ascetic *virtuosi* fed by their laity as part of an unceasing spiritual exchange, by which matter (in the form of food) was offered in return for the ethereal, spiritual goods of prayer and preaching.[42] In following the fortunes of Christian asceticism across the Fertile Crescent, from Syria to Egypt, we have the privilege of listening in to one end of a debate on alms and labor that was as wide as Eurasia itself. The outcome of this debate ensured that large parts of the Christian Middle East and Western Europe did not become what Eurasia east of the Pamirs—northern India, Central Asia, and western China—became, in precisely these centuries. To use the words of the Chinese Buddhist pilgrim of the early fifth century, Fa-Hsien, who had walked all the way from China to India following the route along which the Buddhist sangha had moved from northern India to China, these were "Lands of the Begging Bowl."[43] By contrast, Western Europe, Egypt, and much of Byzantium did not become what most of Eurasia had become: they were not "Lands of the Begging Bowl." In theory at least, they were lands of working monks. Altogether, things look very different depending on where one views them from. What seems a foregone conclusion in the history of Western Christianity is, in fact, the exception that proves the rule for the religious evolution of most of Asia.

So let me end, in Egypt, with the little known words of the great Coptic monastic prayer to the Archangel Michael:

> We find the intercession of Michael in the strenuous work of our hands...in the quietness of the oxen and the growth of the lambs...in the body of the vine and the gladness which is in the wine...in the fatness and the savor of the olives...And we find the intercession of Michael [also] when he is gentle towards those who are weary with toil and when he giveth them strength.[44]

CHAPTER 3

Medieval Monks on Labor and Leisure

JOHN VAN ENGEN

Nearly a century ago historians and historical sociologists singled out work and prayer as especially revealing of human activity. Attitudes toward work and prayer, Max Weber (1864–1920) and R. H. Tawney (1880–1962) contended, significantly shaped the varied histories of early modern peoples: those commercially successful Calvinists (England, Holland, New England), for instance, over against malingering Medieval Catholics and Early Modern Lutherans. These observations were shrewd—if driven as well by debates in their own day over observably different levels of industrialization and capitalization. Fundamental too were methodological disputes, whether society and economy should be approached empirically, or culturally and historically. Since then we have come through at least two more interpretive cycles: a massive turn to the empirical from the 1950s to the 1970s, energized by statistics and computers (pray-ers then given no value unless they could be counted up), followed by an equally sharp turn to the cultural and representational (facts and statistics now put into quotation marks). If we turn to the study of peasant labor in the Middle Ages, Georges Duby, building on Marc Bloch, pioneered bottom-up empirical studies of local societies with his thesis on Mâcon, then made the tripartite schema of pray-ers, fighters, and workers an omnipresent cultural shorthand for medieval society.[1] Paul Freedman began with detailed social and legal studies of serfs and society in Catalonia (which he continues), then sensitively explored cultural and religious representations of agricultural workers in his *Images of the Medieval Peasant* (1999).

Another set of interpreters has approached work by way of religion. Several influential twentieth-century historians attributed the Western world's economic and technological expansion ultimately to its Christian worldview. Monks were key, they held, especially Benedictine monks. They first dignified labor, also took an interest in technology, and opened the way to Europe's productive future—thus Lewis Mumford, Ernst Benz, and Lynn White jr., the last, one of my teachers. Jacques LeGoff objected, rightly, that in medieval culture labor meant first of all travail, the hardship resulting from sin, a punishing or penitential reality thus. In 1987 George Ovitt evinced skepticism about any significant monastic contribution to a revaluation of work, while in 2006 Patricia Ranft argued enthusiastically for a "theology of work" in the eleventh century, and my late and lamented colleague Sabine MacCormack favored Augustine over Benedict as first articulating a Christian revaluation of work.[2]

Such contrarieties should not surprise; they lie deep in our sources. In Freedman's account peasants appear as both Christlike and vile, their work as dignified and beneath contempt, their work's claim on society as nil and as leveraging revolt. About 1160 John of Salisbury famously treated society as a body: the royal head, the priestly heart, the knightly and judicial arms, and so on. The feet on which this whole body stood and moved, he poignantly says, were peasant-workers. To them, however, the overwhelming majority, he devoted only one spare chapter.[3]

Religion thus in the making or the writing of history: Why should we take it up again? Why worry a topic discussed so often, also dismissed so often? By one account religion is disappearing from history as surely and unstoppably as air leaking out of a balloon. Max Weber called this *Entzauberung,* all the magic released, escaping into the ether, leaving us with economy and society. By another history was integral to the sacred and the sacred in turn to history, and remains so. Both are views very much alive, indeed both arguably on the advance in the last while. Historians sensitive to religious experience but committed to transparent intellectual integrity and a conversation that transcends the sectarian find themselves in a nearly impossible middle ground. We also come to this—no matter our own convictions or practices—as heirs, perhaps unwitting, to a multilayered tradition, an inheritance both rich and disastrous. For fourteen hundred years Christianity was accounted the established religion in Europe and then in the lands of its colonial heirs, hence compulsory from birth, while also very big business, social and religious power deeply interwoven. At the same time it was no less intensely local and varied and even—the term rightly and contextually understood—voluntary. Consequently it is not easy, even as historians, to locate a rightful place for religion in our understanding of society, this itself a matter contested for centuries, sometimes at the point of a sword, continuously with the point of a pen.

Such disputes did not disappear two centuries ago with Enlightenment and Revolution. History writing itself often became part of that struggle. In the last two or three generations, by contrast, modern historians tended to exclude religion too much, often still do, only to be surprised or puzzled by its continued presence, while medievalists may be accused of focusing on it too much, particularly again of late. Religion in the Middle Ages, multiple in forms and outlets, and itself ever changing, was wholly bound up with society, hence cannot be separated out from property or law or learning or gender or literature—or labor. By inversion, historians cannot exclude or discount religious approaches to grasping that past any more than they can economic or political or gendered. It always comes down to particulars. Here, briefly, we will turn our attention to particulars concerning labor and leisure as factors in the making of medieval history.

We begin with basics about Scripture and medieval monks, then look at select twelfth-century texts and cases. This was a conversation continuously framed by biblical texts. At the beginning God placed Adam and Eve in the garden of Paradise to tend and care for it: work as delight. After eating the forbidden fruit and being expelled, they had to work to survive, Eve bearing children in "labor," Adam harvesting land now cursed with thorns and thistles and eating by the sweat of his brow (Gen. 3:16–19): work as punishment or penance. The Ordinary Gloss on the Bible, the standard reference work for learned teachers and preachers from about 1150, noted (this ascribed to Augustine): "That these are the labors of humankind on earth no one does not know, and that this indubitably would not be so if the bliss that was Paradise had been kept."[4] Hard labor was self-evident and incontrovertible, the human condition summed up here in tongue-twisting double negatives. Two centuries later (1320s) the Franciscan exegete Nicholas of Lyra updated the gloss, offering a strikingly domestic interpretation that would be read throughout the late medieval and Reformation periods: for taking the apple woman was subjected to man in punishment, and man thus also punished because he had now to procure necessities for her and an entire household. Working the land generated anxiety (*anxietas hominis*), whereas prior to the fall tending it was pleasurable (*recreatio*).[5] Note the amazing reversal, from recreation to anxiety, overshadowed by a pointed gendered turn.

Already in Paradise God had structured human time with six days for work and one for rest (Gen. 2:2–3), a scheme strongly reinforced in the

ten commandments (Ex. 20:8–11). In medieval Europe Sabbath observance
eventually became Sunday worship. For laborers required rest brought relief
but also enforced leisure (problematic if crops or animals needed tending,
or in shops if jobs needed finishing). The twelfth-century Gloss, interest-
ingly, was silent on practice. But in the fourteenth century Nicholas of
Lyra was plainspoken: six days are for sustaining things required for human
life (*necessaria*), the seventh for full focus on divine worship (*diuino cultui
totaliter applices*); or as he also put it, time when you were obliged to be free
for things divine (*homo tenetur uacare diuinis*).[6] Earlier commentators tended
anxiously to distinguish Sunday rest from the Jewish Sabbath but then also
to project it ultimately into the future, the seventh day as the seventh age,
the time of eternal rest. For then, Rupert of Deutz says representatively,
"We, truly wearied, truly pilgrims and captives, will be released from our
present captivity, able to breathe again there as those comforted, refreshed
there after our labors and burdens."[7] But rest would not come without work;
indeed required work. To "sanctify the Sabbath," Rupert explained, meant
"in all your works to look to the reward of God or prepare a rest for yourself in God as a reward: this is truly to keep the Sabbath day holy."[8] Work, if
punishing and wearying, was also penitential: laboring in God and for God
toward an eternal Sabbath. Work, though not itself delight, held out to faithful laborers prospects of delight.

In the 930s, in a very early "mirror" for Christians of differing ranks,
Rather of Verona began his injunctions with the common Christian, the
majority plebs, the peasant. Be a laborer (*Esto laborator*), he says, just and
assiduous, content with your own, defrauding no one. Fear God, invoke
saints, attend church, honor priests, offer the tithes and first fruits of your
labors to God, love your wife and her alone, visit the sick.[9] These were to be
lives defined by work, physical work producing sustenance for themselves
and others, moral work respecting and caring for others. The only form
of prayer noted was to call on the saints (*precare sanctos*). But importantly
presumed, what made them "a good Christian among the many Christians," was that such labor would ultimately receive its reward. In the twelfth
century the Benedictine Honorius Augustodunensis made it explicit: in the
end peasant people would mostly be saved because they lived simply and
fed the people of God by their sweat. Few knights would be saved owing to
their plundering, and few merchants or artisans owing to their fraud—while
priests could be saved only if they lived and taught well. Notably, monks
who failed to keep their rules would end up more pitiably than all others.[10]
Scholars have often singled out Honorius's passage as showing empathy for
peasants and their labor (from whose work he lived too). It turns however on

peasant labor conceived as penitential and ultimately redemptive by contrast with the vicious ways of nearly all other social types. There existed a still higher form of life, as he and most Benedictines saw it. At the outset of the New Testament the Devil had tempted Jesus to make it easy for himself by turning stones into bread. Christ retorted (from Deut. 8:3): man does not live by bread alone but by the word of God (Matt. 4:4). Though humanly impossible, as Rupert (and others) noted, for forty days Moses had enjoyed it atop the mountain by living on the divine "word" or "precept."[11] Rupert, himself a monk, presumed that those living on the "word" in the desert or atop a mountain rose above those human constraints requiring work six days a week to win their bread.

Another juxtaposition of texts proved equally important. Advising the community at Thessaloniki, Paul issued a dictum: "If a person will not work, he shall not eat" (II Thess. 3:10) and claimed to have modeled that rule himself while among them: no free sustenance for anyone who was not productive. Yet in an earlier letter he had enjoined that same community to "pray without ceasing" (I Thess. 5: 17). In short, there was to be productive work and unceasing prayer all at once. Mostly medieval glossators saw the latter as meant primarily for dedicated religious. The Ordinary Gloss nonetheless cited Augustine's "on the work of monks" to the effect that they should work so they would not go out begging. Friar Nicholas anxiously added a caveat: that the former dictum not be aimed at the "able-bodied poor" (thus beguines or mendicants like himself), nor be invoked to halt benefactions.[12] Another image widely invoked in the Middle Ages turned on Jesus's remarks to Martha and Mary, one busy with domestic tasks, the other sitting in rapt attention at the feet of the teacher, the latter designated as the *pars optima*.[13] Rupert conflated all these texts at one point to explain what "sanctifying the Sabbath" meant in gospel counsel rather than legal precept. As a legal precept (i.e., for Jews and laity), it meant working well (*operando bene*) so as to establish your work for a true and holy Sabbath (i.e., heaven). As gospel counsel (for monks) it meant that "even now you sabbatize" by rising above the active life and making yourself free (*uaces*) for contemplation, the better part. One who "uses the world well at present" is a faithful servant; one aspiring to perfection will live in "sweet friendship" as a son.[14] Presumptions about work and leisure entered the Middle Ages, in sum, already informed by many considerations, not least coming out of the new monastic ideal.

Fourth-century men and women had turned their backs on an emerging Christian Empire to seek solitude and simplicity. They went to pray but also worked. In all the early accounts, from the lives of Anthony or Paul to collective histories of monastic communities and the early rules, we find the same: prayer and work, psalms and basket-making or gardening.[15] Romans too had their dedicated priests and priestesses, and had variously tolerated sectarian cults, but in the main they expected their religion to integrate rather than separate society and to reaffirm rather than repudiate social goods: honor and exercise of the will, property and material needs, family and progeny. These "men of God" inverted Roman values and did so by placing prayer first while requiring or expecting work as well. To be sure, Hellenistic thinkers and practitioners had also conceived ways of disciplining spirit and body on behalf of achieving virtue and meditative *otium*, as Pierre Hadot has set out.[16] But these Christian separatists envisioned a way centered on praying the psalms. In the 420s John Cassian introduced Eastern teachings to Western monks in a passage that proved formative for a thousand years: "The end of every monk, and perfection of heart, aims for a constant and uninterrupted perseverance in prayer, and strives after, in so far as this is granted human fragility, an unmoving tranquility and perpetual purity of mind. For this we unwearyingly seek in every work of the body as in contrition of spirit; for this we constantly exercise."[17] The end is *tranquilitas* (sometimes also *quies*), the way unceasing prayer, the human means *labor* and *exercitium* and *contritio*. To avoid disquiet and sloth or tedium monks were to work with their hands like the apostles, not eat the bread of others, not yield to the vice of idle leisure (*otiositas*). This entire section, turning on *accedia* (sloth or tedium), is a sustained blast at idleness and the vice of otium, and work of the hands is offered as the main remedy, authorized by Paul's example and texts.[18] Cassian cites a saying from Egyptian fathers: a working monk might be struck by a single demon, but an idle one (*otiosum*) laid waste by innumerable spirits.[19]

This all played itself out amidst longstanding Roman notions of otium and *negotium*, leisure and worldly affairs.[20] Monastic prayer might be assimilated to otium (in time it certainly was).[21] But choosing to make baskets or cook or harvest crops, to work with rough hands for one's own sustenance, even take up slave labor as penitential exercise, this undercut any dignity accorded Roman otium, which might extend to include dignified pursuits in governance and culture and estate management. This new monastic otium, moreover, was open to people way down the social ranks. Monastic teaching, to be clear, however, treated otium initially as a vice, as ruinous to prayer and discipline, themselves conceived as work, even as the new solitary's most characteristic and subversive vice. They went so far as to invent a new word, otiositas, to stand for all that could go wrong in leisured idleness.[22] The threat was quite concretely that monastic withdrawal would take on all the worst aspects of Roman idleness. Thirty years before Cassian, Augustine, at his bishop's request, assailed some in Carthage who said they were free (*vacare*) for prayer and psalms and the word of God. In his finest rhetorical pique he noted in his *de opere monachorum* that those singing songs could also work with their hands and bring solace to their labor by these spiritual rhythms. Do we not know, he goes on, what vanities and obscenities craftsmen in the theater indulge even as they work with their hands? In this new way of life (monasticism), where senators become workers (*laboriosi*), should artisans, he asks, become leisured (*otiosi*)?[23]—the inversion here rendered rhetorically as only he could.[24]

Just as striking is Benedict. The work of God carried out in the divine office, *opus dei,* structures a monk's day. But labor (*opera manuum*) and reading (*lectio*) was to fill it out: labor to secure necessities, it occupying the first to fourth hours from Easter to October, reading the fourth to sixth.[25] This famous chapter was not in fact about labor, however, even if later Cistercians invoked it to the contrary. It was rather about otiositas, its opening word, that vice most inimical to the soul, the whole here an echo of Cassian. By the mid-sixth century hand labor in practice was mostly domestic, done in the kitchen or cellar or gardens. If monks had also to do rougher field work, Benedict went on, they were not to grieve: because they were truly monks if they lived by the work of their hands as the Fathers had. In the mid-sixth century that ideal was plainly already a fading memory. Monastic houses were becoming endowed and privileged institutions, if still mostly lay ones.

Was the effect of all this, then, to revalue work? Yes, but only if we recognize that work gained its value first of all as penitential as well as self-sustaining and restorative, not as an end in itself. Its redemptive value, mostly presumed, got articulated ironically mostly for peasants. Even then there were theological and social complications. *Labor,* even *labor corporis,* often meant in the first instance "effort," in Cassian a paradoxical effort to pray to become tranquil and to work to become quiet, while work, whether in sung psalms or of the hands, was normally *opus.* In a diatribe to Rusticus on true monasticism Jerome said simply that all Egyptian monasteries required both, work and effort (*nullum absque opere ac labore*), for sustenance and salvation.[26] These early solitaries, male or female, were nearly all laypeople, remaining so into the seventh century, and were enjoined to set aside all social or economic distinctions. This, notably, was the first point in Augustine's rule (*praeceptum*), made very firmly. Their main work became to keep a constant round of psalms and prayers, the second point in Augustine's rule,[27] what Benedict called the opus dei, this work of praying to be leavened by hand work as well as reading with mind and mouth and ear. Otiositas was the enemy, the shadowy but every-present threat.

Five hundred years after Benedict, six hundred after Augustine, large-scale change had transformed monastic practice. Monks ceased to be lay, nearly all now clerics, most priests; the opus dei, with vast expansions and private masses, functioned in good part as intercession for benefactors (hence All Soul's Day); and hand work rested on peasants whose labor supplied income and sustenance.[28] As exemplars of prayer and discipline, monks and nuns represented a set-apart station in society, and if true to their vowed life would sit as judges in the Last Judgment rather than standing among the judged.[29] In social and human experience did their opus dei appear in fact now all that different from Roman otium, cultivated leisure? And in the divine realm would their prayers and vigils and fasts yield that hundredfold (another biblical image) promised monks rather than the layfolks' mere thirtyfold? Did their work truly surpass the penitential labors of peasants? Some had worries. As Rudolphus Glaber tells it in 1045–46, a demon planted precisely that anxiety in a monk, very probably himself, a story we have still in his own hand. This monk had, notably, no real response—except to label it a notion most false, quite demonic, and to insist that not all people would in fact gain glory.[30] How many clericalized Benedictine monks, often privileged and aristocratic in social reality, thought of themselves as a "leisured class"? How many were given to long rounds of intercessory prayer as work and a religious ideal? At the end of the eleventh century new monks and canons castigated them as mostly the former.

Since the 1960s historians have made much of the twelfth-century turn to poverty and simplicity, to a straitened prayer with interior meditation, to manual labor with communal poverty.[31] Interpretive disputes continue: to what degree were monks driven out of choir to do field work? Peasant laborers in turn invited halfway into choir as lay brothers? Was this animated by an idealistic turn to primitive ideals at great personal and economic cost? Was it as much a way to exploit a tight labor market, binding peasant workers to monasteries with hopes of eternal benefits?[32] In any case, work itself, together with its spiritual or economic value, was hereby put back into discussion across society and culture, and most forcefully by monks.

Benedict had drawn up a guide he called a "school for beginners." Around 1100 Cistercians turned it into a legislative document to be kept "to the letter" to assure salvation, Benedict's prescription for single houses made the constitution for a Europeanwide religious order overseen by a legislative body (the general chapter). The Rule's chapter beginning with the word *otiositas* now became positive law requiring manual labor of everyone, if from the beginning *conversi* (lay brothers) remained oriented more to field work and monks to sung choir. Bernard of Clairvaux's opening sermon on the

Song of Songs, preached late in 1135, closes with him saying, "The hour is upon us in which both poverty and the Rule drive us out to manual labor" (*nos exire urget ad opera manuum et paupertas et institutio regularis*)—work thus an economic necessity and a religious rule.[33] We also have a moving image in the twenty-sixth sermon, Bernard's lament over his just-departed brother who as cellarer had handled all the house's internal practical affairs as well as socioeconomic business. In Cistercian teaching the blessing of work rested at least in part on its penitential quality as well, not just obedience to the Rule or its overcoming idleness and providing sustenance.[34] But that did not close the social gap between Latinate monks and illiterate lay brothers. In the earliest of Cistercian *Usages* for lay brothers we find this harsh indictment of current abbatial practices:

> Some, holding them in contempt because of their innate simplicity, think that material food and clothing are to be provided for them more sparingly than for monks, but that they are nevertheless imperiously to be made to do forced labor. Others, on the contrary, giving in to their murmuring more than is expedient for souls, indulge bodies the better to get more work if they treat them with greater indulgence as regards food and greater laxity as regards clothing.[35]

Perhaps there was a real effort to close the social gap in some measure by way of the spiritual value of work: clerical monks brought back to the penitential and potentially redemptive qualities of hand work, lay brothers brought into the spiritual value of sung prayer. But at stake too were the definition and blessings of work. We hear it in the startled response of the Benedictines.

Rupert of Deutz (ca. 1075–1129), originally of St. Lawrence in Liège, watched his own archbishop, just across the river Rhine, begin to patronize these new orders, and Rupert's patron, Abbot Cuno of Siegberg, urgently demanded a written intervention. Rupert complied reluctantly, though revealingly. Some were actually saying, he noted, that a monk could not be saved (*non potes hic saluari*) unless he worked with his hands as set out in the Rule; this had made "simpler brothers in our monasteries [i.e., *hic*] very anxious." More, since Benedict's Rule had barely mentioned priesthood, some monks now were focused (*intenti*) almost entirely on manual labor and gave little attention to the daily celebration of mass.[36] Whence this burning question: Was it better, indeed more apostolic, to live by work of the hands, or from the altar and its income? Rupert, on the defensive, retorted sharply. What Benedict said about acquiring one's victuals, about plowing, planting, and so on, he had uttered as permission, not precept, a concession to necessity, not what he preferred (*non est beati Benedicti preceptum sed tantummodo permissum siue patientie consilium*). Monks, unless driven by necessity, should not leave their cloisters to work in fields. Passing over the Desert Fathers in silence, Rupert cited saints who had endowed monks so they would not need to work in fields.[37] Then he went to the heart of the matter: it is good to work with the hands to flee otiositas, he conceded, citing the Rule verbatim, but best to live a Sabbath rest in holy otium with the Word.[38] To sit at the feet of Christ as Mary did, the better part, meant to serve the altar, there where the mysteries of Christ are set out. More, he added provocatively and defensively, this applied equally to illiterate laypeople who were serving those who served at the altar.

But why then had Benedict said almost nothing about priesthood while enjoining manual labor? Rupert grew bolder, again echoing Benedict. The Rule, he says, was written for beginners, its monastic yoke only a beginning. Those who added to it a clerical life of priesthood attained apostolic perfection. Why would people invest nearly their entire hope in the work of their hands, in pruning trees or picking fruit, when they could be committing themselves to that highest service by commemorating Christ at the altar and coincidentally receiving goods for their labor?[39] Opus dei here gets rendered emphatically as priestly service at the altar—an even greater stretch than Cîteaux's prescribed labor—and that service in turn as labor, with monk-priests the worthiest laborers, theirs the "full daily exercise of spiritual work" (*totum quotidianum spiritualis operis exercitium*). Further, the harvest is great, and the workers few. That is to say: many have given gifts and asked for prayers, but few priests now rise above merchant priests to do their work as prayerful monk-priests. Objecting to work at the altar, then, this supreme and highest work, was beyond comprehension. Rupert's text is key. It came earliest and had forced from him an articulation of the Black Monk's implicit vision of contemplative prayer and priestly intercession as work, indeed as the highest work.

The social and cultural stigmas attached to peasant and artisanal labor did not disappear; for the new monks, paradoxically, this partly comprised its penitential or apostolic character. Work itself, however, was now something to conger with, itself yielding value, also spiritual value, and could be extended to activities other than peasant labor or sung choir. Among Benedictine monks a Theophilus Presbyter (probably Roger of Helmarshausen) wrote up recipes for metal work, painting and so on (a known and even antique genre), but chose to add prefaces justifying these crafts as being work of and for God, even as moved by the seven gifts of the Holy Spirit.[40] Victorine canons regular in Paris, operating at the edges of an emerging university, included the mechanical arts among divinely gifted forms of human knowing. Ever after, mechanical arts entered into encyclopedic traditions along with the logical and rhetorical arts, if below them and with their moral ends in view.[41] In a most unusual combination of prayerful otium and work for reward the Templars and Hospitallers combined the work of fighting (and nursing) with the disciplined leisure of religious life.[42] So too with the emergence of schools and schoolmen, these university men engaged reading and teaching ("clerical" tasks) as labor, eventually forming themselves into a guild (*universitas*). Questions soon arose, even making their way into canon law, about this work's status and nature, quite particularly whether it could or should be compensated.[43] Likewise, those now cultivating the new literature and culture of courtly love in leisured gentility were said to be engaged in "labors of love," if for rewards of refinement, virtue, and fleshly pleasure.[44] Virtue too required labor, and love was itself both a virtue and a source of virtue—this a point on which monks, Cistercians in particular, were at one with troubadours. In his *Mirror of Charity* of 1140–43, written for novices at the behest of Bernard, Ailred of Rievaulx taught that "external labors" (whether of asceticism, discipline, or the hands) were meant primarily to aid the "internal labor" by which monks cultivated a virtuous and loving self.[45]

Opus manuum, work with the hands, we should recall, was only one part of what Benedict had enjoined to ward off otiositas. The other piece was lectio, reading, work done with head and mouth and ear. On the whole we do not find a similar prescriptive program set out with respect to reading. What we do find historically, as scholars know and wholly presuppose, is an unprecedented expansion of writers and readers in this era, quite especially readers and writers of religious literature. Scholars speak of a new "literacy," a "monastic humanism," a "new interiority" with a new "individualistic" expressivity. We might recall two basic realities. With benefactions and private masses cut out for these new monks and hermits, and the opus dei itself cut back, they were left with, so to speak, far more time on their hands: time for internal work, reading especially but also writing. Second, these groups now insisted on "adult" converts, not child oblates; many entering were adolescents or young men recruited from schools. *Lectio divina* had a long history. But for five hundred years writing new spiritual literature as such had largely fallen away. Now it emerged with explosive force and originality and in unprecedented quantities, religious experience articulated in wondrous Latin prose and prayers and hymns, all the yield of internal work.

This new energy was evident in some Benedictine monks as well: the self-conscious composing of Anselm's prayers and meditations, and the fierce mental work of his self-reflective theological puzzling. Here Rupert, though a Black Monk, was no different, and had himself to confront shocked protests from both clerics and fellow monks: Why all this writing, all this interpreting and reinterpreting, when commentaries enough had been passed down from the Fathers?[46] Contemporaries saw his production as unprecedented, even unwarranted, for instance, his massive commentary on the Gospel of John, the first serious rethinking since Augustine seven hundred years earlier. In an apologetic letter to his patron he began: "I was meditating in the night with my heart and was exercised [see Ps. 77:6]... and the fruit of that meditating and exercising appeared to be this, that I would write." In the prologue to his last completed work, also addressed to Cuno, he said quite simply, also its opening sentence, "My spirit cannot leave any [scriptural] material, whatever may be presented to it and however beyond my powers, untried or unworked [intemptatam siue inoperatam]."[47] He commonly invoked two scriptural images for exegesis, both metaphors of labor: to dig fresh wells in the fields of Scripture, and to turn over the field of Scripture with the ploughshare of his own mental acuity (ingenium).[48] Similarly, Abbot Peter the Venerable, consoling a Cluniac hermit reproached for not taking up manual labor, wrote: "What is more useful than to turn the hand to the pen rather than the plow, plowing up divine letters on the page rather than plowing fields, planting the seed of the word of God on little scraps which, the harvest having matured—that is, books completed—may fill hungering readers with its multiplying fruit."[49] Exegetical reading, interpreting, and writing were not simply leisure; they too represented work, indeed the highest work.

More than fifty years earlier Peter Damian, a reforming hermit and cardinal, referred explicitly to the Rule and the role of lectio as a hedge against otiositas. A prolix writer, in the 1060s he asked two nearby bishops to read his works—this an act at once of deference, self-protection, and self-presentation—and to correct whatever might cause trouble for him with the eternal judge. As for writing itself, he justified it this way:

> I have taken it upon myself to write certain little works, not indeed so I should add anything to ecclesiastical pronouncements (literally: pulpits), which would have been presumptuous, but for this reason primarily: because without some kind of exercise I could not bear the tedium of idle leisure (inertis ocii) and a quite remote cell; so I, who did not know how to sweat usefully with work of the hands, might restrain a wandering and lascivious heart with a certain bridle of meditation and more easily drive away the noise of incoming thoughts and the press of creeping sloth (accidiae: melancholy, weariness).[50]

To his own secretary he wrote that in undisciplined convents bad monks in their idleness learned neither to engage in honest manual labor nor to write (meaning here, first of all, to copy).[51] When Damian withdrew for a time from active reforming life at the curia, Pope Alexander II enjoined him to visit them still by way of his writings (*dictaminibus*)—to which Damian objected that he was most happy when he could just fully enjoy the leisure of meditating and writing (*contemplandi quidem atque dictandi perfruor ocio*). But even in his leisure, he complained, he was assailed by worldly cases/causes and requests for spiritual direction.[52] On another occasion (late 1050s) he set out at length an apparent dispute with Hildebrand (later Pope Gregory VII), the abbot of Monte Cassino (later Pope Victor III), and other core members of the reform party over the meaning of the Sabbath. They, already then, sought to understand "Sabbath" as spiritual service, interpreted here in a very activist sense—this redefinition intriguing in its own right for appealing to a kind of work trumping rest or leisure. Damian argued instead for effort and writing, what he would enjoin (*studeamus*), his a Sabbath not of ignoble leisure but of laborious quietude (*non ignobilis ocii sed laboriosae quietis*).[53] Still it could be "wearisome," he noted on another occasion, to write what no "hearer" wants to receive; whereas if he but knew the work was well-received he could equal Demosthenes or Cicero in output.[54] And in a famous letter to the monks of Cluny where he praised their filling every minute of the day with the divine office as a Spirit-designed work of continuous effort (*tam continui laboris exercitium*), he then intimated almost casually that his own normal act on first reentering his cell was to open a book.[55] Lectio was assuming new forms and new rationales, a blend of labor and leisure, of reading and meditating and writing. This, not their manual labor, constituted in retrospect the most significant work of these new monks and hermits.

How does all this fit with that schema of pray-ers, fighters, and workers that likewise began circulating more widely in the twelfth century? Joachim of Fiore (d. 1202), one of last great twelfth-century Cistercians and the foremost prophet of later medieval apocalyptic, offers us insights and a way to conclude. He too, repeatedly in fact, spoke of reading Scripture as his chief labor, his efforts at understanding and writing as laborious. Bodily labor was not the most difficult (*difficultissimus*). What is "more difficult to grasp than wisdom?" he says. It was the stuff of boys to grasp the letter and instruct the exterior person, but the serious work of adults to acquire spiritual understanding (*intellectus*) and form an interior person. Only with a Spirit-filled contemplative does labor cease, or will cease: purified vessels filled with fruit and wine and singing alleluia, for in Sabbath rest there is no labor—thus Joachim expounding Benedict's Rule in the 1180s.[56] Joachim labored to uncover in Scripture a complex set of historical and exegetical concords: an Old Testament "status" of the Father and married laity, a New Testament "status" of the Son and secular churchmen, and a dawning "status" of the Spirit and contemplative religious. This last "status," while first adumbrated in Benedict, moved into being with Bernard and was now awaiting full fruition—a time not yet but within glimpsing.

Of the seven world ages from Adam to the End, six are full of labor and the present (sixth) is the most "laborious" (*laboriosissime etatis sexte:* full of trouble as well as full of work).[57] Consider the Sabbath. Literally, it means periodically to be free (*vacare*) for psalms and divine meditation. Morally, it refers to those who turn from the world to full divine service (*servitium*). Tropologically, it means to stop observing the law according to the letter and in the Spirit to serve in liberty. Contemplatively, highest in this life, it offers a taste of the third "status," of passing over from a life perfected in labor (*de perfectione uite laboriose*) to a life of leisure (*ad vitam otiosam*)[58]—otium here notably envisioned as the end and no longer the enemy. Movement from the second to the third "status," he says repeatedly, is from the labored to the tranquil, *laboriosi* to *tranquillum* or *quies,* to a time of *vacare,* being set free for leisure: the time of Rachel, life in silence and quietude. This third "status" is what true monks pursue now with their labors, to be poor, to be free for contemplation, to be where there is no labor.[59] For when labors cease, the New Jerusalem will dawn in peace.[60] Alluding obliquely to early Cistercians leaving Molesme and himself leaving the Cistercians, Joachim asks rhetorically what then does labor have to do with leisure (otium)? Until now, he says, the monastic order has borne with labors so it can supplant sons of the flesh by way of exercises both corporal and spiritual; but increasingly it will advance only on the spiritual front.[61] Labor thus was the mark of all life until now, also monastic life, even in its interior and exegetical work; but contemplative leisure was the mark of the age about to dawn, of which some Cistercians and Joachites now had a taste, a glimpse.

Joachim's *Psalter of the Ten Chords* turns directly, after an opening reflection on God as triune, to the three life-forms (*uite differentia*) of the elect, a scheme going back to Augustine and Gregory. As a marker of value he seizes on coinage, also of course a measure of compensation. The married are likened to a coin valued at ten (*denarius*), the clergy to one worth twenty (*vicenarius*), and monks to one worth thirty (*tricenarius*). He presents the value as cumulative: all begin as laity in labor; to which the clergy add their sung psalter, and monks their contemplation. Yet it is more complex, for each must, as with the Trinity, co-inhere in the other. Thus laity approaching God should have a denarius of divine praise (basic prayers), a vicenarius in learning (*doctrina*), but a tricenarius in manual labor—more worth thus for them placed upon basic knowledge (Creed etc.) than prayer but most in work. A monk must have a denarius in work, a vicenarius in doctrina, and a tricenarius in psalmody; clerics a denarius in work too but a vicenarius in psalmody and a tricenarius in doctrina (teaching, learning, doctrine), thus less prayer than teaching. Joachim then accounts for these values. The laity with their humbler lives, bound by chains of necessity to wives and labor, cannot abandon those, lest worse befall, and so they walk a slower pace in the Christian life.[62] Yet they are still worth a tricenarius for their work. Elsewhere he puts it more traditionally: the laity represent a denarius by adhering to the letter of the Old Testament in producing children like the patriarchs; the clergy a vicenarius by adhering to the Old and New Testaments in imitating apostles who gathered in churches along with holy women; and the monks a tricenarius by adhering to a spiritual understanding and imitating those perfect fathers who resided in solitude such as Benedict.[63] What's remarkable here is the imagined balancing of work, teaching, and prayer. Some is necessarily present in every human type, in coins of varying worth. Very significantly, true otium and quies, perfect Sabbath quietude and liberty of Spirit, is projected into a dawning new age that will be free from labor. Up until now work—physical, intellectual, spiritual—has remained the order of the age, and indeed for everyone, if variously.

No history of labor and leisure in premodern Europe, or even modern secular Europe, will make sense of persisting attitudes and practices apart from their reshaping by medieval religious teaching and practice, particularly during the twelfth century. But it was a revaluing that moved in paradoxes. Turning monks out into fields and shops validated hand work for everyone, as inviting peasant laborers into the confines of the cloister validated the work of prayer also for the lowest social ranks (that which Joachim thought them least capable of). Moreover, to become penitential and redemptive, hand labor's value rested in part, ironically, on its lesser social as well as intellectual and spiritual standing. But with idle leisure (otiositas) the declared enemy of the human soul, no one dared argue that life was leisure, not even monks praying in their cloisters; all was work. These new monks (and the new schoolmen) revitalized and validated head work, the lectio meant to hedge against the potentially soul-destroying tedium of lives spent in meditation. If the new monks' experiments in agricultural labor and farm management were successful, even wildly and corrosively successful, so too, even more, was the energy that went into the work of lectio. Otiositas remained the foremost vice. Otium, freedom finally from work, was projected by Joachim into an imminent next or third "status." Little could he have imagined—such are the ironies and contingencies of both history and religion—that within a decade of his death "new spiritual men" would indeed arise, as he prophesied. But Francis and Dominic and their mendicant heirs envisioned begging rather than working as the way to sustain simplicity of life. More, they set up religious life in town centers rather than isolated rural retreats, and they declared reading and teaching and confessing their central work rather than praying. The Dominicans organized a craft guild centered on preaching as its central work and product. All this unleashed a whole new debate centered on begging and working and the (false) leisure of the "able-bodied poor," one that would dominate the next three centuries. That is another story. But it is a story that turns still on labor and leisure refracted through a religious prism.

CHAPTER 4

Sibling Rivalries, Scriptural Communities

What Medieval History Can and Cannot Teach Us about Relations between Judaism, Christianity, and Islam

DAVID NIRENBERG

Since 1989, that is, since the collapse of the Soviet Union and the end of the Cold War, the ways in which we think about the geopolitical importance of the history of religion, and particularly of Islam, have been turned on their heads. A brief quote is sufficient to make the point, this one from a 1957 intelligence report by a high-level U.S. intelligence and security interagency group called the Operations Coordinating Board:

> Islam is important to the United States, *because it has compatible values.* The present division of the world into two camps is often represented as being along political lines, while the true division is between a society in which the individual is motivated by spiritual and ethical values and one in which he is the tool of a materialistic state. Islam and Christianity have a common spiritual base in the belief that a divine power governs and directs human life and aspirations while communism is purely atheistic materialism and is hostile to all revealed religion.[1]

Throughout the Cold War such ideas played an important role in our geopolitics, helping to mobilize, for example, evangelical Christian lobbying for U.S. support of the Taliban in the 1980s.

It is difficult to think of an intelligence assessment coming to the same conclusion today. This is not, I submit, because intelligence assessments about Islam were more accurate in 1957 than they are today, or vice versa. It is rather because of rapid changes of conviction about what constitutes the key ideological alignments and differences between friends and enemies. A good example of the sharpness of that change is Samuel Huntington's famous (or infamous) essay and later book, "The Clash of Civilizations," which argued that geopolitical conflict would now take place along the fault lines between competing civilizational blocks, whose cohesion was largely determined by a shared religious tradition and culture (Buddhist China, Western civilization, and the Islamic world were his main categories). We don't have to agree with Huntington on the precise nature of these "civilizations," the inevitability of their "clash," or the reasons for the particular violence of the conflict with Islam ("Islam has bloody borders," as Huntington notoriously put it).[2] But even if we don't, we can still admit that the world is now much more preoccupied with religious conflict, and particularly conflict between Judaism, Christianity, and Islam, than it was when the Operations Coordinating Board made its predictions in 1957.

One curious result of this heightened preoccupation is that history of religion has become a battlefield in something of a proxy war over how we should think about our own time and place. How to use the past in order to understand the present, and how our commitments in the present should shape our understanding of the past: these questions confront the historian of religion with increasing sharpness. Indeed I found the intelligence quote in a 2004 book by a distinguished medievalist colleague, Richard Bulliet, whose *The Case for Islamo-Christian Civilization* emphasizes a long history of affinities between Islam and Europe, and suggests Islamo-Christian is a more accurate term than Judeo-Christian to characterize the history of what we sometimes call "Western civilization."[3] In the first sections of this essay, I will attempt to criticize some of the ways in which we have been asking and answering these questions. But I will conclude with more positive suggestions about what the study of the religious past can offer citizens of, and believers in, the present.

Today there are literally hundreds of writers turning to the Middle Ages in order to make this or that argument about the relationship between Western and Islamic civilization. The topic has attracted some very good novelists—including Salman Rushdie, Amin Maalouf, and A. B. Yehoshua—and also produced some very polemical history. But the proxy war is not only literary. A number of policy projects also turned to the history of Judaism, Christianity, and Islam, among them the Union for the Mediterranean conceived by French president Nikolas Sarkozy as a union of all nations—whether Christian, Jewish, or Muslim—whose shores are lapped by the Mediterranean's waters, including both Israel and the Occupied Palestinian Territories.

According to Sarkozy, the three Abrahamic religions had their origins around the shores of the Mediterranean, and on its waters they traded and related with each other for more than a millennium. This ancient unity of Mediterranean history and culture, he suggested, could serve as a platform for the pursuit of Middle East peace and mutual prosperity. But his historico-geographic definition of the union was immediately resisted by the European powers it excluded (namely Germany) as an attempt to circumvent the EU and create an alternative French-dominated vehicle for regional policy. By the time the Joint Declaration of the Union for the Mediterranean was signed on July 13, 2008, it still invoked the shared history of Judaism, Christianity, and Islam in the Mediterranean as its springboard for the pursuit of peace and prosperity. But the list of signatories included not only Germany but all the EU member states, with the European Commission and the Arab League as additional participants. Apparently the binding force of Mediterranean history reaches from Iceland to Yemen. But it still does not reach the United States, and that, of course, is the geopolitical point.[4]

The Union for the Mediterranean is a large transnational initiative, but a smaller example of how the past is deployed in order to participate in the politics of the present will help me illustrate more clearly the limitations and perils of this approach. Some five years ago, at the suggestion of the prime minister of Spain (seconded by Turkey), the United Nations established a new Secretariat for the Alliance of Civilizations with the mandate (I am quoting from the secretariat's concept paper, a draft of which is in my possession) "to overcome prejudice, misconceptions, misperceptions, and polarization... that foment violence." To quote that concept paper just a bit further, the secretariat was meant as "a call to all of those who believe in building rather than destroying, who embrace diversity as a means of progress rather than as a threat, and who believe in the dignity of humankind across religion, ethnicity, race, and culture." The secretariat hosted a series of working groups, many of them focused on examples of multiculturalism and toleration from the Middle Ages and other historical periods, and then, for reasons that are unknown to me (but presumably not because its mission was accomplished), closed its doors less than a year after it opened them.

The one line I have quoted from the UN's concept paper suffices to make clear a contradiction at the secretariat's very foundation: this "alliance" of all who are for diversity and deplore polarization defines itself through a series of oppositions and exclusions. It is against those who would (apparently) rather destroy than build, strive to eliminate diversity rather than embrace it, and who do not believe in the dignity of mankind. We know, of course, whom the drafters of this constitution have in mind: all American policy-makers who are followers of that rival paradigm, "The Clash of Civiliza-tions." Such people are destroyers, eliminators. They are excluded from the "Alliance of Civilizations" because they are not civilized themselves. In this sense, the "alliance" is itself also a "clash," and the claim to toleration is already intolerant.

This may seem an obvious point. Yet it seems to me important to stress the barbarism that attends many of our claims to civilization (to paraphrase Walter Benjamin),[5] both because our tendency to deploy exemplary histo-ries in order to justify our own politics and criticize that of our rivals is so powerful, and because the complexity of the intercultural and interreligious challenges we confront today is so great. I offer just two short contemporary examples of such claims in order to support the point.

In September 2006, at the University of Regensburg, Pope Benedict XVI gave a speech entitled "Faith, Reason, and the University: Memories and Reflections." In it he used medieval Christian sources to characterize the violent intolerance of Muhammad and his followers. The speech triggered protests, even violence, across large parts of the Muslim world. At the center of the storm were a few short but pregnant lines quoted by the pope from a "Dialogue" that the Byzantine emperor Manuel II Paleologus claimed to have had with a learned Muslim in the winter of 1391, when he was himself a soldier fighting in the armies of the Muslim sultan.

> Show me just what Muhammad brought that was new, and there you will find things only evil and inhuman, such as his command to spread by the sword the faith he preached.... God is not pleased by blood.... Faith is born of the soul, not the body. Whoever would lead someone to faith needs the ability to speak well and reason properly, without violence and threats.[6]

Building on such quotes, Benedict went on to claim that Western European Catholicism represents the only successful synthesis in humanity's dialectical struggle between faith and reason. Modern scientific culture inclines toward an excess of reason. Protestantism, because of its rebellion against scholasti-cism and Greek philosophy, inclines toward an excess of faith. Islam, on the other hand, represents an extreme subjection to God: pure faith, without reason. This is why, according to the pope, Islam is so violent and intolerant.

This is one strategy for using the medieval past in our present conflict: as evidence that one side is inherently rational and tolerant while the other is not. The pope certainly does not have a monopoly on the approach. In fact it is also a common Islamist strategy. Many Muslim thinkers and writers today point to the fact that large communities of Christians and Jews lived under Islamic rule in the Middle Ages, at a time when Western Christendom was bent on converting, killing, or expelling whatever non-Catholics lived within its boundaries. This is the explicit claim of my second example, article 31of the Hamas Charter (1988):

> The Islamic Resistance Movement is a humanistic movement. . . . Under the wing of Islam it is possible for the followers of the three religions— Islam, Christianity, and Judaism—to coexist in peace and quiet with each other. Peace and quiet are not possible except under the wing of Islam. Past and present history are the best witness to that.[7]

Like Pope Benedict, the drafters of the Hamas Charter look back to the Middle Ages and seize on one strand—albeit a very different strand—of its history in order to argue that Islam is the only religion capable of providing both Truth and tolerance. Each of these claims that one religion is more tolerant than another is made in pursuit of claims to that religion's superiority, and to the inferiority or political exclusion of the other. These claims to tolerance in the past are also claims to power in the present.

For an example of similar dynamics at work in the United States, consider the controversy—after the Islamist bombing of the World Trade Center— over plans to build an Islamic center in Manhattan, a short distance from "Ground Zero," and name it "Cordoba House." Some, like the former House Republican leader Newt Gingrich, claimed that the center is intended as a symbol of Muslim conquest over the West, because it is "named for a city in Spain where a conquering Muslim army replaced a church with a mosque. This name is a very direct historical indication that the Ground Zero mosque is all about conquest and thus an assertion of Islamist triumphalism which we should not tolerate."[8]

The imam leading the effort to build the center, Feisal Abdul Rauf, makes contrasting claims: "For many centuries, Islam inspired a civilization that was particularly tolerant and pluralistic. Many Jewish and Christian artists and intellectuals emigrated to Cordoba during this period to escape the more oppressive regimes that reigned over Europe's Dark and Middle Ages. Great Jewish philosophers such as Maimonides were free to create their historic works within the pluralistic culture of Islam."[9] "The . . . name reminds us that

Muslims created what was, in its era, the most enlightened, pluralistic, and tolerant society on earth."[10]

These quotes were provided to me by a news organization called Media Matters for America, which asked me to comment on the rival claims. "Based on your knowledge of Medieval Spain," they wrote, "can you help sort out the distortions from the fact? How are we to understand the symbolism of 'Cordoba'?" Such a question can't be answered simply by separating fact from distortion. We cannot arbitrate between these claims by marshaling rival historical facts—pointing out against Newt Gingrich, for example, that the Muslim conqueror's placement of Cordoba's mosque atop a preexisting church is no more and no less a statement of world-domination than the Christian "reconquerors'" placement of a cathedral atop the mosque; or against Imam Abdul Rauf that although Maimonides was indeed born in Cordoba, none of his work was produced in Muslim Spain, because he was just a child when he and all the other Jews of that city were forced to convert to Islam and exiled from the city by its rulers.[11] In order to answer the question of Cordoba's symbolism, which is also the question about the utility of the past for the present, we need first to come to grips with a much larger question: what kinds of knowledge can the past offer the present?

Let me pause to insist that, in pointing to some similarities in contemporary invocations of history, I am not trying to say that all invocations of the past are the same, or equally valid. Nor am I equating the pope with Hamas, or Hamas with the pope; Newt Gingrich with Feisal Abdul Rauf or vice versa. And I am also not suggesting that only Christian and Islamist movements engage in this use of history, or that it is limited only to questions of religion. We could easily show a similar logic at work in some Zionist arguments about the virtues of a Jewish state, or in some neoliberal arguments about the virtues of American-style democracy. What I am trying to suggest is something much more banal: that when we turn to history—medieval or any other—in order to demonstrate the exemplary virtues of a given culture or religious tradition in comparison with another, we are often re-creating the dynamics we claim to be transcending.

This does not mean that history has nothing to offer us in our present need. But what it has to offer is more or less the opposite of what we often ask it for. So far all the examples I have given are of our asking history to produce exemplary moments to feed our competing fantasies of perfection: it is Europe, or America, or Islam, or Israel that stands for peace, progress, and pluralism, not the other. This demand is as old as history itself: think of Herodotus, deploying his art to imagine the superiority of his Greeks to the "barbarian" Persians.[12]

This use of history to imagine the virtues and the boundaries of one's own community will never disappear: it is one of the primary reasons why people tell stories about the past. But history has something more to offer, and it is that something more that we, as teachers, citizens, and even as policymakers, should be demanding of it. First, we should ask of our histories that rather than confirming our preferred fantasies about the past—our fantasy about the essential tolerance of Christianity and the aggressiveness of Islam, for example, or vice versa—they make us critical of those fantasies. Our sense of the past exercises a powerful influence on how we think we should act in the world. All the more important, then, that our historians help us interrogate that sense of the past, lest we act in the grip of what Johann Gottfried von Herder, referring to European ideas about the history of Islamic Spain, called "a comforting fairy-tale" ("angenehmes Märchen").[13] I've tried to do some of that interrogating in the first part this essay, pointing out examples of such fairy tales in our present political and religious discourse.

We might call this critical function of history its "negative role": to deconstruct the exemplary histories and comforting fairy tales with which we approach our world. But history has "positive" pedagogical functions as well: attention to the long history of Islam, Christianity, and Judaism can help us to rediscover the multiple potentials that exist within all three religions and their scriptural traditions. On questions of pluralism and toler-ance, for example, all three scriptural traditions have the potential to legiti-mate attitudes toward the others which range from extensive toleration to total extermination, from (to choose only among passages in the Gospel of Luke) Jesus's exhortations in the sermon on the plain to "love your enemy" and "offer him your other cheek," (6:27 and 29) to the nobleman's com-mand in Jesus's parable: "But as for these enemies of mine, who did not want me to reign over them, bring them here and slay them before me"[14] (19:27). Which of these potentials becomes dominant in a given time and place has little to do with some "essential" tolerance or violence of a given scriptural tradition, and everything to do with the specific work that tradi-tion is asked to do in the particular historical circumstances of that given time and place.[15]

For approximately fifteen centuries, Christian theologians worked very hard to explain why killing heretics, Muslims, or Aztecs during Crusade or conquest should be considered an "act of love."[16] Today few would do so, not because the Scriptures themselves have changed, but because for historical reasons we read those Scriptures in a different way. Conversely, under the pressure of colonialism, ideas about Jihad that would have seemed like hereti-cal innovations to Sunni Muslims from the entire first millennium of Islam,

came to seem normative, traditional, and conservative to many Muslims in
the modern age.

I do not mean to imply that one of these attitudes is true to the scriptural tradition and the other is false. Nor am I declaring that all interpretations of Scripture are arbitrary. My point is rather that all three scriptural
traditions are rich enough to have generated—and to continue generating—a
vast diversity of potential views. And all of these views—insofar as they are
generated through and authorized by Scripture—can be understood by those
who hold them as continuous with and true to the beliefs of the founding
prophetic communities.

For example, on the question of violence and how to treat one's enemies, we might expect the early Christians, powerless and persecuted, to
pay more attention to the passage about "turning the other cheek to be
struck," whereas it would not be surprising if, as many historians have
shown, saints like Ambrose, Jerome, Augustine, and John Chrysostom,
writing once the emperor had become Christian and put his sword at the
disposal of the church, began to pay more notice to "slay them before me."
Nor would it be surprising—and I add this as something of a response
to Pope Benedict's Regensburg address—if the early Islamic community,
arising as it did in a context saturated by late antique Christian representations of holy war deployed by the Roman Empire in its long struggle
with Persia, should have adopted some of those Christian representations
as its own.[17]

"Historicism" is the technical word we use for approaches that pay attention to the multiple meanings produced by myriad communities at diverse
moments in time, rather than treating the truths of a religion or a culture
as essential and unchanging (a position sometimes loosely associated with
"fundamentalism"). It seems banal to point out that this production of new
meaning continues in all three religious traditions: the interpretation of
Scripture continues to generate not only new beliefs about specific points,
but also new scriptural communities (think of the many different evangelical communities that have proliferated in the United States and the Third
World over the past forty years, or of the new egalitarian, reconstructionist,
and secularist movements in Judaism), and even new religions (such as the
Mormons). But I will focus on Islam, because at this moment the fantasy
that it is monolithic and unchanging is particularly powerful, both within
Islam, and outside of it.

Every student of Islamic history knows that there have always been many
different ways to interpret the Prophet's words and actions, resulting in many
different scriptural communities. Politicians and newspaper readers have of

late become much more aware of differences between Sunnis and Shi'ites, but there are many more Islamic communities, all based on different understandings of the Qur'an and the Sunnah. According to an early tradition, Muhammad himself predicted this process: "Those who were before you of the People of the Book became divided into 72 sects [*milla*], and this community will be divided into 73, 72 in Hell, and one in Paradise."[18]

"The People of the Book became divided": Muhammad is teaching us something important here. The Book, that is to say, the scriptural and prophetic tradition from which Jews, Christians, and Muslims all trace their descent, simultaneously unites the adherents of all three religions into one people, and divides them all into many. This ambivalent promise to unite us in blessing and divide us in dissension seems to me a basic attribute of the scriptural tradition. As the book of Deuteronomy frequently tells the Israelites: read and observe my commandments correctly and you will be blessed, incorrectly and you will be cursed.[19] Much of the Hebrew Bible is a demonstration of how hard it is to get the reading right, and a demonstration of what happens to those who fail to do so.

To put it another way, the very same scriptural "book" that unites all "Peoples of the Book" also divides them, from the first moment of its revelation, in an eternal struggle over how it should be read. It is this struggle that moves the sectarian history of the Abrahamic faiths forward through time, this struggle that explains why God "abhorred the tent of Joseph, and chose not the tribe of Ephraim; but chose the tribe of Judah, the mount Zion which he loved" (Psalm 78:67–68). The same struggle produced the second-Temple Jewish sect that became Christianity. We can see it going on in all the early Christian texts, beginning with the letters of Paul,[20] but my favorite example comes from the Gospel of Luke, chapter 24.

Two men are talking on the road to Emmaus. A third figure, a stranger, appears on the road. "What is this conversation which you are holding with each other as you walk?" "And they stood still, looking sad. Then one of them, named Cleopas, answered him, 'Are you the only visitor to Jerusalem who does not know the things that have happened there in these days?' And he said to them, 'What things?' And they said to him, 'Concerning Jesus of Nazareth, who was a prophet mighty in deed and word before God and all the people, and how our chief priests and rulers delivered him up to be condemned to death, and crucified him. But we had hoped that he was the one to redeem Israel.'" Contrary to their first impression, their new companion proves to be quite well informed. "'O foolish men, and slow of heart to believe all that the prophets have spoken! Was it not necessary that the Christ should suffer these things and enter into his glory?' And beginning with

Moses and all the prophets, he interpreted to them in all the Scriptures the things concerning himself" (Luke 24:13–35). "Concerning himself," the gospel says, because of course the stranger was the risen Jesus, although his two disciples did not recognize him till dinnertime and journey's end. The Gospel is making an important point. If we read the prophecies one way, then Jesus, who was condemned, suffered, and died, cannot be the promised Messiah. But if we read them a different way, then in fact that is exactly what they promised. In order to become Christian you need to learn to read the old books in a new way, and one of the most important tasks of the new books is to teach you how.

The sectarian background of the New Testament is well known. Fewer people are aware that the Qur'an is the product of a similar environment, in which a new sectarian community forms out of the coming together of many existing traditions.[21] The Qur'anic community included rabbinic Jews, Samaritans, Christians of many different stripes, as well as polytheists and followers of earlier prophets to the Arabs. Like the Gospels, the Qur'an sees itself as including and fulfilling all of the prophetic tradition that produced these earlier scriptural communities.[22] Thus at the beginning of Sura 2—"The Cow"—God promises Adam that those who believe in his revelations shall neither fear nor grieve. It is only "those who reject faith and belie our signs," who need fear. "They shall be companions of the fire. They shall abide therein"[23] (2:39).

This would seem to welcome receivers of previous prophecies, especially the Jews and Christians (the "People of the Book") who accept God's prior revelations. But just like the letter of Paul or the Gospels, the Qur'an needs to defend its distinctive readings of those revelations. Thus Sura 2 continues:

> O Children of Israel! Call to mind the (special) favor which I bestowed upon you, and fulfill your covenant with me. . . . And believe in what I reveal, confirming the revelation which is within you, and be not the first to reject faith therein, nor sell my signs for a small price; and fear me, and me alone. And cover not truth with falsehood, nor conceal the truth when you know what it is. (2:40–42)

The sura then revisits many of the episodes of Israelite disobedience to God related in the Hebrew Bible and the New Testament, ranging from their complaints about eating nothing but manna in the desert (2:61) to their attacks on Jesus ("Is it that whenever there comes to you a messenger with what you yourselves do not desire, you are puffed up with pride?—some you call impostors, and others you slay!" [2:87]).

These passages provide excellent examples of how deeply intertwined the Qur'anic community and its emerging Scriptures were with communities and Scriptures of Christians and Jews. The accusation that the Jews always persecute their prophets, frequent in the Qur'an (e.g., 2:61, 87, 91, and in many other suras) has obvious New Testament analogs. Think only of the Acts of the Apostles (7:51–53): "You stiff-necked people, uncircumcised in heart and ears, you always resist the Holy Spirit. As your fathers did, so do you. Which of the prophets did not your fathers persecute?" Today critical scholars of the Qur'an call these analogic moments "intertexts," and the study of these intertexts is one of the most rapidly expanding fields in Western Qur'anic studies. Many Qur'anic stories about earlier prophets— such as the repeated account of the infant Jesus making birds out of clay which then fly away—that were once thought to be eccentric, we now know came from the community's vast store of Christian and Jewish sacred lore long since lost or marginalized as uncanonical—in this case the Infancy Gospel of Thomas.[24]

Let me dwell for a moment on the well-known intertexts from just one Qur'anic verse, verse 93 of Sura 2, a passage that focuses on the moment of scriptural revelation itself:

> And remember we took your covenant and we raised above you (the towering height) of Mount (Sinai) (saying): "Hold firmly to what we have given you and hearken (to the Law)!" They said: "We hear, and we disobey." And they had to drink into their hearts (of the taint) of the calf because of their faithlessness. (2:93)

"We raised above you Mount Sinai?" (cf. Sura 2:60, 4:153) The line is not to be found in the five books of Moses or the Hebrew Bible. Yet even the geographic vocabulary of the phrase marks it as an "intertext," for the Qur'an names the mountain not in Arabic (*jabal*), but Aramaic (or Syriac, the language of Christians in the region: the word is the same in both): *Ṭūr Sīnīn* (compare the Targum's *ṭūrā de-sīnai*). The Qur'an consistently refers (with one exception) to the site of revelation in Aramaic (or Syriac), not Arabic, as in the opening of Sura 52: "By the Mount [*Ṭūr*] (of revelation)! By a decree inscribed in a scroll unfolded!" The passage is a citation, though it comes not from the written but from the oral Torah, that is, from the Talmud. Commenting on Exodus 19:17 tractate Shabbat reports a discussion of the rabbis:

> "And they stood beneath the mount": R. Abdimi b. Hama b. Hasa said: This teaches that the Holy One, blessed be he, overturned the

mountain upon them like an inverted cask, and said to them "If you take upon yourselves the Law, good. If not, here you will find your grave." R. Aha b. Jacob observed: "This furnishes a strong protest against the Law."[25]

Even the devastating line "we hear and we disobey" turns out to be an inter-text of sorts. In Exodus (24:7) and Deuteronomy (5:24) the Israelites declare to Moses, "We hear, and obey." The Qur'an's transformation of that phrase is a multilingual pun, playing on the homophony between Hebrew *shama'nu v-'asinu* (we hear and obey) and Arabic *sami'inā wa-'aṣaynā:* (we hear and disobey) (Deut. 5:24).[26] The play on words reveals the shared scriptural space of these communities at the same time that it shatters it.

The ambivalence of this gesture is constitutional of the scriptural tradi-tion we call Abrahamic. Much like the risen Jesus on the road to Emmaus, the Qur'an is here declaring its continuity with previous scriptures, in this case by maintaining that these prophesied the coming of Muhammad, but that those prophecies were concealed through misreadings or falsifications of the Scriptures by the communities that preserved them. As Sura 4:46 has it, "Of the Jews there are those who displace words from their (right) places and say 'We hear and we disobey'... with a twist of their tongues and a slander to the faith." Our multilingual pun, in other words, underwrites the Islamic doctrine of "*taḥrīf*"—the charge of Jewish and Christian alteration and falsification of previous Scriptures—that allows the Islamic community both to honor the previous Scriptures (unlike, for example, the Marcionites in early Christianity) and to set them aside (unlike the Christianity that became orthodox).

I stress the heuristic potential of these intertexts in part because they are among the more self-consciously dialogic passages of Scripture, and can therefore tell us a great deal about the hermeneutic processes of identification and disidentification that produce and maintain sectarian communities within the Abrahamic tradition. Of course these intertexts also remind us of how "multicultural" the early Qur'anic community—like the early Christian and the early rabbinic communities—could be, and thereby open a path toward a historicism that can relativize each tra-dition's claims to exclusive truth. Such reminders offer an attractive kind of relief in an age when scriptural traditions seem poised in intractable opposition: the relief that, however badly things have turned out, they could have turned out otherwise. This is the relief that we nowadays call contingency, and unlike Nietzsche, I do not mock it.[27] But it is not the relief that I am after.

In fact my goal is rather to suggest that the historian has more to offer than either (1) exemplary histories of the sort I began by criticizing, or (2) a thoroughly relativizing historicism of the sort I've just described. The history of scriptural interpretation can teach us something much more radical: it can teach us that Scripture itself does not force us to choose between historicism and faith, or between an awareness of the constant transformation of the beliefs and practices of historical religious communities, and a belief in our own adherence to revealed truths. It allows us, if we wish, to maintain both. The scriptural tradition itself enjoins the ongoing struggle to read it correctly; legitimates the multiple readings that emerge from that struggle in different times and places; emphasizes the inexhaustibility of those readings; and sometimes even reminds us that it is not given to any human in this world to determine which of those readings is definitive. Seen in this light, historicism can become one of the tools by which Scripture generates its own critique, revealing new truths for new times, but sustaining the understandability of all of these new truths—again, if we so wish to understand them—as implicit in Scripture from its very origins in God.

The Qur'an, for example (I focus my concluding observations on Islam for reasons both political and pedagogical, but the same could be said, *mutatis mutandis,* for the Jewish and the Christian Scriptures), often reminds us that its truths are divine, that those truths have the power to save us, and that we must therefore struggle to read the Scripture correctly. In this sense the so-called Islamist fundamentalists are right, and this is the struggle that they focus on. But we must not forget that the Qur'an itself can correctly be read to comment on its own exegesis in ways that authorize believers to read and interpret it, and that it legitimates the many different readings that emerge from the struggle of those believers to do so in different times and places.

For although the Qur'an often proclaims itself a "book wherein there is no doubt," it is also aware that, when subjected—as it must be—to human interpretation, Scripture will inevitably generate doubt and conflict. In the words of Sura 3:7:

> He ... revealed unto you the Scripture in which there are clear revelations [*muḥkamāt*] ..., and others which are ambiguous [*mutashābihāt*]. But those in whose hearts is deviation [*zaygh*] pursue the ambiguous, seeking dissension [*fitna*] and seeking to interpret it [*ta'wīlihi*]. But *no one knows its explanations except God. And those who are firmly grounded in the knowledge say:* "We believe therein; the whole of it is from our Lord." None will grasp the message except men of understanding.[28]

John Wansbrough once called this passage "the point of departure for all scriptural exegesis."[29] In order to understand why, we have to notice, not only its distinction between clear and ambiguous revelations, but also an ambiguity within the canonical text of the Qur'an itself. Depending on where we choose to insert a reading pause, the passage "wa-mā ya'lamu ta'wīlahū illā llāhu wa-l-rāsikhūna fī l-'ilmi yaqūlūna āmannā bihī kullun min 'indi rabbinā wa-mā yadhdhakkaru illā ulū l-albābi" can be translated in ways that give sharply divergent scope to interpretation. The translation above suggests that only God can interpret the ambiguous passages. But if we pause instead a little later in our reading, the sense is very different: "None knows its explanation save God and those who are firmly grounded in knowledge. Say: we believe therein." In other words, even this self-reflective verse of revelation warning of the dangers of ambiguity is itself ambiguous, claiming simultaneously both that the ambiguous verses of Scripture can be understood by (at least some) believers, and that they cannot.

We know that the earliest Qur'anic communities wrestled with this ambiguity, because we have precanonical variants (that is, versions that predate the canonical Uthmanic redaction) of the verse that avoid it. It seems all the more significant that the canonical version chose to preserve the ambivalence, even if the standard readings (and translations) later editors have offered often attempt to contain it. (The widely reprinted Qur'anic text approved by al-Azhar in 1344/1925–26 places the pausal abbreviation *mīm* [i.e., *al-waqf al-lāzim*] above the word *Allāhu,* making the standard reading obligatory. Other modern editions and printings, however, choose to mark it differently.)[30]

Across the long history of Qur'an interpretation, the canonical ambivalence of these verses has nourished those who would expand human hermeneutic agency. It was, for example, on the basis of this ambivalence that the Muslim philosopher and jurist Ibn Rushd (Averroës, d. 595/1198) erected his doctrine of a twofold path. According to him the mass of believers should restrict their Qur'anic hermeneutics to the clear verses: "They should be told that it is ambiguous, and known by no one except God; and that the pausal stop should be put here after the sentence 'And no one knows the interpretation thereof except God.'" But "those firmly rooted in knowledge" (by which Ibn Rushd meant philosophers) could and should interpret the "ambiguous" verses of the Qur'an in pursuit of allegorical truths, which sometimes seemed to contradict the "clear" ones.[31]

Twentieth-century exegetes, like their medieval predecessors, have also insisted on the Qur'an's multiple teachings. For example, the Sudanese scholar Mahmoud Muhammad Taha taught—in opposition to the attempts of Islamist parties like the Muslim Brotherhood to impose Shari'a law—that the Qur'an has many layers of meaning.[32] In particular, he drew a distinction between the teachings that the Prophet addressed to the needs and circumstances of his followers in the Arabian desert in the seventh-century, and the teachings he addressed to the vast future of humanity.[33] According to Taha, the Shari'a law that Islamic parties wanted to impose on the Sudan was a relic of that early message, whereas the Prophet, through his life and example (Sunnah), had modeled different teachings for different futures, including modernity.[34]

Taha made his points through the Qur'an. In the verse "Every day He (shines) in (new) splendor," (55:29), he saw evidence that the Qur'an is full of teachings that await discovery, teachings that make new and evolving sense of the world as it changes.[35] (Compare the comment of a prominent twelfth-century Jewish exegete: "The *pshat* [the plain sense of Scripture] renews itself every day.")[36] He pointed out that the Qur'an itself emphasizes the inexhaustibility of those readings: "If the ocean were ink (wherewith to write out) the words of my Lord, sooner would the ocean be exhausted than would the words of my Lord"[37] (Q 18:109). (Compare John 21:25: "But there are also many other things which Jesus did; were every one of them to be written, I suppose that the world itself could not contain the books that would be written.") And against claims to supreme exegetical authority, he stressed its insistence that it is not given to any human in this world to determine which of those readings is definitive ("over all endued with knowledge is One, the All-Knowing," Q 12:76).[38] In other words, Taha insisted that the Qur'an itself contains and authorizes the "historicism" and "pluralism" that can constrain its own "fundamentalism."

To pick a concrete example, on the question of Islamic politics toward non-Muslims, the Qur'an had taught—according to Taha—the Shari'a of Jihad to an infant Islam: "Slay the pagans wherever you find them . . . but if they repent, and establish regular prayers and practice regular charity, then open the way for them" (9:5). A more mature teaching came in Sura 3:159: "It is part of the mercy of Allah that you deal gently with them. If you were severe or harsh-hearted, they would have broken away from about you: so pass over (their faults), and ask for (Allah's) forgiveness for them; and consult them in affairs. . . . Then, when you have taken a decision, put your trust in Allah." But the pinnacle of the Qur'an's teaching expressed a very different relationship between prophecy and politics, addressed to a more perfect Islam: "Therefore you give admonition, for you are one to admonish. You are not one to manage (men's) affairs"[39] (88:21–22).

Mahmoud Muhammad Taha was executed by the Nimeiri regime in January 1985.[40] Shari'a law was imposed in the Sudan, with genocidal consequences. But neither Taha's death, nor the defeat of his ideas at that particular moment in history, make his teachings less essentially "Islamic" than those of the victors. They remain a potential vision of Islam, one of the many contained in the inexhaustible sea of ink that is Scripture.

The discovery of these scriptural constraints to the claims of exclusive truth, the revelation of this divinely authorized historicism: this is, it seems to me, an important "positive" task not just for the historian, but for all who teach or study these Scriptures and the communities of belief that have formed around those Scriptures, Christian and Jewish, as well as Islamic. In saying this, I do not mean to endorse specific "policy" projects, such as the White House's "National Strategy for Combating Terrorism" of February 2003. That strategy called for establishing a Muslim World Outreach program that would train Islamic preachers, support Islamic schools that counter the teachings of so-called fundamentalist madrassas, and attempt to reshape the content of religious debate in Muslim countries. That same year the National Security Division of the Rand Corporation published a report entitled *Civil and Democratic Islam: Partners, Resources, Strategies* that called for U.S. government support of Islamic reformers who teach what the report referred to as "historicizing" interpretations of the Qur'an. By 2005 the U.S. budget for all such activities was approximately $1.3 billion.[41]

I do not myself believe that such efforts in religious "reeducation" can prove effective without simultaneous (and vast) political and economic efforts at a global level. The ways in which believers read their Scriptures, the kinds of readings they find convincing, the resonances those readings have for them: these are not independent of the kinds of political, economic, and social pressures those readers and their communities face. But I also do not believe that we should condemn such efforts, as some of my colleagues do, as attempts to impose Western secularism on Islam.[42] As I briefly tried to suggest, "historicist" and "pluralist" positions are just as present in the Qur'an and in the long history of Islam as "fundamentalist" and "Islamist" ones are, and the rediscovery of those positions is no more an un-Islamic imposition than the mid- to late-twentieth century rediscovery of medieval "fundamentalists" through the writings of such medieval theologians as Ibn Taymiyyah.[43] Besides, should those efforts succeed, and "fundamentalist" visions of Islam lose ground to "historicist" ones, it will not be because of American dollars, but primarily for the same reasons that those fundamentalist visions themselves became so influential in the second half of the twentieth century: because they became meaningful and convincing to millions of believers struggling to make sense of their changing world.

The reader will surely be aware, after this mad dash through several thousand years and three Scriptures, that my essay is as much sermon as science. For the sake of clarity, I might summarize the sermon as two reductively opposed lessons. First the "negative" lesson: no scriptural tradition has "the answer." All are capable of generating violence, intolerance, exclusion. It is simply not true that the world would live in peace if Muslims and Jews turned to Pope Benedict's beloved *logos* from the Gospel of John, or if Jews and Christians were ruled by Hamas's Qur'an. Even if the entire world converted to one Scripture, the very nature of the scriptural traditions means that their reading would continue to generate new sects and new conflicts.

And then the "positive": every scriptural tradition has "the answer," insofar as each is capable of generating tolerance, inclusion, equality, freedom, or whatever other values the societies reading them come to deem important. It is simply not true—to choose only one Western version of a widespread fallacy, that of Jean-Luc Nancy—that the teachings of Jesus are capable of generating their own critique, whereas those of Muhammad are not.[44] We can learn to read each of the scriptural traditions in ways that expand the space for religious freedom—extending even to freedom *from* religion!—if that is what we want to do, while at the same time maintaining—again, if we wish to do so—the conviction that these truths we derive from Scripture are God-given.

This is not what the U.S. military calls "actionable intelligence." The ways in which communities read their Scriptures are not random: they are the product of habit and custom, and changing them requires effort on the part of teachers and readers everywhere. But neither is the situation hopeless. All of our scriptural communities have changed their reading habits many times over the centuries. (The shift in Catholic teachings about Jews after WWII provides one notable example.) As the thousands of reform movements in the contemporary Muslim, Jewish, and Christian worlds make clear, they are still doing so today. How can teachers of medieval history best help the efforts of all these "peoples of the book?" Perhaps by reminding them that "the book" is not written in stone, and that the people have the power to reshape its meanings.

PART TWO

*Early Modern
Perspectives on
Spirituality, Culture,
and Religious
Boundaries*

CHAPTER 5

The People and the Book

*Print and the Transformation of Jewish Culture
in Early Modern Europe*

DAVID B. RUDERMAN

In the past several decades, the study of Jewish culture and society in early modern Europe has come into its own with a remarkable explosion of books and essays written on almost every aspect of this fascinating period.[1] Most of this scholarship, however, is exclusively focused on a particular region or locality, denying, it would seem, the very possibility that a distinct early modern Jewish cultural experience can ever be meaningfully described. I wish to assert that such a description is possible and desirable.

I have recently tried to describe a transregional culture in early modern Europe, linking in some sense disparate communities and, more significantly, disparate historiographical traditions rarely in contact or in conversation with each other. In searching for larger patterns of cultural formation common to Jewish communities in Italy, Central and Eastern Europe, the Ottoman Empire, and the Western Sephardic Diaspora in cities such as Amsterdam and Hamburg, I did not expect to efface the specificities and singularities of the subcultures of Jewish life other historians have carefully described. Instead, I proposed only another interpretative layer, a perspective on their work that emphasizes connections, contacts, and conversations over time and across specific localities. I will contend that there was a transformation of practices of transmitting and protecting traditions of religious and intellectual authority within and between Jewish communities in the early modern period. For my analysis, I relied especially on the notion of connected histories, which highlights the dialectical relationship between local conditions and continental patterns and was articulated by Sanjay Subrahmanyam in his own work on early modern world history.[2]

A central theme in this description of a transregional Jewish culture in the early modern period is the knowledge explosion precipitated to a great extent by the printing of Hebrew as well as Yiddish and Ladino books. In this discussion, I would like to focus on this one factor alone in assessing Jewish cultural transformations across Europe as a whole, arguing that the movement of books and the activities of their publishers and salesmen played a critical role in creating a connected history of early modern regional Jewish communities. With the involvement of Christian publishers in the business of Hebrew printing, and the emergence of a Christian readership of Jewish books, the image of Jews and Judaism in early modern Europe was also significantly enhanced.

I begin with a rich illustration of the impact of the printing of Hebrew books on Jewish readers: the publication of Joseph Caro's standardized code of Jewish law, the *Shulhan Arukh*. Caro, legal scholar and mystic (ca. 1488–1575), lived most of his life in the Ottoman Empire, especially Safed.[3] The code was first published in Venice in 1565 as the ultimate digest of legal practice for Sephardic Jews living primarily in Mediterranean regions and reflecting their long-held customs and traditions. However, when this code was republished in Krakow in 1578–80, it was dramatically expanded by the addition of the glosses of the equally famous Rabbi Moses Isserles of Krakow (1525 or 1530–72), who sought to adjust the text to fit the needs of his fellow Ashkenazic Jews living in Eastern Europe. Furthermore, Isserles boldly introduced the text into his rabbinical academy in Krakow, thus reducing the totality of Ashkenazic legal practice to the material referred to in this composite work, and more important, producing a new legal compendium whose traditional boundaries separating Ashkenazim and Sephardim by long established custom were dramatically blurred.

As Elhanan Reiner carefully explains, Ashkenazic culture originating in medieval central Europe was based on a limited library of rabbinic works, learned orally and transmitted through *hagahot* (glosses) written by a later exegete that eventually merged with the original text itself as they were studied, transmitted, and recopied. In contrast to the medieval Christian book, an authoritative text for Ashkenazic Jews was thus not the original text but its latest version consisting of the latest accretions to the text. The authority of the text thus depended on the authority of its most recent rabbinic interpreter and transmitter. This all changed when Isserles decided to print his glosses to accompany Caro's legal digest. By committing his oral comments to writing and linking them to the fixed code of Caro, Isserles hoped to preserve at least a part of the earlier oral and scribal tradition in this new printed book so that, in Reiner's words, a kind of printed manuscript emerged.[4] When his contemporary, the Ashkenazic rabbi Hayyim ben Bezalel strenuously objected to Isserles's innovation, this critic was fully aware of the consequences that would result. A binding code with its privileged commentary in the pages of a printed book would arrest the elasticity of the tradition, diminish the importance of local Ashkenazic customs, and degrade the authority of individual rabbinic commentators. All would be subsumed under the centralizing authority of a supracommunal canon whose ultimate authorities were Caro and Isserles themselves.

Reiner's insightful description of the genesis of the *Shulhan Arukh* with its *Mappah* (the Isserles gloss) offers to the modern observer of late-sixteenth-century Jewish culture a lasting icon that a unified culture fusing Sephardic law with Ashkenazic custom could exist among early modern Jews and that it was made possible through the new invention of the printed book and its circulation. Before print, no one could have imagined the seemingly improbable merger of two distinct legal traditions on the pages of a book or the obliteration of localized oral traditions of authority and transmission. Nor could anyone have imagined the extraordinary layout of multiple commentaries from different eras and regions surrounding the core text of the Talmud and simultaneously appearing on the same page in the first printed edition in Venice in the first decades of the sixteenth century. Equally significant was the publication of the *Magna Biblica Rabbinica,* also published in Venice in multiple editions in the sixteenth century. Initially produced by Daniel Bomberg, the Christian printer, with the assistance of Jewish proofreaders, these newly formatted Jewish sacred texts were clearly imitative of Christian publishing practices of their own canon law.

The truly revolutionary implications of these publication events have only recently been appreciated through Reiner's scholarship as well as that of others. It is now possible to understand how the migration of Hebrew books from Venice into Eastern Europe created a crisis for the rabbinic elites of Poland-Lithuania, one more enduring and more repercussive than even that engendered by the publication of the *Shulhan Arukh* itself. Accustomed to the fluid scribal culture of texts with exegetical notes, rabbinic teachers had long felt comfortable in modifying the law according to local custom and current usage. The appearance of a printed text arrested considerably this creative and open process, establishing a kind of canonical text, one not easily "invaded" by scribal glosses and novel formulations. The text became the ultimate word, not the teacher, and thus diminished his authoritative capacity for interpreting the law. The text now available in multiple copies and purchased by larger numbers of students no longer could be easily supervised and controlled by an overseeing rabbinic elite. Through the elevation of the status of the text through print, the rabbinic master was less in a position to contest its supremacy.

One additional transformation was engendered by the new Hebrew printing houses of early modern Europe. With the publication of multiple commentaries and authors flowing first from Venice, then Constantinople, then Amsterdam as well as other Eastern European communities, Ashkenazic readers living in Poland-Lithuania were ultimately exposed to the classics of the Sephardic library. The Ashkenazic yeshivot soon embraced Sephardic biblical commentaries written initially in Spain and later in the Ottoman Empire; the medieval philosophical tradition was revitalized in Eastern Europe with the appearance of the Maimonidean corpus in print; Sephardic and Italian sermons were regularly disseminated in Eastern Europe, along with a massive library of kabbalistic books; and even astronomical textbooks and a medical encyclopedia written by a graduate of Padua's medical school could be read in Prague and Krakow. Eventually the process was reversed as the library of Ashkenazic culture and traditions meandered southward to Italy, eastward to the Ottoman Empire, and westward to Amsterdam and London.[5]

The significant role of the presses of Venice, Istanbul, Amsterdam, and elsewhere in the formation of a connected early modern Jewish culture is compelling. Printing shattered the isolating hold of potent localized traditions and attitudes as one community became increasingly aware of a conversation taking place long distances away. Writing from faraway Prague, Rabbi Judah Loew ben Bezalel (the Maharal) bitterly denounced the Italian Azariah de' Rossi's scholarly work, the *Me'or Einayim,* published in Mantua in 1575, only a short time after the book was published. Similarly, this time moving in reverse direction from south to north, the Venetian rabbi Leon Modena's compared the structure of his sermons with those published by Ashkenazic and Levantine that is, Ottoman) rabbis he had obviously read. Print made Jews more aware of other Jews than ever before.[6]

Scholars have also delineated another result of the printing revolution, one paralleling closely the reading patterns of Christian readers in the age of Reformation. The emergence of cheap books initiated another form of a cultural transformation. The itinerant preachers, teachers, scribes, cantors, and other secondary elites discovered a forum for disseminating their own views. Print helped to shatter the exclusivity and hegemony of rabbis, who were simultaneously recognizing their own diminished status vis à vis wealthy lay communal leaders. They proved incapable of controlling the outpouring of small books and pamphlets quickly and inexpensively produced for a lay public, opening up new readers and audiences, men, women, and children, and exposing them to aspects of a tradition that had once been the exclusive prerogative of highly educated legal scholars.[7]

One subject whose secrets had been guarded zealously by the rabbis before print was the kabbalah. According to the well-known thesis of Gershom Scholem, beginning with the expulsion from Spain in 1492, the kabbalah became a more potent and significant force, responding directly to the existential challenges of Jewish life not only among the Sephardic refugees but throughout the Jewish Diaspora. His explanation has been refined and challenged by later scholars but the general picture of the elevation and dissemination of kabbalah in early modern Europe remains legitimate and surely the printing press was a major catalyst in generating this development.[8] Christians were actually the first to publish kabbalistic books in the sixteenth century. Contemporary Jews had mixed reactions to the dissemination of what was for them an esoteric lore. By midcentury, a major conflict emerged within the Jewish community over the printing of the classic *Zohar* and other compositions related to it. The final outcome was the printing of two separate editions in Mantua in 1558 and in Cremona in 1560, but not without certain fear and foreboding about the consequences of divulging divine secrets in print. These inhibitions very much paralleled those expressed when the Talmud and *Shulhan Arukh* were published. In both instances, rabbinic control and supervision of knowledge were at stake. But in the case of the kabbalah, the situation was even more complicated and painful to the guardians of Jewish culture because the Christians had jumped the gun, so to speak, by publishing at their will what the rabbis would never have allowed their own coreligionists to do so openly. And these same Christian Hebraists were taking liberties with previously protected Jewish secrets in a manner the rabbis deemed irresponsible and theologically dangerous. Jews were ultimately obliged to publish kabbalistic works in order to present what they considered to be authentic versions of their own cultural legacy.[9]

In the sixteenth century, the number of kabbalistic books was relatively modest compared to the publication of other Hebrew books. This radically changed by the late seventeenth century with the wide distribution of both learned and popular kabbalistic texts emanating originally from Safed, crossing the boundaries between north, south, east, and west in the wake of the messianic movement of Shabbetai Zevi. Indeed, the universal appeal of this messianic figure and his prophets well into the eighteenth century, as Ze'ev Gries persuasively argues, is as much a product of the networks of communication engendered by the publications of his followers and detractors as anything else. Lurianic kabbalah, through the Sabbatean printing press, captured the attention of elites and non-elites alike in both the Sephardic and Ashkenazic worlds and ultimately left its impact on Jewish worship and ritual life as well.[10]

Accompanying the publication of these Hebrew books and others were those in Yiddish and Ladino. In fact, Yiddish, the language spoken and read by Jews in Central and Eastern Europe primarily representing a mixture of German and Hebrew and other languages, and Ladino, the language spoken and read by Jews in the Ottoman Empire, a dialect of Spanish with Hebraic elements, were virtually created by the unique conditions of Jewish life in early modern Europe. Through the flourishing book industry in Italy, in Eastern Europe, in the Netherlands, and in the Ottoman Empire, works in these Jewish languages were widely disseminated, including translations of works in other European languages, challenging the privileged place of Hebrew books and offering modes of popular communication and literary outlets that would transform Jewish culture for centuries to come.

In the case of Yiddish, a wide reading public emerged across the continent truly creating a common Europeanwide Jewish culture transcending localized communities and linking especially the West and the East. While Yiddish books had initially been published in Italy and in Poland, by the seventeenth and early eighteenth centuries, Amsterdam became the center of Yiddish printing in the Jewish world. Between 1650 and 1800, more than five hundred different works were printed. The presses catered both to internal use, appealing to the growing numbers of Ashkenazim who had settled in the city, as well as to Jewish authors and publishers who came from long distances especially to print their volumes. Attracted by the relative lack of censorship and by the liberal printing business that published books in many languages, Eastern European book dealers began to travel to Amsterdam in order to publish their manuscripts and return home to sell their new library of printed books. This image of a Jew from Krakow traveling across the continent, with a variety of other Jewish merchants, to publish a Yiddish book in what had been the center of the Western Sephardic Diaspora is as good a snapshot as any of the actual existence of a transregional Jewish culture by the seventeenth century.[11]

Ladino works in the Ottoman Empire began to appear considerably later than Yiddish ones, but they too were widely distributed because of print and helped to shape an entirely new Jewish reading public. Centuries after the first Hebrew books had been published in Istanbul in the late fifteenth century by the first generations of Sephardic immigrants to the city, Ladino printing came into its own with the publication in 1730 of Jacob Huli's *Me'am Lo'ez,* an encyclopedic biblical commentary and distillation of Sephardic Jewish culture. It was followed over the next century and a half by a flow of popular Jewish books attempting to educate and popularize Jewish knowledge. The heyday of the Ladino book also coincided with the publication of the first Turkish book of 1729. Lacking any prior manuscript tradition on which it could develop, Ladino works represented a bold acknowledgement by rabbinic leaders of the need to communicate in the vernacular and to Jews lacking sophisticated Jewish knowledge. What is most interesting about this blossoming of Ladino literature in print is that it emerged at a time conventionally acknowledged as a period of decline for both Ottoman culture and Jewish culture. Long after the Sabbatean crisis of the late seventeenth and eighteenth centuries, Ottoman Jewish life continued to develop and thrive.[12]

Alongside the publication of Jewish books in Ladino and Yiddish, was the steady accretion of books written in Western languages by Jews, demonstrating, among other things, the need for Jewish authors to speak to Christian readers beyond the immediate community of their own coreligionists or to conversos whose primary language was Spanish or Portuguese. This phenomenon was generally restricted to the West, particularly to Jewish intellectuals living in relatively open environments such as Italy and the Netherlands. Already in the sixteenth century, several Jewish authors such as Elijah Delmedigo, Jacob Mantino, Samuel Usque, and the most famous example of all, Judah Abravanel, alias Leone Ebreo, chose the unusual path of publishing books in Latin or other western languages.[13] In contrast, while Jewish preachers had often addressed their congregations in the vernacular, they often remained reticent to publish the written versions of their oral remarks in any language other than Hebrew.[14]

By the seventeenth century, this development of publishing in the vernacular took on added momentum with the emergence of apologetic works written either to convince conversos to return to the Jewish fold or to counter a negative image of Jewish religion and culture emerging in print among certain Christian authors. Such Jewish intellectuals in Italy as Leon Modena and Simone Luzzatto, and their counterparts in Amsterdam such as Menasseh ben Israel, Isaac Orobio de Castro, and many others, felt compelled to raise their voices in a language accessible to assimilated Jews and Christians alike and within a cultural matrix understandable to both.[15]

A wonderful example of how apologetic writing in the vernacular could redefine the very essence of Judaism when presenting it to others is the sixteenth chapter of the Venetian rabbi Simone Luzzatto's *Discorso circa il stato de gl'hebrei et in particolar dimoranti nell'inclita città di Venetia,* published in 1638. In this chapter, Luzzatto offers an intellectual profile of the Jewish community as one consisting of three distinct groups: Talmudists, philosophers, and kabbalists. The division appears strange from an internal Jewish perspective where Talmudists were also philosophers and kabbalists and the distinction between those who upheld the law and interpreted it and those who were preoccupied with "meta-halakhic [legal]" concerns was artificial. Luzzatto probably borrowed these categories from a similar division written by the Catalan Jewish thinker Profiat Duran at the beginning of the fifteenth century. But his division of Jewish intellectuals is also reminiscent of those of Johann Reuchlin (1455–1522), the famous German Christian Hebraist of the sixteenth century. Reuchlin clearly appreciated good Jewish kabbalists but separated them from those Talmudists he deemed disreputable because they blindly followed the letter of the law. Luzzatto hardly disparaged the Talmudists; on the contrary, he provided an accurate and complementary portrait of the legal development of Judaism. Nevertheless, by isolating the Talmud and its transmitters from the rest of Jewish culture, he gave greater attention to those areas of Jewish culture more accessible to Christian readers and more easily translatable into their terms of references. Thus he demonstrated the glorious traditions of Jewish philosophical reflection and its interrelatedness with common developments in Islam and Christianity. And kabbalah in its close association with Neoplatonism and Pythagoreanism, again reminiscent of Reuchlin's articulation, was to be understood and appreciated as part of the exotic and legitimate occult traditions of Western civilization.[16]

The genre of apologetic works presenting Judaism in the simplest and most attractive manner addressed simultaneously wavering Jews and indifferent or antagonistic Christians. The publication of vernacular works was surely an acknowledgment on the part of Jewish religious leaders of the need to reach out to those who no longer bothered or were incapable of reading Hebrew books. And we should add parenthetically that books eventually opened the possibility of presenting Judaism not only in words but also in icons. The emergence of illustrated *minhag* (custom) collections as early as the sixteenth century in Italy, and culminating in the publication of Leon Modena's manual of Jewish life, accompanied by the famous illustrations of Jewish events and observances of Bernard Picart, are two notable examples of how books could be used to visualize Jews and Judaism in novel ways.[17]

My account up to now has focused primarily on the impact of the Jewish book on Jewish culture and society. But the printing of Jewish books was not only an activity engaging Jews; it also affected profoundly the Christian world as well through Christian publishers of Jewish books, through Christian readers, and through the activity of church censors allowing Jewish books to be sold and disseminated as long as they did not violate the doctrinal purity of the Christian faith. The study of Judaism by Christians has a long history before the early modern period and individual Christian scholars pursued Hebraic subjects throughout the Middle Ages, especially related to biblical exegesis and medieval theology.[18] By the end of the fifteenth century, two significant changes in the cultural landscape of European Christendom profoundly affected Christian involvement with the Jewish book. The first was the influence of the Renaissance and Reformation on Christian Hebraic scholarship; the second was the critical impact of the printing press on the production and dissemination of Hebraica for Christian readers.

The most prominent Renaissance figure to approach Hebrew books in a way radically different from that of earlier Christian scholars was Pico della Mirandola (1463–94). With the assistance of Jewish tutors as well as others who had converted to Christianity, Pico studied Hebrew texts while assembling a most impressive collection of Jewish exegetical, homiletical, and philosophical writing translated from the Hebrew into Latin. But his first passion was the kabbalah to which he devoted his primary energies as a student of Jewish literature. For Pico and some of his associates, the kabbalah was the key to lay bare the secrets of Judaism, to reconcile them with the mysteries of other religions and cultures, and thus to universalize them. Through the kabbalah, the essential differences between Judaism and Christianity could be eradicated.[19]

Pico subsequently became the pioneer figure in the dramatic reevaluation of Jewish literature and the gradual penetration of contemporary Jewish thought into European culture. His Christianization of kabbalistic techniques and his amalgamation of Renaissance magic and Jewish mysticism, while officially condemned by the church, were enthusiastically received by a notable number of Christian thinkers in Italy, France, Germany, and England well into the eighteenth century. The Christian kabbalah of Pico left its mark on Renaissance culture through its integration with Neoplatonism. It also influenced both the Catholic and Protestant Reformation through its impact on such thinkers as Egidio of Viterbo, Francesco Giorgio, Cornelius Agrippa, and especially the aforementioned Johann Reuchlin.

After Pico, Johann Reuchlin was the most prominent Christian scholar to master Hebrew sources and to utilize them in revitalizing Christian theology. In *De Arte Cabalistica,* first published in 1517, Reuchlin followed Pico in considering kabbalah a higher and theologically licit form of magic, a source of divine revelation to be correlated with the highest truths of Neoplatonic and Pythagorean philosophy. Reuchlin's commitment to Jewish texts aroused the antagonism of some of his contemporaries in Reformation Germany, especially the Dominicans of Cologne who initiated a bitter campaign to ban the reading of Hebrew books. Reuchlin's well-reasoned responses to the extreme accusations of a Jewish apostate named Johann Pfefferkorn drew him unwittingly into an acrimonious debate over the value of Jewish learning for Christians and the place of Judaism in Christian society.[20]

But Reuchlin was hardly alone in his appropriation of Hebrew learning in the cause of Christian reform. Other Protestant thinkers in the first half of the sixteenth century focused on the more conventional sources of Jewish knowledge beyond the kabbalah. In their return to the Hebrew Bible, they were especially attracted to the literal sense of the text. They mastered biblical Hebrew and its grammatical foundations, and they also probed rabbinic exegesis in attempting to grasp the original meaning of Scripture. Scholars such as Paul Fagius and Sebastian Münster published Hebrew grammars, examined Jewish rites and customs, and explored the Pharisaic context of the utterances of Jesus. Others, like Michael Servetus, even used Hebrew sources to offer a radical critique of Trinitarian Christianity.[21]

By the seventeenth century, Hebraic studies reached new heights among a gifted circle of Christian scholars who included Johannes Buxtorf I and his son Johannes Buxtorf II, Edward Pococke, Johann Christof Wagenseil, John Lightfoot, John Selden, and Christian Knorr von Rosenroth. The Buxtorfs produced translations of some of the classic philosophical texts of Judaism; Wagenseil published Jewish anti-Christian works in Hebrew and Latin; while Christian Knorr von Rosenroth compiled a vast compendium of kabbalistic texts that he called the *Kabbala Denudata,* making available to Christian readers the most extensive anthology of its kind. By the seventeenth century, scholars such as Lightfoot and Selden mastered the large rabbinic corpus of Jewish law and studied it for the insights it provided in understanding early Christianity and ancient legal systems. Their work was continued by Wilhelm Surenhusius who published the entire *Mishnah* with commentaries in an elegant Hebrew and Latin edition by the end of the century. Well into the eighteenth century, erudite Christian scholars studied Hebraica along with Arabic and other Semitic languages, paving the way for the study of these fields within secular universities as well as Christian seminaries.[22]

Besides their learned tomes of erudition on Jewish literature, Christian authors, including the older Buxtorf himself, composed the first ethnographic accounts of Jewish customs for Christian readers. This interest in contemporary Jewish practice was fundamentally ambivalent. It still reflected the older medieval polemical stance toward Judaism, but on the other hand, its ethnographic depictions preserved a relative posture of objectivity and neutrality toward their subject. Jewish practices were normalized and demystified by these descriptions and presented as simply those of another ethnic group alongside Muslims, Hindus, and the other peoples of the world that European society was encountering by the seventeenth century.[23]

The centers of Christian printing of Hebrew books were generally concentrated north of the Alps in the German principalities, France, and the Netherlands. While the Italian and Ottoman Hebrew presses catered primarily although not exclusively to Jews, these presses in the North focused on the needs of Christians publishing, for the most part, works dealing with biblical scholarship. In the case of Amsterdam, however, with its significant resources for Jewish publications, often exported to the East, the distinction between Christian and Jewish presses becomes more confusing. The press of Menasseh ben Israel, Amsterdam's best-known Jewish public intellectual, was surely a case in point, producing books read by both Christians and Jews. In other centers of Christian printing in the North a close correlation existed between the printing of Hebrew books and the presence of Hebrew professors at Protestant universities.[24]

Christian Hebraism thus constituted an intellectual explosion fed by print and university learning; a Christian spiritual quest rooted in the essential notions of rebirth and reform propelling the intellectual and religious developments of the sixteenth century and beyond; and also an appropriation and aggrandizement of the Judaic element of Western civilization to be utilized and appreciated for Christians alone. As has been often remarked, the new Christian scholars were often infatuated with Jewish books with little regard for actual living and breathing Jews.

This last point was sorely appreciated by contemporary Jews who noted with mixed feelings the emergence of the new Christian Hebraism. On the one hand, they initially were flattered by the attention Christian scholars were giving their own religious heritage, even seeking out Jewish teachers with whom to study.[25] For some Jews living in Renaissance Italy, this attention appeared to reflect well on their own self-image; Jewish culture, especially its esoteric dimension, was in vogue. Jews and their postbiblical libraries "were in" among the most elite of Christian intellectual circles. But as time went on, some Jews began to realize the unsettling fact that Christians, to an unprecedented degree, could master Judaic traditions without recourse to Jews. The Jewish intellectual could ignore his Christian rival or challenge his mastery of Judaism. He could also choose to collaborate with him at the risk of losing control of his own sources and their specific Jewish meanings.

In the final analysis, Christian Hebraism thus became a new factor in the intellectual and psychological development of Jewish scholars. From Pico and Reuchlin in the fifteenth century to Benjamin Kennicott, Robert Lowth, and Johann David Michaelis at the end of the eighteenth century,[26] Jews faced a formidable challenge in understanding their own cultural legacy. They were no longer the sole arbiters of the sacred texts of the Jewish tradition, and certainly not of the Hebrew Bible. The more Christians mastered the Hebrew and Aramaic languages and the more they could consult medieval Jewish authors, the more they could also claim to understand the Jewish tradition, especially the Hebrew Bible, better than the Jews themselves. To some extent, the mastery of Jewish books by Christian scholars was an expression of power relations, of aspirations to dominate Jews by acquiring intimate knowledge of their intellectual legacy. And in the new cultural space populated by Christian Hebraists and an increasing number of converts to Christianity, Jewish scholars were surely losing their hegemony over the interpretation of their own texts and their own traditions.[27]

One final dimension of the printing of Jewish books by both Christians and Jews revolves around the censorship of Hebrew books by the Catholic Church, beginning in the sixteenth century. According to Amnon Raz-Krakotzkin, Hebrew censorship should be treated as part of the Catholic campaign to censor all books as well as in the context of an emerging Christian readership of Hebrew books. Raz-Krakotzkin emphasizes the fact that censors did not necessarily prevent readings; rather they strove to preserve the text in a way noninjurious to a potential Christian reading public. Furthermore, Hebrew books emerged in a new setting unique to early modern Europe: the print shop usually owned by Christians where converts and Jews worked side by side. In this unique setting, editors, typesetters, and censors worked together, often making it difficult to determine where editing had concluded and censorship had begun. The ultimate effect of this shared endeavor was to reach a kind of consensus whereby Judaism could be fully expressed without deprecating the Christian other and Jewish self-definition could be articulated in a neutral and nonpolemical manner. The print shop offered an intimate space of nonbelligerent encounter between Jews and Christians. The censor extended to the Jewish community an official legitimization of its literature while participating in a new articulation of Jewish identity. Thus the social context of printing Hebrew books offers yet another novel direction in which Jewish-Christian relations were emerging in early modern Europe.

In light of what I have argued above, it would be fair to conclude that the more tangible linkages existing across Jewish cultural boundaries and localized subcultures in early modern Europe were due in large part to the printing press. Print radically changed the manner in which the Jewish tradition was transmitted to Jews as well as to Christians, expanded the intellectual horizons of many Jews, and made them more aware of their cultural connections with their own coreligionists scattered in far-off regions. It also elevated the study of the classical texts of Judaism and contemporary customs and rituals within the space of Christian high culture through the presses of both Jewish and Christian printers. Finally, it significantly enhanced the knowledge and appreciation of the "other" for at least some Christians and Jews while opening new opportunities as well as new challenges for Jewish-Christian relations for centuries to come.

CHAPTER 6

The Jewish Book in Christian Europe

Material Texts and Religious Encounters

ANTHONY GRAFTON

Between the fifteenth and the seventeenth centuries, European Christians confronted and tried to make sense of many different religions. They reconstructed the religious beliefs and practices of the ancient Greeks and Romans whose works they studied at school and university. They studied the origins and history of Christianity—a subject that led to fierce debates, as the Reformation and Counter-Reformation gave it new urgency—and those of what they saw as its most dangerous opponent, Islam. They destroyed the temples of the Aztecs and Incas, only to find that they could not turn the surviving inhabitants of the New World into believing Christians if they did not gather as much information as they could about their previous beliefs and practices. They struggled to understand the religions of China, Japan, India, and Persia, chiefly in the hope of learning how to mount effective missions—but also out of curiosity about the strange new worlds, so much richer and more sophisticated than Western Europe, to which it was bound by emerging systems of trade and empire. As Guy Stroumsa has recently argued, the historical and comparative study of religions first took root and flourished not in the Enlightenment, but in this earlier period.[1]

No religion received more attention from Christians—or stirred them to greater extremes of empathy and antipathy—than Judaism. Jews lived inside as well as outside the Christian world. They apparently possessed vital knowledge about part of the Christian Bible; they certainly practiced their strange and distasteful rites in Christian cities, and many thought they did so as murderously vicious opponents of Christianity. And two great fifteenth-century events—the introduction of printing to the West and the expulsion of Jews from Iberia—sent both Jewish texts and Jews moving across Europe in great numbers. No short paper can survey all of the ways in which Christian theologians and censors, scholars and ministers encountered and thought about Judaism in this period. But by sticking to one thread—the material texts of Judaism and the reactions they provoked—and by examining a limited number of Christian thinkers, all of them scholars deeply interested in Jewish thought and life, we may appreciate the complexities, and some of the ironies, of a vital episode in the history of both Jewish and Christian religion and culture.

Early in the seventeenth century, Joseph Scaliger looked back with satisfaction on the rise of Hebrew studies in Christian Europe. "Two hundred years ago," he told the French students who lodged in his house "if anyone had taught or known Hebrew, he would have been considered a heretic." In Scaliger's time, by contrast, Christians were free to learn Hebrew and other Jewish languages, and even to live in proximity with Jews. Scaliger liked seeing the women of the Portuguese community in Amsterdam sitting in front of their houses, observing the Sabbath, and he contrasted the enlightened policy of the Estates of Holland with that of Swiss cities like Basel, which had exiled their Jews: "The Jews should never be expelled, they bring us profit and we learn from them."[2]

The second point mattered much more to Scaliger than the first. For Jewish learning was one of his central passions. He treasured the Semitic books that he owned, which included everything from a book in Provençal written in Hebrew characters to the Leiden manuscript of the Jerusalem Talmud, and he left his Hebrew, Aramaic, and Samaritan manuscripts to the Leiden University Library, which set them aside as a treasure.[3] He boasted to his friend Francois Vertunien about how much he had spent on these books even before he left France for Leiden, where he received a high salary, in 1593: "The Talmud," he explained, "costs 100 livres."[4] And he told his students much more. Scaliger disliked Jewish poetry, but praised the Jews' letters, in which he found "wonderful sentences," and their subtle commentaries on the Bible. Again and again he urged contemporary Christians to go beyond reading the Hebrew Old Testament (though, as he also cautioned them, "the rabbis are hard").[5] And he made wicked fun of friends who lacked his critical sense and historical command of the tradition. When one friend tried to convince him that a medieval Hebrew text was ancient, he replied, "I flatter

myself I could write Hebrew as well as he can." If Hebrew had seemed out-
landish, even heretical, a century before, it now counted as a third classical
language, next to Latin and Greek. "The Hebrew language," Scaliger told his
pupils, "has a majestic beauty"—and an expert like Scaliger could tell the
real thing from a late and derivative version.[6] In fact, the one letter of his in
Hebrew, a very rough draft of which survives, is a fairly mechanical set of
inquiries about books, addressed to the Samaritans. It suggests that his written
Hebrew did not match his Latin and Greek for fluency.[7]

Scaliger's confidence in his power to write Hebrew may have been
misplaced. But he was right to think he had witnessed a revolution in
scholarship—even if he did not realize that Jews had done as much as Christians to bring it about. From the 1470s, Jewish books of every kind tumbled
from both Jewish and Christian presses. Imagine yourself as a Christian
scholar, confronted with the vast range of Jewish books that reached print:
the Zohar, the classic text of Jewish mysticism, in its first edition of 1558,
printed on blue paper as a special mark of distinction; the Rabbinic Bible,
with its sea of commentaries breaking over small islands of text; the responses
of a great thirteenth-century rabbi, Shlomo ben Aderet, or Rashba, to formal
questions of Jewish law; a Yiddish-Hebrew-Latin-German dictionary by the
sixteenth-century Jewish scholar Elias Levita; a vividly illustrated description
of Jewish customs in Yiddish. Any Christian humanist or theologian who
hoped to make the Jewish world his own confronted books from many different centuries, written in several distinct languages and printed in a baffling
variety of scripts and type faces.[8]

Adding to the difficulty were the screens, woven of assumptions and prejudices, through which Christians read Jewish texts. Attitudes toward the
Jews varied widely in Renaissance Europe, but two symmetrical extremes
perhaps shaped responses most deeply. One set of Christians argued that
the Jews were irredeemably stuck in their evil ways, and that knowledge of
their religion could only be harmful. In the late fifteenth and early sixteenth
centuries, Christian authorities arrested, tortured, and convicted Jews for the
ritual murder of Christians—Christian boys, in particular, whose blood the
Jews supposedly needed to make matzo. In March 1475, when a two-year-old
Christian boy named Simon was found dead in the cellar of a Jew's house
in the beautiful city of Trento, in the Dolomites, the leaders of the Jewish
community—eighteen men and five women—were arrested and tortured.
Almost all confessed, and eight were executed, while another killed himself.
While never sainted, Simon became a powerful presence in Catholic devotion, the doer of many miracles. Though the Roman Curia disapproved
of these proceedings and eventually stopped them, vivid printed texts and

images carried the charges against the Jews of Trent, with their implication that Jewish ritual was directed against Christians, across regions and social orders—and helped to provoked more persecutions, including torture, executions, and expulsion of ancient communities.[9] Less radical—but no less critical—treatises by Jewish converts and Christians offered detailed, polemical descriptions, visual and verbal, of Jewish religious observances, designed to show they were strange and uncanny as well as pointless. Johannes Pfefferkorn, a convert who pioneered this form of writing, did so as part of a concerted campaign to confiscate Jewish texts from their owners. One form of Jewish book, or book about Jews, powerfully conveyed the message that they were a dangerous people, and that their own literature should be confiscated or destroyed.[10]

Yet the idea that Jews had concealed an ancient revelation—one somehow connected with their status as an uncanny, magically empowered people—could take a positive form as well. Charismatic converts like the Sicilian exile Flavius Mithridates and Christians like Johann Reuchlin announced to Christians the great news that ancient Jewish texts confirmed the fundamental truths of their religion.[11] Flavius made this point for two hours in a famous, brilliant Good Friday address to the papal curia, in the course of which his elegant pronunciation of Hebrew and Aramaic charmed his listeners. These men offered, in addition to scrambled citations from the Talmud that supported the doctrine of the Trinity, genuine passages from texts of the kabbalah, or mystical tradition, which they identified with the Hebrew Oral Law. Flavius translated thousands of pages of genuine Jewish mystical material for Pico della Mirandola in a mad, magnificent rush during 1485 and 1486.[12]

Although the bulk of these texts lay hidden for centuries, unexploited and unknown, many other teachers offered similar lessons. In 1513, the Spanish convert Matthaeus Adrianus taught the brilliant young Basel scholar and publisher Boniface Amerbach to read the Psalms, first in transliterated Hebrew and then in the original, to which Boniface learned to add the vowels. An ambitious man, Adrianus called himself "doctor of medicine, knight of the Holy Land, and expert in the sacred language and in Cabala," and did his best to persuade Boniface's father Johannes to fire the pioneer Hebraists Johann Reuchlin and Conrad Pellicanus and hire Adrianus as his Hebrew proof corrector in their stead (this would have been a bad idea: Adrianus's fluent Latin obeyed no known rules of Latin grammar or syntax).[13] His lessons on the Psalms were also ambitious. At Psalm 22:17, the transmitted text reads, "The assembly of the wicked have inclosed me: like a lion, my hands and my feet." Adrianus carefully informed his pupil that the Masora—the Hebrew marginal apparatus—noted that in reading the text, one should vocalize the consonants differently. In this form, the phrase at issue meant "they dug [or pierced] my hands and my feet"—a Christian mystery deeply buried in a Jewish source.[14] As Boniface worked with Adrianus, he drank the full cocktail of the Christian kabbalah: an inspiring mixture of the Jewish mystical tradition and traditional, nonsemantic forms of exegesis, which inspired Adrianus to defy the theologians of Louvain, where he taught Hebrew a little later at the Collegium Trilingue and insisted on the transcendent value of the Jewish language and tradition.

In new institutions like the Collegium Trilingue, administrators and scholars viewed Jewish textbooks and texts as a new foundation for Christian learning. For the Christian Scriptures, as Saint Jerome had pointed out, included not only the Greek New Testament but the Hebrew Old Testament: "hebraica veritas," Hebrew truth.[15] High Renaissance humanists like Erasmus found it second nature to argue that one must study texts in their original languages, including Hebrew. This required a new level of discipline. Soon the ebullient converts who had taught the first generation made way for learned Christians. Some of them, like Conrad Pellikan and Johann Reuchlin, shared Pico della Mirandola's enthusiasm for kabbalah and the belief that the Jewish tradition, properly understood, confirmed and deepened the understanding of Christian doctrine.[16] But they developed a far deeper linguistic mastery than he had, and they and their successors gradually produced a range of grammars and commented texts that Christians could work their way through with relative ease. The Basel scholar Sebastian Münster, for example, composed Hebrew and Aramaic grammars and dictionaries. He edited portions of the Bible and other texts for use by students—from the Book of Jonah, which he printed with the Aramaic translation or Targum and translations of both, to the medieval rabbi Ibn Ezra's commentary on the Ten Commandments, which the great Zurich scholar Conrad Gesner used to learn his Hebrew.[17] Munster did all this so effectively that his star pupil, Erasmus Oswald Schreckenfuchs, was able to compose a funeral oration in Hebrew when his teacher died.[18] Similar traditions grew up across Europe—at Paris, for example, where Gilbert Génébrard, who held a royal lectureship in Hebrew, produced an edition of Maimonides's statement of the thirteen basic principles of Judaism, which students worked through, word by word.[19]

Even these pioneers often viewed Jews and their beliefs from the traditional polar positions: with inordinate dislike or inordinate awe. Jewish books, accordingly, aroused emotions that ran the gamut from love to horror. Many encountered both. In 1521 the Christian printer Daniel Bomberg told Reuchlin that he had undertaken to print the Talmud "at the command of the supreme Pontiff"—the highest of High Renaissance Popes, Leo X. In 1553, as the Catholic Church geared up to respond to the challenge of Protestantism, piles of copies of the Bomberg Talmud and other editions were publicly burned in Rome.[20] The grandest products of Christian Hebraism often revealed the same opposed prejudices at work. The Antwerp Polyglot Bible was one in a series of similar projects that began with the polyglot psalter of Agostino Giustiniani and the Complutensian Polyglot Bible of Alcalà. This great collaborative reached its climax with the London Polyglot edited by Brian Walton in the middle of the seventeenth century, with its shocking new material from the Samaritan textual tradition. All of these enterprises were distinctly Christian, and in multiple ways. They were inspired by one of the greatest scholarly enterprises of the early church, the Hexapla, or six-column manuscript edition of the Bible, assembled by Origen at Caesarea in the middle of the third century. More important, modern editors often remained at one pole or the other of normal attitudes towards Jewish writing. Giustiniani, fascinated by kabbalah, introduced material from Reuchlin into his commentary, and proclaimed that his countryman Columbus had fulfilled the prophecy of Psalm 19:4. By contrast, Cardinal Ximenes, the patron of the Complutensian Polyglot, notoriously compared the Vulgate text of the Old Testament in his edition, lined up between the Hebrew and Greek versions, to Jesus, crucified between the two thieves. Benito Arias Montano, a Spanish cleric and scholar, spent years in the house of the Polyglot's publisher, Christopher Plantin, overseeing the production of the Polyglot. He signed every page of the proof sheets. He saw to it that the edition included such up-to-date aids to readers as Hebrew grammars, a literal, word-for-word translation of the Hebrew Old Testament, and splendid illustrations that drew on the new antiquarian scholarship of the sixteenth century. But he argued, in his own treatment of the ancient Jewish world, that Solomon's ancient Jewish wisdom had matched that of his modern counterparts. When Solomon sent ships to what the Bible called Ophir and Parvaim for treasure, Montano argued, he was already drawing on the mines of what sixteenth-century Spaniards called Peru. The wisdom of ancient Judaism had unified the world long before modern times and was partly transmitted in the world of mystical exegesis. Here and elsewhere the inspired, visionary Judaisms so dear to Christians of the High Renaissance lived on.[21]

And yet, as we have learned in the last two generations, many Christians learned a vast amount that was new to them from Jewish texts—even as they continued to work within lines laid down long before. Historians of this movement have generally called it Christian Hebraism and have concentrated on the scholarly work of Christians who wrote Hebrew grammars or edited one or more books of the Bible. Such scholars did work of great erudition and originality. A Semitic scholar by vocation, Johann Buxtorf produced a great series of grammars, lexica, and other aids for students, as well as a massive edition of the Hebrew Bible and a polemical history of the development of the Hebrew text.[22] But two other scholars less embedded in the historiography also developed complex attitudes toward the Jews and considerable skill at reading Jewish texts. Their work, and their experiences, complement Buxtorf's in many ways. Joseph Scaliger, the French philologist and historian whom I have already mentioned, reconstructed the entire chronological framework of ancient history as a professor at the new university of Leiden, where he worked from 1593 to 1609.[23] Isaac Casaubon, a Swiss Hellenist and classical scholar, wound up his life in England, writing polemics against Catholic scholars about the early history of the church. In this work he showed, with a famous set-piece philological argument, that the dialogues ascribed to Hermes Trismegistus were not really ancient.[24] No two of these three men ever met, and each had his own interests. But they corresponded with one another on a wide range of questions, they have left us a vast amount of information about their use of Jewish books, and they give us a rich period sense of the many forms of Christian scholarly engagement with Jews and Judaism. By examining their experiences and setting them into context, we can begin, perhaps, to draw a profile of the fates that awaited Jewish books in the Christian world.

Each came to Hebrew in a different way. Buxtorf learned the language formally at Herborn and devoted himself to further study at Basel, where he was soon made professor of the language. Casaubon studied with the Geneva Hebraists Corneille Bertram and Pierre Chevalier, and was himself pressed into service to teach the Hebrew Bible to students at the Geneva Academy. Scaliger taught himself. For all the personal differences, two points of similarity emerge. All of them began with the Bible. As good Protestants, they knew the text intimately, verse by verse, before they ever looked at the Hebrew. As good humanists, moreover, all of them read the Hebrew Scriptures with a ferocity that the term *reading* does not evoke in the blurry-eyed age of Google and the hot link. Christian humanists read pen in hand. They physically mastered the texts they studied in conditions of strenuous attentiveness, and sometimes assisted by elaborate equipment. Their books—whose margins they wreathed with annotations—and their notebooks—which bulged with carefully transcribed extracts, often annotated as well—were their primary information-gathering devices. Some laid out literal commonplace books with neatly arranged "loci"—"places," or subject headings—and literally placed their excerpts under the proper topic. Others simply summarized their texts, in order, as they read. What mattered was the disciplined approach that underpinned these techniques and its results. Almost sixty of Casaubon's notebooks and dozens of his annotated books survive, as well as a thousand-page Latin diary that lets us trace how he created them with unique precision, not to mention some pity for his furious Calvinist self-discipline ("I arose at five," he writes at one point: "alas, how late!"). These documents show us how seriously Casaubon took copying as a tool of scholarship. Early in his diary he mentioned that the Greek orator Demosthenes had copied the histories of Thucydides eight times. By contrast, Casaubon copied out the biblical book of Esther.[25] Scaliger did the same, starting—as many did—with the medieval Hebrew text of the Gospel of Matthew, part of a commentary on which he copied out in his own hand.[26]

None of these three men stopped with the Bible (in fact, all of them ridiculed Christians who did so). Casaubon worked his way systematically through major texts of Jewish law, history, and religion, as his late, appreciative notes on Maimonides's *Mishneh Torah* show. He liked everything about the book, including its handsome title page.[27] Buxtorf chewed his way systematically through the sections of the Talmud that dealt with blessings and prayers, translating, collating, and noting divergences between editions as he took notes.[28]

None of these men was a kabbalist: in fact, through most of their lives, each tended to treat the Jews as sunk in folly and obstinacy. Yet each at some point cherished an enthusiast's conviction that systematic study of Hebrew would offer him the keys to intellectual kingdoms. Late in life Scaliger recalled how Guillaume Postel had convinced him "that there were marvelous mysteries in the eastern languages, and that the Hebrews had excellent and very worthwhile authors, who had not yet been translated."[29] Casaubon, as he confessed to a friend, hoped to travel in the Eastern Mediterranean, where great works of philosophy in Arabic awaited the attention of Christian scholars. Spoken rabbinic Hebrew, he thought, would serve him as a lingua franca there.[30]

Buxtorf, in some ways, dreamed the most ambitious dreams of all. He was the reigning expert in late Renaissance Europe on the religious practices and customs of the Jews, which he described in great detail in his *Juden-Schul* of 1603. Inspired by Martin Luther, Buxtorf did his best to prove, from the disorderly, unpleasant rituals and conduct of the Jews, that they were sunk in folly and superstition: "They say that they know God, but belie it by their works, since they are those whom God abominates." As Scaliger remarked,

"It's remarkable how much the Jews seem to like Buxtorf, given how sharply he criticizes them in the *Synagoga Judaica*."[31]

But Buxtorf loved the languages of the Jews, from Hebrew and Aramaic to Yiddish, and he dreamed of doing for Hebrew what earlier generations of European scholars had done for Greek: wresting the language from the control of those who had inherited it and making it wholly available to western Christians. Contemporary Hellenists like Martin Crusius of Tübingen not only read Greek—contemporary as well as ancient—but also wrote it fluently: Crusius wiled away the three sermons he attended every week by translating them into classical Greek (more than six thousand of these transcripts survive, awaiting the attention of scholars).[32] Why not gain the same fluency for and command of Hebrew? To this end Buxtorf provided, for Hebrew, what dozens of authors had already provided for Latin and Greek: a book of model letters on all the subjects that a humanist might need to address. To his delight, he found in an apothecary's shop a treasure trove of letters to Israel Sifroni, the Jewish corrector of the press who had overseen an edition of the Talmud at Basel in 1578–81. Like Casaubon and Scaliger, Buxtorf read these texts pen in hand, and excerpted from them model passages on important subjects. How do you explain, for example, why you have not written to a friend in a long time? Tell him, in flowery language, that no messenger was available. Why, having waited so long, did you write so little? Tell him, eloquently, that you were very, very pressed.[33] After assembling these and many other useful passages in his notebooks and purchasing Jewish collections of model letters, Buxtorf published a collection of his own, with commentary—a book he regarded as a first step in what would eventually be the wholesale takeover, by Christians, of Jewish eloquence and learning. Scaliger and Casaubon—both of whom occasionally received letters in Hebrew themselves—received this hybrid text with warm enthusiasm.[34]

To attain the deeper mastery that Scaliger, Casaubon, and Buxtorf dreamt of, it was first of all necessary to know Jewish literature. But that too was a tall order. For decades, Christian scholars had been arranging Greek and Latin books in lucid series in the new secular libraries of the Renaissance. Where would all the newly available Jewish books fit in this lucid, clearly defined order of knowledge? The first problem Christians faced—and one of the most serious—was that of bibliographical control. As usual, the Jewish situation had some distinctive features. A near-terminal condition of information overload afflicted the scholars of sixteenth- and seventeenth-century Europe. Floods of books on every subject washed into their libraries, threatening to overwhelm them with new continents, new cosmologies, and new

commentaries on authoritative texts. Jewish books were also widely varied, but they proved strikingly hard to find—especially in northern Europe.
Reuchlin and other early Hebraists had to collect manuscripts and printed
editions of individual treatises one by one, often—as he remarked of his copy
of tractate Sanhedrin of the Jerusalem Talmud, now in Karlsruhe—with
some effort.[35] But even the new age of print did not always bring Christian scholars into an age of Jewish bibliographical plenty. Casaubon, for
example, brought with him to England a relatively modest collection of
Hebrew books: some forty survive, a few are lost. It was not a great Hebrew
library, and Casaubon himself regretted its lacunae—which became worse
when friends borrowed his copies of Azariah de' Rossi's *Me'or Einayim* and
Abraham Zacuto's chronological work, the *Sefer Yuhasin,* the latter of which
never made its way back into his hands. Yet this small collection became the
nucleus of the Royal Library's, and then the British Library's, holdings in
Hebrew, where its very existence was eventually forgotten. Scaliger owned
a bigger collection, including some now famous manuscripts: yet even he
wrote wistfully that Daniel Bomberg had printed so many rabbinical texts
that one could not buy them all for eight hundred gold coins.[36] It was hard
to know what books actually existed; which offered new information; which
editions were reliable.

To overcome these difficulties, Christian Hebraists constantly exchanged
books and information. In 1593 Buxtorf's friend Caspar Waser returned to
Zurich from a stint in Italy, bringing with him a collection of rare Jewish
books, Buxtorf teased and flirted in order to obtain a look at Waser's catalogue. "I am translating another Hebrew book," he wrote, "for my private
use, and I can scarcely tell you how much I enjoy reading it. I don't doubt
that you bought it and other books like it in Italy. But I don't want to tell
you the title until you send me the list of your books."[37] Only after Waser
coughed up his list did Buxtorf identify his find and explain that he had
ordered three copies, one of which he now sent to Waser, asking in return
for rarer books.[38]

Going deeper into the different ranges of Hebrew books eventually
meant dealing with Jews. Israel Sifroni, after a protracted period of work
in Basel, returned to Venice, where he worked for the printer Giovanna
di Gara and took advantage of his contacts to sell Hebrew books to visiting
Swiss scholars. Buxtorf turned to him, via his Swiss friend Jacob Zwinger,
when he wanted to buy special books for his classes and his scholarship. He
asked for five or six small-format copies of the Torah with the prophetic
readings ("The Jews," Buxtorf carefully wrote to his Christian friend, "call
the Pentateuch the Chimmusch and the readings from the prophets added

to it Haphtaroth") and a collection of *Minhagim* ("it's a Hebrew-German book," he explained, "that contains the ceremonies of the Jews for life and worship.")[39] More direct contacts between Christian collectors and Jewish bookmen were not always so smooth and pleasant. Buxtorf, for example, told his friend Waser that "you would not believe how much I have to sweat in order to buy some little pamphlet, by begging and for a high price, from some disgusting Jew."[40] More than once he used the same set phrase, "prece vel pretio," to emphasize his fury at a Jew who had refused to sell him anything at all. Buxtorf explained that his own knowledge of Hebrew letters would inevitably remain incomplete, so long as he had no one to daub his face with aromatic powder or pomegranate juice "so that I could penetrate the smoky, stinking vaults of the Jews," where the rarest books were no doubt to be found.[41]

Even the scholar who somehow collected or gained access to a Jewish library still faced problems. First of all, there was the great one of control. Who were the main Jewish authors? When had they lived? What had they written? In 1545 the Zurich botanist and polymath Conrad Gesner published a massive bibliography. According to its title page, Gesner's *Universal Library* covered the three holy languages of culture, Latin, Greek, and Hebrew, describing books ancient and modern, books that existed and, in a nice piece of Borgesian symmetry, books that did not exist. Gesner, as we have seen, had studied Hebrew, and he felt warm sympathy for Postel's version of Christian kabbalah. He even transcribed a letter from Postel to their mutual friend, the Hebraist and Arabist Theodor Bibliander, into the magnificent patchwork of handwritten notes and pasted-in additions that was his working copy of his book.[42] But he gave far less information about Jewish writers than about Greek or Roman ones, and sometimes what he offered was false. On Maimonides, for example, he told his readers that "his Guide in theology is in print, in Latin and Hebrew. The Jews hold him in high esteem and call him Ramban." In fact, Maimonides, Rabbi Moses ben Maimon, was called Rambam. Eventually Gesner became aware of his basic slip. In his working copy, Gesner corrected Ramban to Rambam and noted: "This needs an m at the end. For Ramban with an n is Moses the son of Nachman."[43] Yet this information did not make its way into the authoritative corrected summary of Gesner's work that Josias Simler published in 1555.[44] Most of the names of Jewish writers listed by Gesner came, in fact, not from Jewish sources or publications but from the work of Christian Hebraists, above all the Franciscan Pietro Galatino, whose 1518 treatise *De arcanis Catholicae veritatis* would serve for decades as a storehouse of information for Christians interested in Jewish texts.

By the early seventeenth century, Buxtorf was working on a wholly different, much more comprehensive level. In 1612 he described his project to
create "a formal list of Jewish books." He suggested, a little chillingly, that
the Frankfurt magistrates should require Jews to deposit the names and titles
of their books—or copies of them—in the Frankfurt library. And he specu-
lated on the total size of his task; "I have heard from a certain Belgian who
has put in some work on this topic that he knows that there are not more
than 500 Jewish books in print. On that point I have my doubts." Buxtorf
was right to nourish doubts about the Belgian's figures. Daniel Bomberg
alone had printed more than two hundred titles. But he was also right to be
confident. His own library extended to many reaches of Jewish literature—
from three versions of the Talmud, censored and uncensored, to the little
Hebrew-Yiddish version of prayers for the table published in 1600 by a
Jewish acquaintance of Buxtorf's, Jacob Mocher Seforim (Jacob the book
peddler) from Messeritz. The *Bibliotheca Rabbinica* offered lucid, informative,
and helpful accounts of hundreds of Jewish books, listed in alphabetical
order. Entry after entry reveals the depth of Buxtorf's familiarity with a wide
range of types of books and with their place in Jewish life: "Machzor.... This
is a prayer book used for the more important festivals. Almost all the prayers
are poetic in form and in a difficult language that few understand. Most of
the Jews say these prayers the way our Vestal Virgins [Catholic nuns] say
their Psalter in Latin and the Pater noster."[45] Equally expert, equally objective, were the other aids Buxtorf provided for Christian readers: for example,
a field guide to the hundreds of abbreviations used in Jewish books.

Whatever the practical difficulties that Scaliger, Casaubon, and Buxtorf
confronted, their mastery of the Jewish book world was of a different order
from Gesner's. Their notebooks tell the tale. Buxtorf excerpted many texts
that few Christian humanists ever saw: for example, the *Sefer Ha-Terumah,*
a medieval German legal work which he combed for evidence of prohibi-
tions against Jews' doing business with Christians. Both he and Casaubon
eagerly read and collated as many Jewish prayer books as they could.[46]

Yet the notebooks—and the scholarship they made possible—tell another
story as well. Scaliger, the great student of ancient calendars, used the material
he gathered from the Talmud to argue that the rabbis had not understood
the historical development of the Jewish year—and that they had wasted
much time on fanciful speculation. Buxtorf copied out the relevant passages
from Scaliger, with their sharp words about rabbinical erudition.[47] He himself spent most of his time as a text collector and deployed his remarkable
expertise to hunt out passages in which he scented, rightly or wrongly, Jewish efforts to curse Christians or blaspheme against the Savior—or to argue

against Jews, like the thirteenth-century Tosafist Yechiel ben Yoseph, who had claimed that Talmudic references to Nazarenes had not been directed against Christians.[48]

Buxtorf's most famous book, the *Juden-Schul,* often reads like a notebook: one passage after another, selected to be used against the Jews. It grew naturally from its author's practices.[49] The vivid descriptions of ritual and conduct in the *Juden-Schul* that have led many modern scholars to take Buxtorf as an unsympathetic but perceptive witness to real Jewish life were chiefly constructed by excerpting texts. He began with systematic works, as he himself explained to the Bremen scholar and theologian Matthias Martinius, from Jewish texts: the Yiddish collection of customs, the *Minhagim;* the mid-sixteenth-century codification of Jewish law by Joseph Caro, the *Shulhan Arukh* ("Set Table"); and the great codification of law, rabbinical debates, and so much else, the Talmud, especially the Babylonian Talmud.[50] Perhaps the vivid Venetian illustrations that Buxtorf knew from his own working copy of the *Minhagim* helped the author to give his book its feel of eye-witness testimony. In the world of the notebook, after all, deep scholarship could take place, without much need for deep contact with actual Jews. Yet Buxtorf's notebooks show that he had some informants— for example, a young Jew who explained what Buxtorf took as a kabbalistic way to transform the toast "Lechayim tovim" into a curse.[51] More remarkably, his readers cared deeply that he drew some of the material in his *Juden-Schul* from living Jews. Casaubon, like his friend Scaliger, read Buxtorf's book with the greatest care. On the title page—his favorite place for serious data dumps— Casaubon pointed out that Buxtorf knew the rabbis so well he had actually gone to parties with them, and noted down, systematically, every page on which Buxtorf wrote from personal experience or Jewish oral tradition.[52]

Interactions of even more complex, human kinds took place in the world of the Jewish book. Many—perhaps most—projects for large-scale publication of Jewish works brought Jews and Christians, not just Jewish and Christian texts, together. The great Antwerp entrepreneur Daniel Bomberg printed in Venice his precedent-setting editions of the Rabbinical Bible with multiple commentaries and of the Babylonian Talmud—which he published, in its entirety, three times between the 1520s and the 1540s. His workforce was as cosmopolitan as the Venetian Jewish world more generally: the learned men who corrected the proofs of his Talmud edition came from as far afield as Frankfurt and Tunisia, as well as a range of Italian cities. The texts Bomberg printed were Jewish, but the models of mise-en-page that he used for them clarified the traditional forms of Jewish manuscripts by combining them with a new formal repertoire from the great Christian tradition of variorum commentaries. This had flourished in the fifteenth century not only in the Bible, but also in classical scholarship and Roman law. Karniel Adel Kind, the Jewish printer who designed the layout of Bomberg's Talmud editions, converted to Christianity and changed his name to Cornelio, though he continued to turn out editions of the Talmud.[53] Meanwhile Bomberg, at least according to the German humanist and Reformer Justus Jonas, moved for a while in the other direction. "Bomberg," he wrote to Luther, "seems to me to be have become Judaized, as happens to those who do too much work in Hebrew without being adequately prepared and forewarned in their piety." (Bomberg had told Jonas that the numerical values of the first word of Genesis in Hebrew, Bereshit, amounted to the number of years from the Creation to the Crucifixion).[54]

No big editorial project better illustrates the richness and complexity of these cross-cultural currents in the book world than the Hebrew Bible that Buxtorf published in Basel in 1619. Buxtorf and his publisher, Ludwig König, engaged a Jewish scholar, Abraham Braunschweig, to serve as co-corrector with Buxtorf (as Buxtorf explained with reference to an earlier project, otherwise Jews simply would not buy the final product).[55] Jews and Christians worked together intimately, though not always effectively, in König's shop. Braunschweig described the complex situation in an afterword to the edition: "We would be talking about one sheet of proofs and suddenly another would appear to be read, since three leaves were printed every day. The corrector can speak sharply to them and say: 'Finish your work in accordance with what is indicated on the proofs!'"[56] But sometimes the workers did not pay attention, and sometimes König—who was, after all, the boss—simply declared that a particular sheet was correct enough and must be printed off. On Saturdays, real disasters happened regularly, since the workers had to hurry in order to have time to make ready for their own Lord's Day, while the Jewish corrector, observing the Sabbath, could not be there to examine their work.

The final product impressed many readers with its elegance and accuracy. From our point of view, though, what seems more remarkable than the quality of the edition is the amount of mutual ethnography that went on during its creation, as Jewish correctors learned the customs of Swiss Lutheran workmen, and a Christian scholar lived for two years with Jews. Most remarkable of all is the evident sympathy that developed between Buxtorf and his Jewish colleague—a sympathy deep enough to bring Buxtorf into deep hot water. While in Basel, Braunschweig had a son. On his invitation, Buxtorf attended the ritual circumcision. Enraged local clergy reported this to the city council, which expelled Braunschweig's wife and son from the city and fined Buxtorf a hundred gulden. Angry and humiliated, Buxtorf protested to a friend that he had attended the briss only in order to rebuke the Jews for their superstitions and grumbled that some of the Baslers thought that he and his Bible should be thrown out of the city too.[57]

It seems unlikely that theological convictions and a wish to scold actually drew Buxtorf to the ceremony. For he had clearly developed some intimacy with Braunschweig. In a letter written earlier the same year to his friend and colleague, the Zurich Hebrew professor Caspar Waser, Buxtorf explained how "my Jewish fellow-corrector had whispered in my ear" gossip about a troublesome Jewish confidence man and sometime convert, Julius Conradus Otto.[58] It even seems possible that, thanks to his collaborative work with Braunschweig, Buxtorf found himself softening toward Jews more generally. That may help to explain why he argued in his late work on the Bible that medieval Jewish correctors had done a perfect job of preserving the accents and punctuation of the Old Testament. After all, he believed that most rabbis supported him in his fight against those who held that the vowels were recent. Even buying books from Jewish dealers became less unpleasant. In 1623, after Buxtorf published his Tiberias, a detailed study of the vocalization of the Hebrew Bible, he told Louis Cappel that he expected to obtain "two or three Hebrew books from Jews in Frankfurt, in which I hope to find older material" that would prove that the vowel points and accents were as old as he believed them to be.[59]

These contacts helped to determine more than the shapes taken by major editions of Jewish books. Reading, in this period, was not always solitary or silent. Christians interested in Hebrew and Judaism—even the most brilliant and original of them—often read Jewish texts in Jewish company. In the private space of his notebooks, Buxtorf recorded that Jews had called important aspects of Hebrew texts to his attention. On one page, where he described Jewish customs for cutting of nails, he noted that a Jew had shown him a passage in the *Orach Chayim,* part of Jacob ben Asher's fourteenth-century code *Arba Turim,* according to which the cut nails should be burned lest magicians put them to evil use. On another, he recorded an explication of a word in Deuteronomy 19:6 that had been offered him by Menachem ben Jacob, a Frankfurt rabbi whom he praised for his "outstanding knowledge of the Jewish law."[60] Casaubon read passages in the Talmud and other Jewish texts with a young Sephardic Jew named Jacob Barnet, whom he met in Oxford and took with him to London. He used these passages to powerful effect when he set out to show that the great Catholic Church historian Cesare Baronio had misunderstood early Christian burial customs because he did not realize that they derived from the Jews.[61] And no wonder. As

Scaliger told his students, "There's just no way to read the Talmud without the living voice of a Jew."[62] Scaliger enjoyed that experience for six months or so, in Leiden, where he studied with a Jew named Philippus Ferdinandus, who was made professor of Arabic on his recommendations.[63] These experiences proved transformative, at least for Casaubon and Scaliger. In the lonely solidarity of hard, collaborative reading, confessional barriers did not depart, but they seemed lower than before. Jewish texts became accessible to new kinds of reading, in which Christian prejudices played a smaller role, and the value of Jewish teachers became clearer. Casaubon defended Jacob Barnet from British prelates and theologians who tried to force him to convert. Scaliger's happy days of work with Ferdinandus, at whose death he lost his taste for reading the Talmud, helped to transform his understanding of what a Jewish text actually was, by making him look back with new eyes on his earliest experience of discussing texts with a Jew.

As a young man in Avignon, Scaliger had met a Jewish woman, who was poor but decently dressed—a fact that led him to admire Jewish charity. She was willing to eat with him: only fish and bread, no meat. She impressed him with her ability to read Hebrew. And she told him many interesting things—including the story that the Jews of Avignon, in order to save their best scholars from papal tyranny, had sent them away and made their most incompetent circumcised Jew become their rabbi. When Scaliger laughed, she replied: "Don't laugh, my lord: your Jesus was circumcised too." From that date on, Scaliger never ceased thinking about the Jewish elements in the Gospels. By the end of his life, he told his students that many of Jesus's teachings in the Gospels were actually Jewish proverbs, which Ferdinandus had identified for him. More strikingly still, Scaliger proclaimed that "I approve of certain Jewish ceremonies that Christ took over," and made clear to them that Jesus had dressed and worshipped as a Jew.[64]

At this point—as twenty-first century readers can see more easily than some of Scaliger's contemporaries could—he had devised a truly powerful thesis. In the 1570s and 1580s, Azariah de' Rossi and Scaliger had arrived, simultaneously, at the realization that many ancient Jews had written and spoken Greek, and had extended the realm of the Jewish book to include the works of Philo, Josephus, and the letter of Aristeas.[65] Now Scaliger argued, at least to his students, that the most important Jewish books, for a Christian, were the constituent books of the New Testament, and that Christians could not hope to understand these without setting them before the context of contemporary Judaism, insofar as the Mishnah and Talmud could reveal them. No kabbalist in his sympathies, Scaliger joined Pico and Reuchlin in their insistence that the Christian religion could not be complete until Christian scholars mastered the universe of Jewish texts. He thrilled and shocked the readers of his great book on chronology, which appeared in 1583, when he argued that to reconstruct exactly what Jesus and his disciples had done at the Last Supper, the Christian reader must bear in mind that they had carried out a full Passover ritual before the sharing of bread and wine described in the Gospels. To know what that had been like, one must read the Jewish Passover Haggadah—subtracting those elements, like the expression of hope, "Next year in Jerusalem," which would not have belonged to the Passover ritual before the destruction of the Second Temple.[66] Scaliger's dangerous idea found strong support. Casaubon insisted that Baronio had gone wrong in his account of the origins of Christianity because of his ignorance of Jewish texts, and Buxtorf lectured his students on the need to use the Talmud to explicate the New Testament. In milieus like theirs—as in the milieu of Pico or Egidio da Viterbo long before—Christianity continued to set the terms of discussion. But the relation between Christianity and Judaism was turning out to be something more complex than simple supersession—a suggestion that would live on long after the pleasant talks in Scaliger's garden had themselves become memories, passed down by later scholars to their students. These encounters deserve chapters of their own in the full story of the Jewish book in Christian early modern Europe.

At times, these men could even bring themselves to read for a moment or two—and feel for a moment or two—as Jews. Of the three Christian scholars I have concentrated on, only Casaubon has never been identified as a Judaist. Yet Casaubon's Jewish reading extended very widely. He loved Jewish prayer books, for example, which he collected and compared. Some prayers—like the one with which Orthodox Jewish men thank God for not making them women—seem to have baffled him. But he loved the *selihot,* the prayers of repentance, which he found "very beautiful," and criticized Buxtorf for describing Jewish prayers—as many experts did—only in terms of their anti-Christian content.

One Jewish book that Buxtorf, Casaubon, and Scaliger had all read was the *Sefer Hasidim,* or *Book of the Pious* of Judah the Pious. Composed in the Rhineland in the late twelfth century, this rich text describes the lives of a circle of pietists passionately dedicated to the pursuit of holiness and to devotion to the Torah—the material book as well as the Law it taught. On the flyleaf of his copy, Casaubon summarized the book, as he often did: "It teaches the basis of piety and then explains the duties of the pious, which are exemplified by many stories about the righteous as well as the wicked."[67]

Casaubon found the book striking and valuable, both for its prayers and for its technical terms for books and manuscripts. One story, in particular, fascinated him:

> There was a woman who was charitable but whose husband was stingy and did not wish to buy books or to give charity. So when the time came to perform her monthly immersion [ritual bath] she did not wish to do so. He asked her, "Why do you not immerse yourself?" She said: "I will not immerse myself unless you agree to buy books and give money to charity." And he was not willing to comply with her request, and she refused to immerse herself until he would agree to buy books and give charity. He complained about her to the sage who told the man: "May your wife be blessed that she forced you to perform a religious duty." To his wife he said, "If you are able to ensure that he performs good actions, all well and good, but with regard to sexual intercourse, do not put an obstacle before him, lest he contemplates sinning, and you therefore will be prevented from conceiving and he will become even more incensed."

"Elegant" is the way Casaubon refers to this story, his marginal summary of which oddly omits any mention of male desire.[68] It exemplifies the ways of the Jewish women of the Rhineland, who made it their business to ensure that the books were copied by scribes and then loaned to students. Casaubon was as passionate a book buyer and as dependent for all practical purposes on his wife as any *yeshiva bocher.* On May 19, 1611, he recorded in his diary a typical book buyer's vain resolution to improve: "Today I paid the booksellers what I owed, except for Norton, my debt to whom is the largest. I have emptied my purse. 'It is too late to save when all is spent' [Seneca]. I take no thought for my wife, I take no thought for my children. Today I decided that until my wife arrives I will not spend more than a gold sovereign on books—unless something truly rare turns up!"[69] No wonder, then, that this medieval short story, contained in a Jewish book, combining the acquisition of books, marital life, and charitable deeds, appeared to epitomize the things that mattered most in his life.

Casaubon, in this case, could see his own reflection in a text about pious Jews. Scaliger, by contrast, dismissed the work, in a letter to Casaubon, as neither old nor profound.[70] Buxtorf described it neutrally in his bibliography of rabbinical texts: "It contains the rules for a good life, which are illustrated by a variety of examples and stories."[71] And he used it, as he used so many other Hebrew texts, as a source not of inspiration but of ammunition to fire off against the Jews. In the varieties of their responses to this single text—as in the varieties of their enthusiasms, irritations, and denunciations—the three men illustrate something of the range of ways in which early modern Europeans responded to contact with the Jewish books that suddenly filled their libraries, and sometimes challenged their parochialism.

CHAPTER 7

Mission and Narrative in the Early Modern Spanish World

Diego de Ocaña's Desert in Passing

KENNETH MILLS

In the early modern Spanish world, thirst for all manner of information and "news" from abroad appears to have been rivaled only by the enthusiasm of various willing informants to provide it. These participant-tellers delivered in a stunning variety of forms. Amidst the array of communications, there rests a vast range of spiritual reportage by members of religious orders from abroad. Often urgent and dramatic in nature, sometimes quite self-contained, these writings represent a kind of "intelligence" which, while demonstrably vital for sixteenth- and seventeenth-century contemporaries, can be particularly challenging for twenty-first century readers. In the spirit of this volume, concerned with our ways of presenting religion in history, I seek to demonstrate in this chapter that the challenge of such early modern religious narratives is best met by near-immersion—by endeavoring to appreciate the world that people "lived through," and how and why spiritual reportage not only persuaded but moved them.[1] "Immersion" signals my attempt to enter into the world experienced by a range of contemporary historical subjects. That such entry is always an unreachable aim is signaled by "near." "Near" immersion offers distance that also allows one to bring more information to bear than a historical subject could have done in interpreting an utterance, an action, or the context surrounding an event. The impossibility of immersing fully in a past thought-world makes me—and my enthusiasms, priorities, and judgments—an inescapable part of the puzzle.

For this near immersion, I have selected the narrative of a difficult portion in a journey made by the Castilian Hieronymite friar Diego de Ocaña, who traveled throughout the Spanish viceroyalty of Peru between 1599 and 1606. I contend that movement and obstacles experienced by Catholic churchmen such as Ocaña in the "exterior" world were almost always accompanied by interior spiritual journeys sought and found along the way. These sweet and necessary exiles drew on a deep Christian tradition and were expected by the early modern Spanish imaginary, which is to say, by readers as much as by the travelers themselves. With respect to their encounter with difficulty in the extreme, holy wanderers who became participant-tellers in early modern times needed to emulate exalted predecessors. They needed especially to demonstrate their ability to seek and to reembody the apostolic ideal, "traveling far," as an early seventeenth-century Franciscan put it, "to come close to God."[2] "Those who embark on this enterprise," asserted another contemporary, the Jesuit Jerónimo Pallas, "undertake something scarcely less than what the apostles themselves embraced in the conversion of the world." Each *operario* should be thought of as "God's prized possession," continued the allusive Pallas, reaching even further back and twisting his Plato toward the description of Paul as "a chosen vessel" in Acts—the missionary body as special instrument passing along trails in which the trials would be many and the trophies few.[3]

The untitled but so-called "Relación de viaje" of the Hieronymite Diego de Ocaña was many things at once.[4] In focusing here on one aspect, that of a personal and emulative spiritual journey,[5] I explore what many early modern missionaries saw themselves as doing, what they conceived their written records to be *about* and, ultimately, *for.* As much as early modern missions in foreign environments justified themselves through empirical results, tales of a mission's progress, and hard-won lessons about little-known peoples and new corners of the exterior world, the mission abroad also offered the contemporary religious an invaluable opportunity to make and tell of an interior journey. I present these inclinations—outward and inward—as ultimately linked, as part of the author's broader reckonings about the spiritual potential of peoples and places.

The turn inward, the impulse to write about the spiritual side of experience for the benefit of oneself and other people and, ultimately, to render an account in praise of God was a complex performance, an ideal that not all missionaries were able to reach, much less so successfully. Yet for others it beckoned as the ultimate and most necessary response to the dynamic challenges and hostilities of the world, a narrative response that hinged on seeing and interpreting real spaces, people, and events through the lens of a vibrant spiritual imagination.

I do not have space here to discuss Diego de Ocaña in relation to his religious contemporaries, much less to his many predecessors. Suffice it to say that, as Ian Wood has observed in the context of early medieval Europe, I proceed conscious of the fact that modern scholars' inclination to apply a single kind of "missionary varnish" and genre label to vastly divergent narratives has led to a yawning and misrepresentative gap between "mission and its portrayal."[6] Sixteenth- and seventeenth-century missionary accounts, like their medieval (and indeed their late antique and apostolic) predecessors, were notoriously flexible written forms, scripts that still manage to defy easy generic designations. Indeed, noting just two pertinent examples from among Ocaña's contemporaries indicates our Hieronymite's particular and more representative qualities. The *Descripción breve de toda la tierra del Perú, Tucumán, Río de la Plata y Chile* (ca. 1595–1609), composed by the Dominican Reginaldo de Lizárraga, shares with Ocaña's account a remarkable attempt to survey Andean cities, regions, and local histories, yet features little of Ocaña's tendency toward personal reflection. Similarly, the *Viaje* recounted by a Hieronymite successor of Ocaña, Pedro del Puerto (1624), who reports prominently on alms-collection and his inspection of devotional sites, offers tight-lipped and dutiful reportage by comparison, underscoring the variety within and between contemporary missionary accounts, even those which, on the surface, appear to meet similar needs and traverse very similar territories.[7]

Quietude, a state of inner stillness, was sought by many early modern missionaries as the stage from which truly to begin. Somewhat paradoxically to our lights, for many in the sixteenth and seventeenth centuries, this state of mind and spirit was not only to be found in quiet prayerful seclusion with their brothers or sisters at home. Quietude might come most powerfully of all in the rigors of a radical road, when the missionary was battling alone against the elements. St. Paul's epistles, the Acts of the Apostles, portions of Scripture, the teachings of the Church Fathers, and Christian appropriations from classical learning—all drummed on the constant relationship between the harsh tests of the exterior world, on the one hand, and a religious person's spiritual development and understanding of God's will, on the other. Aristotle had taught that difficulty was what most summoned people to heroic acts. The Psalms, for their part, trumpeted just who God's heroes were, singing the praises of the long suffering.[8] The apostles' frontier labors in taking the gospel to Gentiles proceeded in similar spirit, leaving the conveyers of the precious message exposed and at risk, tested at many turns.

In early modern times, Ignatius de Loyola (1491–1556), founder of the Society of Jesus, reportedly made no secret of his admiration for movement and experience as a form of knowledge that might surpass all others and, thus, of the pilgrim as "the one who knew the most."[9] Articulating the association between difficult travel and interior journeying, between exterior movement and spiritual growth, became a mark of Jesuitness.[10] The aforementioned Jesuit Jerónimo Pallas explained that there was nothing more effective at wrenching God's possession away than a purposeful voyage to the Indies. A journey so far away "frees the religious of the ties that bind him most tightly," the ties that distract and "try to keep him within." The goal was to avoid snares, the various "quarrels and thickets of temporal things."[11] Extremity is what "one finds perfectly in a mission to the Indies," Pallas enthused, presenting the "enterprise" (*empresa*) of a foreign mission as a "great interval" (*grande intervalo*)—a kind of exile from the life of the world, an orphanhood from which incalculable benefits might be drawn.[12] Despite the fact that early modern Spanish contemporaries such as Santa Teresa de Ávila (1515–82) had managed to free themselves in a heroic manner by entering a convent,[13] many religious contemporaries contended that one's monastery was an insufficient barrier against human love. Rather, suffering and privation abroad offered themselves up as their own protective balm of fellowship and endeavor.

The plotline for finding oneself utterly alone in the New World was well established. It was just as important to do something with these rewards, to reflect on and record one's experience—for personal spiritual growth, to be sure, but also for others and, ultimately, for God. Saint Francis Xavier (1506–52), one of the earliest and most articulate missionary voices in an expanding early modern world, wrote of living with a sense of indebtedness because of the "dangers" and "difficulties" he had been "granted." The sense of debt was partly to his predecessors and current brethren; he saw himself and his enterprise in a highly relational manner, attributing his ability to make his way to the similar "battles" that had been, and were being, fought by others.[14] Writing—leaving a personal record of an interior journey—amounted to a reciprocal offering. The missionary who had been inspired to emulate by the writings of others now looked to inspire and be emulated in turn. The companions of the future St. Ignatius were not alone in understanding him—themselves, and missionaries everywhere—as riders whose sense of God's control over their fate (and even of God dwelling within) was such that, in metaphorical terms, they simply dropped the reins of their mules, embracing whatever happened next. Missionary accounts of such experiences—of undertaking a mission, dropping one's reins, and enduring the results—were also composed, in part, to fulfill what Marjorie O'Rourke Boyle has called an "epideictic" function—which is to say that their accounts were declarations "invented *from* the self *about* God."[15]

Next to the explicit reflections on these matters of near contemporaries such as the Jesuit Jerónimo Pallas, Ocaña's engagement with apostolic parallels can at first appear nonchalant. Yet he treats them as multiform invitations to his own ends. Indeed, we should not be misled into thinking him less "genealogical" or emulative a narrator than his contemporaries. He possessed an alert and allegorical understanding of himself as a wandering instrument of God, buffeted and tested along an earthly journey. His awareness of apostolic narrative models and of the expectations of his Hieronymite and wider readership are acute. His apparent sense of freedom in adapting the metaphor and literary form is entirely in keeping with the deeper Christian tradition that Scott Fitzgerald Johnson has called the practice of "literary paraphrase." Ocaña works as a vernacular missionary reporter whose relationship to the "shared tools and techniques of Christian story-telling across the centuries," as Johnson succinctly put it, is deducible but often implicit.[16]

An author engaging in literary paraphrase—as much in early modern times as in late antiquity—mobilizes the narrative patterns and guiding metaphors of a revered apostolic past to illuminate the present. "To bring the apostolic past" into another present involves, as Johnson points out, a process of "reiterating and claiming [what amounts to a] foundation myth." Idiosyncrasy and even significant changes are permitted, so long as intended readers of the retellings recognize and feel persuaded by the author's analogies and appropriations. While no case is precisely the same, a generalizing principle gains force for both authors and readers: the apostolic storyline and metaphors in question grow more and more symbolic, even atmospheric. A familiar story-shape is created also by establishing a mood and texture, by playing on a cultural code that the author feels utterly comfortable appropriating toward his own vision and ends. The relationship to an original metaphor or story is not about accuracy but, rather, about "elasticity" and broader consistency.[17]

For early modern readers, tales of terrible storms and shipwrecks, of droughts and plagues, captured in dramatic fashion that the God of the Bible, of the Acts of the Apostles, and of saints' lives commonly expressed himself as *the* force of nature. The natural world is a setting for divine action. Ocaña would have been additionally familiar with the equation of God and his mother Mary with natural forces from the corpus of miracles attributed to the Virgin of Guadalupe de Estremadura from the fourteenth century forward, and recorded in a series of volumes begun in the early fifteenth century.[18] For example, working with this close metaphorical association, the anonymous Hieronymite author of the early sixteenth-century prologue to the third Guadalupan miracle volume presented the world as a massive ocean within which humans could scarcely help losing their way and going under, "swallowed up by the storm of desperation." Terrible winds and waves would threaten—winds of arrogance, ambition, slander, envy, avarice, and lust—blowing people off course, and in all directions. The only hope of rescue in such circumstances, the only fixed point for navigation amidst these worldly predicaments, was the fabled Guadalupan advocation of the Virgin Mary, a true "port of salvation," the prologue's author assures.[19]

Like the unruly ocean, the desert landscape was depicted as a vast and treacherous domain in which demons and temptations lurked, and in which a human could so easily become lost. And yet the desert's very barrenness and featurelessness, the primal nature of the isolation it made possible, simultane-ously made it a place of considerable spiritual opportunity. In a desert, the religious would be truly tested, purified, and there he might grow closer to God. The desert—where God communicated with Moses, where John the Baptist preached, where Christ himself retreated to pray and where he was tested before triumphing over the Devil—nurtured what Bernard McGinn has called a "spirituality of Exodus" well in place even before the faith's first monks set out into the deserts of Egypt and Judaea, making the desert the emblematic landscape for their spiritual journeys. From the Greek *eremos* and *eremia* comes our "eremetical," and the associations of "inexpressible height" and a wilderness space "removed from all things," where a soul might be fed and new understandings found.[20]

Accordingly, early modern missionary authors and their readers thought often in terms of the desert. Like the original desert solitaries in fourth-century Egypt such as Antony and Pachomius, who came to welcome the company of visitors and even gathered fellow monks into regulated communities, early modern missionaries invoked the desert landscape because it helped make sense of themselves, their communities, and their enterprises. Suffering "desert places" which, by the time of the monastic articulations of the twelfth and thirteenth centuries, had become as metaphorical as lit-eral, bolstered the self-image of religious as spiritual ascetics and persuaded informed and sympathetic readers.[21] In paraphrasing their own experiences of wilderness, the early modern missionaries mobilized the radical isolation of the desert to appeal to a readerly community.

Ocaña's equations of forbidding American surroundings with the desert, and of himself with an instrument, are thus powerful keys to his sense of how adversity becomes a religious act and expression. In what he perceives to be depopulated wastelands, among those whom he judges to be abject peoples, and as he is suffering what feels like rejection and apathy in others, Ocaña experiences a desert. In these passages of his manuscript, the emotional arc of his narrative is heightened. In remembering the experience in ink on paper, the suffering, itinerant "stranger" (*peregrino*) turns inward. The exterior world becomes God's testing ground, where his true instruments would be marshaled to reflect on their service, their mission, and look within. For the Hieronymite Ocaña, the memory of what happened in such desert places merges with the need to represent an understanding of what happened. Diego de Ocaña's physical body and his state of mind converge and become the page from which we learn.

Ocaña's "deserts" punctuate his experiences of more straightforward hope, the latter being predominantly in urban Hispanicizing centers where this agent of the Extremaduran image and shrine might create or correct American "Guadalupes," and establish devotional communities and schemes for alms collection that were securely linked back to the image and home sanctuary. All else was in-between, earthly experiences to endure.[22] By punctuating his narrative with episodes suffered in the apostolic spirit, Ocaña set hopeful zones in greater relief, while simultaneously positing that it was the *demandador*'s place to travel, be jarred, and suffer privations in the name of the Virgin Mary and in the interest of her guardians, his Hieronymite brethren.

We join Diego de Ocaña en route from Cusco to Lima in late November 1603, during the Hieronymite's final crossing of the Andes. He has just left the warm abundance of Jauja and the Mantaro River Valley, and has passed into the upper reaches of the province of Yauyos, climbing the rugged, westernmost mountain range of the high Andes from the east. He knew the name of an infamous pass ahead, and what the place had come to signify for Spanish and Hispanicizing minds in Peru. If he had learnt anything of the place's far older meanings and transformations for indigenous and mixed-race peoples, such knowledge does not show.

The pass of Pariacaca and its range of snowy peaks refers to one of most illustrious ancestral beings of the region (*huaca*), a divinity who once shook the earth with his beneficent presence and raucous adventures, and, after lithomorphosis was revived in sacred histories, once danced and sung. His resting body was itself a twin-peaked snowcap in the cordillera, whose other selves or children had multiplied across the land. Pariacaca's seat and craggy likeness could be seen from great distances on either side. By the end of the sixteenth century, melting snows and the sacred songs and dances from his heights had long explained the social as well as the geographical landscape, and gave vital if transforming meaning to people in the surrounding regions who made regular festive commemorations and pilgrimages to his shrine.[23] Diego de Ocaña passed through the territory of the Andean divine Paria-caca without knowing it, immersed in his alternate ontology, marveling at first over how the melting snows and rushing waters fed deep lakes and the seasonally raging rivers that flowed down sloping valleys to the west and the South Sea (the Pacific Ocean) and east into what he knows as the Jauja River (today, the Mantaro). The experience of the pass of Pariacaca demanded further engagement, too, but as other Spaniards had done for over the half-century already, Diego de Ocaña created his own meanings from an admixture of what he experienced and what he had read from others.

Sixteenth-century Spanish officials, chroniclers, and traveler-commentators expressed astonishment at just how it was that they managed to move through places such as the pass of Pariacaca at all. Even without the force of their Christian metaphors in play, such mountain passes connoted wilderness and danger to human existence, the antithesis of the valleys and plains as places for human order and civilization, with their ports the gateways to oceans leading home. The arrangement between indigenous people and this vertical environment of the Andean interior was disorienting to most Spanish eyes. How was one to master such a place, let alone grow as prosperous as the Inkas and their Andean subjects evidently had been? How was one even to move about?[24]

As was the case with so much of what the Spanish were eventually able to do in Peru, the means to move about had been created by native Andeans, and by the Spaniards' imperial predecessors the Inkas in particular. A network of about forty thousand kilometers of roads had been engineered and maintained by Inka rulers to join some eighty provinces of their vast, four-part realm. The two principal highways running north-south—a first artery through the mountains and a second hugging the western foothills and following the coastline—had facilitated long-distance movement of armies, messages, and supplies, and were achievement enough. But the lateral roads over the high mountain passes of the central Andes, such as the stretch of "royal highway" along which Ocaña moved, were still more overwhelming to behold. These constructions did not so much defy the seemingly harsh

natural environment of high winds, snowy peaks, and *puna,* as resign themselves to its nature.

Native Andean molding of the terrain went well beyond the practical
needs of soldiers and llama caravans, let alone messengers and small bands
of travelers on foot. Surfaces of roadways—generally between one and four
meters wide—were paved with cobbles and flagstone whenever possible, and
there were drainage canals, retention walls, causeways and bridges.[25] Staircases
had been carved into the rock faces, many early colonial travelers marveled,
easing the climb over the steepest portions of passes such as that of Pariacaca.
Spaniards in the immediate postconquest years guessed that their descriptions
of the lateral roads through the central Andes would be difficult to believe
for anyone who had not seen them with their own eyes. Such roads seemed
like ostentatious exhibitions of power over the environment and the native
Andean subjects who built and maintained them as part of their turn (*m'ita*)
of labor on the Inka state highways.

When Pedro de Cieza de León told of his crossing of the Pariacaca range
in the 1550s he felt the need to canvas specialized readers in search of a little
support for his assertions. "Let those who read this book and have been
to Peru recall the road that goes from Lima to Jauja," he wrote, "through
the rugged peaks of Huarochirí and the range of Pariacaca, and those who
hear them will understand whether what they saw is even more than what
I describe."[26] For Spanish and Hispanicizing travelers in the last third of the
sixteenth century, the notorious pass still stood out, drawing its visitors and
their commentary. But its meaning was shifting. It was becoming not so
much a marvelous example of the Inkas' taming of Andean space as a route
along which different kinds of difficulties for Spaniards appeared, questions
might be posed, and opportunities seized.[27]

When the Jesuit José de Acosta crossed the range in both directions in the
1570s, the pass of Pariacaca seems to have offered principally an opportunity
to research the natural world around him, to collect empirical information,
and articulate his findings. Yet it was also an ideal moment for dramatic
story-telling, for luring his expectant readers toward the meanings he most
wished to convey. He climbs up the rolling slopes through a succession of
microclimates, across the bleak high tablelands, and into the thin air of the
snow-covered mountain passes. Acosta's account becomes an opportunity to
describe carefully the cruel test of this place on not just *the,* but *his* human
constitution. His body in transit becomes the laboratory for natural history.
His account turns on his firsthand experience of altitude sickness embedded
in a chapter of the *Natural and Moral History* in which he extrapolates on the

active powers of different kinds of air, the "wondrous effects of winds" at sea and on land in various parts of the Indies.

Acosta claimed that he would never forget that first crossing in 1573, an ascent from sea level, up the so-called "Steps of Pariacaca" and across the watershed at an altitude of nearly five thousand meters. He had arrived in the foothills scientifically primed, having consulted the best local advice on what would lie ahead, on what "alterations" (*mudanza*) he was likely to experience, and on how best to keep his senses in order to observe, record, and analyze data. Yet no amount of local consultation and advance reading could prepare him for the physical effects of this first leg of the journey. "When I climbed the Steps, as they are called, the highest part of that range," he writes, "almost immediately I felt such mortal distress that I thought of throwing myself off my mount onto the ground. "Indeed, Acosta saw one man do just that, "cast himself to the earth, screaming, in [reaction to] the enormous pain that the crossing of Pariacaca had caused him."

Yet, steadied by a more reliable companion, the Jesuit stayed on his horse, bearing the personal burden, he notes, of the some "three or four hours of suffering" it took to reach a "more moderate altitude." Acosta's readers are invited along: he remembered for them the panic, confusion, and helplessness spreading through his traveling party, with some people even seeking to confess their sins, perhaps for the last time. Given the similar narrative of suffering and abandonment Ocaña would later spin, Acosta's description of the physical chaos sown by the place is worth our attention:

> Although many of us were making the journey together, each one fell about hurrying for himself and not waiting for the others in order to escape that evil place. I was left with only one Indian, whom I begged to help me grip my mount. I gave myself over to such bouts of retching and vomiting that I thought I was done for and that my soul would depart. For after vomiting up my food and phlegm there came bile and more bile, some yellow and some green, and I soon even brought up blood from the violence stirred in my stomach.[28]

Whereas, in roughly the same spot a few decades earlier, Pedro de Cieza de León had worried that readers might not trust his account of the mastery of Inka roadworks over the environment, Acosta wonders if readers will ever credit his descriptions of the dramatic physical effects of altitude on the human body experienced by him, his Indian servant, and their fellow travelers. The crossing of the Pariacaca pass is, for the Jesuit, principally a site of improved knowledge, a marvel in the natural and medical sense. Yet it is also a personal experience and test to report on as carefully and memorably as possible.

Some three decades later, Diego de Ocaña ascended the same pass, but more gradually and from the east. He had been living at altitudes of greater than three thousand meters for the better part of three years, thus the shock of existing at nearly five thousand meters was lessened.[29] His narrative priorities are different from those of Cieza and Acosta; both the Inkas' taming of fierce Andean spaces and the opportunity to observe bodily effects fade into the background or, rather, become foundation and fodder for what he wishes to express. Although he does not make reference to his commentating predecessors, Ocaña doubtless knew of them, especially the account left by Acosta, as we shall see. The practice of active paraphrase—of elaborating from firsthand experience and from the records of others—emerges in full. The inspiring source, Acosta, had bolstered his disquisition on the biting nature and killing capacity of high-altitude winds and air by relaying the vivid near-death experience of one of his informants, a friar, in those same "uninhabited zones." When this unnamed "Dominican, and a prelate in his order," had negotiated the pass of Pariacaca, he had very nearly died along with the other less fortunate members of his traveling party. According to Acosta, the Dominican had survived a night alone in the bitter cold only by gathering a number of his companion's dead bodies as shelter from the wind. He "made a kind of wall of them, a head for his bed," Acosta recorded, "and there he slept, the dead giving him life."[30]

In November 1603, the Hieronymite Diego de Ocaña is just as clear as Acosta had been that the range of Pariacaca was a *despoblado,* an "uninhabited zone"—a punishing stretch of some eighteen leagues of royal road between the Jauja Valley and a road-side travelers' inn (*tambo*) at Huarochirí. Here was one of a number of regions in the vast Indies designated as such by Spanish and Hispanicizing observers that was viewed as essentially empty and signifying danger. *Despoblado* was, and still is, a subjective and highly connotative term. It is someone's idea, a designation, a summary judgment about civilization deemed wanting or missing. Writing in 1586, some seventeen years before Ocaña's transit of the pass of Pariacaca, the long-serving *corregidor* and the administrative author of many of the resettlements of Huarochirí's indigenous peoples into "ordered" towns, Diego Dávila Brizeño, reported to King Philip II that the traffic of passengers on horses and mules along this royal road was brisk—too brisk, in fact, for its people to be able to endure.[31] The travelers were abusive and the area through which they moved was becoming lawless. Among other things, Dávila Brizeño objected to the lure and corruption of the *tambos* in between, and more generally to the service and provisions all these Spanish and Hispanicizing travelers demanded.

Like his *corregidor* predecessor, Diego de Ocaña thought in terms of a Christian Renaissance humanist dichotomy in which ordered urban concentrations of people existed in contrast to their boundless and threatening negations. If a *despoblado* could not be changed, it had to be endured. What meanings such a zone is allowed to contain are of negative value, a set of indications about what is found wanting, impossible or "not present." In passing through, there is a cold colonizer's assumption from Ocaña that people such as him would require not just assistance and service, but empathy and divine protection.

And yet, the idea of so deserted a place is also inviting. Here was a blank page that a person might fill. Its very uncrowdedness—in terms of modes of habitation one can understand, and more broadly in terms of subjectively valuable meaning—is an invitation to fear, reflection, and commentary. Because nothing of exterior value is thought to exist in the *despoblado* (outside of its testing nature), the commentator of ascetic spiritual bent is stirred and turns inward. In making writerly meaning of the experience, he is liable to reveal something of himself. Indeed, as even my brief excursus on the serial nature of commentary on the pass of Pariacaca suggests, it would not be an exaggeration to observe that something of a narrative competition was developing among literate travelers negotiating these heights—with this or that strand of emphasis in an earlier description of the experience of the pass of Pariacaca being picked up, examined, perhaps reshaped or rejected for new emphases and paraphrase by a later participant-teller.

Diego de Ocaña sets up his narration of experience on the pass in two ways. First, he pointedly contrasted his experience of earthly bounty in the Jauja Valley, where he spent two days gathering supplies and commissioning assistance, with what lay ahead: the "uninhabited zone called Pariacaca, the most severe *puna* [high-altitude plateau] of them all in Peru." Second, he characterized his experience as a stern test from which his survival is a deliverance that was nothing short of miraculous. "What happened to me [on the pass of Pariacaca] was the worst misfortune to befall me in five years of continuous traveling," wrote Ocaña, referring especially to "a night from which I miraculously emerged with my life."[32]

Ocaña signals the experience of suffering from the very first moments he describes, as he climbs out of a rustic shelter in the *tambo* on the morning in which his small party is to begin its crossing of the pass. The entire doorway of his hut was obscured by snow that had fallen in the night, and it had to be dug away in order for the Hieronymite to emerge. From that moment on, the portents grew even worse. Animals were missing. Not far away, members of Ocaña's traveling party discovered one of its strongest horses—the one that had been transporting the friar's effects—dead on a frozen riverbank. Ocaña's theory is that the beast had been parched and taken in the icy water too quickly, shocking itself to death.

Much of the experience of traveling over the high puna and mountain pass is, by Ocaña's own characterization, too painful to recall. "I will want to pass over [all this] in silence so as not to restart the tears I shed in that desert, a place I will remember for the rest of my life."[33] But this pretense of silence about experiences too painful and plentiful to recall is highly performative. For—as in description of other painful "deserts" in his manuscript—Ocaña does write on, and, his readers in mind, with considerable care. The sense of a bitter outer expanse triggering an "inner desert" in which the soul, deprived of the world, begins to concentrate and rejoice in silence, begins what Alain Saint-Saëns has characterized memorably as a nostalgic, "sublimated eremiticism," would have appealed not only not only to the Hieronymite Ocaña, but also an entire religious culture in early modern Spain.[34] Ocaña calls out a desert. His intended readers are to understand the pass of Pariacaca to be an unbounded wilderness that is as much the subject of eremetical longing as dread. In so arduous a space, a divine instrument would be severely tested, but there, too, the mobile soul might learn things of infinite value.

The snow continued to fall, Ocaña recorded later, and in such quantities "that it seemed to me as if the sky was falling to pieces from its celestial sphere."[35] Loads were abandoned one by one in desperation. Ocaña and his fellow travelers trudged single file, and soon began to lose track of each other. The group was spreading out along a trail that was becoming impossible to follow. One of the two native Andean guides whom Ocaña had commissioned in the Jauja Valley had already abandoned them, fleeing without his pay and leaving only a blanket. As night descended, they crossed a high, flat plain where the wind cut through them. The Hieronymite presented himself, a remaining native Andean guide, and a single mule as, increasingly, alone before God and all the snow falling from the heavens.[36] At a certain desperate point, unsure of how many in their traveling party were still following, they decided that the guide would return in the direction from which they were ascending to see to it that any others did not lose their way. Ocaña claims that he promised to get the native man a drink once they were safe, trying to ensure his return—coldly commenting on his page "that to give an Indian a drink is to offer a thing he esteems more than a hundred ducats."[37]

Diego de Ocaña was not writing to impress the likes of us with his sensitivity. Indeed, right down to his careful recollection of reliance on a mule—

long the animal of choice for the Christian religious traveler[38]—Ocaña is setting the stage, once more, for a purposeful meditation on himself and on the torments he endured. The indigenous guide, turning back and possibly never to return, heightens the drama and is part of the suffering Ocaña means to convey. "So there I remained, out in the open," he writes, "crying out from time to time, as the snow continued to fall."[39] Two hours passed and no one returned.

Yet having been so alone does not, of course, mean that in recording the experience afterward, Acosta's sparse account of the Dominican's terrible night on the pass of Pariacaca would not come to mind. Indeed, it appears to have spurred Ocaña's own remembering and telling, providing a frame into which his own experiences on the pass could be tipped. The Hieronymite is comfortable inventing interior monologues, his own, as well as those of others.[40] He imagined, for instance, what the others would have been thinking as darkness descended, and they could not see the trail: "The friar has gone ahead with the Indian; by now they will have reached the little inns; as for ourselves, we can't even see where we are going and our beasts can't take another step; let's take shelter here beneath these rocks." The passage is a retrospective teller's artifice, in that Ocaña later learned that this is indeed what happened. He went on to explain that the Indian guide had come on the stragglers in their refuge, but not until about eleven in the evening. The party judged it futile to go out in search of Ocaña at that hour, since they might not even reach him before dawn. Ocaña imagined their desperately hopeful guesswork starting up again: "The friar will have made his way, little by little," they will have thought, "and by now he will already have made it [to shelter]."[41]

With the night growing colder and hope of rescuers fading, with Acosta's unadorned account of the Dominican shielding himself beneath the dead bodies to ponder alongside the even more deeply internalized storylines of Scripture, saints' lives, and miracle narratives, Diego de Ocaña presents himself as having approached a tipping point, presuming all was lost. The predicament was coming into view—the moment of utter desperation, the climax for which readers yearned. But he was not quite there, not yet; for now came the crucial moment when God's human instrument would truly struggle.

Alone in a trackless void of frigid desert, a man whose purpose depended on making starts, on leaving traces, grew contemplative. Diego de Ocaña was thinking over what he was doing in the Indies as a messenger, alms-collector, and image-maker in the service of a famous advocation of the Virgin, thinking over God's will, and suffering along in thought, word, and deed.

His attention turns to the mule that, at this point, could scarcely keep her feet. "I took a covering and threw it over the mule's head, then wrapped myself into its reins, close up to the mule's neck, my face next to the animal's, and with my hands tucked for warmth within the folds of her neck. Tied in and covered thus, with her in my company and she in mine, God allowed that we would spend the night." The resemblance to Acosta's account of the Dominican religious taking shelter in the same howling expanse, making his macabre bed and drawing life (if not quite warmth) from his dead companions' bodies, is striking. With this search for warmth from his mule, Ocaña's interior dialogue with his readers continues, picking up pace.

There were just so many reasons, Ocaña reflected, why he and his four-legged companion should have died. Mules were accustomed to nights in the bitter cold, it was true. But they could usually walk about, take in water, and enjoy some food. Ocaña's mule—like him—enjoyed no such luxuries or sustenance. Surely, he remembers thinking, they would soon both drop dead in the snow. "From time to time," he wrote, "I took out my hands to shake off the snow that was rising like a tower above my hat." He chronicles the gradual process of losing hope, of weeping into the mule's neck in that blizzard. At his moment of least resistance, in time-honored narrative fashion, he made his "pious entreaties" to Our Lady, saying:

> How can it be, Señora, that my fortune is so twisted or my sins so great that I would die in this desert, buried in snow, while the monks of Gua-dalupe are well-fed and tucked up in their cells? [And how can it be that I am] unable to go about my business, which is in fact your busi-ness, gathering alms to feed the pilgrims who turn to your house, [and that, instead,] I must starve and freeze to death tonight in this desert?[42]

The explanatory Ocaña continues, underscoring the extent of the test in the desert:

> I could not even form these words without shedding copious tears, and I now tell and confess that in full truth, with all that snow and the cold tapping my strength, I felt that it would have been best to die that night, for it seemed impossible that I would wake up alive, but rather frozen right through.[43]

Extremity in the pass of Pariacaca offered solitude for thought, which had fortified his memory of the home sanctuary and his connection to the community of Hieronymite brethren who would be (he imagines) his prin-cipal readers. Further, the near-death experience has focused his mind on the purpose of his journey and such sufferings: the "business" of collect-ing alms to sustain the beloved pilgrims arriving, year in and year out, at the Extremaduran shrine. Perceiving this "American desert" as "severely dislocated space...uninhabited by God," Ocaña retreats in mind to the Christian ideal of the desert, reacting to the exterior world by effectively elevating the isolated place into a position of interior exemplarity, a place for penitence, suffering, and the contemplation of one's purpose before God.[44] In the terms of reference employed by far-flung missionaries in his time, the snowy desert becomes the test he needs. It is true that he had almost died in the snow, but in more important emulative terms, Ocaña drew comfort from the fact that his crossing of the pass of Pariacaca had gone according to God's plan. His prayerful beseeching of the Mary of Guadalupe and the unlikely survival suggest a miraculous deliverance, but it is unseemly—unapostolic—to claim miracles for oneself. Characteristically, Ocaña chooses a suggestive, roundabout route that will allow his readers to draw their own conclusions. He compares his sufferings that night to Job's travails, then builds further on the drama of a survival that would not have been possible without the Virgin's miraculous intercession and God's attentive mercy and will—worked through the sustaining warmth of the mule. But he records this understanding with a characteristically lighter emotional touch. "It is certain that the warmth of my mount sustained me," he wrote, "so much so that, later, I cared for [and treasured] that mule, and never wanted to sell her or to be served by another."[45]

Ocaña leaves no doubt about the point of telling of his crossing of the pass of Pariacaca. The pass is a desert in which his purpose has come into focus, a "lens" through which he and his readers are able to examine the obstacles and opportunities of his mission.[46] "I shall always have the memory...of being as if newly returned to life," Ocaña insists, of feeling "like a resurrected body...half of me inside the tomb and half without, because, in truth, as dawn broke, the mule and I awoke to find ourselves half-covered in snow."[47] With that—with the evocation of a "rebirth" in the desert, an entering into a life in which meanings are clearer—his point has been made, and the meaning which the experience had for him is inscribed. Moving about, clad in the covering he had thrown over them, there was no sign or track of anything in the total white of the snow, a desert of "divine Nothingness" for which a long Christian tradition of spiritual expression has conditioned him and his reader to long.[48]

Diego de Ocaña comes to earth again, returning to the mundane. He writes of finding a few pieces of *íchu* grass to feed to the trusty mule. He first told of his passing of a night in the desert of Pariacaca a few hours later, when, at about ten in the morning, his Indian guide—in whom he had held such scarce hope—returned with wine and a sandwich for the freezing monk.[49]

Diego de Ocaña's firsthand reflections of personal travails and spiritual focus such as the crossing of the pass of Pariacaca in late November 1603 characterize significant portions of the manuscript that treats his six-year journey through Spanish South America. I believe that Ocaña fears he will lose his mental and spiritual footing entirely if he proceeds in any other way. Several of his turns inward, and his most pointed emulations of apostolic suffering, occur when the missionary sees the least chance for tangible fruits from his enterprise—in Ocaña's case, when prospects for alms and devotional foundations are at their lowest. As Ocaña moves, experiences, and records in his most personal and spiritual ways, it bears noting that the spiritual prospects of entire peoples and regions of late sixteenth- and early seventeenth-century Spanish South America are being surveyed, put at issue, avoided and pronounced on by this vernacular reporter. What is a *despoblado?* In whose eyes? What vast expanses of human experience—in this case those of indigenous and mixed-race persons in processes of religious and cultural change in the wake of the consolidation of Spanish Catholic rule—are neglected or treated as obstacles? What is this passage through such a purported desert *about* and *for?*

I have contended that at such points, Ocaña's record represents a cumulative kind of missionary knowledge. While purportedly descriptive, it is most powerfully "genealogical" and universalizing. He draws on a wide and rich sacred narrative tradition of apostolic movement and suffering and of miraculous deliverance to narrate the interior journey of an instrument of the Guadalupan Virgin and of God. His purpose at such times and in such places is to persevere, to open himself to the ordeal, and to reflect on what he is doing and thus why his miraculous survival might matter—preparing himself for a time when material and spiritual prospects improve. The turns inward might be fruitfully described as performative responses to extreme difficulty, the function of Ocaña's realization that as a timeless ascetic traveler refuge and meaning must ultimately be sought elsewhere, in rekindled devotion and within himself. His beloved narrative *exempla* were there, within reach—elastic enough to ensure that, in a spiritual sense at least, he was always headed home. Exploring Ocaña's pattern of personalizing sorrow, pain, and torment is to take seriously his self-conception and authorial attempt to draw in his prospective contemporary readers, to draw them inside the kind of interior journey they will feel and with which they will readily identify. The personal spiritual journey of passing through and chronicling the experience of an American desert is what, for Ocaña the instrument of the Guadalupan Mary and of God, matters most.

CHAPTER 8

Incombustible Weber

How the Protestant Reformation Really Disenchanted the World

CARLOS EIRE

> When we ignore the awkward realities and contradic-
> tions of any period, we shortchange the past. We short-
> change ourselves as well. If we choose to remember only
> the "progressive" parts of history, the ones that read-
> ily "make sense" to us, we oversimplify the past and
> our own lives. We cultivate an artificially naive view
> of the world.
>
> —H.C. Erik Midelfort, *Exorcism and Enlightenment*

Why does Max Weber continue to haunt vari-
ous disciplines a century after he made very large claims for the impact of
Protestantism on Western civilization?[1] One would think that Weber and his
theses would have been forgotten by now. Instead, despite various attempts to
declare him worthy of oblivion, he simply will not vanish from view.[2] Much
like those images of Martin Luther that were rumored to be fireproof—a
belief once cited as evidence that Weber was wrong—Weber, too, seems to
be incombustible.[3]

Ever since Weber proposed that Protestants had caused "the disenchantment of the world," (*entzauberung der Welt*) this thesis has been the focus of
close scrutiny.[4] At issue in this ongoing discussion is the very definition of
religion, and how it differs from "magic" (*zauber*). Also at issue is the role
played by Protestantism in the secularization of the West. This essay has as
its central focus that large issue of secularization, not just in reference to
Weber's "disenchantment" thesis, but to our present-day understanding of
the Protestant Reformation. In brief, this essay will examine the concept
of "disenchantment" in non-Weberian terms, particularly as manifested in
three distinguishing characteristics of Protestantism: the redefinition of how
"matter" and "spirit" relate to each other, which led to iconoclasm and a new
approach to symbols and rituals; the redefinition of the boundaries between
the "natural" and "supernatural" realms, which led to the denial of miracles

and mystical ecstasies; and the separation of the living from the dead, which led to a reconfiguring of conceptual and socioeconomic structures.

Though tightly focused on theological and philosophical concepts, this essay will also consider lived religion and popular piety, that is, the practical day-to-day changes wrought by the larger shift in thought and belief.

Contemporary Interpretations of the Protestant Reformation

Secularization.[5] *Confessionalization.*[6] *Social Disciplining.*[7] *Transition to Modernity.*[8] These are the reigning paradigms for understanding the Protestant Reformation in our own day. Whether it is state building, or the emergence of the public sphere, or the triumph of lent over carnival, or the revolution of the common man, or any other such entry point into the realm of grand summation, all of us who study the early modern period are stuck with these conceptual formulations—like it or not—that make much more sense to us now than they would have to the very people who are the subject of our studies.

Discerning what differentiates "modern" from "medieval" is an obsession of our times, too.[9] And in this search for boundaries, the concept of secularization looms large, with "medieval" as synonymous with religion, superstition, and mumbo-jumbo, and "modern" as the liberation from such dreck. And in most formulations of the transition from medieval to modern, all changes in religion tend to be seen as wrinkles within some other matrix that is more tangible, as modes of social exchange that flow from deeper material needs. What people *do* rather than what people *believe:* that's the *real* thing, the stuff of history. Religion is an activity: "consecrated behavior," "symbolic behavior," or "social glue."[10] In brief, beliefs, in and of themselves, are never the ultimate or proximate cause of anything.[11]

This is not to say that all such theorizing is necessarily wrong. Not at all. The insights gained through such materialistically inclined perspectives on religion are valuable in and of themselves.[12] But should this be our sole perspective? What if we consider "disenchantment," a concept that takes the innate value of ideas and beliefs very seriously and grants them a causative role, at least in part?

As Weber saw it a century ago, one of the most unique effects of the Protestant Reformation was its reconfiguring of the Western European worldview. Weber, it seems, took his mother's Calvinism very seriously, even though—by his own admission—he was not attuned to religion. On a personal level, he understood the formative potential of beliefs, and on the professional level he never lost sight of the world-shaping power of faith. This is why, at times, his theorizing verged on wistfulness.

> The fate of our times is characterized by rationalization and intellectualization, and, above all, by the "disenchantment of the world." Precisely the ultimate and most sublime values have retreated from public life either into the transcendental realm of mystic life or into the brotherliness of direct and personal human relations. It is not accidental that our greatest art is intimate and not monumental.[13]

Disenchanting the Disenchantment

Reformation historians have engaged with the legacy of Weber's theorizing for decades,[14] but none has wrestled with it more strenuously than the late Robert Scribner. His negative take on Weber was contextual: Weber simply could not extricate himself from nineteenth-century prejudices. Seeking to expel Weber from the Reformation for good, Scriber declared: "I do not think that the thesis about the 'disenchantment of the world' will any longer pass muster as a historically accurate description."[15]

Scribner's rejection of Weber offers us a useful entry point to the larger issue of the changes wrought by the Protestant Reformation, and more specifically to the issue of "disenchantment." Is there some valuable insight embedded in *entzauberung*? If one focuses on the German term, and especially the word *zauber*, which translates as "magic" or "thaumaturgy" in English, it is difficult to conceive of "disenchantment" broadly and easy to think that Protestants were still embedded in a "religio-magical space," just like Catholics, simply because of continuities in ritual. Throw the devil and witchcraft into the mixture, and the similarities seem more intense.[16]

This way of thinking goes back to the sixteenth century, when Catholics and Protestants alike began to root out all beliefs and behaviors they deemed magical or superstitious, even though their takes on "magic" and "superstition" were very different. "Religion" and "magic" are fluid terms, wide open for interpretation, and in the era of the Reformation, they became highly charged with polemical value.[17] Although Tridentine Catholicism identified many popular beliefs and practices as "magical" or "superstitious," and strove to do away with them, Protestants went much further.[18] As Protestants saw it, Catholic piety was naught but fiendish hocus-pocus: consecrated hosts—mocked as "white gods"—were no different from the witches' "eye of newt."[19] Herein one finds the root of the nineteenth-century German Protestant understanding of "magic," or *zauber*, inherited by Max

Weber. And herein one also finds the root of the blind spot shared by Weber and many of his critics.[20]

But what if one were to look beyond this troublesome magic/religion dialectic, so central to Weber and to Scribner? Might it be possible to identify some other traits of the Protestant Reformation that reveal it as a rupture in Western history rather than some murky transitional era? What if one were to think outside the German *zauber* box? Could "disenchantment" have a wider and deeper meaning missed by Weber and his critics that includes magic and superstition, but is not limited by these categories?

What about *desacralization:* a redefinition of the sacred? Not a redrawing of the line between "magic" and "religion" or "superstition" and "religion," as Scribner and many others have seen it,[21] but rather a fundamental shift in the way in which reality is conceived.

If one turns to three metaphysical concepts championed by Protestants—concepts that were philosophical and theological, but had immense practical ramifications—the Protestant Reformation can be seen as a major paradigm shift, and a crucial step in the secularization of the world. These three conceptual shifts point to a "desacralization," that is, a reinterpretation of the *sacred* and its place in human life rather than a redefinition of the magic/religion dialectic. All three concepts redefine one of the crucial elements of every civilization: the way in which ontological categories are sorted and reality is conceived. Significantly, all three were perceived by Reformation era Catholics as essential markers of the difference between themselves and Protestants.[22] They also have to do with the divine and supernatural, not the demonic and preternatural or the "religio-magical."

First and foremost, the great ontological difference between the physical and spiritual realms upheld by Protestants, especially in the Reformed tradition, drove a wedge between *matter and spirit*. Iconoclasm was its initial manifestation, but it extended much further than religious imagery, to other symbols: shrines, relics, the Eucharist, and all rituals. The most extreme version of this reinterpretation of matter and spirit found voice in the Reformed Protestant tradition, and in two of their guiding principles: *Finitum non est capax infiniti* (the finite cannot contain the infinite); and *quantum sensui tribueris tantum spiritui detraxeris* (the physical detracts from the spiritual).

Second, despite the differences among them, Protestants redrew the boundaries between *natural and supernatural,* and rejected the commonplace irruptions of the sacred favored in medieval religion. In other words, Protestants rejected miracles, and especially those practically oriented supernatural events that historians now classify as *thaumaturgy*. God could work miracles, certainly, but as Protestants saw it, the age of miracles had passed, and God's supernatural interventions were a thing of the past, strictly limited to biblical times. Thus, with just a few exceptions among the Radicals, Protestants denied the possibility of mystical ecstasies, visions, apparitions, revelations, levitations, bilocations, and all other supernatural phenomena associated with intimate encounters between the human and divine.

Third, Protestants redefined the relation between the here-and-now and the hereafter, sundering the links between earthly time and eternity, and the *living and the dead*. This reconfiguration of the *communio sanctorum* led to the creation of a segregated society in which the living and the dead could no longer mingle, physically or spiritually. Not only were the bodies of the dead removed from the churches, but their souls were made inaccessible, beyond the reach of prayer. The dead were now truly *dead and gone:* the saints in heaven could no longer be approached for favors, and the souls of the departed in purgatory could not be aided by prayer either.

Relying on the original meaning of the word *secular* (Latin: *saeculum* = "this age" or "earthly time"), one can argue that these changes contributed substantially to the *secularization* of the West by creating societies that were more this-worldly than ever before—societies that rejected the medieval *sub specie aeternitatis* worldview in which human existence and all history had an eternal backdrop.[23] These three major paradigm shifts were much more than a mere change in thinking: they also had a profound and immediate impact on the cultural, social, economic, and political structure of Protestant communities, and on Western Europe as a whole.

Matter and Spirit

The Protestant Reformation was a metaphysical and epistemic revolution, a new way of interpreting reality and of approaching the ultimate. To put it in the simplest terms: it redrew the boundaries between heaven and earth, the sacred and the profane.[24]

Ever since the first century, Christians had accepted a binary understanding of the cosmos: God was spirit, and He had created a material world, ontologically related to Him, but metaphysically different and inferior. Humans were the pinnacle of this creation, part matter and part spirit, composed of a mortal body and an immortal soul. Bridging these two essential realms of existence was the role of religion, or, more specifically, of the Church and its clergy, and the bridging was effected in myriad ways through rituals and symbols. In sum, the medieval Christian world pulsated with accessibility to the divine, replete as it was with material points of contact with the spiritual realm.[25]

Protestants made matter and spirit much less compatible. And their rejection of material access points to the spiritual realm made all Protestants iconoclasts, literally and figuratively.[26] Protestants did not always agree on the meaning and function of symbols, but all of them agreed that the veneration of matter was wrong. It was "idolatry," one of the worst of sins. The Protestant critique of idolatry was strongest among those of the Reformed tradition, and it flowed from a set of interrelated principles. At one level, Protestant iconoclastic theology was rooted in the principle of *sola scriptura,* and on the prohibition of religious imagery found in Exodus and Leviticus. At a deeper level, Reformed Protestant iconophobia was also driven by certain key assumptions about the relationship between matter and spirit and the natural and supernatural realms. The guiding principle of iconoclastic metaphysics—and therefore also of iconoclastic hermeneutics—was the incompatibility of spirit and matter. This principle, in turn, was derived from three assumptions.

First, the Reformed Protestant tradition assumed that God was radically transcendent and that the supernatural realm was wholly "other," above and beyond the natural and created order. Ulrich Zwingli argued that the things of earth were "carnal," and that they were "enmity against God." He also argued that matter and spirit were as incapable of mixing as fire and water and that "those who trust in any created thing whatsoever are not truly pious."[27] John Calvin was equally adamant: "Whatever holds down and confines the senses to the earth is contrary to the covenant of God; in which, inviting us to himself, he permits us to think of nothing but what is spiritual."[28]

Second, Reformed metaphysics proposed that matter is not just incapable of bridging the gap between heaven and earth, but actually an obstacle. "The more you give to the material," said Zwingli, "the more you take away from the spiritual."[29] John Calvin, as shown in the aforementioned quote, agreed.

Third, Reformed Protestants thought that idolatry threatened the well-being of society as a whole: it was a sin that polluted everyone and invited the wrath of God.[30] In addition, iconoclastic theology also argued that the material resources "wasted" on idols were an affront to Christian charity and a reification of wrongful class distinctions. The medieval church had long argued that images were the *libri pauperum,* or books of the poor and illiterate. Protestant iconoclasts rejected this argument because, as they saw it, images kept the laity under the thumb of the Catholic clergy.[31]

The Protestant redefinition of matter and spirit was thus revolutionary on two fronts. First, it was a theological upheaval, and a redefinition of the sacred. Reformation iconoclasm was also revolutionary in a sociopolitical and economic sense, for it was an act of violence against the costly symbolic code of medieval Christianity and its guardians, the Roman Catholic clergy. The young men who led the iconoclastic riot that turned Geneva into a Reformed city knew this, for they called the images they destroyed "the gods of the priests."[32] By redefining the meaning of Catholic symbols and rituals, then, Protestants also redefined the nature and function of the clergy.

So it was that by redefining the relationship between matter and spirit and denying the possibility of physical access to the divine, Protestants changed the social and political order.

The Natural and Supernatural

Redefining the relation between matter and spirit also entailed redrawing the boundaries between the natural and the supernatural. This led Protestants to reject miraculous phenomena and the possibility of merging with God in mystical ecstasy.

In many ways, this second paradigm shift was a desacralization of the world much more intense than that brought about by the Protestant war against idolatry and also more profound than that against those non-Christian practices labeled as "magic" or "superstition." This was the ultimate demystification, and a Copernican revolution in worldview, even though Weber failed to see it as such.

In the whiggish view of history miraculous phenomena and mystical ecstasies are powerful markers of cultural difference, telltale traits of an older, inferior civilization, of the "superstitious" and "magical" culture of the ancient and medieval worlds.[33] Supernatural phenomena are modernity's foil, significant foci for the articulation of the norms of "modernity" itself.[34] And this is not only true of whiggish history, which sees the Protestant rejection of medieval piety as the first step toward "modernity," but also of postmodern history.[35] Lately, a few historians have emphasized the significance of this redrawing of boundaries.[36]

In their contest for souls, Protestants and Catholics realized very quickly that miracles played a key role in polemics and therefore also in self-definition. Catholics defended the truth of their claims through countless ancient and contemporary miracles, performed through the agency of sacred sites and objects or holy men and women. Catholics also argued that the lack of miracles among Protestants proved the falsehood of their teachings beyond a shadow of a doubt. Protestants rejected these claims on several grounds, but especially on these two: that the age of miracles had ceased at the end of the Apostolic age, sometime in the first century; and that the miracles claimed by the Catholic Church were either fraudulent or of demonic origin.[37]

Martin Luther was among the first of the Protestant Reformers to reject the possibility of postbiblical miracles, even though he was inclined to emphasize God's absolute power over His creation. Religion was not about miracle-seeking, he argued, but about faith and salvation.[38] As he put it: being rescued "from the power of the devil and from eternal death" and being led to "eternal life in heaven...far surpasses all outward signs and wonders."[39] Yes, he admitted, the Bible was full of miracle accounts, and especially the Gospels, but Christ and the Apostles had performed these miracles simply to convince unbelievers; miracles, in and of themselves, had no power to arouse faith in those who already believed in Christ. This meant that the miracles recorded in the New Testament had been necessary in their day and age— and only then—to establish Christianity.

> Those visible works are simply signs for the ignorant, unbelieving crowd, and for their sakes that are yet to be attracted; but as for us who know already all we do know, and believe the Gospel, what do we want them for?...Wherefore it is no wonder that they have now ceased since the Gospel has sounded abroad everywhere, and has been preached to those who had not known of God before, whom he had to attract with outward miracles, just as we throw apples and pears to children.[40]

As if this were not enough, Luther added one crowning objection to miraculous claims: the devil could manipulate nature and deceive people. Luther's devil was a prolific and creative artist, capable of thousands of tricks, each a masterpiece of deception. Luther's wonder-working *Tausend-Künstler*[41] could cause people to see or hear the most preposterous things. He could trick hunters into thinking he was a hare, or show up as almost any animal— especially as an ape. Once, Luther found a dog in his bed and flung it out the window, convinced that it was a demon.[42]

Martin Bucer, the Strassburg Reformer, made much of the demonic in his argument against miracles.[43] Arguing against the cult of the saints and the miracles attributed to them, Bucer proposed that it was Satan who worked these "miracles" through his preternatural powers.[44] Bucer's argument would later be picked up and expanded on by Calvin and also by English Reformers.[45] It is important to emphasize, however, that this polemically charged Protestant tradition of attributing Catholic miracles to the devil was above all an affirmation of their conviction in the inviolability of natural laws. Nature might be manipulated by Satan, yes, and humans might be easily fooled, but genuine *supernatural* miracles were restricted to biblical times.

Ulrich Zwingli also argued against miracles, but it would be his French disciple, John Calvin, who would give the Protestant denial of the miraculous its definitive contours. Like Luther before him, Calvin argued that the only function of miracles was to confirm the authority of God's messengers, and that they were restricted to those rare occasions when God had something to reveal. But Calvin also took a metaphysical turn, explicitly stating that the ultimate purpose of all biblical miracles was *not* to alter the fabric of the material natural order, but simply to authenticate revelation.[46] Since Protestants were not revealing anything new, then it was wrong for Catholics to demand miracles from them. Moreover, Calvin also argued that the countless miracles claimed by the Catholic Church came straight from Hell:

> We may also fitly remember that Satan has his miracles, which, though they are deceitful tricks rather than true powers, are such a sort as to mislead the simple-minded and untutored [II Thes, 2:9–10]. . . . Idolatry has been nourished by wonderful miracles, yet these are not sufficient to sanction the superstition either of magicians or of idolaters.[47]

Satan had no supernatural powers, however: his manipulation of nature was preternatural, a result of his angelic nature, which, while fallen, still granted him an intimate and superhuman knowledge of the laws of nature.[48] This means that scholars in our own day who speak of "magic" or "thaumaturgy" without distinguishing between the truly supernatural (the divine) and the merely preternatural (the demonic) fail to take into account a distinction that was immensely significant to those who lived in the Reformation era.

The worldview that Calvin bequeathed to his followers was thus very naturalistic: only when God decides to break into this world to communicate with humans does He appoint specific instances where the natural, material order is changed.[49] Religion, then, does not seek to change the course of nature, as Catholics claimed, but rather to understand it as it is: eternally subject to God's will and as always incapable of transmitting any spiritual power in and of itself. To believe otherwise, said Calvin, was to fall into the trap of idolatry.[50]

So, even though some Protestants continued to believe in natural signs and portents that conveyed messages, such as cloud formations, astronomical and meteorological anomalies, or monstrous births—"wonders" (*mirabilia*) rather than "miracles" (*miraculi*)[51]—and even though supernatural miracles eventually worked their way back into Protestant piety in various limited ways during the late seventeenth and eighteenth centuries, Protestantism did much more to disenchant the world through its take on miracles than it ever did by its rejection of anything that could be called "magic" or "superstition."

Even more significant, it could be argued, was the disenchantment that Protestants brought to the relationship between human beings and God. Save for a few Radical extremists, all Protestants rejected the ultimate goal of medieval Catholic piety and of monasticism in particular: that of mystical union with God.

Purgation, illumination, union: These were the three basic steps in the mystical quest that the Christian tradition, both east and west, had accepted and elaborated on since the second century of the Christian era. Becoming ever purer and more Godlike, even to the point of experiencing supernatural encounters with Him in this life was the goal of monasticism, ostensibly, and the promise held out to every potential saint. This quest and its attending experiences were based precisely on those core metaphysical assumptions that Protestants discarded, especially concerning matter and spirit, the natural and the supernatural, and the human and the divine. In other words, the claims made by Catholic and Orthodox mystics reified their soteriology: salvation was something to be lived out; theology, belief, and practice were all of one piece. And the most significant manifestation of this mentality was monasticism, a penitential and contemplative way of life discarded as useless by Protestantism.

The Protestant rejection of monasticism, based as it was on a very different understanding of human nature, figures prominently as a social change effected by theology: it was not only the largest redistribution of property in Western history before the Bolsheviks came along, but also a social and economic revolution. Suddenly, an entire social class was abolished, along with their sizeable assets. In addition, on both the material and conceptual level, a way of life that focused intensely on *otherworldliness* was extinguished. The "disenchanting" or secularizing impact of the extinction of monasticism seems obvious enough and needs little elaboration. The impact of the rejection of mysticism—the main goal of monasticism—is harder to discern, but no less significant.

Those men and women who reached the pinnacle of holiness were considered living proof of the divinization of matter. They not only conversed with Christ and the Virgin Mary, but had ineffable encounters with the Godhead; they also swooned in rapture, went into trances, levitated, bilocated, read minds, prophesied, manifested the wounds of Christ on their bodies, and healed the sick and lame. Once they died, their corpses could emit a wonderful aroma and remain intact.[52]

All this was rejected by Protestants, save for a few Radicals.[53] Even Martin Luther, who was influenced by the mystics Tauler and Suso, could not abide the ultimate claims made by medieval ecstatics.[54] Luther came to despise all who claimed direct contact with the divine as *schwärmer,* that is, as unhinged fanatics. John Calvin recoiled in horror at the thought that humans might claim any sort of divinization, for his God was "entirely other" and "as different from flesh as fire is from water."[55] Though he sometimes quoted the twelfth-century mystic Bernard of Clairvaux, Calvin had no place in his theology for the Catholic tradition of *unio mystica,* or for its raptures, trances, visions, and miracles.[56] Such a crossing of boundaries was impossible, argued Calvin, for the human soul "is not only burdened with vices, but is utterly devoid of all good."[57]

The significance of this radical desacralization can be best appreciated by contemplating how Catholics responded to it. The sixteenth and seventeenth centuries were a golden age for mysticism, during which the miraculous physical phenomena associated with mystical ecstasy became more pronounced than ever before among Catholics.[58] And few other Catholic mystics serve as a better contrasting backdrop than Joseph of Cupertino (1606–66) and María de Jesús de Ágreda (1602–65).

Joseph of Cupertino, a Franciscan friar from Italy, gained renown in his own day for his frequent ecstasies and levitations. Friar Joseph not only hovered a few feet off the ground repeatedly, in full view of many witnesses, but also rose dozens of feet into the air on many occasions or flew great distances. One time, when he flew from one end to the other of the enormous basilica of Saint Francis in Assisi, his miraculous aerobatics even managed to convert a Lutheran prince from Saxony.[59]

María de Jesús de Ágreda, a Spanish nun, pushed the miraculous to new limits. As if levitating frequently were not enough, she claimed to have visited America through mystical trances, and to have preached the Gospel to the natives in New Mexico. Eyewitness reports of her visits to America seemed to confirm this extreme bilocation as fact, even to the point of convincing the Inquisition and the King of Spain. Sor María also claimed that she had been visited by the Virgin Mary repeatedly, and that the Mother of God had dictated her autobiography to her. This enormous book—over two thousand pages long—related intimate details about the Virgin Mary's childhood, her life with Joseph and Jesus, and her work with the Apostles after Jesus's death and resurrection.[60] News of her miraculous feats reached King Philip IV, who ended up relying on her as a spiritual advisor through hundreds of intimate letters.[61]

Given such phenomena, it is no surprise that a reform-minded Spaniard would complain about his own culture in 1600, as if in prescient affirmation of Weber's disenchantment thesis: "It seems as if one had wished to reduce these kingdoms to a republic of *enchanted* beings, living outside the natural order of things."[62]

Is it possible to imagine a world more "enchanted" than the one inhabited by St. Joseph of Cupertino and Sor María de Ágreda, or a world more
"disenchanted" than the one inhabited by Calvin's followers? Perhaps. But
imagining is not the same as dealing with the cold hard facts of history. The
Protestant rejection of the miraculous and mystical was a giant step toward
disenchantment, and "magic" had nothing to do with it.

The Living and the Dead

One of the most profound changes brought about by the Protestant Reformation was its redefinition of death and the afterlife.[63] Luther and all other
Protestants would reject not only belief in indulgences and Purgatory, but
also belief in any kind of interrelationship between the here and the hereafter. "The Scriptures forbid and condemn communication with the spirits of
the dead," Luther warned, citing Deuteronomy 18:10–11. Moreover, Luther
also demonized all of the medieval apparition tales that undergirded belief
in Purgatory, saying: "Whatever spirits go about, making a noise, screaming,
complaining, or seeking help, are truly the work of the devil."[64] Masses for
the dead, then, were nothing but demonically inspired sorcery and necro-
mancy.

For Luther, death was the deepest abyss of all, an unbridgeable metaphysical and ontological chasm in time and space. Luther summed it all up in
1522, in a sermon.

> The summons of death comes to us all, and no one can die for another.
> Every one must fight his own battle with death by himself, alone. We
> can shout into each other's ears, but everyone must himself be prepared
> for the time of death: I will not be with you then, nor you with me.[65]

Protestant popular literature made much of the cult of the dead, singling it
out as one of the surest signs of the falsehood of the Roman Catholic Church,
and of its exploitation of the people. A Swiss playwright, for instance, had
the pope's character say:

> Church offerings, weekly, monthly, and annual masses for the dead
> Bring us more than enough. . . .
> We also put a lot of stock in Purgatory,
> Although Scripture doesn't have much to say about it.
> The reason is that we must use every chance
> To scare the Hell out of the common folk.
> For that is what keeps the cover on our deception.[66]

Along with the death of Purgatory came also a rejection of all of the "works" or suffrages that supposedly helped to free souls from it. Gone were the masses for the dead, the prayers, anniversaries, chantries, and all else that went with such rituals. Moreover, the physical remains of the dead were subjected to apartheid as well, for it became common among many Protestants to remove burials from the churches and churchyards to suburban sites where there could be no routine mingling of the living and the dead.

The spiritual and cultural consequences of this sea change are hard to reckon, but the material consequences are not.[67] The disappearance of all postmortem rituals was an economic revolution. Suffrages for the dead always involved money: whether it was a single mass or a perpetual chantry, some cost always had to be borne by the living, who constantly saw part of their inheritance consumed by the dead, or to be more precise, by the clergy who said mass. Many postmortem rituals were funded in one way or another through real estate: either through rents or outright gifts of property to the church. Over the decades and centuries, the transfer of funds and property to the church snowballed into a gargantuan inheritance.

Though no one has yet tallied how many clerics were funded directly or indirectly by the cult of the dead in pre-Reformation Europe, we do know that the financial bond between the living and the dead held much of the church's fabric together. In 1529, a young Protestant lawyer named Simon Fish complained to King Henry VIII that Purgatory had placed "more than the third part of all your Realm" in the hands of the clergy.[68] The young John Calvin, writing to his former friend Gerard Roussel—who had just accepted a bishopric—upbraided him for growing rich off the dead. "It is indeed fair to say," Calvin told Roussel, "that you do not own any piece of land that has not been placed in your hands by Purgatory."[69] Calvin was right about this, and Catholics agreed, too. Writing in the 1560s, the exiled English cardinal William Allen acknowledged that the whole world knew that the doctrine of Purgatory had "founded all Bishoprics, builded all Churches, raised all Oratories, instituted all Colleges, endowed all Schools, maintained all hospitals, set forward all works of charity and religion, of whatever sort soever they be."[70]

To reconfigure the hereafter in the sixteenth century was to redefine many social, political, and economic realities. The most immediate practical effect of the abolition of the cult of the dead is easy to reckon: all of the property and funds that the clergy had been consuming in the name of the dead were redistributed, and usually put to secular use.[71] And, as this happened, Catholics began to embrace their dead even more tightly than before, intensifying the differences between the two rival religious cultures.

The Council of Trent (1545–63) decreed that indeed "there is a Purgatory, and that the souls there detained are aided by the suffrages of the faithful and chiefly by the acceptable sacrifice of the altar." Further, it also enjoined all bishops to "strive diligently to the end that the sound doctrine of Purgatory, transmitted by the Fathers and sacred councils, be believed and maintained by the faithful of Christ, and be everywhere taught and preached."[72] The council was equally firm concerning the veneration of the saints in Heaven, asking all bishops to "instruct the faithful diligently in matters relating to intercession and invocation of the saints, the veneration of relics, and the legitimate use of images, teaching them that the saints who reign together with Christ offer up their prayers to God for men."[73]

This reaffirmation of tradition was extremely successful at all levels, not so much because it was decreed from on high, but because it seems to have been eagerly embraced throughout the Catholic world, both by elites and common people. The best evidence we have of the triumph of Purgatory after the Council of Trent comes from wills. In Catholic Spain, for instance, the amount of money invested on the dead during the time of Philip II and his successors Philip III and Philip IV (ca. 1550–1665) would add up to much more than several years' worth of treasure from the New World.[74] In Cuenca, the bequests that funded the masses over nearly two centuries resulted in transferring more than half of the city's properties and nearly half of all of the surrounding land to the church.[75] One is forced to ask: What could have become of Spain if the dead had not claimed such a large share of its envied wealth?

Catholics enhanced their links with the dead in other ways, in response to the disenchanting challenge of Protestantism. Devotion to the saints escalated, along with apparitions of the dead—especially of souls who confirmed the existence of Purgatory and the efficacy of prayers for the dead.[76]

In contrast, Protestants scoffed at incorruptible corpses and apparitions, at least in part. Though belief in ghosts continued to be part and parcel of Protestant culture, their theologians insisted that all such events were really demonic in nature. Chances are that the afterlife described by the ghost of Hamlet's father in Shakespeare's play brings us closer to popular beliefs than nearly anything else:

I am thy father's spirit,
Doomed for a certain term to walk the night;
And for the day confined to fast in fires,
Till the foul crimes done in my days of nature
Are burnt and purged away.[77]

Given the trouble that Hamlet's dead father causes, could the audience doubt that he was anything other than a demon?[78]

Once Purgatory was extinguished and eternity was dismissed from theological discourse as a distant, unreachable dimension, the social, political, and economic claims that held together the very structure of the medieval church collapsed like a house of cards. If clergy were not the keepers of the keys to eternity, then what was their function? How on earth could they claim a superior status? As Protestants saw it, every claim to clerical supremacy was voided, from the gilded pope all the way down to the most slovenly parish vicar.

Luther began this redefinition by speaking of "the priesthood of all believers." At a popular level, dozens of pamphleteers immediately denounced all clerical claims of superiority. As an ex-monk put it: Why should the clergy turn themselves into "sacred cows," promoting the illusion of separateness and special "spiritual right," claiming "all kinds of exemptions and privileges from Heaven"?[79] One of the leaders of the Protestant faction in Strassburg summed up his party's argument by saying that all clergy should instead be subject to the same civil obligations as the laity, instead of being "treated as gods," and that any claim to the contrary was "against God, against the love of one's neighbor, against all sense of fair play, against human nature and reason, and detrimental to the community at large."[80]

As the clerics were desacralized, so were time and space. Gone were shrines, pilgrimages, processions. Gone were the images and relics that connected the faithful to heaven. Churches were still special places, yes, but there was nothing inherently sacred about them. A barn would be just as good, or even a pasture. The calendar was also redefined, in one brutal sweep. Only the Sabbath remained sacred. Gone were all the feasts and the fasts, gone were all public celebrations that surrounded the cult of the saints. As all places were equally good for finding God, so were all days.

And as time and space were desacralized, so was the world itself.

Conclusion: Reconstruing Disenchantment

Protestants did more than simply change beliefs by redefining the relationship of matter to spirit, and the natural to the supernatural, and by segregating the living and the dead: they reordered their society and their economy. In the sixteenth century, as in our own, a change in beliefs led to changes in the world.

Catholics had a way of interweaving metaphysical strands that Protestants segregated, and of doing so in very concrete ways, not just through ritual and symbol, but also through social, economic, and political structures. Among Catholics the world was at once sacred and profane. Take the case of the dead, for instance: they were not merely remembered, as was the case among Protestants, but actually *re-membered* and reintegrated into the social and economic fabric of the community.[81] Masses for the dead, like images and relics, reified social bonds and obligations of all sorts, linking not just the living and the dead, but all of the living. Among Protestants, what do we find in place of masses and relics or images of the saints? What, if anything, fills the void left by the disappearance of the dead in Purgatory and Heaven? On a personal and social level, the shift from a communally shared responsibility for each death to a very personal and private one signified a turn toward individualism; a turn that has been identified as the key to "modernity."[82] Protestants faced the divine tribunal and their eternal destiny *alone,* at the end of *this* life. Without the Catholic communion of saints *this* life and *this* world became the sole focus of religion, as did the *individual* over the community and even over all of history itself.

In *The Protestant Ethic and the Spirit of Capitalism,* Max Weber argued that Protestants gained an economic edge over Catholics because they developed a "this-worldly asceticism" and that Protestantism hastened "the elimination of magic from the world."[83] Though he did not focus on death rituals per se in order to defend his thesis, perhaps he should have, for the economic repercussions of this individualistic, "this-worldly" turn were profound and much easier to discern and quantify than any turn away from something as tangential to essential material structures as "magic." The same can be said for those two other essential Protestant traits: iconoclasm and the rejection of the miraculous.

The Protestant Reformation is a key turning point in Western history for many reasons, so anyone who singles out one or two or three of the changes brought about by Protestantism does so at great risk. But way up on the list, among the most profound changes, we can identify a sea change best described as *desacralization,* in which we see the earth becoming less charged with the otherworldly and supernatural.

It matters little that the devil was still around for Protestants, fooling people with his preternatural tricks, wreaking havoc through his witches and warlocks. Protestants saw the devil as a creature, and as only capable of manipulating the laws of nature, not of altering them. Sure, if one thinks of the wonders attributed to him as no different from divinely derived "thaumaturgy" or "magic," or as part of a "religio-magical" spectrum, it is easy to argue that the Protestant Reformation did not disenchant the world. But if one thinks of the devil as the Protestant Reformers did, as a mere creature who can never undo the laws of nature, but only work with them, much as our modern scientists do, then it becomes much more difficult to mount such an argument.

The Protestant realignment of heaven and earth and the natural and supernatural was a Copernican revolution of sorts with immediate, practical consequences. It was also a significant step toward the elevation of this world as the ultimate reality and, eventually, toward the rise of rationalism and the secularization of the West. To ask whether this process of "disenchantment" took place exactly as Weber said is to miss two much more significant points: first the undeniable fact that the world was substantially desacralized by Protestants, and that this change had much more to do with core metaphysical concepts than with "magic" (*zauber*); and second, that the beliefs and conceptual structures of Protestantism did have a direct and immediate impact on the world of the sixteenth and seventeenth centuries.

In sum, to deny or downplay the desacralization effected by Protestants— or to think of it as mere "disenchantment"—is to shortchange both the past and ourselves, as the epigram to this essay avers; even worse, it is to enchant ourselves through an artificially naive view of the world.[84]

Max Weber's disenchantment thesis, flaws and all, could very well be his most valuable insight. It's what makes him incombustible and gives him the right to haunt us still.

PART THREE

From the Premodern to the Modern World

Sacred Texts, Individual Agency, and Religious Identity

CHAPTER 9

Religion and Gender in Enlightenment England

The Problem of Agency

PHYLLIS MACK

This is the story of two women who lived and preached in the parish of Madeley, in Shropshire, in the second half of the eighteenth century. Abiah Darby (1716–93) arrived in 1745 as the second wife of Abraham Darby II when he took over the management of the family-owned ironworking company.[1] Her parents were Quaker ministers in Durham and her relatives were coal-fitters and mining engineers, so she was comfortable in the atmosphere of an industrializing town and wrote knowledgeably about the techniques of smelting iron and transporting coal.[2] In 1751 she began traveling as a minister, accompanied by a female friend and occasionally by her husband. These journeys were carried out mostly on horseback, often for months at a time, in most parts of England and at all seasons of the year. Like most eighteenth-century Quaker leaders, she preached chiefly at Quaker meetings and visited those in prison for refusing to pay tithes (church taxes). But she also engaged in activities that were outside the pale for a respectable eighteenth-century woman, Quaker or otherwise, preaching before army garrisons, town mayors, and out of doors at the market cross. Once she walked into church when services were in progress and upbraided the minister, John Fletcher, for what she called his "copyhold on priest craft." She also invited him to dinner and lent him books.[3] Near the end of her life, she wrote to Fletcher, with whom she had pursued a friendly theological debate over many years, proposing to speak to the Methodist congregation after services about a plan to solicit donations and establish a network of Sunday schools.[4]

Down the hill from the Darby house stood the Anglican and Methodist church and parsonage, presided over by John and Mary Fletcher.[5] Mary Bosanquet Fletcher (1739–1815) belonged to a wealthy Essex family (her brother was governor of the Bank of England) and converted to Methodism at age eighteen.[6] In the following decades she founded and managed an orphanage and home for impoverished women, sustained a vast written correspondence, and composed several short works. She was one of the earliest Methodist women to preach in public and the author of the only extant formal sermon by a woman. In 1781 she married John Fletcher and moved the following year to Madeley, where they carried out what amounted to a joint ministry in a parish of a few thousand people, mainly laborers and colliers (miners). After his death in 1785 she continued to run the local Methodist Society, preaching every Sunday morning before services, conducting parish business, and appointing ministers, the only female leader in early Methodism to exercise such authority. She died in 1815.

So we have before us two exceptional women, married to exceptional men, highly eminent in their respective religious communities, public preachers and published writers, who lived at the center of two momentous historical events, the early Industrial Revolution and the evangelical revival. Both were wealthy—Mary by birth, Abiah by marriage—and both experienced the same long widowhood of about thirty years, when they continued to be active as public figures.[7] They knew each other, though their religious habits and the twenty-two year difference in their ages probably precluded an intimate friendship. Abiah wrote a condolence letter to Mary after John Fletcher's death in 1785 in eloquent and conventional Quaker language: "I trust thy mind is so center'd upon the living Rock and Jesus, that no storms or oppositions can hurt or molest thy safe hiding place!"[8] Five years later, after Mary had been a dinner guest at the Darbys', Deborah Darby (Abiah's daughter-in-law) remarked that Mary was "a solid and truly pious woman" but "rather too full of conversation."[9]

As exemplars of female leadership in their respective communities, Abiah Darby and Mary Fletcher can teach us a good deal about the relationship between modernization and religion. We can learn how the concerns of middle-class Quakers—technological innovators, traders, and industrialists—differed from those of Methodists, whose legacy, according to some historians, was the creation of a docile laboring class. We can observe how the religious sensibility of a prominent Methodist, whose theology emphasized Jesus's suffering and atonement, differed from that of a Quaker, whose theology emphasized the Inner Light in the depths of every soul. We can compare the public persona of Quakers, who strove for equanimity and emotional control, with that of Methodists, who sought emotional intensity and a heightened sensibility. We can see how two middle-class women applied the emerging paradigms of public and private spheres in their own domestic settings. And we can get a sense of what was at stake for a woman preaching in public in the era of the Enlightenment. Indeed, this essay argues that the history of secularization was a story, not about the marginalization of religion, but about the interaction of religious and Enlightenment values, an interaction that played out differently among different individuals and religious groups.

Abiah Darby and Mary Fletcher felt themselves to be both denizens of the Enlightenment and seekers of the supernatural. They were in the vanguard of movements we view as modern, including the industrial revolution, the crusade for the abolition of slavery, reforms in education, and feminism. They were also in the vanguard of the evangelical revival that began in the mid-eighteenth century and continued into the nineteenth-century social welfare and missionary movements. Quaker and Methodist women leaders were a minority, but they were a minority with an inordinate influence on the dynamic of mainstream culture. Their religious experience, far from being a precursor of or a reaction to modernity, was part of the process of modernization itself. Their stories therefore do more than increase our knowledge of and sympathy for women's experience; they also call into question the traditional narrative of modernity in which religion is viewed as an interesting but anachronistic phenomenon that is essentially marginal to the main story.

But the lives of Mary and Abiah offer the historian much more than the fact of Christian piety joined to social change. Indeed, what is most intriguing about these two women—so close in spatial terms and so allied in their social commitments and moral values—is that their morality as preachers developed out of two different spiritual epistemologies, two different views of the sources of their own moral authority and agency, and two equally different understandings of the relationship between spirituality and emotion. Like earlier seventeenth-century Quaker prophets, Abiah's impulse to preach or prophesy was felt as an involuntary, almost physical compulsion—she was "seized upon with a mighty power" to speak—and both her speech and her written works reproduced the language and passion of angry Old Testament prophecy: "Oh! Call to remembrance the fatal End of those who were mighty *to drink strong drink,* who sat *till Wine inflamed them,*...For these, the Lord declared by his prophet, *Hell hath enlarged herself, and opened her Mouth without Measure; and their Glory, and their Multitude...shall descend into it.*"[10]

The summons to preach reached Mary Fletcher not as a kind of mental seizure, but through her insights into biblical passages and her own emotions and dreams. Of course, the universal strictures on women's preaching meant that, whatever her religious affiliation, it was impossible for a woman to become an official, ordained minister. Hence any woman who preached publicly in this period had to claim unique, divine inspiration, what John Wesley termed "an extraordinary call"; in that sense, every female minister was a visionary or prophet. But there is a difference between Abiah's biblical language and affect, which implied a kind of spiritual ventriloquism—God speaking through the mouth of the prophet—and the exhortations of Mary Fletcher, which were consciously crafted essays and meditations, written in her own voice and keyed to the realities of contemporary life. She actually produced a set of sermon notes or Watchwords, one for every letter of the alphabet. Another of her sermons was taken from Acts 27:29: "They cast four anchors out of the storm, and wished for help":

> The situation of the ship wherein Paul and his companions were, seems to me to illustrate the state and situation of many of us here.... Satan... keeps the mind in a continual agitation. Sometimes they are sunk, and almost crushed under the weight of care; and again raised high on the waves of some expected pleasure.... By all this, the soul becomes restless.... Dear souls, is not this the case with some of you?[11]

Judging by its self-presentation and religious language, Mary Fletcher's personal agency appears far more developed than that of Abiah Darby. However, if Abiah's prophetic authority was experienced as an involuntary and painful compulsion to speak, her *earthly* authority as a minister depended on no one but herself. The children's catechism she wrote posed the question, "Is the ministry of Christ confin'd to men only? Are not women also called to that work?" The answer is, yes they are, because "male and female are one in Christ."[12] She traveled in the ministry with a certificate from her home Meeting, and had she needed it, she would have been given funds for her expenses as well. Her second marriage to Abraham Darby was a spiritual partnership solemnized at Friends' Yearly Meeting after she had met him only once. Not only did he support his wife when she became an itinerant minister; "It was fully understood by Abraham and approved by him," writes her biographer, "that her religious concern counted before all other considerations, even when he or the family were unwell." (Nevertheless, Abraham was the ultimate authority in earthly matters. When he wanted to have their children vaccinated against smallpox, Abiah was terrified and unable to give her full consent; the children were vaccinated anyway.) Mary Fletcher's authority to preach was bestowed on her primarily by the Methodist leader John Wesley, who gave a small cohort of women permission to tell in public what God had done for their souls, and secondarily by her husband, John Fletcher. Indeed, her life with Fletcher exemplified that new eighteenth-century phenomenon, companionate marriage, an intimate sharing of domestic activities and a merging and subordination of her psyche and spirit to his; that was how she saw the relationship.[13]

In short, here in this small but seminal place, at a highly significant historical moment, were two neighbors who knew and respected each other and who shared not only a spiritual and social mission but a perceived tension between current ideals of feminine domesticity and the spiritual ideals of their respective religious communities. Yet despite their common claim to spiritual authority, their dedication to social reform, and their willingness to challenge contemporary gender roles, their religious consciousness put them at very different places on the cusp between preindustrial culture and modernity. I suggest that these religious and emotional juxtapositions, these different modes of language, feeling, and consciousness, were characteristic of many encounters in eighteenth-century British culture. More broadly, their different understandings of their own agency and emotions demonstrate the complexity of the processes that scholars have defined as secularization and the creation of the modern self. In the remainder of this essay, I'll discuss several aspects of Quaker and Methodist consciousness by analyzing the writings of Mary and Abiah, including their interpretation of dreams and beginning with some general points about eighteenth-century Quakerism.

Quakerism and Women

During his visit to England in 1726–29, the French philosophe Voltaire made the acquaintance of a retired Quaker merchant who received and entertained him in his simple country house.

> The Quaker was a hale and hearty old man who had never been ill because he had never known passions or intemperance; never in my life have I seen a more dignified or more charming manner than his.... He kept his hat on while receiving me and moved toward me without even the slightest bow, but there was more politeness in the frank, kindly expression on his face than there is in the custom of placing one leg

behind the other and holding in one's hand what is meant for covering one's head.[14]

So the Quaker took his place alongside the Incas, Tahitians, and other exotics who provided the philosophes with a mouthpiece for debunking their own corrupt society. He also stands as an exemplar of the ideal Enlightenment citizen as seen through the eyes of a premier exponent of Enlightenment values.

Seventeenth-century Quakers (or Friends, as they called themselves) had used the language of biblical prophecy to preach to audiences of non-Quakers in places as remote as the Caribbean, Malta, and the forests of the American wilderness. Eighteenth-century Quakers were both more limited in their preaching and more integrated into the larger community. Indeed, as social reformers and innovators in science, industry, education, medicine, mental health, and the administration of prisons, they seemed to be breathing the clear air of the Enlightenment; the Darbys of Madeley parish were pioneers in the early industrial revolution that would transform Britain and the world. Yet these same Quakers were also religious seekers striving for self-transcendence, spiritual insight, and radical pacifism, all of which isolated them from the social and political worlds of their contemporaries. Abraham Darby I, inventor of the process of smelting iron ore with coke, was also a Quaker minister. Abraham Darby II, husband of Abiah, who refined the process of smelting and ran the business, was equally devout. He once wrote to an unnamed Friend, "What can be the meaning of this general depravity? Men and women endued with such excellent understandings, to act so diametrically opposite to all sense and reason...to all the convictions in their own minds, as if there was no god, no afterlife, no retribution!"[15]

The central principle of Quaker theology was the doctrine of the Inner Light, the existence of a spark of divinity in the soul of every human being. That Inner Light is the essence of both individual conscience and universal truth, and the source of each person's capacity for moral and spiritual restoration. The first Friends, preaching in the chaos of the Civil War period, expressed these principles by chastising the moral laziness of their neighbors, attacking corrupt institutions, and witnessing to Truth by following their own individual "leadings" to speak or act, which often caused them to leave their families, assault the magistrates, or preach naked in the marketplace.[16] A Quaker meeting his social superior on the street would not show deference by removing his hat, but he might well embrace him or begin shouting in his face.

Following the Toleration Act of 1689 (which granted freedom of worship to religious sects), and the ensuing decrease in overt physical persecution, Quakers became business people and family people.[17] English law or their own religious principles prevented them from entering either the university or the military, and continued penalties for nonpayment of tithes made farming precarious, nor could they engage in luxury trades or the manufacture of products used in warfare. So Friends became involved in the textile and clothing trades, iron foundries, the production of domestic iron ware and porcelain, mining, and banking; by 1802 the largest coal dealer, tea merchant, druggist, tinman, and pewterer in London were Quakers. Because of strictures against marrying outside the community, all of these enterprises came to be dominated by large manufacturing and trading families, whose kinship ties reinforced Friends' sense of corporate responsibility for solvency and honest dealing, as well as their devotion to private property. In short, by the time Abiah Darby and Mary Fletcher met each other, Quakerism had evolved from a movement of radical visionaries into a community of upstanding citizens with an anxious respect for law and order and a terror of overly emotional behavior or "enthusiasm." For Friends, as for other denizens of the British Enlightenment, reason and emotional balance were privileged over passion and enthusiasm, simplicity of manners over unconventional shock tactics, humanitarianism and social reform over contentious politics, family and Meeting over public prophecy. Salvation was achieved and demonstrated not through asceticism or visions, but through moral integrity and economic prosperity: the quality of one's bearing in the world.

In this new external environment, the home assumed equal importance with the Meeting for worship as a social and spiritual refuge and as a school for character. The busy trader, teacher, or capitalist was elevated to a higher spiritual plane when he retired into his family, divested his mind of all aggression and greed, and transcended class differences by treating his workers, servants, and children as his moral apprentices. Called by an admirer "the Princess of the Dale," Abiah Darby presided over an endless stream of guests and a vast household (walnut trees, a lawn populated with deer, a pond, an island with a summer house) and often preached to guests at dinner. "This is the most uncommon place I was ever in," wrote a visitor. "There is such a deal of religion and worldly business, human learning and Christian simplicity among the people—such a native wild irregularity, subdued and cultivated by art and opulence about the place."

From a more modern perspective, it might seem that Friends' religious ideals had been effaced by the secular ideals of the Enlightenment; indeed, many Quaker writings used "God" and "Wisdom," "conscience" and "the inner light" as interchangeable terms. From the Quakers' own perspective, their restrained language and behavior was an attempt to formulate a new conception of the right way to discern and express spiritual authenticity. Friends had always believed that salvation—being "in the light"—was expressed through the ordinary gestures of daily life; the earliest Friends were noted for honesty and sincerity as well as their flamboyant public prophecy. For later Friends, who believed that salvation was expressed through calmness, moral clarity, and personal restraint, social behavior had to be both authentic and respectable—a model of public virtue rather than a challenge to it; so a male Quaker admired the minister Mary Ridgeway, "in whom were united the seriousness of the minister, and the courtesy of the gentlewoman."[18]

The addition of the Victorian pedestal to the Quaker woman's persona did not imply any diminution of respect for women as ministers or helpmeets. Several writers defended not only a woman's capacity to be inspired but her capacity for intellectual discourse. Hundreds of women received certificates to preach, which entitled them to financial support from their home meetings as well as support for the families they left behind; many other hundreds of women were elders, overseeing the pastoral care of their home meetings; and every woman who married participated in a ceremony that was more egalitarian than any other comparable Christian rite.[19] What the pedestal did imply was an awareness of the Quakers' vulnerability as a religious minority and a desire to assimilate to the norms of British middle-class culture. Unlike the ecstatic political prophets of the seventeenth century, a woman could not act like a man in the public spaces now reserved for men alone. Nor could she convey the presence of the Inner Light by the physical gestures that distinguished earlier Friends. On the contrary, it was the physical reserve and quiet authority of women elders and ministers that conveyed authenticity. This created problems of interpretation for the men who listened to Quaker women ministers. Seventeenth-century audiences, watching a female prophet disrupting a church service and shouting at the top of her lungs, had to decide whether the prophet spoke with the voice of God or the Devil; eighteenth-century audiences, listening to the measured, sing-song tones of a female preacher delivering a sermon, had to decide whether she spoke with God's voice or the voice of an ordinary woman using ordinary intelligence to tell men what was wrong with them and what they should do about it.

Relieved of the struggle for physical survival and educated in the values of the Enlightenment, Quaker women now struggled to understand themselves and their place in the world in an entirely new language; rather, they struggled to graft a new vocabulary of reason and sensibility on to their original language of Old Testament imagery and bodily signs. In one tract, Abiah Darby's biblical language was a replica of seventeenth-century Quaker preaching ("Oh! Call to remembrance the fatal End of those who were mighty to *drink strong drink,* who sat *till Wine inflamed them,* who loved *Instruments of Music in their feasts...*). But she also wrote in the same tract, a diatribe against horse-racing, cock-fighting, throwing at cocks, gaming, plays, dancing, musical entertainments, or any other vain diversions:

> [Do not] conclude [that] this Address cometh from a melancholly Enthusiast,... for I can assure you I am not one of those;... I am not of that Opinion, that we ought to recluse ourselves from the World, but that we keep ourselves from *the Evil* thereof; *using this World as not abusing it;* enjoying the Blessings bestowed, *as good Stewards of the manifold grace of God....* [Thus] our Understandings as Men will be polished, our Faculties brightened, and qualified for Converse and Commerce among Men. So that in a spiritual and natural Sense, we shall become as *Lights in the World.*[20]

In those two final sentences, the languages of the Inner Light and the Enlightenment finally meet. Later Abiah wrote in her journal that God expects more from her own generation than from earlier Friends, "For we are favored to live in a much more enlightened age—we enjoying the promises they only saw at a great distance."

The tension between the Quakers' desire to maintain their uniqueness as a group and their equally strong desire to assimilate to modern society is also evident in their private writings. Quaker journals of the period are filled with accounts of preachers—male and female—straining to recapture the zeal of the earliest Quakers, riding for miles on horseback to meetings, but remaining silent before assembled Friends because they did not feel the Light or could not overcome the constraints dictated by their own spiritual inhibitions and good manners. I know of very few Quakers in this period who preached in the marketplace to strangers, or standing before the mayor of the town, or who interrupted a church service in order to prophesy, as the earliest Friends did, and as Abiah did in 1755, when she and her friend Ann Summerland went on a preaching tour to Hertfordshire and Bristol. At one meeting she felt oppressed, needing to speak to the leading men of the city. Her friends did not think it was a suitable time, so they gave up the idea, but Abiah was "very distressed" all night. The next day, still upset, she went to the Mayor's house and asked permission to hold a meeting in the town hall and presented her certificate "that I was no impostor." That night she was very anxious, and the next day she went to the bishop. "I told him...I was engaged to come to speak to him from the Holy Spirit, he said 'we don't hear such things.'" She wrote to the bishop, urging him to combat vice, but,

> Still my distress was so great I could have no peace without *giving up* to go into the street, to proclaim repentance...I stop't short before a shop door and lifted up my voice as a trumpet. The people were surprised, one man sprung out to me asking "What is the matter Madam?"...After being clear I went to the inn, but *a profusion of weeping came over my mind,* and all the way out of town I wept exceedingly for the people, who seemed to sit in darkness.[21]

We can see in these accounts how humbling it was for a respectable bourgeois woman, well-known in the community, to surrender her dignity and position in this way, even though her husband and the Quaker Meeting clearly supported her. In 1755 she preached at the dinner table shortly after giving birth: "A great, very great cross to my natural will: but always condemned when I put it by...but when I give up, oh the comfort and joy that redounds to my soul, that I then admire how I ever dare disobey—but the next time it's as hard as ever."[22]

I can only speculate about the religious consciousness that moved Abiah to carry her public performance to these extremes. Clearly, intense piety and self-criticism were important elements of her religious temperament. As a child she used to visit a Presbyterian woman to read Scripture and sing psalms, and as a young woman she felt guilty for letting an impulsive and very brief early marriage divert her from her call to preach. The nightmares she had around this time were remembered and recorded many years later in a journal written for her children. In one dream, she was chased by huge men on horses who threw stones at her; in another she tried to hide from Christ, who gazed at her through a window in horror. This is the only dream I have found in either Quaker or Methodist records in which God is terrified by the dreamer, and it testifies to her intense feelings of guilt about avoiding the burden of prophecy: "In great terror I run up stairs into a chamber to hide myself: when looking towards the window, I saw him at the outside, looking full upon me astonished—I ran into the inner chamber: and at the window, there I saw him standing also. He looked awfully solemn and piercing upon me—with amazement and horror filled."[23]

If Abiah's spiritual struggles were generated by a conflict between religious zeal and personal timidity, I suspect that her wealth and social prominence were equally important in shaping her vocation as a prophet. She records in her journal that as a child her father and his brother argued over an inheritance and her father surrendered part of his estate to keep the peace. Her first husband had less material wealth than her own family, and the disapproval of her parents cast a pall over the marriage and increased her guilt at resisting the call to preach. "All the time I was married, which was about two years or upwards—I remained poor and barren in spirit, as one left alone."[24] As the wife of Abraham Darby, she must have experienced an opposite pressure: both a greater scope for good works and a sense of spiritual danger in her life as "princess of the dale." Her awareness of the obligations attendant on wealth is apparent in her tract on horse-racing, where she basically says, take up your burden as exemplars in the community, be vigilant against your own acquisitive nature, and God will make you wealthy and inviolable.

> To you then, whom the Beneficent Father hath blessed with Affluence...a double Obligation is laid upon you to walk in awful Reverence and Circumspection before your God, as *faithful Stewards* of his manifold Mercies and Grace.... People's Eyes are upon you, they love to imitate, they conclude ye know better than they, and implicitly follow your steps.... [God] expects more from us in this enlightened Age.... [If you] obey the holy Will...he will bless you in all your Undertakings: the Fields will yield their Increase, and Plenty shall abound in your Dwellings; and nothing shall be permitted to hurt or destroy you.[25]

Methodism and Emotion

Abiah Darby's concerns about material success are a common affliction of successful reform movements, where the second and third generations are both more secure and less single-minded than their forebears. Turning our attention to Methodism and Mary Fletcher, we see a movement younger by almost a century, where there was no shortage of spiritual energy and emotional heat. Eighteenth-century Quakers were modern in terms of their engagement with the world of science and business and their concern for social justice, but they looked backward in attempting to emulate the fervor of the earliest Quakers while eschewing their flamboyant enthusiasm or acts of civil disobedience. Methodists were far less sophisticated in terms of their engagement with the secular world, but they were modern in their focus on feelings, tapping into the contemporary concern with sensibility and styles of emotional expression that would later emerge as nineteenth-century romanticism.

Methodism began in the late 1730s as a renewal movement within the Anglican Church, led by John and Charles Wesley and a small cohort of ministers, lay leaders, and lay preachers. By the time of John Wesley's death in 1791, it had attracted more than seventy-two thousand members in Britain and sixty thousand in North America.[26] Until the end of the century, Methodists were also Anglicans, remaining within the body of the national church and attending baptism, communion, and so on. Wesley's Methodists were also Arminians: believers in free will, but emphasizing the power of Jesus's atonement to justify sinners. In short, Methodism was both a charismatic movement and an organized system of worship, ranging from huge revival meetings to classes of men and women, and small bands or meetings when worshippers were separated by gender and marital status. Most important for our purpose, Methodism, or "heart religion," was a movement that privileged the emotions. Not only did revivalist preaching elicit wildly demonstrative responses; emotional perception was valued above mere reason or intellectual effort. John Wesley once wrote in a moment of desperation, "I do not love God. I never did."[27] Undoubtedly Wesley *believed* in God at that moment, but it was his *relationship* with God, the affective connection, that was the goal of Methodist worship and discipline.

Mary Bosanquet Fletcher joined the movement when she was about eighteen (her parents having expelled her from their home so that she wouldn't pollute her siblings with her new spirituality and disreputable friends) and quickly became part of a community of women living and praying together in London. From the beginning, her connection to the movement was rooted in her emotional connection to individual members, who became her mentors and intimate friends. If Abiah Darby's vocation developed out of her parents' example and feelings of guilt for her daughterly disobedience and current wealth, Mary Fletcher's spirituality developed out her parents' lack of sympathy and the intense relationships she cultivated within the movement. One of these relationships was with Sarah Ryan, a woman ten years older who had been a servant, laundress, and bigamist. For many Methodists, Sarah Ryan was an embodiment of the primitive, sanctified Christian, whose past suffering and intuitive insight imbued her with an authority out of all proportion to her status as a housekeeper of the Methodist centers in London and Bristol. She and Mary Bosanquet planned to establish an orphanage and haven for poor women. They also exchanged letters of a quite romantic intensity. Mary wrote to Sarah:

> I believe you will return but I observe you never say *when*...I know not how it is but I have lost all that assurance I had of your unchangeableness. And don't you remember when you went you said the first letter you wrote or at the least the second, you would assure me of your intention of returning at the time appointed....O Jesus what wouldst thou have me learn by this dispensation?...does [the Lord] now show you anything concerning my soul as he used to do, I shall read your letter over and over and draw out all the honey I can.[28]

Sarah reassured her,

> O my dear your *thoughts* your *thoughts* catch them as they flee bring them into the pure presence of God and there hold them till he hath scattered them by his eye or cleansed them by his holy spirit as to me my dear enjoy me in God look for me in God find me in God love me in God and live with me in God then shall you die with me into God and *we* shall live with God together...I am happy very happy.[29]

Before her marriage at age forty-two, Mary Bosanquet had repeatedly advised single women to avoid marriage as at best a hindrance to the exercise of piety and at worst a form of tyranny:

> How many married persons are at a loss to determine to what length they may oblige their partners in those things not absolutely forbid: and yet such as may be great hindrances in their way....But from all this *you* are free—whatever shines on your soul...you are at full liberty to follow it without difficulty or interruption....If you are entrusted with...money...you can consecrate it all to God....Again, if you led to cry to God in public, to visit the sick, or in any way to rescue souls from perdition—you have not to ask leave of man...if a man have a bad wife he is still his own master—but the woman is not her own mistress—therefore to these I say take care how you part with the liberty you now enjoy....I say again you are now your own mistress— beware how you become subject.[30]

Nevertheless she was unwilling to challenge the norm of patriarchal marriage that made such subservience possible. In a later passage, she writes in terms that would have been anathema to Abiah Darby,

When you are married you can no longer be mistress of yourself—
You ought not, for you have made him (whether good or bad, wise
or foolish) your superior.... [So] let me entreat you never to entertain
a thought of taking any man as your head, unless he be such a one as
your highest reason chooses to obey.[31]

Perhaps one reason for this conservatism was that her concern for wom-
en's moral autonomy coexisted with a powerful desire for those she loved to
behave not as equals, but as loving parents:

Nov. 12, 1783: [God] showed me he would make his will known to me
through that of my dear husband, and that I was to accept his directions
as from God, and obey him as the Church does Christ. That I must
give myself to his guidance as a child, and wherever we were called, or
however employed in the work of God, I should always find protection, and glorify God, while I renounced all choice by doing the will
of another rather than my own.[32]

Throughout her life, Mary Fletcher used dreams and the emotions they
elicited as a way to think about the nature of her various roles as teacher,
spiritual counselor, wife, and overseer of her late husband's parish. Indeed,
dreams were generally important for Methodists as a justification and direct
inspiration for female preaching. Unlike Quaker women, whose authority
to preach was formalized by a certificate given by the meeting for worship,
Methodist women's authority to preach was based on an "extraordinary call,"
a divine commandment to preach. This commandment did not entitle them
to behave either as ordained ministers, preaching from a biblical text, or as
political prophets, but only to relate their own personal experience (Mary,
we have seen, ignored this rule). Dreams were thus a part of women's public
vocation far more than men's. Not only did they convey a visionary authority and a symbolic language that justified and elevated women's preaching;
they also implied that the call to preach was both spontaneous and innocu-
ous. Mary Fletcher often used her own dreams in the same way she used
biblical texts; thus she introduced her dream of the Tree of Life as a sermon
text that was also a divine message:

She thought she saw a large tree, the branches, trunk, and roots, were
very beautiful, but all transparent.... She thought the sap run through
a part of the branches very swiftly, and that part was very green,
lively, and flourishing, but in some part of the branches that ran slowly,
and... were but languid.... She informed us, that the dream was immediately explained to her. She said the trunk and roots, represent God

the Father. The human form within the trunk [was] Jesus Christ. The sap represents the Holy Spirit. The branches and leaves the Church. The knots and crooked parts...were the remains of unbelief, self will, [and] carnality.[33]

In many of Mary's dreams, she encountered a succession of deceased figures who had been her mentors in life and who assisted her in her struggle to balance her emotional intensity with the detachment of the sanctified Christian whose sole love object is God. The main character in these dreams was John Fletcher, who invariably appeared as a godlike, parental figure who affirmed his eternal love and concern, but cautioned Mary to detach herself from her dependence on him and direct all of her desire toward God. In one dream, unable to think clearly enough to talk to him about religious matters, she could only ask plaintively whether he ever visited her. Characteristically, he responded by reminding her that though he did visit, she should not rely on these visits, but on God.

> At length I asked, "My dear, do you not visit me sometimes?" He answered, "Many times a day."... "and may I always know that thou art near me when I am in trouble, or pain, or danger?" He paused and said faintly, "Why, yes"; then added, "but it is as well for thee not to know it, for thy reliance must not be upon me."[34]

Abiah Darby's relationship to her husband appears to have been one of spiritual equality and immense respect, but the lines of authority were more balanced and the emotional register was more subdued. When Abraham died, she recorded a very moving dream in which Abraham appeared as the suffering Christ:

> I was sitting in a parlor...when looking on my left hand I saw a large cross, and a person hanging thereon, with his arms extended. I considered who it should be,...and presently knew him to be my husband, he had only his shirt on fastened close about him—he took me by the hand, looking upon me with a solid sweet countenance but said nothing...[then] the wall and house behind us opened wide, and...my husband mounted up...I got up and held his hand as far as I could reach, when he gently drew his hand out of mine, and ascended into the air.[35]

Mary Fletcher's dream of her dead husband was more gruesome and intimate, and more focused on the lesson he had to teach her:

> I thought the side of his tomb was opened...and I saw him lying under it, while I lay at his side....He then said, with a sweetness which

I cannot describe, "Put thy arm over me and feel what companions I have; they must be thy companions too." I put my arms, and felt bones and broken coffins, at which nature seemed to shrink, but I did not speak. He tenderly answered my thought, "Thou will lay thy head upon me."[36]

Not surprisingly—and in strong contrast to the self-presentation of Abiah Darby—Mary's great talent as a writer and preacher was empathy, the capacity to express theological principles in terms of concrete human experience. In her sermon on Acts, she wrote,

Look through the creation,—observe the tender love of the birds toward their young, yea, even the most savage beasts! . . . It is a shadow of that infinite compassion that reigns in [God's] heart. Rise a little higher. Fix your eye on man. How does he love a stubborn son who will neither serve God nor him? True, he frowns on him, and corrects him. . . . But if that son shed but a tear of sorrow . . . if he but come a few steps, how do the father's bowels yearn toward him! How doth he run to meet him! Now carry the idea a little higher;—are ye not the offspring of God?[37]

Conclusion

Compared to the flamboyant religiosity of seventeenth-century visionaries, the scope of Mary's and Abiah's religious activities was narrower in spiritual, social, and geographic terms. Seventeenth-century prophets used the language of biblical prophecy to preach to audiences of non-Quakers in places as remote as the Caribbean, Malta, and the forests of the American wilderness. Abiah Darby preached mainly to other Quakers, and her forays into the non-Quaker world—"a gentlewoman riding in her carriage"— were a perpetual source of anxiety and embarrassment. Mary Fletcher was attracted by the ascetic practices of the early saints and martyrs, but her own experiments in self-denial were almost ludicrously limited. One night she woke up from a dream about her husband and considered the possibilities for living a more ascetic life:

Last night I dreamed my dear husband wrote a line for me to read. I took up the paper with desire, and read, "Those who closely follow Jesus Christ can discern the mark of the thorn in his steps". . . Lord, show me how to walk thus! Give me a steady power to rise the very moment the alarm goes off. To watch against sloth all day, and to use more abstemiousness in my food. . . . I am quite clear I have no right to hurt my body. I am not, I think, in any danger of that. . . . I propose to keep a watch over my appetite each day . . . to this I would add a shadow of a fast, twice a week. On Mondays and Fridays I would omit butter in the morning, eating dry bread, and as usual rosemary tea without sugar. For dinner, water gruel, with salt and pepper, and, as on other days, tea for my supper. This cannot hurt my health, and may be a kind of remembrancer that there is such a duty as self-denial.[38]

Clearly, Fletcher never imagined that she could achieve a religious epiphany by giving up butter, only that her small sacrifice might serve as "a kind of remembrancer" of the need to imitate Christ.

This said, it is also true that both women pushed far beyond the limits—both social and spiritual—that hampered women in late eighteenth-century culture. Abiah Darby continually obliterated the boundaries between the public and the private spheres, prophesying in the street, preaching at the dinner table to assembled guests, and discussing religious matters with male visitors who visited her in her bedroom shortly after she had given birth. Mary Fletcher preached at revival meetings and, as John Fletcher's wife, her preaching and pastoral work paralleled that of her husband. In her widowhood, still resident in the vicarage, she preached twice every three weeks while the newly incumbent vicar preached only once (covering for him when he preached elsewhere in the parish).

As preachers and religious leaders, these Quaker and Methodist women had agency in the modern, liberal sense: an embodied authority to act based on their own free choice and intelligence. They also had a strong sense of their own individuality, based as much on the religious practices of individual prayer and diary-keeping as on Enlightenment values. But this new agency was limited by increasingly rigid standards of bourgeois femininity. Quaker and Methodist women also had agency in a spiritual sense, an authority based in the Quakers' case on the Inner Light and in the Methodist case on their acceptance of God's love and the efficacy of Christ's atonement. But the expression of this spiritual agency was limited by new inhibitions about openly ecstatic behavior.

Judged in terms of their own spiritual goals, Mary and Abiah's attempts to achieve both inner peace and a purity of intention clearly failed. But if we consider their efforts in relation to the wider culture, their relentless pursuit of spiritual perfection looks both genuinely impressive and historically significant. For women, the new evangelical Christianity meant a transmutation of their spiritual authority, an acceptance of a more circumscribed self-definition and spiritual ambition. It also meant a renewed energy to convert and educate, and a vastly increased scope for the use of their own spiritual education and worldly position in careers of philanthropy and missionary work. The contradiction between the ideal of self-transcendence and the cultivation of a competent self was resolved by turning the energies of the individual outward, in charitable impulses toward others; the ecstatic prophecy of the seventeenth century was transmuted into the aggressive altruism of the nineteenth century. By helping to effect a change of direction in the history of their religious communities and by expanding the community's activities in the world at large, they influenced the nature and importance of religion as an element of the modern psyche.

CHAPTER 10

Constructions of Jewish Identity through Reflections on Islam

SUSANNAH HESCHEL

Can one discover one's own religious identity by exploring another religion? Philological examinations of the Qur'an by Jewish scholars, starting with Abraham Geiger (1810–74), initially were a project of restoration. By pointing to significant parallels between the Qur'an and rabbinic texts, including Mishnah and Midrash, they thought they were offering Muslims and all those interested in Islam a foundational context, namely, early Judaism. No gift, of course, was ever without an expectation of reciprocity. Although the anthropologist Marcel Mauss analyzed gift exchange within the context of Pacific island societies, his demonstration of the politics of the gift bears implications not only for modern social and economic theory, but also, I would like to argue, for the field of what has come to be known as "Oriental studies" or, more recently, as "comparative religion."[1] For Jewish scholars, demonstrating parallels between the Qur'an and rabbinic literature was not only a gift to Islamic studies, it was also a display of the importance of Judaism's influence in the history of religion, and a tool for affirming the Jewish presence within Europe. The positive view of Islam that prevailed among Jewish historians and theologians, at least prior to the end of the nineteenth century, allowed Islam to function as a template for presenting central Jewish ideas, such as monotheism, rejection of anthropomorphism, and religious law as divine revelation.

Scholars of Islam for the past two centuries have credited the beginnings of their field to the work of Geiger, whose study of parallels between the Qur'an and rabbinic literature, *Was hat Muhammad aus dem Judenthume aufgenommen?*, was published in 1833. The work was hailed throughout Europe as marking a breakthrough in scholarship by demonstrating for the first time that Islam arose within the context of Judaism and not, as previously believed, as a result of Christian heretical influences on Muhammad. Yet the reception of Geiger's work has also varied. Prior to World War II, his work served as a model for numerous other scholars investigating additional parallels, many of whom concluded that Islam was not original, but derived its major ideas and religious practices from Judaism. In recent years, some scholars, such as Michael Pregill, have criticized Geiger and the tradition his work spawned for having confined early Islam to a primarily Jewish context and ignored other influences, including the possibility that some Jewish texts were transmitted to Muhammad via Christians.[2] The nineteenth-century philology that searched the Qur'an to uncover influences also came to be viewed, in recent decades, as an effort to pull the Qur'an into pieces of Judaism (or Christianity), making the work a passive recipient of the ideas of other religions. The important recent work of Angelika Neuwirth on the Qur'an, by contrast, restores agency to the Qur'an by asking, in methods drawn from intertextual theory, how the Qur'an reads and interprets the texts, traditions, and ideas of the polysemic and multireligious context in which it arose. She argues, for example, that sections of the Qur'an should be understood as insightful commentaries on the Hebrew psalms, both incorporating and altering its language through its own, original Qur'anic poetic voice.[3]

Geiger's gift to the study of Islam was accompanied by his expectation that rabbinic literature would come to be appreciated as an essential part of the study of religion, including Christianity and Islam as well as Judaism. Even more, he developed an older Jewish theory of "mission"—that Jews have a mission to bring monotheism to the world—into a broader theory, asserting that Christianity and Islam are daughter religions of Judaism, carrying its message to Greco-Roman and Arab pagans, respectively.[4]

Jewish interest in the study of religion—Judaism, Christianity, and Islam—began in the midst of a Jewish struggle in Europe for political emancipation and social integration. The context was molded by intellectual currents of the Enlightenment, romanticism, and historicism, but also by wider political movements of imperialism, racism, and nationalism, all of which shaped scholarship well into the twentieth century. Although Germany did not possess colonial holdings until late in the nineteenth century, Susanne Zantop has demonstrated the extensive "colonial fantasies" that dominated German belles lettres for the prior hundred years. Such fantasies focused on both the southern hemisphere—Africa and South America—and on the east, the imagined Orient.[5] More recently, Suzanne Marchand, in her study of the German field of Oriental studies, has argued that the major motivation was not imperial conquest, but rather much older, theological questions about the origins of Christianity, ancient Near Eastern influences on the Old Testament, as well as problems shared more widely, such as whether human progress occurs; whether monotheism is an intrinsic part of human nature; how cultures can influence one another apart from conquest; and just how necessary religion might be to a stable society.[6] German Orientalists, in their search for the context of Christian origins, and frequently, searching for a context other than Judaism, tended to be less interested in Islam, which arose after Christianity was established, than in the religions of India, China, and pre-Islamic Persia.

Jewish scholars, by contrast, were drawn to Islam not because they were searching for the context out of which Judaism had developed, but rather because they wanted to demonstrate the religious fruit that Judaism had produced: not only Christianity, but Islam as well—three monotheistic religions. Oriental studies, as it was then known, became a template through which a new kind of Jewish identity could be explored, and historicism was a substitute for revelation: whether or not Judaism was the product of revelation could not be proven through historical method, but historical method could demonstrate the productivity of Judaism's inspiration. Historical narrative not only described the path, it assured a future, inasmuch as narrativity implies futurity, at least in the heteronormative plot of reproduction: a child is born, be it Christianity or Islam, from the mother religion, Judaism. Given that Judaism was termed a "dead religion" by theologians from Luther to Schleiermacher, as Amy Newman has pointed out, progeny would imply not only continued existence, but also futurity.[7] Lacking fruitfulness, that is, the ability to generate new religious ideas, a religion was "dead."[8]

The Jewish engagement in the study of Islam was motivated by additional factors that changed over the course of the era, from the 1830s to the 1930s. Foremost is the political factor: Jews, as Germany's most significant and visible minority, were often targets of the Orientalist imagination, functioning as a kind of colonized Oriental community within Germany.[9] Entering the field of Islamic studies, then, had political as well as intellectual motivations for Jewish scholars. Anti-Semites often described Judaism as an "Oriental" religion—that is, primitive, degenerate, and outside the sphere of Western civilization. Breaking that linkage between Judaism and the Orient was one response; another approach was the Jewish argument that, indeed, Judaism had given birth to Islam, and that Islam was a religion of significance—of strict monotheism, religious ethics, abjuration of anthropomorphism, and religious tolerance. Indeed, it was within the Islamicate context, Jewish scholars argued, that Judaism was able to flourish, in contrast to the persecutory ambience of Christian Europe.

Scholarship

From the 1830s until the 1930s, Jews came to be among the finest scholars and greatest admirers of Islam in Europe. Indeed, simply in writing Jewish history, the *Wissenschaft des Judentums* devoted a disproportionate amount of attention to the history of Jewish life in Muslim lands, emphasizing the tolerance of Islam for Jews (the "Golden Age" of Muslim Spain), the intellectual and cultural exchanges in the fields of science and philosophy, the Muslim discovery and transmission of classical Greek texts and ideas that fertilized medieval Jewish thought, and the use of Arabic for Jewish philosophy and poetry. We also see the identification expressed concretely in the architecture of European and American synagogues, which abjures Gothic, occasionally accepts Romanesque, and more frequently employs Moorish style. Gothic, it seems, was so Christian a signifier that it would swallow Judaism, whereas the Islamic Moorish would point to the "Golden Age" of Jewish life in Muslim Spain. The Jewish alliance with Islam thus also served as a tool for the ongoing polemic against Christianity and stands in sharp contrast to the prevailing view held by most Christian scholars in Europe; as an example, the Austrian scholar of Islam, Joseph von Hammer-Purgstall, considered Islam "the most intolerant of all religions, which strives for world domination and thus for constant conquests."[10] In short, Jews became mediators of Islam for Europeans on both a scholarly and popular level, and Islam became a tool for configuring the position of Jews and Judaism on the map of Western civilization.

The First Generation of Jewish Scholars

The story of the Jewish fascination with Islam, as well as modern scholarship on Islam, began with Geiger. When Geiger left his Orthodox family in Frankfurt am Main to become a student at the University of Heidelberg in 1829, and then at the University of Bonn from 1830 to 1833, he joined a small group of male Jewish students; Jewish men were newly welcome to study at German universities, while Jewish women had to wait until the 1890s when women students were finally admitted.[11] Several of Geiger's fellow students at Bonn were interested in becoming rabbis; in those days, Bonn "seemed to be truly a Hochschule for Jewish theologians."[12] Lacking a rabbinical seminary to attend, they formulated their own course of learning, gathering regularly to practice delivering sermons. Geiger's studies emphasized Oriental languages and he enrolled in Arabic classes with the philologist Georg Freytag, who had held the professorship in Arabic studies since 1819.[13] They were remarkable students; some became outstanding scholars: Salomon Munk, in medieval Arabic Jewish philosophy, translated Maimonides's *Guide for the Perplexed* from Arabic into French; Josef Derenbourg wrote on Second Temple Judaism and later, with his son, Hartwig Derenbourg, worked on the medieval Arabic texts of Saadia and Averroes; Ludwig Ullmann translated the Qur'an into German.[14] At Heidelberg, Geiger had been together with Gustav Weil, who later published extensively on early Islam. Ullmann died at a very young age, and Geiger became a rabbi in Germany, while Munk, Derenbourg, and Weil moved to France and developed academic careers there. Germany's universities suffered a brain drain.

Geiger's own work at Bonn resulted in his monumental study of rabbinic influences on the Qur'an that he completed in a remarkably short period of time. His prize essay, which earned him a Ph.D. at the University of Marburg, was published and hailed all over Europe as inaugurating a new way of understanding the origins of Islam within Judaism.[15] Geiger placed the text of the Qur'an under historicist scrutiny and contextualized it within the history of transmission of rabbinic Judaism in Arabia. He was the first to demonstrate that passages in the Qur'an repeat passages from the Mishnah, and that Qur'anic accounts of biblical stories are taken from Midrashic commentaries. Islam, in other words, was born of Judaism, and Muhammad, he writes, while convinced of his divine mission, did not want to found a new religion, but to align his teachings with those of the biblical prophets.

The study of Islam was in its infancy in the 1830s in Germany; the basic scholarly tools had not yet been developed: dictionaries, critical editions of texts, and methods for analyzing them. As Geiger wrote, his analysis of the Qur'an was based simply on the "naked Arabic text." Freytag and Heinrich Lebrecht Fleischer, who became professor of Oriental languages at the University of Leipzig in 1835, both trained under Sylvestre Antoine de Sacy in France, where scholars were busy analyzing the treasure trove of documents that Napoleon's scholars had brought back from Middle East expeditions.[16] Bonn remained a smaller center than Leipzig for studying Islam; in Leipzig,

Fleischer had more than three hundred students, Jews and Christians, and of the 131 dissertations he directed prior to his death in 1886, 51 were written by Jews, including Daniel Chwolsohn, Morris Jastrow, Immanuel Loew, Wilhelm Bacher, Eduard Baneth, and Ignaz Goldziher.[17] Fleischer was also the founding editor of the *Zeitschrift der deutschen morgenländischen Gesellschaft* and welcomed contributions by Jews, making his journal one of the only prestigious German academic journals studying religion in which Jews were permitted to publish their scholarship, and creating Islamic studies as a particularly welcoming field for Jewish scholars.

Geiger's Study of the Qur'an

Geiger opens his book by arguing that the major theological and moral ideas of Islam, as expressed in the Qur'an, were deliberately taken over by Muhammad from Judaism. Convinced of his own divine mission,[18] Muhammad did not want to found a new religion but to align his teachings with those of the prophets.[19] Muhammad himself felt ambivalent toward Jews and Judaism, according to Geiger; at first he wanted to please the Jews and win them over with promises of equality and efforts to accommodate their customs, but later he became hostile when their response was not positive.[20] In that way, Qur'anic passages sympathetic and unsympathetic to the Jews could be dated and interpreted by Geiger as earlier and later texts. Early Islam, then, took shape as did early Christianity, around questions of Judaism and its religious practices. Ultimately, Muhammad wanted to persuade the Jews that "his views were on the whole the same as theirs with some few differences,"[21] yet at the same time to "borrow from Judaism...so long as the Jewish views were not in direct opposition to his own."[22]

Geiger traced fourteen central themes in the Qur'an, including hell, paradise, divine presence, divine providence, resurrection and judgment, several heavens, religious law, as well as the basic Islamic belief in the unity of God, and argues that they had entered Islam either directly from rabbinic literature or from the Hebrew Bible as mediated by Jewish interpretation. For example, he traced unclear associations within a Qur'anic sura to parallels within rabbinic literature, such as a correspondence between Sura 5:32 and Mishnah Sanhedrin 4:5: "Whoever killed a human being...shall be deemed as though he had killed all mankind; and that whoever saved a human life shall be deemed as though he had saved all mankind."[23] See also Sura 5:31: "Then God sent a crow, which scratched into the earth to show him how he might hide the corpse of his brother." In Pirke de Rabbi Eliezer, the same story appears—but it is Adam who buries Abel.

Studying the Qur'an also gave Geiger a template for defining Judaism. For example, Geiger's evaluation of Muhammad's borrowings from Jewish sources allows him to assert that early Judaism was strictly monotheistic and abjured anthropomorphic imagery. In analyzing Sura 38:73–77 of the Qur'an, a passage in which the angels fall down in honor of Adam, he concludes that the passage cannot reflect Jewish tradition because worship of any being other than God would have seemed to any Jewish interpreter inconceivable.[24] Instead, he writes,

> The legend bears unmistakable marks of Christian development, in that Adam is represented in the beginning as the God-man, worthy of adoration, which the Jews are far from asserting. It is true that in Jewish writings great honor is spoken of as shown by the angels to Adam, but this never went so far as adoration; indeed when this was once about to take place in error, God frustrated the action.[25]

Geiger's analysis of the Qur'anic passage is both an interpretation of Islam and of Judaism: here he is using the Qur'an to demonstrate the boundaries of the three religions. His certainty regarding the limits of Judaism is also a denial of the possibility of Christian influence and of Jewish syncretism, or of alternative traditions within Judaism. Instead, the Qur'an serves to demonstrate an inviolable boundary between the two religions, a boundary that then makes Geiger turn to Christianity as the source of influence, a Christianity that Geiger represents as a kind of corrupted version of Judaism.

In most cases, however, Geiger asserted that Muhammad brought into the Qur'an Midrashic versions of Old Testament narratives. Those Midrashic sources could not have been transmitted to Muhammad by Christians, Geiger argued, because Christians would not have been familiar with rabbinic embellishments of biblical texts. One example is the Qur'anic and Midrashic recountings of the tower of Babel (Genesis 9:8–9). In both cases, the biblical punishment of dispersion and confusion of tongues is intensified to a curse according to which those who built the tower will be absolutely annihilated by a poisonous wind or will have no place in the next world (Sura 11:63 and Mishnah Sanhedrin 10:3).

Geiger maintained the Islamic belief that Muhammad was illiterate (as proof that the Qur'an was received from God, not written by Muhammad), in order to claim that Muhammad learned Jewish sources orally from teachers, rather than through his own study of written texts. That Muhammad was not well-educated in rabbinic texts is demonstrated, Geiger suggests, by his apparent ignorance that the biblical injunction of "an eye for an eye" had been given a monetary reinterpretation in rabbinic law. He was not an independent, learned scholar, in Geiger's portrayal, but a student who simply repeated what he happened to be told.

Geiger's book became a model for many subsequent studies of parallels between the Qur'an and Jewish texts. His work was also a "dry run" for his subsequent scholarship on early Christian texts, which Geiger similarly claimed were influenced by rabbinic ideas. Less often noticed, however, is that Geiger's argument sparked a new tradition in Jewish self-understanding, crafting a position of significance of rabbinic literature in Western history as the source out of which the Qur'an emerged. Subsequent scholars followed Geiger's model. These included the work of Isaac Gastfreund, *Mohammed nach Talmud und Midrasch* (1875); Hartwig Hirschfeld, *Jüdische Elemente im Koran* (1878); and Israel Schapiro, *Die haggadischen Elemente im erzaehlenden Teil des Korans* (1907); among others. These works were understood not only as contributions to Islamic studies, but also to the Wissenschaft des Judentums, the scholarly study of Judaism, inasmuch as they argued for the important contribution of Jewish texts to the shaping of early Islam; indeed, Schapiro's dissertation was published by the Gesellschaft zur Foerderung der Wissenschaft des Judentums.

Governing Jewish interpretations of Islamic origins included parallels with Judaism on monotheism, morality, law, theological concepts, ritual practice, and the rejection of anthropomorphism. Since Islam was not considered a product of divine revelation, Geiger's positive image of Muhammad was necessary to explain the power of his impact. Islam's greatness came through Muhammad's efforts, so he has to be a powerful personality. Furthermore, Muhammad's conquest of paganism plays an important role in Jewish self-understanding, linking Islam to Jewish claims to have been given the mission of destroying paganism. Islam then becomes a handmaiden of Judaism, furthering the antipagan cause and demonstrating the power of the Jewish monotheistic idea. Once again, there is no original religious idea in Islam. In his survey of Jewish history, written in the 1860s, Geiger wrote, "Whatever good elements Islam contains, whatever enduring idea appears in it, it has taken over from Judaism.... Judaism is the only fruit-bearing and world-conquering thought contained in Islam."[26] His claim was echoed by other Jewish scholars, such as Schapiro, who spoke in the introduction to his study of aggadic influences on the Qur'an and of the Qur'an's "dependence on Jewish texts." The Qur'an elaborated on Jewish texts as a kind of "bejeweling" of the original, Schapiro wrote. One generation earlier, Hirschfeld had written that the "Qur'an, the textbook of Islam, is in reality nothing but a counterfeit of the Bible."[27]

Subsequent Echoes

Geiger was echoed by the nineteenth-century German-Jewish historian Heinrich Graetz, whose eleven-volume *History of the Jews* popularized the kind of argument Geiger put forth. Graetz wrote that Islam "was inspired by Judaism to bring into the world a new religious form with political foundations, which one calls Islam, and it in turn exerted a powerful impact on Jewish history and the development of Judaism."[28] Graetz was also one of many Jewish historians and intellectuals who emphasized the tolerance of Islam vis-à-vis Judaism, in contrast to the intolerance of Christianity. Jewish life under Muslim rule in Spain was a "Golden Age," according to Jewish descriptions, whereas Jewish life in Christian Europe was constantly punctuated by persecutions. Shortly before his conversion to Christianity, Heinrich Heine emphasized precisely that point in his play, *Almansor,* which describes a love between a Jew and a Muslim that was forbidden and persecuted by the new Christian rulers of medieval Spain who conquered the prior Muslim rulers.[29]

Other popularizers of Jewish history wrote in a similar vein, claiming Islam as the product of Judaism, even as they distinguish (as did Geiger himself) between the religion of Islam, on the one hand, and the warfare and violent conquests carried out by Muslims, especially by Ottoman Turks, over the centuries. Yet the battlefield did not represent the religion, nor undermine its relationship to Judaism. Here is the voice of the German-Jewish philosopher of the turn of the century, Hermann Cohen: "The Jewish philosophy of the Middle Ages does not grow so much out of Islam as out of the original monotheism. The more intimate relationship between Judaism and Islam— more intimate than with other monotheistic religions—can be explained by the kinship that exists between the mother and daughter religion."[30] A sharp contrast, of course, from Cohen's well-known polemics against Christianity. Muslim society permitted the emergence of the so-called "creative symbiosis" that emerged between medieval Jewish and Muslim cultures; S. D. Goitein writes, "It was Islam which saved the Jewish People."[31]

Travelers and Converts

During the nineteenth century, some Jewish scholars were also inaugurating contacts with the Muslim world, and some left important imprints. Gustav Weil traveled with French expeditionary forces through North Africa and spent four years in Cairo studying Arabic and Turkic dialects and teaching European languages at a medical college. His time in Paris and in Cairo overlapped with the travels of the noted Egyptian philologist, Tahtawi, and it is likely they had contact, though no written record of their relationship has as yet been uncovered. Geiger, by contrast, seems not to have had relations with Muslims, nor to have traveled to Islamicate countries. Among the non-Jewish nineteenth-century scholars of Islam, Alfred von Kremer, Joseph von Hammer-Purgstall, C. H. Becker, and Aloys Sprenger spent time in Muslim countries. But the last decades of the century show a new development. From 1907 to 1914, shortly after completing his doctorate at the University of Berlin, Josef Horovitz held a professorship of Arabic at the Aligargh Muslim University; the Hungarian Max Herz, after studying at the University of Vienna, became a consultant for architectural restoration of mosques and preservation of Islamic antiquities in Cairo; Goldziher established personal relationships with scholars, religious reformers, and political leaders during his trips to Cairo and Damascus, and several of his studies of hadith and Qur'an exegesis were later translated into Arabic and published in Egypt in the mid-twentieth century.[32] Those translations, according to Josef van Ess, came primarily at the direction of Ali Hasan Abdalqadir, who taught at al-Azhar University during the 1930s and 1940s.[33] Controversies broke out in Egypt in the 1940s over the use of Goldziher's historicist approach, primarily in conjunction with the rise of the Muslim Brotherhood; Mustafa al-Sibai, founder of the Muslim Brotherhood in Syria, came to al-Azhar to study under Abdalqadir in 1939 and objected to the latter's citations of Goldziher in his lectures on Islamic law. The controversies over historicist approaches to Islamic texts limited the impact of Goldziher's work, as well as that of other European historians, in Egypt.[34]

The numerous travelogues written by Europeans who visited Muslim countries during the eighteenth and nineteenth centuries have been analyzed by scholars tracing Orientalist motifs. Fine art, music, dance, and fashion complemented the growing European textual enthrallment with the "Orient," an amalgam of India, China, the Ottoman Empire, and the Middle East. Among the travelogue writers were Christian missionaries, but also some Jews, who, far from attempting to missionize Muslims, became fascinated with Islam and began to pretend to be Muslim or even convert to Islam. These travelers include Arminius Vambery (né Hermann Bamberger), Henry Aaron Stern, William Gifford Palgrave (né Cohen), Muhammad Asad (né Leopold Weiss), and Joseph Wolff, Essed Bey (aka Kurban Said and Lev Nussimbaum). Christians such as Ernest Renan sought in Arab culture, which they held to be stagnant, a taste of the culture Jesus had experienced in first-century Palestine. While sexual fantasies fill the vast travelogue literature, such anecdotes and fantasies are generally absent from the Jewish-authored accounts.

Conversion to another religion also writes a narrative. Not only a repudiation of one's own religion, conversion also implies a narrative of the religion one enters: the new religion may be idealized, or at least be assumed to meet the needs absent from the old one. Some Jews converted formally to Islam, while others pretended to convert, wished they might, or fostered uncertainty about their religious identity. Among these were Lev Nussimbaum, aka Kurban Said and Essad Bey; Eduard Schnitzer, aka Mehmet Emin Pasha; Arminius Vambery; Margaret Marcus aka Maryam Jameelah. Of these, some became influential leaders and theologians. Jameelah, for example, claimed in later years that her conversion was largely motivated by the superficiality of her parents' Jewish commitments and the hostility of her Jewish professor, Abraham Katsh, at New York University, toward the Islamic texts he was teaching.

Perhaps the most interesting convert is Muhamad Asad. Born Leopold Weiss in 1900 in Lemberg, he studied art history and psychoanalysis at the University of Vienna in 1918–20, where two of his maternal uncles, Aryeh and Dorian (Isador) Feigenbaum, also from Lemberg, were studying medicine. Weiss then moved to Berlin and worked as a journalist, specializing in Middle Eastern politics. In 1920 his uncles moved to Jerusalem to practice ophthalmology (Aryeh) and psychiatry (Dorian). In 1922, at the invitation of his uncles, Weiss went to Jerusalem, via Egypt, for an extended visit; he stayed two years with Dorian Feigenbaum, a bachelor. Dorian had trained as a psychoanalyst in Vienna and was close to the circle around Freud. His own analyst was Otto Gross, notorious as an anarchist, who died in 1920 from a drug overdose.[35] In January 1921, Dorian was appointed head of the only psychiatric hospital in Palestine, located in Jerusalem, Ezrat Nashim, which served a heterogeneous population of Jews, Muslims, and Christians.

Both Weiss and Feigenbaum published similar criticisms of Zionist efforts in Palestine that were inattentive to the subjective, spiritual condition of the Jews. The high suicide rate among Zionist pioneers was due, according to Feigenbaum, to the trauma suffered by Jews not only in the harsh economic conditions of Palestine, but prior experiences of persecution in the countries they had abandoned.[36] Weiss wrote of a "malady" of Zionism in assuming that a homeland was the cure for the "bitter fate of the Jewish people." In an article he published in a German newspaper in 1923, Weiss wrote, "Those who advocate this idea [homeland] act blindly regarding the reasons for the people's misery and longings; they seek to circumvent them and cover them up—and this is precisely the reason for Judaism's sickness!"[37]

In his purported autobiography, *Road to Mecca,* written thirty years later, Asad wrote that going to Palestine was a return: "My coming to this land, was it not, in truth a home coming?"[38] While in Palestine, Weiss met with Arabs and with Zionist leaders and intellectuals, including Menachem Ussishkin (president of the Jewish National Fund), Chaim Weizmann (later the first president of Israel), and Jacob de Haan. A turning point came in 1924, when Weiss witnessed the public humiliation of his uncle, Dorian Feigenbaum, who was fired from his hospital after delivering the Yishuv's first lectures on Freud, whose ideas outraged the reactionary intellectuals of Jerusalem. Protests against the firing abounded, including letters to the local newspaper from Hugo Samuel Bergmann, one of the leading intellectuals of Jerusalem and a patient of Feigenbaum's, but to no avail. Dorian Feigenbaum eventually left for a position at Columbia University's medical school in New York City, where he became a leading psychoanalyst and cofounder, in 1932, of the distinguished journal, *Psychoanalytic Quarterly.* Palestine's psychoanalytic community was not reconstituted until the arrival of Max Eitingon in 1935, when the Berlin Psychoanalytic Institute closed its doors to Jews.

Weiss left Palestine as well, returning to Berlin, where he married a German woman and joined his wife in converting to Islam. Neither Zionist politics nor family troubles fully accounts for the conversion of Leopold Weiss into Muhammad Asad, but the kinds of issues he debated in the Zionist context—nationalism, colonialism, and the inadequacy of a political response to Jewish suffering—continued at the forefront of his writings within the Islamic context. During the 1930s, he entered into correspondence with Muhammad Iqbal, a distinguished writer and influential political theorist in India who wrote extensively on the nature of an Islamic state and is credited with inspiring the creation of Pakistan, issues not without parallel to Zionist discussions. In examining Asad's writings of the 1930s, Yossef Schwartz has compared his concerns to those of the Jewish philosopher Franz Rosenzweig; both, Schwartz argues, were looking for religiosity, not for the dogmatic religious establishment, and both saw the act of prayer as basic to religion and were unsatisfied with the Jewish religious environment in which they were raised.[39] Certainly the corpus of Asad's writings demonstrate both religious and political concerns, and reveal an intellectual who kept a critical distance from the dogmatic positions prevalent in his day. His 1934 book, *Islam at the Crossroads,* rejects both the nascent religious extremism within the Muslim world and also serves as a precursor to postcolonial theory in its critique of the West. A similar voice can be heard in his magnum opus, his multivolume translation and commentary of the Qur'an, originally published in the 1980s, which is widely read to this day and regarded as a banner of liberal Islamic theology.

No study has gathered demographic data on European Jewish converts to Islam, and conversion narratives are notoriously unreliable, so no definitive conclusions regarding motivation can be drawn. However, the conversion of Jews to Islam at minimum suggests an additional dimension to the Jewish admiration for Islam. It also raises the question of the transfer of ideas from Judaism to Islam; when Muhammad Asad left behind the intense Jewish debates over statehood in which he engaged for many years in Lemberg, Vienna, Berlin, and Jerusalem, and joined Muhammad Iqbal in trying to conceive the nature of a Muslim state in Pakistan, did he bring Zionist debates to the nascent Pakistan? The question requires further study. .

Zionism

Judaism, Sidra Ezrahi writes, is a mimetic religion. A culture of substitution in all the lands of their dispersion, such as Zionism, implied a reconnection with the original space that was "perceived as the bedrock of the collective self."[40] What is longed for in Zionism is supposed to be what is remembered: the spaces and moments of biblical history. Yet, as Ezrahi writes, memory is imagined, "as mimesis takes on the authority and license of memory and memory becomes an article of faith."[41]

The role of mimesis in the Jewish fascination with Islam and, especially, Arab Muslims and the Bedouin of Palestine, intensified in the early Zionist movement. As Gil Eyal writes, early Zionists, arriving in Palestine at the turn of the century, required a "myth of autochthony, a project of inventing a new Hebrew culture, almost out of whole cloth, and for this very reason it required the mask of the Arab."[42] Zionism meant a negation of exile, but also a romantic appropriation of Orientalism; the Jew was now the Arab. In a pamphlet published in 1946, Shlomo Dov Goitein, who trained in Islamic studies under Josef Horovitz at the University of Frankfurt, wrote that Zionists, children of the Orient, should learn Arabic as part of their "return to the Hebrew language and to the Semitic Orient."[43]

Zionism meant a negation of Jewish exile, a rejection of Europe and its anti-Semitism, but at the same time, Zionism began with an appropriation of European Orientalism, despite its links to anti-Semitic discourse. Zionists in Palestine, recently arrived from Europe, rode camels and wore keffiyahs. Joseph Klausner gives us a cynical description of the phenomenon: "If a Jew happens to adopt Bedouin customs; if he manages to ride a horse and shoot a gun and wear an Arab robe—right away our Hebrew writers get excited.... If the establishment of a Jewish Yishuv in Erets Israel [means]...assimilation into Arab backwardness, it is better to stay in the Diaspora and assimilate into the enlightened Western culture."[44]

Early Zionist writers embraced the Orient as the original, authentic Jewish identity, even while rendering the Arab population obsolete and holding the Mizrahim, Jews from Muslim and Arab countries, in contempt. "From the outset," writes Amnon Raz-Krakotzkin, "Zionist discourse was premised upon the adoption of orientalist attitudes, and orientalism was essential to the nationalization of the Jewish collectivity and the ways in which the nation was imagined."[45] Performance and mimicry were, of course, essential components of Orientalism. The Orient was an identity to be assumed and performed; its authenticity lay in its appropriation by Westerners and the Orient's negation lay with Arabs and Mizrahi Jews, much like Christians who celebrate Hebrew but vilify the Jew. The adoption of Bedouin customs and the encouragement of Arabic language study by Jews seemed to be tools to fashion a new Jewish identity. Who, then, was to be the real Oriental, the Jew or the Arab? Was authenticity rooted in the mimetic efforts of the European Jews adopting Oriental dress, or in the lives of Jewish immigrants from Arab lands?

Initially, Zionist historiography was devoted to Jews of the Arab world; the first series of the journal *Zion* was devoted to Oriental and Palestinian Jewry. Yet in that same year, 1936, the denial of Mizrahi history began and historians shifted to the study of European Jews, while anthropologists were assigned to study Orientals.[46] Those shifts were accompanied by a growing ambivalence toward the Orientalist nature of the Zionist project. Arabic language study in Jewish schools in Palestine fell into disfavor, Mizrahi immigrants were viewed as uncultured, and the Hebrew University did not implement the curricular plan formulated by Josef Horovitz in the mid-1920s for its Institute for Oriental Studies. Horovitz had called for dual languages at the Institute, in Hebrew and Arabic, and in addition to the European philological methods of Islamic studies, classes taught by Islamic imams on contemporary theological and legal debates in the Muslim world.[47] For a variety of reasons, including Horovitz's sudden death in 1931, his vision was not realized. Nonetheless, the study of Islam became an important and admired field in Israeli universities.

Conclusion

Where does this lead? Jews dominated the field of Arabic and Islamic studies in Germany in the 1920s and 1930s, a field that was devastated by Hitler and took decades to recover in postwar Europe. But the fascination has left other legacies. The scholarship of Geiger, Goldziher, and the many other Jews fascinated by Islam continues to be profoundly appreciated to this day. At the same time, already in the nineteenth century there were always some Jewish countervoices, such as Ludwig Philippson, and Jewish views of Islam shifted in the twentieth century.[48] The German-Jewish theologian Franz Rosenzweig, for example, was far more ambivalent toward Islam than was Hermann Cohen. On the other hand, another significant German-Jewish thinker, Leo Strauss, forged an important alliance between Judaism and Islam on the question of modernity and secularization.[49]

There is also a more popular legacy of Islam. Few Jews developed a comparable interest in other areas of the Orient, such as India, China, or Japan. Orientalism in the Jewish context usually implied Islam, or at least fantasies about Islamicate culture. Such fantasies were expressed in broader Jewish cultural terms. The Moorish architecture of a vast number of synagogues built in Europe, Britain, and the United States suggests that Islam was perceived to be able to stand as a signifier for Judaism, whereas the Christian Gothic architecture, virtually never employed, cannot. Gothic architecture, for example, is too closely identified with Christianity and thus swallows other traditions into its own framework.

Finally, there are the politics of the field. Edward Said determined too much of our thinking in his insistence that Orientalism was the product of empire—ignoring, of course, German scholarship and Jewish scholarship. Suzanne Marchand views German Oriental studies as a set of practices in Central European institutions, frequently motivated by a desire to find the origins of Christianity in the East—anywhere, in fact, apart from Judaism.[50] European historiography of Islam continued to be impregnated with theological assumptions. Christian scholars denigrated its system of religious law, while Jewish scholars fashioned an image of a liberal, acculturated Islam not dissimilar from their image of modern, liberal Judaism.

For Jews, the study of Islam was a tool for reshaping Judaism. In contrast to Said's claims regarding European Orientalism, Jewish scholarship on Islam was not the product of nationalism or imperialist interests, but rather it blunted the forces of nationalism, seeking theological alliances between West and East, Judaism and Islam, blurring distinctions of religious practice and belief between the two religions. Most Jewish scholars emphasized Judaism's role in creating Islam, denying Islam's originality, as well as Christianity's. Yet that ethnic chauvinism has its limits, too, as Patricia Crone has pointed out in relation to Goldziher, who "could have made an effortless case for the theory that Jewish law contributed heavily to the Shari'a; yet time and again he opted for the view that it was 'a bygone stage of Roman legal history' which made the contribution."[51]

Nonetheless, there is an undeniable insistence on the part of Jewish scholars that Judaism is the progenitor of Islam and Christianity. Why do Jews claim this so strongly? Rather than a process of disenchantment or secularization, the strong Jewish interest in Islam was a process of intertwining, of understanding one religion—Judaism—through the other, by establishing linkages and influences.

Ultimately, Jews saw in Islam that which was important to them within Judaism, an ethical monotheism, and just as they created a *Kulturjudaismus*, a Judaism in accord with the liberal culture of their era, they did likewise for Islam. Their scholarship created a *Kulturislamismus*, describing Islam as a rational, philosophical, law-adhering, family-centered, highly moral religion. Yet could we not also consider the reverse: a Judaism reconceived by Jewish thinkers after the image they created of Sunni Islam, as a rational religion without mysticism, apocalypticism, or anthropomorphism, rooted in philosophical ideas, monotheism, sexual restraint, patriarchal family, ritual law, and stringent morality. These German-Jewish thinkers created an alliance between Judaism and their idealized image of Islam to bolster their definition of Judaism as a religion of ethical monotheism. And always, Jews insisted that Islam, like Christianity, was born of Judaism, even as their newly conceived, modern, liberal Judaism was born, in part, out of their imagined Islam.

Chapter 11

Bible, Translation, and Culture

From the KJV to the Christian Resurgence in Africa

Lamin Sanneh

While Christianity has been in sharp decline in its historic European heartlands, it has been undergoing a striking resurgence in modern Africa and elsewhere, taking knowledgeable observers by surprise.[1] The normal expectation was that in the age of nationalism Christian missions would come to an end to signal the end of Christianity in Africa. In the meantime, unable to make a dent on Islam in its impregnable North African heartlands, Christian Europe accepted the situation as "the end of an era," the title of a sober appraisal by a veteran missionary.[2] From its origins Islam has presented a challenge to Christian Europe. In North Africa the Islamic wave washed away the remnants of Roman civilization. About three hundred columns from the nearby Roman and Byzantine buildings were used by the Muslim victors in the construction of the great mosque of Qayrawan that emerged as an eminent seat of Islamic legal scholarship with an influence extending over Muslim West Africa. The only evidence of the long Roman occupation in Ghadames were a few Doric and Corinthian columns incorporated into the two principal mosques there.[3] Following their swift conquest in the seventh century, the new Muslim rulers in Egypt allowed the hard-pressed Coptic Christian community to exist as a restricted enclave, while Ethiopia could be discounted in the drive to subdue Christian Nubia and beyond.

Medieval missions attempted but failed to penetrate the Muslim shield in Egypt and North Africa, and that produced a negative outlook on prospects further south in sub-Saharan Africa.[4] Ethiopia had been sending emissaries to Rome since 1402 without obtaining any response. Finally, in 1443 Ethiopian observers turned to the Council of Florence to appeal for mission to the kingdom. The Ethiopian overture, followed shortly by the debacle of the Fall of Constantinople in 1453, awakened the interest of Portugal in opening channels of outreach beyond the Islamic confinement and was a stimulus in the organization of the maritime explorations of Spain and Portugal. In that effort the Portuguese built in 1482 a massive trading fortress, called São Jorge da Mina, or Elmina, on the Gold Coast.[5] As bastions of trade, these fortresses dispensed with the idea of mission, and when convenient, which was most of the time, with the idea of religion as well.[6]

When in the first half of the nineteenth century Catholic missions in North Africa were challenged to venture beyond their Islamic quarantine and expand into sub-Saharan Africa they rejected the idea as unfeasible because of the barrier of the desert, though it should be pointed out that for Islam the desert was a centuries-long well-trodden pathway. At any rate, by the nineteenth century small settlements of Christians had been established in Freetown and Liberia on the west coast of Africa within striking range of Nigeria as a particularly promising field. Despite prevailing ideas about mission as essentially a narrative of European interests and values, by this point African pioneers had turned the Christian narrative into one that is reflective of their own history and hopes. It is with this indigenous narrative that Christian fortunes in modern Africa became intertwined.

This narrative, however, stands in stark contrast to late-twentieth-century assessments of the role and impact of colonialism. The huge response to Edward Said's argument in his book, *Orientalism,* that the West's goal of hegemony and domination was achieved by essentializing the Other as remote and strange, shows the potency of the imperialist stigma. With particular reference to the rise of Christianity in modern Africa, anthropologists Jean and John Comaroff contended that mission "hinged upon the effort of a few men, with loosely shared social origins, to impose an entire worldview upon their would-be subjects." The missionaries

> set out to save Africa: to make her peoples the subjects of a world-wide Christian commonwealth. In so doing they were self-consciously acting out of a new vision of global history, setting up new frontiers of European consciousness, and naming new forms of humanity to be entered onto its map of civilized mankind.... Their assault [was] driven by a universalizing ethos whose prime object was to engage the

Africans in a web of symbolic and material transactions that would bind them ever more securely to the colonizing culture. Only that way would the savage finally be drawn into the purview of a global, rationalized civilization.[7]

The unfolding picture of Christianity in the course of the nineteenth century is unquestionably one in which the African narrative became dominant as the religion reached a turning point on the continent. That narrative was about new possibilities for the religion as a historical intercultural movement invested in the rising aspirations of a new generation of Africans. It placed a new and special responsibility on the educated class of African leaders to make credible the idea of modern Africa as a postslavery society that is as committed to reform as it is to renewal of custom and tradition. The instrument for this double task belonged with the idea of mission as an intercultural process, and that was the vernacular Bible, where the new Africa and the old Africa came into creative convergence. A 1982 report published in the *New York Times* revealed how old and new Africa found extensive common ground in Christianity. The report noted that "travelers will still be treated to scenes such as that reported by a Westerner here, of 21-year old Irish missionaries, deep in the bush, stammering through the liturgy in the local Chinyanja language, under roofs of thatch in distant villages—incongruous redeemers."[8] The vernacular idiom adopted in Bible translation realigned the role of missionary and local agent in a common enterprise.

Shortly after my studies in classical Islam at the American University of Beirut, Lebanon, I arrived in Ibadan, Nigeria, to assume the position of tutor in Islamic Studies. A senior colleague, a long-serving English missionary who first came to Nigeria during colonial rule, agreed to accompany me to Dugbe market to purchase some furnishings for my flat. Being fluent in Yoruba, the missionary was known by the local name of Adebayo. As we were doing the round of the stalls it slowly dawned on the people that the white man was translating for his African companion, and that caused quite a stir. Whole corridors of stall-keepers erupted into laughter with clapping, rolling, and calling out their neighbors to watch the incredible spectacle. Was it true or was it contrived for their mid-afternoon amusement, they wondered? As the dust settled and the hubbub subsided the people started visibly to absorb the information that Adebayo acquired his language expertise in the course of his duties as a missionary to the Yoruba, whereas the African came from another part of the continent.

The missionary crossed the language boundary by becoming fluent in the idiom; the African as African had no need to be fluent without the missionary vocation. It was not the standard picture of mission, but, on reflection, the stall-keepers welcomed the fact. It took several decades for a corresponding shift of perspective to dawn on me, namely, that Christianity in Africa had been a multilingual affair at home in the idioms and dialects of the people. The religion's cultural breakthrough was a centuries-long development, not a momentary diversion on an afternoon shopping jaunt. Built on the basis of the orthographies, grammars, and dictionaries the missionary movement created, Christianity was inscribed into indigenous forms and expressions to become a stimulus for awakening and renewal in Africa, with consequences not only for indigenous societies but also for claims of uncontested colonial hegemony. Christianity was invested in languages and cultural materials that existed for purposes other than for Christianity and whose acknowledgment powered the Christian movement. These materials were there before Christianity, and subsequently thrived in it and by it. The question of cultural and linguistic diversity as an integral part of Bible translation was taken up by the translators of the King James Bible.

Language and Translation from the KJV to the Yoruba Bible

We should emphasize that scriptural translation is not alien to Christianity even though in much of its premodern history it has been marked by sectarian bad blood. After all, Tertullian (ca. 160–ca. 240), who converted to Christianity in 195, expressed supporting ideas about the Gospel in the languages of the peoples of the world, as did Irenaeus (ca. 130–ca. 200) and numerous others after them.[9] The translators of the King James Bible cited Theodoret of Cyrrhus (d. ca. 458) to the effect that by his time Scripture had been translated into the languages of the Greeks, Romans, Egyptians, Persians, Indians, Armenians, Scythians, Sauromatians, "and, briefly, into all the languages that any nation useth." In the list of translations they included Gothic, Arabic, Saxon, French, Slavic, and Dutch. "So that, to have the Scriptures in the mother tongue is not a quaint conceit lately taken up... but hath been thought upon, and put in practice of old, even from the first times of the conversion of any nation; no doubt, because it was esteemed most profitable to cause faith to grow in men's hearts the sooner, and to make them able to say with the words of the Psalm, 'As we have heard, so we have seen'" (Ps. 48: 8).[10]

All this suggests that the Bible was a major force in providing a measure of unity and continuity for the scattered communities of faith across space and time. As Peter Brown has shown, this was especially true in the age following the collapse of the Roman Empire, including the centuries of the ascendancy of Islamic power.[11] The sense of oneness that infused the many members of the body of faith was in specific respects often more meaningful than political ties.

It is not merely that the different languages of the world, including English, constituted an obstacle the church must overcome to establish the faith, but that Christianity is invested in languages and idioms that existed for purposes other than for Christianity, and whose basic value system flourished with the Christian impact. Accordingly, the translators of the King James Bible affirmed their "desire that the Scripture may speak like itself, as in the language of *Canaan,* that it may be understood even of the very vulgar." The originality of the religion resides in the common idiom of translation, an originality that resembles the incarnation in which the "word became flesh."[12]

That is the fundamental case the King James Bible stood to make, as the translators affirmed when they argued that the Apostles intended to include all languages in the witness of Scripture, and to except none,

> not Hebrew the ancientest, not Greek the most copious, not Latin the finest. Nature taught a natural man to confess, that all of us in those tongues which we do not understand are plainly deaf.... Therefore as one complaineth that always in the Senate of Rome there was one or other that called for an interpreter; so lest the Church be driven to the like exigent, it is necessary to have translations in a readiness. Translation it is that openeth the window, to let in the light... that removeth the cover of the well, that we may come by the water; even as Jacob rolled away the stone from the mouth of the well, by which means the flocks of Laban were watered. Indeed without translation into the vulgar tongue, the unlearned are but like children at Jacob's well (which was deep) without a bucket or something to draw with.[13]

The experience of Pentecost (Acts 2: 1–13) had among its disconcerting effects the loosening and anointing of the Gentile tongue, and scriptural translation established that fact as an enduring witness to God's unforgettable promises. If Pentecost was a novel experience, the truth of it is original to God's sovereign design of universal redemption and reconciliation. For Christians, the one God is "in all the world" by virtue of, not in spite of, the sundry and manifold tongues of witness cultivated—and yet to be cultivated—in Scripture, worship, prayer, and devotion. In that witness no language is forbidden, and none is a prerequisite.

In the hands of Bible translators, the religious view of language can be construed as far more radical in its unqualified welcome of language, any language, than a purely utilitarian view in which languages of scale weigh more heavily in the balance of merit. The translators of the King James Bible asserted that before God, all languages are equal as much in their merit as in their demerit, for which reason none has an in-built advantage or disadvantage. For them, all languages share in the consequences of fallen human nature, just as, by virtue of Bible translation, all languages share equally in the benefits of God's intervention in Christ. Scriptural translation is not an exercise in linguistic perfection; it is a willing and attentive inquiry into God's mind and purpose. "We never thought," the translators declared, "from the beginning that we should need to make a new translation, nor yet to make of a bad one a good one;... To that purpose there were many chosen, that were greater in other men's eyes than in their own, and that sought the truth rather than their own praise."[14] Undeterred by the pitfalls of human fallibility, the biblical writers set to work with the unwavering confidence that their commission was from God. It is in that sense that the Bible is sui generis. A focus other than that may produce a technically correct translation, but not the Bible as the heritage of faith and devotion. The translators emphasized the role of the Spirit in conveying the truth of Scripture, saying their own role was ultimately dispensable.

> Therefore, the word of God, being set forth in the Greek, becometh hereby like a candle-stick, which giveth light to all that are in the house; or like a proclamation sounded forth in the market-place, which most men presently take knowledge of; and therefore that language was fittest to contain the Scriptures, both for the first preachers of the Gospel to appeal unto for witness, and for the learners also of those times to make search and trial by. It is certain, that the translation was not so sound and so perfect, but that it needed in many places correction; and who had been so sufficient for this work as the Apostles or apostolick men? Yet it seemed good to the Holy Ghost and to them to take that which they found... rather than by making a new, in that new world and green age of the Church, to expose themselves to many exceptions and cavillations, as though they made a translation to serve their own turn; and therefore bearing witness to themselves, their witness not to be regarded.[15]

The importance of language as a native treasure that was at stake for the translators of the King James Bible was also taken up by Shakespeare with characteristic eloquence in his *Richard II* where Lord Mowbray, the Duke of Norfolk, anguishes about what the foreign exile the king imposed on him implied for his native tongue.

> The language I have learned these forty years,
> My native English, now I must forego;
> And now my tongue's use is to me no more
> Than an unstringed viol or a harp,
> Or like a cunning instrument cas'd up
> Or, being open, put into the hands
> That knows no touch to tune the harmony.
> Within my mouth you have enjail'd my tongue,
> Doubly portcullis'd with my teeth and lips...
> What is thy sentence then but speechless death,
> Which robs my tongue from breathing native breath.

As to Shakespeare's religious views, his biographer describes them simply as calculating and rational, unlike those of Christopher Marlowe, his contemporary, which are hostile or cynical.[16] The unchained native tongue that is well attuned to natural harmony becomes the vehicle of the imaginative life, and as such the heart of the cultural process.

The great popularity of the KJV in the English-speaking world established it as a standard for the idioms of subject populations of the colonial empire. The promoters of vernacular Bible translation invoked the KJV in their efforts in Nigeria. In a coauthored book designed to introduce the teaching of the vernacular in schools in Nigeria, the writers cited a tribute to the KJV that they rendered into Igbo in a parallel translation. "No book has had an equal influence on the English people. Apart from its religious considerations, it gave to all classes alike an idiom in which the deepest emotions of life could be recalled. It gives grace to the speech of the unlettered and entered into the style of the most ambitious writers. Its phrasing coloured the work of poets, and its language has so embedded itself into our national tradition that if the Bible is forgotten, a precious possession will be lost."[17]

For Samuel Ajayi Crowther and his African contemporaries it was the KJV that supplied the dignified language of religion and the norms of translation, of which Crowther was the distinguished African leader. A linguist and the first African bishop of Nigeria, he translated and published portions of the Bible into Yoruba between 1850 and 1851, with the full New Testament appearing in 1862, and the first complete Bible in 1884. Born in about 1806 in Oshogun, the boy Crowther was captured by Muslim Yoruba forces and sold as a slave to a Portuguese slave ship in Lagos. By a series of remarkable circumstances he and hundreds of other African slaves were eventually rescued in the course of their trans-Atlantic passage in April 1822, by the British Naval Squadron and disembarked in Freetown. There Crowther came under missionary instruction that led in time to his ordination. Crowther's Yoruba New Testament translation was the first in an African language—done by an African with African materials for African use. Rendered in the Oyo dialect, his Bible became the Yoruba KJV, as revered and honored today as it ever was. A common criticism is that Crowther's translation has so dominated the field that it has discouraged a fresh and more contemporary translation to be undertaken.

For his linguistic labors, Crowther turned field anthropologist long before the discipline existed. Yet even by the standards of those antediluvian days his method of inquiry can withstand today's stringent tests. His edition of the Yoruba *Grammar and Vocabulary,* published in 1852, had the benefit of extensive consultations with leading linguists of the day, including Samuel Lee of Cambridge, Max Müller of Oxford, and Carl Lepsius of Berlin whose orthography helped open avenues into the documentation of several Nigerian languages, including Hausa, Kanuri, Igbo, and Ijaw. Crowther reflected on the challenges of reducing a language to writing for the first time, saying he did so by working diligently to get behind colloquial speech and slang. To do that he befriended informants without respect to their religious affiliation, and in his words, "watched the mouth of elders," in order to note down "suitable and significant words," pondering how the words would have been uttered with "the eloquence of the native assembly," in the words of David Livingstone.[18] When he came on words that were on the verge of extinction, he said their historical value persuaded him to retain them because in time, transfused with the merits of Christian usage, "to the rising generation, they will sound sweet and agreeable." He continued: "In tracing out words and their various uses, I am now and then led to search at length into some traditions or customs of the Yoruba."[19] When his house burned down in a fire in 1862, he wrote that his collections of language research, all eleven years' worth, had perished in the fire. To him that work was invaluable, and he now recalled their loss like a dream gone. Undeterred, Crowther continued with his work in language and Bible translation. Eventually his revised dictionary was published in 1870.

Few people saw more clearly the imperative and value of custom and culture for vernacular Bible translation, and few were more assiduous at such an early date in cultivating an indigenous direction for the enterprise.

In important ways Crowther was the William Tyndale of Africa, his extraordinary labors the KJV project writ small. Even in his lifetime he was a living legend, what one historian called "missions' greatest propaganda weapon,"[20] thinking specifically of his value to the antislavery cause. Like Tyndale, Crowther considered his translation work his life's bequest. Writing to London in January 1860, he pleaded with the Church Missionary Society, his employer, to allow him to relinquish leadership of the mission to Nigeria. His age and declining health, he appealed, had made the road life particularly onerous. When approached to be consecrated as the first African bishop, he again pleaded to be exempted. "I should like to spend the remainder of my days among my own people, pursuing my translations as my bequest to the nation."[21] London would not budge in either case. Crowther would soldier on against European missionary colleagues who resented his standing as a leader among them. The resentment reveals the scope of the impact of Bible translation in mission on relations between Europeans and subject populations, and Crowther's career, checkered as it was, was an endorsement of the indigenous cause and an inconvenient obstacle for a hegemonic colonial order. Still, the rising resentment would haunt his final days.

In any event, on the issue of custom and culture for Bible translation, Crowther addressed in 1869 a meeting of clergy under his direction, giving them instructions about the background research necessary for communicating the Gospel. He said he knew opinions differed on the subject but insisted that it was not given to the Christian witness to despise local culture just because of its unfamiliar and elemental expressions. It would be wrong and unproductive to fabricate or impose a replacement. Instead of condemning amusements as immoral, indecent, and corrupting, for example, they should be studied in the light of Scripture for the value that sustained them. Without that intentional attitude, as the translators of the KJV observed in their case, the old materials would appear to the uninstructed as beggarly rudiments, merely musty and full of contagious heresies.

The Gospel is invested in the vernacular materials that preceded it, and whose cultivation boosted knowledge of salvation among unevangelized populations, leading them to reclaim their cherished tribal ways as "an inheritance immortal, undefiled, and that shall never fade away."[22] Crowther made it a rule consistently to employ terms already in use rather than to invent new ones, including amusements.

> Of these kinds of amusements are fables, story-telling, proverbs and songs which may be regarded as stores of . . . national education in which [people] exercise their power of thinking [because such amusements

tend to relieve the mind and sharpen the intellect]. Their religious terms and ceremonies should be carefully observed; the wrong use made of such terms does not depreciate their real value, but renders them more valid when we adopt them in expressing Scriptural terms in their right senses and places from which they have been misapplied for want of better knowledge.[23]

Under the new religious dispensation, the old rites and ceremonies did not exist for memory only, but for salvific instruction. It is a rule of translation "that which they falsely or vainly attributed to these things for bodily good, we may justly and with full measure ascribe unto Scripture, for spiritual [good]."[24] When it is true to its calling, Christianity is not sent "to destroy national assimilation," Crowther insisted. Through Bible translation Christianity refashioned a faithful narrative of indigenous reorientation in a period of challenge and change.

That brings up one more time the invaluable role of local agents for mission. More than "college-trained men," Crowther pointed out, the real agents of the spread of the Gospel were "farmers, carpenters, merchants, masons, court messengers, stewards on ships and the like by profession...as men of proven character."[25] The cause of the vernacular Bible spawned confidence in local agency, and the fact that Scripture in the vernacular loses nothing of its divine merit, as the KJV translators emphasized, offered a moral challenge to the entitlements of colonial suzerainty. Thomas Cranmer was invoked in this context to support calls for creating an African liturgy to consolidate the gains of the vernacular Bible.[26]

Indeed the key to having the Bible in the mother tongue is worship and the liturgy it gives rise to. While still living in Freetown, Sierra Leone, where he was resettled after his miraculous rescue from a slave ship in 1822, Crowther was at the center on the occasion of the first celebration of the Yoruba liturgy in 1844. The surviving account portrays the occasion as historic.

A large number of Africans crowded thither to hear the words of the prayer and praise for the first time in their own tongue in an English church. "Although it was my own native language," says Rev. S. Crowther, "with which I am well acquainted, yet on this occasion it appeared as if I were a babe, just learning to utter my mother-tongue. The work in which I was engaged, the place where I stood, and the congregation before me, were altogether so new and strange, that the whole proceeding seemed to myself like a dream.... At the conclusion of the blessing, the whole church rang with *ke oh sheh*—so let it be, so let it be!"[27]

In the people's idiom Christian Scripture supplied the requisite text for personal self-realization. Africans rushed to the translated Bible to seek answers to their pressing problems, and also because amidst the restrictions and other disadvantages of colonial domination the Bible offered them written assurance of continuity and solidarity with the promises of the family of Abraham.[28] When a local Christian held a translated Gospel in his hands for the first time, he declared: "Here is a document which proves that we also are human beings—the first and only book in our language."[29] Equally exultantly, a Christian in Angola celebrated holding the Gospels in his hands for the first time, affirming, "Now we see that our friends in the foreign country regard us as people worth while."[30] At an assembly of local Christians when a Wesleyan missionary produced the complete Bible, an elder declared, "I know that in my body I am a very little man, but to-day as I see the whole Bible in my language I feel as big as a mountain." Another echoed him: "I wish that I were as big as an ox, or had the voice of an ox, so that I might shout the great joy which I feel."[31] These examples had in common the fact that vernacular translation amounted to a historic event for indigenous populations, and that the mother tongue was fertile soil for the new religion. It presented Christianity as arriving where it belonged, its new message brimming with the narrative power of the mother tongue. The excitement was understandable.

Mission and Vernacular Translation: Challenging Enlightenment and Colonialism

Much of what came to transpire in Africa with the post-Western Christian resurgence was predicted by writers who made the shift of perspective regarding the importance of the indigenous narrative. Even though he was dogged by much foot-dragging and official obstruction, Diedrich Westermann, for example, the German missionary-linguist, contended that Bible translation would contribute to African advancement in education and sow the seeds of cultural renewal as the assured basis for an acculturated Christianity, with an effect on the rest of society far greater than anything secular education alone could achieve. Writing in 1925 from his academic chair at the University of Berlin, Westermann advanced reasons why vernacular translation was essential to the whole psychology of recasting Christianity in the idiom and psyche of an indigenous culture. Translation was empowerment. "In this sense we speak of the soul of a people, and the most immediate, the most adequate exponent of the soul of a people is its language. By taking away a people's language, we cripple or destroy its soul and kill its mental individuality. . . . If the Christian

Church in Africa is to be really African and really Christian, it must be built upon the basis of the indigenous peculiarities and gifts of the people, it must become part of the African genius, and these will for ever be embedded in the mother language."[32] In views identical to those of Westermann, Edwin Smith, a translator of the Ila New Testament in Zambia, observed that the mother tongue is the music of the heart and home. Persons may learn many languages, but they will pray in their own, as they make love in their own. The speech that comes to people in their mother's milk is the most precious thing they have. "Every language is a temple in which the soul of the people who speak it is enshrined. If it is sinful to exterminate them bodily, it is no less sinful to destroy their individuality."[33] Smith opposed foisting a ready-made Christianity on Africans, saying the African "cannot be treated as if he were a European who happened to be born black. He ought not to be regarded as if he were a building so badly constructed that it must be torn down, its foundations torn up and a new structure erected on its site, on a totally new plan and with entirely new materials," because "to insist upon an African abandoning his own language and to speak and think in a language so different as English, is like demanding that the various Italian peoples should learn Chinese in order to overcome their linguistic problem."[34]

Smith stated the reasons, as he saw them, why scriptural translation coalesces with mother tongue impulses to fuel sources and forms of narrative expression, why Bible translation avoids artificial or foreign materials that restrict the imagination to little beyond current or contemporary fashion. He observed that

> men need two kinds of language, in fact; a language of the home, of emotion, of unexpressed associations; and a language of knowledge, exact argument, scientific truth, one in which words are world-current and steadfast in their meanings.... To express the dear and intimate things which are the very breath and substance of life a man will fall back on the tongue he learnt not at school, but in the house—how, he remembers not. He may bargain in the other, or pass examinations in it, but he will pray in his home speech. If you wish to reach his heart you will address him in that language.[35]

The development of mother tongues under the aegis of Bible translation was a radical departure from the Enlightenment legacy of the quest for one language as the *Ur-sprache,* as the mother of all languages.[36] Bible translators were confident that linguistic diversity was integral to the richness of cultures and societies, a position that often conflicted as much with the interests of colonial power as with the language policy of nation building and educational reform.

The linguistic diversity that was a consequence of the policy of Bible translation called for a fundamental change in colonial policy in spite of the disadvantages involved in promoting African languages without much of a written literature suitable for use in schools. In 1923 the Education Committee of the Conference of Missionary Societies in Great Britain and Ireland submitted a memorandum to the Secretary of State for the Colonies on the subject of education in the colonies in Africa, calling for greater resources to be devoted to the issue than the missions commanded. In the memorandum, the mission societies stressed the importance of religion broadly understood and moral instruction as a safeguard against cultural alienation and disenchantment.[37]

In colonial north Nigeria the administration introduced an education code in 1926 called the Education (Colony and Southern Provinces) Ordinance. It prescribed vernacular languages in primary and secondary education. The preamble stated: "Among infants and younger children all instruction should as far as possible be given in that vernacular or language [sic] by means of which the new ideas presented to their minds are most readily explained.... The free development of their minds must not be hampered by making the assimilation of new ideas unnecessarily difficult by presenting them in a language not readily understood."[38]

The future first prime minister of an independent Nigeria, Abubakar Tafawa-Balewa, became a teacher at Bauchi Middle School under the terms of the education code. Intending to hold the attention of his pupils, Tafawa-Balewa devised an ingenious pneumonic piece on pedagogy called, "The City of Language," in which he compared the grammatical parts of speech to the parts of a hierarchical Hausa city.[39]

Tafawa-Balewa appreciated what the vernacular channel offered by way of a creative outlet for young minds—and for gifted teachers. Without the development of the vernacular in Bible translation, for example, there would have been such a dearth of materials as to make the task an almost impossible one to conceive and to undertake. A teacher in Benin Province pointed out that problem, lamenting the fact that no textbooks existed in the language in question, and no standard orthography, either, all of which confronted teachers and students with daunting challenges. The one ray of hope came from missionary efforts—so many Adebayos made the task seem less daunting. The Benin teacher wrote: "As for text-books the rudimentary but laudable efforts of Rev. J. Corbeau may be regarded as pioneer work."[40]

The writer in the last reference made no claims about Europeans having the power to name new forms of humanity in order to promote their agenda of colonial hegemony, as the Comaroffs argue. Instead, the writer turned his attention to the imperative of developing an African consciousness radically different from the Western tradition.

> We English-speaking Africans very often forget that the atmosphere, both physical and moral, which shaped the European mind is quite altogether different from ours; and that European literature is the written expression of [the] European mind and the atmosphere which shaped it. If an Englishman wants to study Latin or French he will not be required to make very strenuous mental efforts to enable him to "think" a Latin or French sentence. The atmosphere is all European, it is there already. But with African languages the position is different; the gulf between the two intellectual developments is wide.[41]

It was that gulf that Tafawa-Balewa, and Adebayo before him, tried to bridge with his bicultural approach. The challenge of bringing the benefits of modern education to children reared in traditional society led Tafawa-Balewa to expound linguistic principles by analogy with established Hausa political institutions and ideas, thus achieving the double goal of respect for the old amidst the new. It might be a new form of consciousness, a narrative of empowerment, but if so it was one of the Africans' devising. Because of its vernacular inspiration, such creativity exceeded by far the superficial import variety of imitation and repetition, and encouraged all concerned to look again with fresh, discerning eyes at the world of everyday life. The *malam* (derived from the Arabic *mu'allim*), as the teacher is called in Hausa, was quintessentially an agent with a dual role: he brought frontier ideas to bear on heartland traditional values without undue strain or distortion. The malam as transmitter of new ideas was the community's contact point with historical developments and its shield against cultural dispossession, as Malam Tafawa-Balewa so well demonstrated. Westermann's contention that an education that uprooted the child from the soil of its nurture could not achieve much of lasting value seems valid. The vernacular allayed that fear by connecting the child to things of mother tongue originality and assurance. Faithfulness to mother tongue values was not incommensurate with willingness to embrace new ideas and challenges.

Current Awakening and New Directions

D. H. Lawrence's pessimism about Christianity's future has been disproved by developments in the mission fields where statistics show that with expanding horizons as a result of the surge in conversions we are, in Lawrence's language, in the midst of a new venture toward God.[42] In all its complex vitality and variety religion has emerged to dominate the African landscape, with Christianity staging a surprisingly vigorous surge in the midst of the widespread disenchantment of the postcolonial era. In his sociological study of the phenomenon J.D.Y. Peel locates the revival phenomenon in the early decades of the twentieth century, showing its strong American connections.[43] In his continent-wide survey, David Barrett traces the roots of the awakening to the 1960s,[44] a period coinciding with the accelerating pace of the decolonization movement. In either case the scope and momentum of the resurgence have taken observers by surprise, and while explanations are many and various all are agreed that a new reality has taken hold.

Accounting for this new reality and estimating its significance constitute a critical challenge to historical as well as religious scholarship. Religion's return has forced a reappraisal of the received wisdom about secularization because of the way the revival has attached itself so tenaciously to ideas of indigenous renewal, institution building, education, public health issues, social engagement, accountability, and transparency. On the ground the debate seems to have shifted from colonial grievances to local empowerment and from Messianic nationalism to free association of civil society.

Historians have noted that because of its millennia-long presence Islam has been by far the more significant of the two world religions that have shaped the social terrain of tropical Africa. Yet the realization that since the middle of the twentieth century Christian expansion has more than doubled has demanded a redrawing of the religious map of the continent. In 1960, for example, Muslims still outnumbered Christians by a ratio of nearly three to one, constituting more than 34 percent of the continent's population, with Christians about 8.7 percent. Yet by the year 2000 Christians increased to some 380 million compared to 316 million Muslims. Today Christians are estimated to be about 418 million, which is about 50 percent of Africa's population. By 2025 this figure is expected to increase to over 600 million. Such an increase in Christian numbers was scarcely conceivable in 1960 when Christians numbered about 60 million, according to Barrett, and when writers predicted a rout in the wake of the retreating colonial powers. Historians recognize that the change is not merely a question of size; social scale brings about a realignment of cultural priorities and a fundamental change of perspective.[45]

As can be appreciated, the change is more than a question of numbers. At the time of the partition of Africa in 1885, apart from the ancient kingdom of Ethiopia and the settlements of Sierra Leone, Liberia, and South Africa, Christians were statistically insignificant in nearly all sub-Saharan societies. The emergence in the twentieth century of Kenya at one end of the continent and Ghana at the other end as Christian strongholds, for example, indicates that Christian Africa is set to dominate affairs in African societies in a way that will rival Islam, if not exceed it. No one was confident to make that prediction barely fifty years ago, and it renders nearly moot the debate about Christianity as a colonial construct. Although the issue persists in academic holdouts in the West, it is not what commands the attention of scholars and leaders in Africa today. The change offers challenges as well as opportunities for a fresh perspective on the intersection of culture and history.

In light of the shift of Christianity's center of gravity, scholars must review the nature of the origins of the modern missionary movement in the West. Europe launched the missionary movement intermittently in the fifteenth century, then in earnest from the sixteenth century with uneven and disparate results in colonies in Latin America, Africa, and Asia. The colonial-mission partnership foundered on ground contested by local populations. After three hundred years of dogged but futile attempts, from the era of Vasco da Gama to the year of the American Revolution, missions reached a turning point when in 1792 a drive from the New World led by former slaves and ex-captives, and supported by a trans-Atlantic philanthropic movement, breached the maritime slave corridor and secured a free colony at the source of the slave trade in Sierra Leone on the West African coast. It led to the passage of the Slave Trade Abolition Act of 1807. A spell was broken, and chiefs and rulers gave way to freed slaves and ex-captives as the new agents of conversion and social change. On the frontier, power and privilege, as represented by chiefs and rulers, were not the expected natural advantages of Christianity; for three hundred years they were immoveable barriers.

That recognition inserted a wedge between the project to transplant a heartland, Constantinian Christianity, and the untapped potential for change and leadership of hinterland societies. We see glimmers of this potential in light of what today is manifest in the exponential growth of Christianity in former mission fields, in contrast to its steady decline in the old heartlands of Europe. In the disarray following the fall of Rome the religion picked up momentum as it penetrated boundaries beyond the world of classical learning. That was how the conversion of northern Europe released fresh vernacular energy into the Christian stream as revealed in works such as *Beowulf, The Dream of the Rood,* and *La Chanson de Roland.* As exemplified by King Alfred of England, it led to the first bloom of vernacular literature outside the classical heritage. From its European transposition, the biblical heritage in time expanded and flourished in its post-Western mother tongue phase.

Thanks to vernacular Bible translation, the Christian movement entered a vigorous, expansive indigenous course with the gift of tongues. In contrast to Islam, Christianity's translated status, including the fact that the Gospels in Greek are a translation of the preaching and teaching of Jesus, means that the religion has a built-in vernacular disposition, and therefore, cross-cultural tendencies. The name "Jesus Christ," that combines a Jewish appellation and a Greek title, indicates precisely such a cross-cultural transposition. The perspective-altering sense of Christianity's center of gravity is the consequence of the religion's successful naturalization in the people's idiom. It echoes the shift of the religion from Jerusalem to Athens, from the temple to the Lyceum, requiring the acceptance of a polycentric territorial orientation of the religion and multiple concurrent cultural forms, as is evident in present-day manifestations taking place in the southern hemisphere and in significant waves that are breaking on American shores through the growing immigration tide.[46]

It is to this hemispheric shift of the religion's center of gravity that we must go to understand how the Christian movement crossed multiple borders as it broke out in new directions and in new cultural forms and idioms.[47] In the course of being conveyed to regions of the colonial field, the Christian movement became naturalized in new settings, thanks to the cultivation of the mother tongue in Scripture, worship, and national life. The rise of the modern West ironically helped bring about the rediscovery of indigenous narrative as the answer to colonial domination and the key to critical self-understanding. Proliferating new forms of the religion, as well as the accompanying exegetical work, demonstrate that the boundaries of Christianity are among the most dynamic and the most penetrable. The accompanying statistics of conversion reflect that, especially when we take into account the interpretation that belongs with translation, a point C. S. Lewis makes when he argues that translation is necessarily interpretation.[48] In the primal cultures of Africa and elsewhere, translation and interpretation together assume a self-conscious urgency that religious inquiry feeds.

Writing under the pseudonym of Fiona Macleod, William Sharp notes the importance of language as a unique cultural asset when he affirms that the last tragedy for broken nations is not the loss of power and distinction, or even of country. "The last tragedy, and the saddest, is when the treasured language dies slowly out, when winter falls upon the legendary remembrance of a people."[49] That narrative fate Bible translation and its ancillary activities averted for the vanquished subjects of the colonial empire.

Statistical Summaries

Table 1   The worldwide religious profile

Year	1900	1970	2000	2006	2025 estimate
World	1.6 Billion	3.7 Billion	5.7 Billion	6 Billion	7.8 Billion
Buddhists	127 million	233.4 million	364 million	382.4 million	418 million
Christians	558 million	1.2 billion	2 billion	2.15 billion	2.6 billion
Hindus	203 million	462.5 million	811 million	877.5 million	1 billion
Muslims	200 million	553.5 million	1.1 billion	1.3 billion	1.7 billion
Pentecostals/ Charismatics	981,000	72.223 million	523 million	588.502 million	800 million

Table 2   The world Christian resurgence: New center of gravity

Year	1900	2000	2005 (projected)	2025 (projected)
Africa	8.75 million	346.4 million	389.304 million	600 million
North America	59.57 million	212 million	222 million	250 million
North America and Europe (combined), includes Russia in 1900	427.779 million (82% of the world's Christians)	748 million	757.765 million (35% of the world's Christians)	767.9 million
Rest of the World (i.e., without North America and Europe)	93.7 million	1.2 billion	1.378 billion (65% of the world's Christians	1.85 billion

Table 3   Comparative resurgence in Africa

Year	1900	1985	2000	2025
Africa's population	107.8 million	520 million	784 million	1.3 billion
Muslims	34.5 million	216 million	315 million	519 million
Christians	8.7 million	270.5 million	346.5 million	600 million

Sources for tables 1–3: Adapted from various sources, including the *World Christian Encyclopedia,* 2nd ed. (New York: Oxford University Press, 2001); *International Bulletin of Missionary Research,* January issues for 2004 to 2007; and Stanley M. Burgess and Eduard M. Van Der Maas, eds., *The New International Dictionary of Pentecostal and Charismatic Movements,* revised and expanded (Grand Rapids: Zondervan, 2003).

CHAPTER 12

Reflections on the Bible and American Political Life

MARK A. NOLL

"This country is, as everybody knows, a creation of the Bible, ... and the Bible is still holding its own, exercising enormous influence as a real spiritual power, in spite of all the destructive tendencies."[1] These words, spoken more than a century ago, came from an unexpected source as part of an address delivered by Solomon Schechter at the dedication of the main building of the Jewish Theological Seminary in New York City. Yet although this opinion came from the Jewish margin of American society, it echoed what was then a common assertion about the biblical character of the United States. Much more frequently, of course, such words came from Christian commentators and with specific reference to the Christian character of the Scriptures.

Thus, only two years after Schechter's address, David J. Brewer, an associate justice of the United States Supreme Court, lectured at Haverford College on the theme, "The United States a Christian Nation." In these lectures, Brewer quoted his own opinion from an 1892 Supreme Court judgment that had affirmed "this is a Christian nation," and he went on to say specifically of the Bible—"No other book has so wide a circulation, or is so universally found in the households of the land.... Our laws and customs are based upon the laws of Moses and the teachings of Christ."[2] What Schechter the Jewish scholar and Brewer the Christian Supreme Court justice wanted to say is that without full consideration of the Bible, no account of American national history or of American national ideals was possible.

A century and more later, much has changed in the attention that North Americans pay to Scripture, the place they accord it in their lives, and the editions of the text that are available when they put it to use. Even more has changed in the American cultural environments where Scripture, though never the only force, was once clearly preeminent. One set of changes concerns the demography of American religion. As compared to a century ago, the United States is now home to more Protestants not of British background and so who have never used any English-language Bible, much less the King James Version (KJV) that once exerted such an immense cultural force throughout the English-speaking world. Many more Christians who are not Protestants now live in the United States, and so read their Bibles without the Protestant assumptions that once dominated American public life. There are also many more religious believers who are not Christians, but whose sacred texts deserve equal status in an open democracy alongside the Jewish and Christian Scriptures. And there are many more citizens who do not practice any religious faith or recognize any writings as sacred, but whose right not to practice religion demands equal protection alongside the rights of those who do.

Other changes extend far beyond the religious pluralism of contemporary society. The linguistic and narrative place occupied by the KJV from the first English settlements into the early twentieth century has now been taken by the omnipresent electronic media. Bible-based materials—including movies like Mel Gibson's *Passion* and the *Jesus Film* from Campus Crusade for Christ, or a number of successful children's adaptations of Bible stories like *Veggie Tales*—do quite well in this new electronic marketplace. But the subjects that have been most successfully popularized by television, the movies, and the internet—which now constitute the driving engines of ideas and images in modern culture—are sport, crime, pornography, political battles, warfare, modern medicine, and the media itself. In treating these subjects, there is minimal place for biblical themes, much less the specific language of any one biblical version.

And yet. In still another strike against the now tattered remnants of once-dominant secularization theory, Americans in very large numbers continue to buy, read, and defer to the Scriptures. Survey numbers probably overestimate such matters, but they are still impressive. In 2000, 14 percent of Americans told Gallup pollsters that they were participating in a Bible study group, which translates into roughly 40 million or more each week (or many more each week than the total attendance for an entire year of the National

Football League).[3] A Gallup Poll from January 2005 found that 95 percent of American regular church attenders, and 69 percent of the total American population expressed agreement with one of the two conservative opinions provided: "The Bible is the actual word of God and is to be taken literally, word for word"; or "The Bible is the inspired word of God but not everything in it should be taken literally."[4] In 2006, the Barna Group reported that its surveys found 47 percent of the American population reporting that they read the Bible at least once a week, a figure that had risen from 36 percent in 1988.[5] Making sense of such numbers, as also of the long history of Bible usage lying behind them, is not a simple task. Yet the American story of the Bible reflects the dominant place of Scripture in the Christian churches and Jewish communities, illustrates the power of democratic practice to shape the use of sacred texts, and is itself influenced almost as much by political, economic, and racial realities as by religion.

This chapter sketches the larger dimensions of the Bible's presence in American history before turning to the question of how Scripture has featured in political life. It argues a point about modern American life: the Bible (like other scriptural traditions) can be used either "for the common good" or as a weapon that heightens conflict over debated positions across the social-political spectrum. Because Scripture remains potent in many ways for private lives, it will inevitably remain potent for public life. The rich, but also complex history of the Bible in America has revealed that potent force working to heal as well as to destroy. Moreover, this account of Scripture in American life underscores several of the theoretical issues considered in this volume—most pointedly, the degree to which religious texts, beliefs, and practices are by nature so deeply embedded in the fabric of history that they have become invisible or at least indecipherable to many contemporaries, whether scholars, students or the general public.

Before addressing the Bible and American politics directly, I would like to briefly survey the many spheres of life in which Scripture has been prominent throughout American history. The Bible has been important in public life only because of its ongoing religious significance for individuals and for worshiping communities. Private reading, liturgical use, group study, and regular sermons constitute the *cantus firmus* underlying the more visible, and polyphonically complex, presence of Scripture in public life.

The publication of the Scriptures has also been a large and significant commercial enterprise from the first printings in Spanish, German, and Indian languages during the colonial period to the more than $500 million annual sales of today. The business practices of publishers that have specialized in

Bibles, like the early Harper & Bros., as well as nonprofits like the American Bible Society, firmly situate the American history of the Bible in the history of the American marketplace. Once American printers began publishing their own editions of the King James Version after the War for Independence, they began an industry that booms to this day. Mason Weems, who is famous for making up the story about George Washington confessing to chopping down a cherry tree, sometimes earned his living as a traveling Bible salesman. Shortly after 1800 Weems wrote from Virginia to his publisher in Philadelphia about the various KJV editions he was retailing: "I tell you this is the very season and age of the Bible. Bible Dictionaries, Bible tales, Bible stories—Bibles plain or paraphrased, Carey's Bibles, Collin's Bibles, Clarke's Bibles, Kimptor's Bibles, no matter what or whose, all, all, will go down—so wide is the crater of public appetite at this time."[6] Market success with the Bible hastened the emergence of great publishing firms like Harper & Bros. A different kind of marketing was perfected by the American Bible Society, which has distributed hundreds of millions of Bibles, at home and abroad, since its founding in 1816.

The Authorized or King James Version (KJV) of the Bible has always been the preeminent translation for English-speaking Protestants, but that preeminence has not prevented an incredibly diverse production of alternative English translations and an even vaster array of Bibles in non–English languages. Scripture has occupied a central place for Catholics who long employed the Douay-Challoner-Reims version; among Jews who have produced a number of significant translations of the Hebrew Scriptures; and among many religious communities using languages other than English. It is instructive to remember that the first complete Bible published in the new world was a translation into Algonquin prepared by the Massachusetts Puritan minister John Eliot in 1663. Later, as another noteworthy example, between 1860 and 1925, a hundred separate German-language editions of the Bible were published in the United States. In recent years the number of American Bibles published in Vietnamese, Korean, Chinese, and especially Spanish has grown rapidly. Understanding why the KJV was so dominant for so long, as well as why the KJV's centrality coexisted with so many competitors in English and other languages, opens up the wider dimensions of the subject as a whole.

The Bible has provided a bulging cornucopia of resources for many of the nation's most revered artists and writers as well as for uncountable hoards who purvey pop culture. Its sophisticated employment by the artists like Edward Hicks, who in the nineteenth century painted many versions of *The Peaceable Kingdom*—alongside the protean producers of songs, billboards, tracts, Bible-themed playing cards, T-shirts, and refrigerator magnets—testifies to the broad significance of Scripture for popular consumption.

Robert Alter recently published a short book that records how the nation's elite literature has exploited the universal presence of the KJV.[7] His study shows how much the taken-for-granted status of the KJV influenced the prose or the literary structure of novels from Herman Melville, William Faulkner, Saul Bellow, Ernest Hemingway, Marilynne Robinson, and Cormack McCarthy. For Alter, the payoff of these novelists' debt to the KJV goes beyond prose, metaphors, themes, and rhythms. By evoking in very different ways the language of the KJV, they also evoke the moral universe of the KJV. Even when their fiction subverted that morality, Alter believes that without the universal awareness of the KJV, the humane seriousness of these works would be immeasurably reduced.

The Bible has always functioned as a source of empowerment for racial, ethnic, and linguistic minorities. Its resources have been critical for African Americans such as the poets Phillis Wheatley and James Weldon Johnson, for advocates of women's rights like Sarah Grimké and Elizabeth Cady Stanton, for promoters of new translations of the Hebrew Bible like Solomon Schechter or Harry Orlinsky, and for many others on the margins of cultural influence. How that empowerment could function was illustrated in the 1890s when Elizabeth Cady Stanton and other prominent feminists published *The Woman's Bible*. This Bible was a mixed-genre combination of Scripture and commentary that promoted the reinterpretation, or the overthrow, of scriptural texts that the editors considered harmful to women. One of the prominent women whom Stanton recruited to comment on the project offered a particularly telling testimony. Frances Willard, head of the Women's Christian Temperance Union, was then at the height of her influence as a reformer, active not only against alcohol abuse but for a wide range of women's and children's rights. When she replied to Stanton's request for a contribution to *The Woman's Bible,* she provided a sophisticated defense of the Bible that had so dominated American civilization: "No such woman," she wrote, "as Mrs. Elizabeth Cady Stanton, with her heart aflame against all forms of injustice and of cruelty...has ever been produced in a country where the Bible was not incorporated into the thoughts and the affections of the people and had not been so during many generations." Moreover, it was to Willard precisely the Bible that made possible "a hallowed motherhood...because it raises woman up, and with her lifts toward heaven the world...it has produced the finest characters which I have ever known; by it I propose to live; and holding to the truth which it brings to us, I expect to pass from this world to one even more full of beauty and of hope."[8]

The Bible has also been the object of sustained, often contentious, but always prodigious academic attention, with that attention always complexly connected to the vast reservoirs of popular biblicism. How modern scriptural scholarship came to the United States and how it has developed in conflict with (but also supporting) popular usage is such an immense subject that it would take a small library even to outline the story.

In sum, the Bible has played an extraordinary role for the American public at large because it has been so securely rooted in private and corporate religious life, because it has been a vigorous commercial property, because it has served as an inexhaustible literary resource, and because it has been read in one unusually dominant translation (the KJV) alongside thousands of other versions. Given the comprehensive presence of the Bible as a social and cultural force, it can be no surprise that it has also enjoyed a nearly continuous political presence as well.

From the beginning the Bible provided powerful themes for Americans to define themselves politically, both as a people and then as a nation. During the American Revolution, countless preachers exploited the words of Scripture to drive home their vision of a liberated America. In 1773, a Connecticut Congregationalist based a discourse on the virtues of home rule and the folly of government by a foreign power on Exodus 1:8—"Now there arose up a new king over Egypt, which knew not Joseph." A year later a Presbyterian *Sermon on Tea* took Colossians 2:21 for its text—"Touch not; taste not; handle not."[9] Such creative use of biblical phrases has been repeated at many other moments, both great and small, in American history.

Significantly, these political uses of Scripture are by no means restricted to ancient history. On January 20, 1961, John F. Kennedy quoted the KJV twice at strategic places in his presidential inaugural address. Eight years later, Richard Nixon took the presidential oath of office with his hand placed on a Bible opened to the same text that Lyndon Johnson had chosen for his inauguration in 1964: Isaiah 2:4 ("And He shall judge among the nations, and shall rebuke many people: and they shall beat their swords into plowshares and their spears into pruning-hooks; nation shall not lift up sword against nation, neither shall they learn war any more").[10]

Although some pundits in the early twenty-first century have treated the Bible as a campaign document of the Republican Party, it is noteworthy that one of the most adept citers of Scripture in the modern period has been Bill Clinton. In his acceptance speech as the Democratic candidate for president on July 16, 1992, Clinton quoted or paraphrased three passages and also used three other biblical phrases at strategic moments.[11] And in January 2008, perceptive observers noted that President Barak Obama's inaugural address included an injunction from the Apostle Paul: "In the words of Scripture, the time has come to set aside childish things." (Obama's was also the first presidential inaugural to mention Islam positively, though no such address has yet quoted from the Koran.)

Political use of the Bible in formal or informal national occasions includes two of the greatest speeches in American history: Abraham Lincoln's Second Inaugural Address, delivered from the east side of the Capital Building on March 4, 1865,[12] and Martin Luther King Jr.'s climactic address at the Lincoln Memorial during the March on Washington for Civil Rights, August 28, 1963.[13] The orations by King and Lincoln were unusual in large part because they drew on biblical testimony at unusual public moments during times of great national crisis. King's dramatic address underscored a turning point in the nation's moral history when, nearly a century after the end of the war to end slavery, the United States was moving haltingly to confront the bitter realities of racial discrimination. For Lincoln, a calm meditation near the conclusion of the nation's bloodiest conflict became the occasion for profound reflections on the costs of justice delayed, the blessings of charity for all, and the unfathomable mysteries of divine providence. In both cases, the Bible was indispensable for shaping what the speakers said. Before examining these speeches, however, it is useful to show that they illustrate four different ways that the Bible has been put to use in American politics.[14]

First is a *rhetorical* or *stylistic* echoing of Scripture, where speakers, in order to increase the gravity of their words, employ a phraseology, cadence, or tone that parallels the classic phrasing of the King James Version. This usage was illustrated in another one of Abraham Lincoln's famous speeches, the Gettysburg Address, with its famous opening words, "Four score and seven years ago."[15] To a lesser extent, Lincoln's Second Inaugural Address used the same kind of rhetoric. But among the most dramatic examples of such a biblical style was Martin Luther King Jr.'s speech in August 1963, which was filled with biblically sounding phrases: "The Negro... finds himself in exile in his own land...; now is the time to rise from the dark and desolate valley of segregation to the sunlit path of racial justice...; Let us not seek to satisfy our thirst for freedom by drinking from the cup of bitterness and hatred...; Let us not wallow in the valley of despair..."

A second usage of the Bible is *evocative,* where speakers put actual Bible phrases to use, but as fragments jerked out of original context in order to heighten the persuasive power of what they are trying to say. William Jennings Bryan was an acknowledged master of this style, as in his memorable oration opposing the gold standard, delivered as part of the platform debate at the 1896 Democratic national convention in Chicago: "You shall not press down upon the brow of labor this crown of thorns; you shall not crucify mankind upon a cross of gold."[16] Abraham Lincoln used the Bible in this way when he took a phrase from Matthew 12:25 as the keynote for his famous "house divided" speech of 1858, and when in the Second Inaugural he used words from Genesis 3:19 to say it was "strange that any men should dare to ask a just God's assistance in wringing their bread from the sweat of other men's faces." In his "I Have a Dream" oration, King quoted words from Amos 5:24 similarly in order to proclaim, "We will not be satisfied until justice rolls down like waters and righteousness like a mighty stream."

Needless to say, rhetorical and evocative uses of the Bible have been the most common in American public speech. But in the orations by King and Lincoln there were also a *persuasive* use and a *theological* use.

In *persuasive* deployment of Scripture the Bible is quoted or paraphrased to make a direct assertion about how public life should be ordered. The difference from mere rhetoric or evocation is the speaker's implicit claim that Scripture is not just supplying a conceptual universe from which to extract morally freighted phrases, but that it positively sanctions the speaker's vision for how public life should be ordered. Toward the end of his memorable address, King quoted Isaiah 40:4 in order to enlist a divine sanction for his vision of a society free of racial discrimination: "I have a dream that one day every valley shall be exalted, every hill and mountain shall be made low, the rough places shall be made plain, the crooked places shall be made straight and the glory of the Lord will be revealed and all flesh shall see it together." The fact that this passage from Isaiah was also applied in Luke 3:5 to Jesus at the beginning of his public ministry only heightened the moral significance of what King wanted to assert about the desirability of a racially healed society.

In his Second Inaugural, Lincoln did something similar when he combined resignation before the workings of providence with an indictment of the ones who had asked God's assistance in wringing their bread from the sweat of other men's faces. For that combination of opinions a quotation from Matthew 18:7 was Lincoln's clincher: "The prayers of both [sides] could not be answered; that of neither has been answered fully. The Almighty has His own purposes. 'Woe unto the world because of offences! for it must needs be that offences come; but woe to that man by whom the offence cometh'!"

Persuasive political use of Scripture is more effective, but also more dangerous, than the merely rhetorical or evocative. The risk is the sanctified polarization that has so often attended the identification of a particular political position with the specific will of God. At its most extreme, that sanctified polarization can become an excuse for self-righteous violence. More often, the danger is that a worthy mandate from Scripture is simply disregarded as impractical, untimely, or quixotic. Lincoln's paraphrase in the Second Inaugural from Matthew 7:1 ("Let us judge not that we be not judged"), which he used to short circuit the assignment of blame for the continuation of slavery, illustrates this more prosaic danger. Despite Lincoln's scriptural mandate for charity, judgment from all sides of all sides has never ceased for interpretations of the Civil War.

Yet persuasive political use of Scripture can also be remarkably effective. When a specific political position is successfully identified with the purposes of God, that position can be defended, promoted, and advanced with tremendous moral energy. In the speeches of Lincoln and King, strategic quoting from the Bible played a significant part in reassuring many Americans that Lincoln's opposition to slavery and King's opposition to racial discrimination really did embody a divine imperative. Without widespread acceptance of the fact that these were divine imperatives mandated by Scripture, it is hard to imagine that either opposition to slavery or opposition to racial discrimination could have carried the day. As historian David L. Chappell has argued for the Civil Rights movement in which King's "I Have a Dream" speech figured so prominently, only such a biblically rooted motivation possessed the moral energy to galvanize and sustain the movement.[17]

Finally, after rhetorical, evocative, and persuasive usages, there is the *theological* deployment of Scripture, where the Bible is quoted or paraphrased to make an assertion about God and the meaning of his acts or providential control of the world. In American public life, Lincoln's Second Inaugural may represent its only instance. What he said pertained not primarily to the fate of the nation, and not even to a defense of his own political actions, but to the sovereign character and mysterious purposes of God. For that statement, a quotation from Psalm 19:9 provided the last word:

If we shall suppose that American Slavery is one of those offences which, in the providence of God, must needs come, but which, having continued through His appointed time, He now wills to remove, and that He gives to both North and South, this terrible war, as the woe due to those by whom the offence came, shall we discern therein any departure from those divine attributes which the believers in a Living

God always ascribe to Him? Fondly do we hope—fervently do we pray—that this mighty scourge of war may speedily pass away. Yet, if God wills that it continue, until all the wealth piled up the bond-man's two hundred and fifty years of unrequited toil shall be sunk, and until every drop of blood drawn with the lash, shall be paid by another drawn with the sword, as was said three thousand years ago, so still it must be said, "the judgments of the Lord, are true and righteous altogether."

A good case can be made that Lincoln's public articulation of scripturally derived theological principle about the sovereignty of God over human events explains the unprecedented humility that followed in the Second Inaugural's peroration. In other words, without a scriptural theology concerning the righteousness of God's ultimate judgment, there would have been no proclamation of "malice toward none" and "charity toward all." Both Lincoln's theological use of Scripture and his profession of charity to political foes have been extraordinarily uncommon in American history.

Most Americans, regardless of personal religious conviction, would probably agree that the deployment of Scripture in the two great speeches by Abraham Lincoln and Martin Luther King Jr. advanced the common good. The Bible helped the nation survive the nearly fatal wounds of war; the Bible helped the nation to push democratic ideals closer to reality. Sadly, however, the political functioning of Scripture has not always been as positive for political well-being, as can be illustrated by the nation's history of race and public education.

The extensive prevalence of the King James translation in early American history certainly contributed to the horrific disaster of slavery. The KJV's translators had regularly rendered the Greek word *doulos* as "servant." "Servant" and the more accurate translation, "slave," were already differentiated in the sixteenth century, and became even more so as time passed. Yet in America the gentler word *servant* provided a cover for those who defended slavery as a biblical institution since they could refer euphemistically to their "servants" long after "slave" had become the accurate word for a person held in chattel bondage.

The broader cause for complaint among African Americans was that quoting verses from the KJV often succeeded in having abolitionists labeled as infidels. Because of the unquestioned authority of the KJV, those who could quote its chapter and verse to defend slavery gained great authority for their arguments. Slave defenders were expert at citing texts that showed Abraham holding slaves, Paul sending the slave Onesimus back to his owner

Philemon, and many more. These passages regularly trumped efforts to reason from, rather than just to quote, the Scriptures—for example, that slavery in Bible times was usually of white people or that broad principles in Scripture (like the Golden Rule) could speak against the slave system in the United States.[18] It was, thus, no surprise when in 1899 Henry McNeal Turner, a bishop of the African Methodist Episcopal Church, called for a new translation. He complained that "the white man" had "colored the Bible in his translation to suit the white man, and made it, in many respects, objectionable to the Negro. And until a company of learned black men shall rise up and retranslate the Bible, it will not be wholly acceptable and in keeping with the higher conceptions of the black man.... We need a new translation of the Bible for colored churches."[19]

A different set of problems came from the unquestioned popularity of the KJV as *the* Protestant Bible in a nation where Protestants organized the institutions of public life. When tax-funded public education began in the United States, educators properly sought ways to inculcate morality as part of ordinary school experience. Since in the Protestant minds of these pioneering educators, the Bible was far and away the best single source for encouraging morality, they mandated Bible readings as a regular part of daily instruction. But because the KJV was so instinctively the preferred Bible of the educators, they simply equated Bible reading with reading the KJV. Protest against use of the KJV in schools was therefore taken to be a protest against the Bible. When this confusion was joined with rising worries about increasing waves of non-Protestant immigrants, violence could be the result.

In late spring and early summer of 1844 deadly riots left parts of Philadelphia in ruins, several Catholic churches burned to the ground, more than a dozen people killed, scores wounded, and many millions of dollars in damage.[20] The spark of this conflagration was a request by a Philadelphia bishop, Francis Kenrick, that Catholic schoolchildren be excused from readings of the KJV or be allowed to substitute readings from the Douai-Rheims translation. When nativist groups twisted this request into a charge that the pope was demanding the removal of Scripture from Philadelphia schools, rioting commenced that flared off and on for almost two months.

In contrast to King and Lincoln, who used biblical language to initiate change, public evocation of Scripture could also mask hypocrisy that violated the universal morality that many adherents of the Bible see so plainly in its pages. American history is replete with political figures who used the Bible to imagine a nation populated by masses united around an ideal of unity in diversity, while using the same source to reinforce the dominant social hierarchy or racial prejudices. Anniversary commemorations near the start of the twentieth century illustrate the potential for such hypocrisy.

On May 7, 1911, the sitting governor of the state of New Jersey addressed a great crowd who gathered in Denver to hear him speak on the subject, "The Bible and Progress." The speaker was Woodrow Wilson, the former president of Princeton University who by the spring of 1911 had come to enjoy a nationwide reputation for his efforts as New Jersey's progressive reforming governor. The next year he would be elected president of the United States. Then as the American leader who committed his nation to the armed struggle of the Great War, he would proclaim a biblical ideal of "covenant" as the key for a League of Nations that he hoped would forever make such international conflicts impossible.

In the course of his address, which had been arranged by local officials to commemorate "the tercentenary of the King James Version of the Bible,"[21] Wilson waxed rhapsodic about the democratic spirit of the Scriptures: "Isn't this the book of the people?" he asked. He answered by declaring that "these pages teem with the masses of mankind! ... These are the annals of the people—of the common run of men." The Bible was nothing less than "the 'Magna Carta' of the human soul."[22]

While Wilson's attachment to Scripture was sincere, it did not help him to rise above racial prejudice. Wilson told his Denver auditors in 1911 that the Bible "has made democracy and been the source of all progress." Yet his actions belied his profession when in 1916 he was asked to take part in public ceremonies marking the one hundredth anniversary of the American Bible Society. When this staunchly segregationist president was told that, since the Bible Society was a national organization with an extensive work among African Americans, it would have to include a black person in the platform party, Wilson objected. The ceremony was, therefore, duly segregated so that Wilson, echoing phrases he had uttered in 1911 about "the masses of mankind" drawing inspiration from Scripture, could unabashedly extol the Bible before his (all white) audience for "weaving the spirits of men together" throughout the world.[23]

Today in American political life, it might be suggested that the Bible is being put to use more for divisive polemics than for ennobling purposes. Partisan use of Scripture is a mainstay on the Right, especially in appeals for traditional moral positions on abortion, same-sex marriage, and stem-cell research. But it also appears as a useful tool on the Left for advocating ecological reform and supporting economic assistance for the poor.

In the divisive political climate of recent years, religion in general seems only to add fuel to polemical fires. For use of the Bible, the situation seems particularly dire. Thus white evangelical Protestants, who find it easy to deploy Scripture in political speech, have succeeded in organizing support for the Republican Party, but also in deeply offending many of their Democratic opponents and even some of their own Republican colleagues. By contrast, churchgoing African-American Democrats have shown an equal facility in using the Bible to address their own constituencies, though using different parts of the Bible than white Republicans employ; such African Americans are rarely answered directly by their Republican opponents nor are they much heeded by their fellow Democrats. Consequently, political leaders who act against type—that is, Democrats who deploy the Bible to support their positions or Republicans who warn about the dangers of exalting Caesar over God—receive little attention for their efforts. The results are especially unfortunate for issues with foundational moral dimensions—like the wars in Iraq and Afghanistan, health care reform, abortion, immigration policy, the environment, and even sometimes racial discrimination. Such debate is often distorted, confused, or trivialized by partisans who wield Scripture like a meat axe; it is likewise distorted, confused, or trivialized by partisans who panic over considering even a hint of authoritative moral guidance for public policy.

Thus both earlier examples from American history and recent polemical uses of the Bible for partisan political purposes point to a similar dilemma. The more irrelevant or partisan or superficial the Bible becomes in a religiously plural nation, the less likely that leaders can use Scripture for the self-sacrificing, altruistic, or prophetic purposes for which Abraham Lincoln and Martin Luther King Jr. put the Bible so dramatically to use. Such a dilemma brings us back, in conclusion, to Solomon Schechter and the perspective he brought to bear on both the nature of the Bible and its uses in American public life.

As even a moment's reflection might predict, Jewish reflections on the Bible and the United States have been unusually rich. To be sure, Jewish organizations continue to be understandably nervous about efforts to define the United States as a Christian nation, Jewish voters shy away from appeals by the Republican Party featuring "biblical values," and influential Jewish spokespersons regularly protest against any trespassing of the division between church and state. At the same time, it is noteworthy that from the founding of the nation, a prominent strand of Jewish opinion has embraced the proposition that the United States can be identified as an unusually biblical nation and has defended this identification as a positive good.[24] Recently, for example, a Jewish commentator, David Gelernter, used the

pages of *Commentary* to defend what he calls "Americanism" and to claim
that "the Bible is not merely the fertile soil that brought Americanism forth.
It is the energy source that makes it live and thrive; that makes believing
Americans willing to prescribe freedom, equality, and democracy even for a
place like Afghanistan, once regarded as perhaps *the* remotest region on the
face of the globe."[25]

More often, however, ambiguity has prevailed in Jewish assessments of the
Bible and American life. The tension between Jewish identity and American identity defined the context in which Solomon Schechter expressed the
opinions quoted at the start of this chapter. Commentary from Schechter (1849–1915) is especially intriguing, since his wide range of experience
before coming in 1902 to the United States and New York's Jewish Theological Seminary included birth and early years in Romania; education in
Poland, Austria, and Germany; teaching assignments at Cambridge and the
University of London; and greatly esteemed work on ancient biblical texts
in Egypt. The signal impression made on Schechter by reading Abraham
Lincoln's Second Inaugural Address as a youth in Foscani, Romania, perhaps
in a Yiddish translation, may have influenced his later views, for Schechter
reported that when he contemplated Lincoln's words, he could "scarcely
believe that they formed a part of a message addressed in the nineteenth century to an assembly composed largely of men of affairs." Instead, Schechter
imagined himself "transported into a camp of contrite sinners determined
to leave the world and its vanities behind him, possessed of no other thought
but that of reconciliation with their God, and addressed by their leader when
about to set out on a course of penance."[26]

A fuller account of what Schechter had to say in defending the biblical
character of the United States is particularly pertinent since his words from
1903 were spoken when Schechter was actively supporting Jewish efforts
to end Christian Bible readings in New York public schools, when he was
working to establish an independent network of private Jewish day schools,
and when he was offering full support to the Jewish Publication Society's
efforts at producing its own translation of the Hebrew Bible.[27]

Given these activities, Schechter's willingness to assert that "this country
is, as everybody knows, a creation of the Bible" deserves careful attention.[28]
First, he suggested that it was "particularly the Old Testament" that gave the
United States its biblical character. Then he expanded on problems he saw
when Americans took such a conviction seriously—including an "excess of
zeal," a spate of "caricature revelations," and the presence of "quacks" who
"create new Tabernacles here, with new Zions and Jerusalems." Schechter was
using a Hebrew vocabulary, but students of America's churches could describe

all of these excesses, and more, in any fair-minded account of how American Christians have also exploited their zealous attachment to Scripture.

Yet though Schechter was willing to acknowledge problems in the Bible-centric character of the United States, even more did he want to defend that character. He was pleased that trust in the Bible was standing up well against what he called "all the destructive tendencies, mostly of foreign make." He was also convinced that, despite genuine difficulties, "the large bulk of the American people have, in matters of religion, retained their sobriety and loyal adherence to the Scriptures, as their Puritan forefathers did."

Schechter's final point in praising the biblical character of the United States came back to the Bible rather than to America. For his audience in New York City in 1903 he wanted to emphasize that they were celebrating the foundation of "a *Jewish* Theological Seminary." As he spelled out what such a foundation meant, Schechter explained that it would be appropriate for ancient Jewish teaching to adapt to the American environment—for example, by respecting American democratic traditions and so downplaying aristocratic, centralizing, or autocratic tendencies in Jewish life brought from Europe to the new world. Yet, in the end, he contended that Judaism transcends America: "Any attempt to confine its activity to the borders of a single country, even be it as large as America, will only make its teachings provincial, narrow and unprofitable." Rather, the point of a *Jewish* theological seminary must be "to teach the doctrines and the literature of the religion which is as old as history itself and as wide as the world." An American setting was important precisely because of how much the Bible had gone into the shaping of the United States. But because the study of Judaism took in all of history and implicated the whole world, it had to remain the highest concern of the Jewish Theological Seminary.

Schechter's understanding of the Bible in America offers much for reflection more than a century later. To those who downplay the importance of scriptural grounding for the American experiment, he would appeal for a more positive assessment of what biblical convictions have contributed to American history and American ideals. To those who focus only on excesses of Christian imperialism in American history, he would claim—as a Jew—that this Christian heritage has provided a commodious home for Judaism to thrive. But to those who equate the Bible and America, he would assert that because Scripture embraces all of history and all of the world, it must continually assess, evaluate, and even judge the United States rather than the reverse.

Schechter's comments in 1903 parallel in important ways what the translation committee of the New Revised Standard Version (NRSV) wrote when

it published its revision in 1989. The chair of this committee was the venerable Bruce M. Metzger of Princeton Theological Seminary. The perspective
he proposed provides an essential beginning point for those, like myself, who
regard Scripture as only secondarily important as a political artifact. It also
provides a basis for making concluding comments about the use of the Bible
in American political life. Here is the conclusion of the NRSV's prefatory
remarks:

> In traditional Judaism and Christianity, the Bible has been more than
> a historical document to be preserved or a classic of literature to be
> cherished and admired; it is recognized as the unique record of God's
> dealing with people over the ages. The Old Testament sets forth the
> call of a special people to enter into covenant relation with the God of
> justice and steadfast love and to bring God's law to the nations. The
> New Testament records the life and work of Jesus Christ, the one in
> whom "the Word became flesh" as well as describes the rise and spread
> of the early Christian Church. The Bible carries its full message, not
> to those who regard it simply as a noble literary heritage of the past or
> who wish to use it to enhance political purposes and advance otherwise
> desirable goals, but to all persons and communities who read it so that
> they may discern and understand what God is saying to them.[29]

Following Schechter's commentary and Metzger's NRSV preface, then, it
is imperative for those who believe that Scriptures teach, reveal, or embody
the Word of God to look on the sacred books as universally valid, as
important for America only because they are important for all humanity.
Once this foundational premise is secure, believers are all but compelled to
follow their understanding of Scripture into political life, as into all other
dimensions of existence. Yet because the Bible can never be the possession of
only one modern nation or of only one faction within a particular nation,
Bible believers err grievously by allowing any particular use of Scripture to
rule out or marginalize other uses. Another way of putting this matter is to
say that while everything in the Bible can be construed as political, politics
can never exhaust, equal, or contain the message of the Bible.[30]

If these assertions about Scripture are correct, a number of implications
follow. First, American society would be immeasurably poorer if it was no
longer possible to bring the universal message of Scripture to bear on the
particulars of political life as Abraham Lincoln and Martin Luther King Jr.
did with such memorable effect. But it is also true that narrow use of the
Bible for partisan political advantage violates its own teachings about the
dignity of all human beings under God and about political power as only a

stewardship bestowed by God for the maintenance of order, the guarantee of justice, and the care of the powerless. Finally, given the current situation where temptations abound for rejecting political use of Scripture entirely or enlisting Scripture for only partisan objectives, those who want to use the Bible politically for the common good must attend to what it says about everything and not only political questions. Or to apply the conjunctions of Abraham Lincoln's Second Inaugural Address to the current situation: those who believe that the Bible speaks truly the word of God must be the first also to display "charity toward all" and "malice toward none."

This account of Scripture in American life echoes much that has come before in this book. In particular, the other essays of the last section grapple with questions related to textual authority in the modern era. They illustrate the way scriptural authority has changed over the last two centuries, how allegiances to different scriptural interpretations have shaped religious identities in modern, often secular societies, and why modern notions of citizenship have complicated identification within religious communities. Yet even in the premodern era, questions of scriptural interpretation and application shaped the political, social, and economic landscape as well as the cultural identities of whole peoples from the Levant to colonial Peru and from the Rhineland to New York City. The story of the Bible in American life is, thus, an epitome, not only for how Scriptures function in the modern world, but also for most of the possibilities—for good and for ill—of religion throughout history more generally.

NOTES

Introduction

1. Among many recent assessments of trends in religion and society worldwide, see Grace Davie, "Religion in Europe in the 21st Century: The Factors to Take into Account," *European Journal of Sociology* 47 (2006): 271–96; and Woodrow Wilson International Center for Scholars, "Religious Revival in the 21st Century: What Impact on Politics?" February 14, 2011, http://www.wilsoncenter.org/event/religious-revival-the-21st-century-what-impact-politics.

2. See Lizette Alvarez and Dona Van Natta Jr., "Pastor Who Burned Koran Demands Retribution." *New York Times,* April 1, 2011. http://www.nytimes.com/2011/04/02/us/politics/02burn.html; Paul Harris and Paul Gallagher, "Terry Jones Defiant Despite Murders in Afghanistan Over Qur'an Burning," *The Guardian,* April 2, 2011. http://www.guardian.co.uk/world/2011/apr/02/pastor-terry-jones-burning-koran; Thomas Erdbrink, "Iran Denounces Florida Pastor," *New York Times,* April 30. 2012. http://www.nytimes.com/2012/05/01/world/middleeast/iran-denounces-florida-pastor-over-koran-burning.html.

3. The press coverage of this event has been voluminous, locally and internationally. See Jason Lieser, "Gainesville Pastor: Deaths Acceptable Cost for Spreading Anti-Islam Message," *Palm Beach Post,* September 12, 2012. http://www.palmbeachpost.com/news/news/national-govt-politics/gainesville-pastor-deaths-acceptable-cost-for-spre/nR9Jf/; Terry Jones (Pastor), *New York Times,* September 13, 2012. http://topics.nytimes.com/top/reference/timestopics/people/j/terry_jones_pastor/index.html; and Sarah El Deeb, "'Innocence of Muslims' Protests: Egypt Issues Arrest Warrants for Terry Jones, 7 Coptic Christians," *Huffington Post,* September 18, 2012. http://www.huffingtonpost.com/2012/09/18/innocence-of-muslims-egypt-terry-jones_n_1893315.html.

4. Sociological notions of religion formulated in the nineteenth century have continued to shape scholarly views of religion in our own day. Particularly influential in this regard are the theories of Max Weber and Emile Durkheim. For further discussion of Max Weber's disenchantment thesis and its influence on subsequent understanding of religion see the essay of Carlos Eire in this volume.

5. Sanford Levinson, *Constitutional Faith* (Princeton: Princeton University Press, 1988); Beau Breslin, "Is There a Paradox in Amending a Sacred Text?" *Maryland Law Review* 69, no. 1 (2009): 66–77; and Emilio Gentile, *Politics as Religion* (Princeton, NJ: Princeton University Press, 2006).

6. Several observations in this opening section of the Introduction were articulated by contributors to this volume who served as panelists in a session devoted to Faithful Narratives, jointly sponsored by the American Historical Association and the

American Society of Church History in Boston (2011). We are especially indebted to John Van Engen for submitting a draft of his informal comments, some of which have informed our reflections here.

7. A few examples must suffice to illustrate this point. George M. Marsden, *The Soul of the American University: From Protestant Establishment to Established Non-Belief* (New York: Oxford University Press, 1994), concluded his survey of the role of Protestantism in the history of higher education in the United States with a short "Unscientific Postscript" proposing that the academy make room for traditional religious voices alongside feminist and multicultural perspectives. The brief postscript may have received more attention than that 450-page historical study sparking responses not only in academic journals and the *Chronicle of Higher Education,* where the notion of relating religious faith to academic scholarship was described as "looney" (May 4, 1994, A18), but also in the *New York Times.* Similarly, Brad Gregory's recent reassessment of the Protestant Reformation, *The Unintended Reformation: How a Religious Revolution Secularized Society* (Cambridge, MA: Harvard, 2012), concludes with a plea for the contemporary academy to "unsecularize itself" (386). Though Gregory does not discuss his religious identity, the book has been described as "an exercise in Catholic apologetics," sure to provoke debate. And Daniel Boyarin has repeatedly made a point of announcing his religious and theoretical commitments as the framework for his scholarship and his scholarly interests. In his *Preface to Border Lines: The Partition of Judaeo-Christianity* (Philadelphia: University Pennsylvania Press, 2004), Boyarin speaks of his marginality within his community as an orthodox rabbinic Jew "drawn to Christianity," and even of "the love of this Orthodox Jew for Christianity." While in other works he attempted to express and make sense of his powerful commitment to and "greater love" for rabbinic Judaism, his motivation in this work, he explains, was "to make some sense of my other love [Christianity] and how it drives the text that follows" (x).

8. See, for example, *Religious Advocacy and American History,* ed. Bruce Kuklick and D. G. Hart (Grand Rapids, MI: Eerdmans, 1997). This volume brings together a diverse group of prominent American historians to consider whether religious commitment precludes objectivity in scholarly pursuit.

9. For example, the Center for Cultural Judaism promotes academic programs at universities worldwide in order to promote a living model of cultural or secular Judaism in which the religious ritual and liturgical elements are marginalized, if not completely excluded. The center is the institutional branch of the umbrella philanthropic organization that carries the name of its founder, Felix Posen, and the following objectives: "to support secular Jewish education and educational initiatives on Jewish culture in the modern period and the process of Jewish secularization over the past three centuries. At a time when the majority of world Jewry defines itself as secular and is not well educated in Jewish culture, the Foundation offers this growing community the opportunity to deepen and enrich the study of its cultural and historic heritage—from a secular, scholarly perspective." http://www.posenfoundation.com/goals.html. At the time of writing, the Posen Foundation was providing substantial grants to twenty-nine American universities that house Jewish Studies programs.

10. See for example the multivolume series, Denis Janz, ed., *A People's History of Christianity,* 7 vols. (Minneapolis: Fortress Press, 2010).

11. In addition to his article in this volume, see David Nirenberg, "Judentum und Islam in der europäischen Dialektik von Glaube und Vernunft: Anmerkungen zur Geschichtstheologie Papst Benedikts XVI," in *Religionskontroversen im Verfassungsstaat,* ed. Hans G. Kippenberg and Astrid Reuter (Göttingen: Verlag Vandenhoeck & Ruprecht, 2010), 181–207.

12. See also in this regard Peter Brown, "Conversion and Christianization in Late Antiquity: The Case of Augustine," in *The Past before Us: The Challenge of Historiographies of Late Antiquity,* ed. Carole Straw and Richard Lim (Turnhout: Brepols, 2004), 103–7.

13. The methodological difficulties inherent here are analogous to any "identity studies" discipline, but the example of Jewish Studies seems especially apt. Scholars of Jewish history necessarily focus almost exclusively on Jewish culture and society in the historical time and place under review. The broader swath of Jewish life and culture throughout history and the wider cultural context in which communities of Jews have lived are hardly considered. See Moshe Rosman, *How Jewish Is Jewish History* (Oxford: Littman Library of Jewish Civilization, 2008), 19–55.

14. There is a vast literature on secularization and its discontents. The following list includes only a small sampling of the recent literature: Jeffrey L. Cox, "Secularization and Other Master Narratives of Religion in Modern Europe," *Kirchliche Zeitgeschichte* 14, no. 1 (2001): 24–35, and Cox, "Master Narratives of Long-term Religious Change," in *The Decline of Christendom in Western Europe, 1750–2000,* ed. Hugh McLeod and Werner Ustorf (Cambridge: Cambridge University Press, 2003), 201–16; Charles Taylor, *A Secular Age* (Cambridge, MA: Harvard University Press: 2007); Peter E. Gordon, "The Place of the Sacred in the Absence of God: Charles Taylor's Secular Age," *Journal of the History of Ideas* 69, no. 4 (October 2008): 647–73; The *Power of Religion in the Public Sphere: Judith Butler, Jürgen Habermas, Charles Taylor, Cornel West,* ed. Eduardo Mendieta and Jonathan Van Antwerpen (New York: Columbia University Press, 2011).

15. For excellent examples, in addition to the writings of Jeffrey Cox and Hugh McLeod cited above (n.14), see David Sorkin, *The Religious Enlightenment: Protestants, Jews, and Catholics from London to Vienna* (Princeton: Princeton University Press, 2008), and James E. Bradley and Dale K. Van Kley, eds., *Religion and Politics in Enlightenment Europe* (Notre Dame, IN: University of Notre Dame Press, 2001).

16. Besides Gregory, *The Unintended Reformation,* see Taylor, *Secular Age,* and other works listed in notes 14 and 15.

17. Lamin Sanneh, *Whose Religion Is Christianity? The Gospel Beyond the West* (Grand Rapids, MI: Eerdmans, 2003); Lamin Sanneh and Joel A. Carpenter, eds., *The Changing Face of Christianity: Africa, the West, and the World* (New York: Oxford University Press, 2005); Philip Jenkins, *The New Faces of Christianity: Believing the Bible in the Global South* (New York: Oxford University Press, 2008), and Jenkins, *The Next Christendom: The Coming of Global Christianity,* 3rd. ed. (New York: Oxford University Press, 2011).

18. John Van Engen, "The Christian Middle Ages as an Historiographical Problem," *American Historical Review* 91, no. 3 (1986): 544.

19. Besides her essay in this volume, see Phyllis Mack, "Religion, Feminism, and the Problem of Agency: Reflections on Eighteenth-Century Quakerism," in *Women,*

Gender, and Enlightenment, ed. Sarah Knott and Barbara Taylor (New York: Palgrave Macmillan, 2007), 434–59.

20. See Richard Schaeffer, "Let's Talk About Religion," *Perspectives* 48, no. 5 (May 2010): 48.

21. Mark Noll and David Nirenberg are more explicit in this regard, but the treatment of context, perspective, and religious belief in all the essays has applications to teaching as well as scholarship. For more direct autobiographical reflections on religion and pedagogy in the context of the humanities and social sciences see the essays in Part III of Andrea Sterk, ed., *Religion, Scholarship and Higher Education: Perspectives, Models and Future Prospects* (Notre Dame: University of Notre Dame Press, 2002). For recent trends vis-à-vis religion in the broader university context, see Douglas Jacobsen and Rhonda Hustedt Jacobsen, eds., *No Longer Invisible: Religion in University Education* (Oxford: Oxford University Press, 2012).

Chapter 1

1. I would like to thank Nina Caputo and Andrea Sterk for inviting me to Gainesville to present an early version of this paper. For Julian's rise see Shawn Tougher, *Julian the Apostate* (Edinburgh: Edinburgh University Press, 2007), 16–21, 31–43. Joachim Szidat's view that Julian was technically not a usurper has not found widespread scholarly acceptance. See "Die Usurpation Julians. Ein Sonderfall," in *Usurpationen in der Spätantike,* ed. François Paschoud and Joachim Szidat (Stuttgart: F. Steiner, 1997), 63–70. For a comprehensive account of Julian's reign see Klaus Rosen, *Julian: Kaiser, Gott und Christenhasser* (Stuttgart: Klett-Cotta, 2006).

2. See the important contributions in Christian Schäfer, ed., *Kaiser Julian "Apostata" und die philosophische Reaktion gegen das Christentum* (Berlin: Walter de Gruyter, 2008).

3. For a summary of the scholarly debates regarding this edict Emilio Germino, *Scuola e cultura nella legislazione di Giuliano l'Apostata* (Naples: E. Jovene, 2004). For discussions about religion in scholarship see the important collection edited by Andrea Sterk, *Religion, Scholarship, and Higher Education: Perspectives, Models, and Future Prospects* (Notre Dame: University of Notre Dame Press, 2002). Here, I found the contributions by David Hollinger and Brian Daley especially stimulating. I entirely agree with Professor Daley that there has to be far more work on editing texts, and that matters religious would be well served by being examined more by nonreligious scholars. Italian scholarship on early Christian authors could serve as a model, since it tends to be done by persons trained as classicists, who do not shy away from Christian authors with the exception of Augustine and his *Confessions.* For an insightful analysis David Brakke, "The Early Church in North America: Late Antiquity, Theory, and the History of Christianity," *Church History* 71 (2002): 473–91.

4. Peter R.L. Brown, *Power and Persuasion in Late Antiquity: Towards a Christian Empire* (Madison: University of Wisconsin Press, 1992), remains the essential discussion of *paideia* in late Antiquity; see also Barbara E. Borg, ed., *Paideia: The World of the Second Sophistic* (Berlin: Walter de Gruyter, 2004).

5. See Susanna Elm, "Hellenism and Historiography: Gregory of Nazianzus and Julian in Dialogue," *Journal of Medieval and Early Modern Studies* 33 (2003): 493–515, for additional bibliography, and Susanna Elm, *Sons of Hellenism, Fathers of the Church:*

Emperor Julian, Gregory of Nazianzus, and the Vision of Rome (Berkeley: University of California Press, 2012). Jean Bouffartigue, *L'Empereur Julien et la culture de son temps* (Turnhout: Brepols, 1992); Dominic J. O'Meara, *Platonopolis: Platonic Political Philosophy in Late Antiquity* (Oxford: Clarendon Press, 2003); and now Christian Schäfer, "Julian 'Apostata' und die philosophische Reaktion gegen das Christentum," and Dirk Cürsgen, "Kaiser Julian über das Wesen und die Geschichte der Philosophie," in Schäfer, *Kaiser Julian,* 41–64 and 65–86.

6. For a social historical approach see especially Raymond Van Dam, *Kingdom of Snow: Roman Rule and Greek Culture in Cappadocia* (Philadelphia: University of Pennsylvania Press, 2002); Van Dam, *Families and Friends in Late Roman Cappadocia* (Philadelphia: University of Pennsylvania Press, 2003); Van Dam, *Becoming Christian: The Conversion of Roman Cappadocia* (Philadelphia: University of Pennsylvania Press, 2003); and the important papers now collected in Neil B. McLynn, *Christian Politics and Religious Culture in Late Antiquity* (Farnham, UK: Ashgate, 2009). See John A. McGuckin, *St. Gregory of Nazianzus: An Intellectual Biography* (Crestwood, NY: St. Vladimir's Seminary Press, 2001); and Francis Gautier, *La retraite et le sacerdoce chez Grégoire de Nazianze* (Turnhout: Brepols, 2002).

7. The best and most recent work devoted to Gregory's theology is Christopher A. Beeley, *Gregory of Nazianzus on the Trinity and the Knowledge of God: In Your Light We Shall See Light* (Oxford: Oxford University Press, 2008).

8. See in particular Bryan Ward-Perkins, *The Fall of Rome and the End of Civilization* (Oxford: Oxford University Press, 2005); Christopher Kelly, *The End of Empire: Attila the Hun and the Fall of Rome* (New York: W. W. Norton, 2009).

9. John F. Matthews, *The Roman Empire of Ammianus* (London: Duckworth, 1989), 181; Tougher, *Julian the Apostate,* 63–71.

10. For example, Jul. *Letter to Themistius* 267a; *The Works of Emperor Julian,* vol. 2, trans. Wilmer C. Wright. Loeb Classical Library (Cambridge: Harvard University Press, 1998).

11. Jul. *Hymn to King Helios* 152d–153a; *The Works of Emperor Julian,* vol. 1, trans. Wilmer C. Wright. Loeb Classical Library (Cambridge: Harvard University Press, 1980).

12. Ammianus Marcellinus, *Res gestae* 22.2.3; *Ammianus Marcellinus History,* vol. 2, Trans. John C. Rolfe. Loeb Classical Library (Cambridge: Harvard University Press, 2000).

13. Jul. *Against the Galileans* fr. 36, 171e; fr. 43, 194d; *The Works of Emperor Julian,* vol. 3, trans. Wilmer C. Wright. Loeb Classical Library (Cambridge: Harvard University Press, 1998).

14. Jul. *Ep.* 36; *Works,* vol. 3.

15. Jul. *Against the Galileans* fr. 55, 229cd; *Works,* vol. 3.

16. Jul. *Ep.* 36; *Works,* vol. 3.

17. For Gregory's engagement as rhetorician after returning from Athens, see Neil B. McLynn, "Among the Hellenists: Gregory and the Sophists," in McLynn, *Christian Politics,* 213–38, esp. 220–24; for biographic details Beeley, *Gregory,* 7–14.

18. Brian E. Daley, *Gregory of Nazianzus* (London: Routledge, 2006), 1–61.

19. Gr. Naz. *Or.* 2.38; *Grégoire de Nazianze Discours 1–3,* trans. Jean Bernardi. Sources Chrétiennes 247 (Paris: éditions du cerf, 1978); English trans. my own, but see also C. G. Browne and J. E. Swallow, eds., *Gregory of Nazianzus.* The Nicene

and Post-Nicene Fathers of the Church, 2nd series, vol. 7 (Edinburgh: T&T Clark, 1989).

20. For Gregory's reception of the honorific "the Theologian," and for his later impact see McGuckin, *St. Gregory,* xxii–xxvii, 399–402.

21. For an overview of scholarly constructions of the bishop, see now the seminal work by Claudia Rapp, *Holy Bishops in Late Antiquity: the Nature of Christian Leadership in an Age of Transition* (Berkeley: University of California Press, 2005), esp. 3–22 and 24–33; also Andrea Sterk, *Renouncing the World yet Leading the Church: the Monk-bishop in Late Antiquity* (Cambridge: Harvard University Press, 2004), esp.119–40. Still foundational is Hans von Campenhausen, *Kirchliches Amt und geistliche Vollmacht in den ersten drei Jahrhunderten* (Tübingen: Mohr, 1953).

22. Beeley, *Gregory,* 3–16, 34–62.

23. For bibliographic details, see Susanna Elm, "Family Men: Masculinity and Philosophy in Late Antiquity," in *Transformations of Late Antiquity,* ed. Philip Rousseau and Manolis Papoutsakis (Farnham: Ashgate, 2009), 279–302, here 281–82.

24. *Gregorio di Nazianzo. Contro Giuliano l'Apostata: Orazione 4,* ed. and trans. Leonardo Lugaresi (Florence: Nardini, 1993), 15; *Gregorio di Nazianzo. La morte di Giuliano l'Apostata: Orazione 5,* ed. and trans. Leonardo Lugaresi (Florence: Nardini, 1997); Ugo Criscuolo, "Gregorio di Nazianzo e Giuliano," in *Talariskos. Studia Graeca Antonio Garzya sexagenario a discipulis oblata,* ed. Ugo Criscuolo (Naples: M. D'Auria, 1987), 165–208, here 205.

25. Tougher, *Julian the Apostate,* 55–62 for a discussion of scholarly views.

26. Rosen, *Julian,* 287; translation mine.

27. Only the tip of the iceberg has been examined such as explicitly anti-Julianic texts, e.g., Gregory's orations *Against Julian* (Or. 4 and 5) and other direct responses to Julian's writings, especially to his *Against the Galileans,* most notably by Cyril of Alexandria.

28. Ward-Perkins, *Fall of Rome,* 180.

29. Elm, *Sons of Hellenism,* 312–35. There are notable exceptions, especially Felix Thome, *Historia contra mythos: die Schriftauslegung Diodors von Tarsus und Theodors von Mopsuestia im Widerstreit zu Kaiser Julians und Salustius' allegorischem Mythenverständnis* (Bonn: Borengässer, 2004); and María Dolores García Garrido, *Las homilias "In hexaemeron" de Basilios de Cesarea: ¿Una respuesta a la política religiosa del emperador Juliano?* (Louvain-la-Neuve: Fondacio Barceló, 2000).

30. Jean Bernardi, *Grégoire de Nazianze: Discours 4–5 contre Julien.* Sources chrétiennes 309 (Paris: éditions du Cerf, 1983); translation mine.

31. Johannes Quasten, *The Golden Age of Greek Patristic Literature,* vol. 3 of *Patrology* (Utrecht: Spectrum, 1974), 242; Glen W. Bowersock, *Julian the Apostate* (Cambridge: Harvard University Press, 1978), 5, considers Gregory's work a useful collection of gossip; Van Dam, *Kingdom,* 194–95.

32. Bernardi, *Discours 1–3,* 91.

33. P. Godet cited by Lugaresi, *Orazione 4,* 13–14, translations mine.

34. For the dating, see Elm, *Sons of Hellenism,* 341–44; Bernardi, *Discours 4–5 contre Julien,* 11–37; and Lugaresi, *Orazione 4,* 39–48; Peter Sarris, "Rehabilitating the Great Estate: Aristocratic Property and Economic Growth in the Late Antique East," in *Recent Research in the Late Antique Countryside,* ed. William Bowden, Luke Lavan, and Carlos Machado (Leiden: Brill, 2004), 55–71, esp. 62; Jairus Banaji, *Agrarian*

Change in Late Antiquity: Gold, Labour, and Aristocratic Dominance (Oxford: Oxford University Press, 2001), 49–51.

35. Blake Leyerle, *Theatrical Shows and Ascetic Lives: John Chrysostom's Attack on Spiritual Marriage* (Berkeley: University of California Press, 2001), 13–20, quote 18.

36. Compare denunciations of the Roman senators' lust for the theater in Leonardo Lugaresi, "Ambivalenze della rappresentazione: riflessioni patristiche su riti e spettacoli," *Zeitschrift für antikes Christentum* 7 (2003): 281–309, at 299.

37. Richard Lim, "Converting the Un-Christianizable: The Baptism of Stage Performers in Late Antiquity," in *Conversion in Late Antiquity and the Early Middle Ages: Seeing and Believing,* ed. Kenneth Mills and Anthony Grafton (Rochester: University of Rochester Press, 2003), 84–126, at 87–91.

38. As Gregory elaborates in *Or.* 4.113–19, Julian's claim to Greek culture and the sacred was nothing but a recourse to the "fictions and vain words of the poets" (4.118), particularly those of "Homer . . . the great comediograph, or better tragediograph of your gods" (4.116).

39. Recall that the men whom Gregory here addressed, all Christian, were also the ones who continued to fund just such theatrical games for public enjoyment and at immense costs to themselves; Lim, "Converting," 84–86; also Sarris, "Rehabilitating the Great Estate," 63.

40. This is the widely quoted characterization of Julian's physique; Bowersock, *Julian the Apostate,* 12; Rosen, *Julian,* 18.

41. John F. Matthews, *Laying Down the Law: A Study of the Theodosian Code* (New Haven: Yale University Press, 2000), 195–99.

42. Severin Koster, *Die Invektive in der griechischen und römischen Literatur* (Meisenheim am Glan: Hain, 1980), 7–17, 38–39, focuses on Latin authors (and does not treat Christian writers) but is nonetheless fundamental.

43. Alois Kurmann, *Gregor von Nazianz, Oratio 4 gegen Julian: Ein Kommentar* (Basel: Friedrich Reinhardt, 1988), 19–20.

44. Neil B. McLynn, "The Transformation of Imperial Churchgoing in the Fourth Century," in *Approaching Late Antiquity: The Transformation from Early to Late Empire,* ed. Simon Swain and Mark Edwards (Oxford: Oxford University Press, 2004), 235–36.

45. A few years later Gregory reversed the call to support Valens as evident in his famous description of the hostile encounter between emperor and bishop in a church. Again, Gregory used the term *stele.* Now the bishop, Basil, was the solid pillar and the public display of power took place in the church. The emperor, now Valens, twitched again. The winner was, of course, the bishop, Basil (*Or.* 43.52).

46. As shown in Thome's excellent monograph (n.29).

47. Susanna Elm, "Translating Culture: Gregory of Nazianzus, Hellenism, and the Claim to *Romanitas,*" in *Intermedien: Zur kulturellen und artistischen Dynamik,* ed. Alexandra Kleihues, Barbara Naumann, and Edgar Pankow (Zürich: Chronos Verlag, 2010), 17–26.

Chapter 2

1. This theme has been thoroughly studied of late: see Richard D. Finn, *Almsgiving in the Later Roman Empire: Christian Promotion and Practice, 313–450* (Oxford:

Oxford University Press, 2006); Peter Brown, *Poverty and Leadership in the Later Roman Empire* (Hanover, NH: University Press of New England 2002), and *Through the Eye of a Needle: Wealth, the Fall of Rome, and the Making of Christianity in the West, 350–550 AD* (Princeton, NJ: Princeton University Press, 2012); Susan Holman, *The Hungry Are Dying: Beggars and Bishops in Roman Cappadocia* (New York: Oxford University Press, 2001), and *God Knows There's Need: Christian Responses to Poverty* (New York: Oxford University Press, 2009); Andrea Sterk. *Renouncing the World and Leading the Church: The Monk-Bishop in Late Antiquity* (Cambridge: Harvard University Press, 2004), 67–70; Emily A. Hanawalt and Carter Lindberg, *Through the Eye of a Needle: Judeo-Christian Roots of Social Welfare* (Kirksville, MO: Thomas Jefferson University Press, 1994); *Per foramen acus. Il cristianesimo antico di fronte alla pericope del "giovanni ricco"* (Milan: Vita e Pensiero 1986).

2. J. B. Ward-Perkins, "Frontiere politiche e frontiere culturali," in *Atti del convegno sul tema: La Persia e il mondo greco-romano? (Roma 11–14 aprile 1965),* Problemi attuali di Scienza e di Cultura. Quaderno, N. 76; Accademia nazionale dei Lincei. Anno, 363 (Roma: Accademia Nazionale dei Lincei, 1966): 395–409 at 395.

3. Pseudo-Clement, *Ad Virgines* 2.6, *Patrologiae cursus completus: Series graeca* [= PG], ed. J. P. Migne (Paris: Migne, 1857–86), 1: 433A. See Peter Brown, *Body and Society: Men, Women and Sexual Renunciation in Early Christianity.* Twentieth anniversary ed. with a new introduction (New York: Columbia University Press, 2008), 196.

4. Peter Brown, "The Diffusion of Manichaeism in the Roman Empire," *Journal of Roman Studies* 59 (1969): 92–103, now in *Religion and Society in the Age of Saint Augustine* (1972; reprint Eugene, OR: Wipf and Stock 2007), 94–118; S.N.C. Lieu, *Manichaeism in the Roman Empire and Medieval China,* 2nd ed. (Tübingen: Mohr, 1992).

5. M. Tardieu, "La diffusion du Bouddhisme dans l'empire kouchan, l'Iran et la Chine d'après un Kephalaion inédit," *Studia Iranica* 17 (1988): 153–80.

6. *Psalms of Heracleides,* ed. Charles R.C. Allberry, *A Manichaean Psalmbook,* Part II. Manichaean Manuscripts in the Chester Beatty Collection (Stuttgart: Kohlhammer 1938), 195.8–12; now ed. S. G. Richter, *Die Herakleides-Psalmen* 5: 56–61, *Corpus Fontium Manichaeorum: Series Coptica* 1, Part 2, Fasc. 2 (Turnhout: Brepols 1998), 80–81.

7. Iain Gardner and Samuel N.C. Lieu, "From Narmouthis (*Medinat Madi*) to Kellis (*Ismant al-Kharab*)," *Journal of Roman Studies* 86 (1996): 146–69. Much of this material is now available in Iain Gardner and Samuel N.C. Lieu, *Manichaean Texts from the Roman Empire* (Cambridge: Cambridge University Press, 2004).

8. Athanasius, *Life of Saint Anthony* 2.3, ed. G.J.M. Bartelink, *Sources Chrétiennes* 400 (Paris: Le Cerf, 1994), 132; *The Life of Anthony: The Coptic Life and the Greek Life,* trans. Tim Vivian and Apostolos A. Athanassakis, Cistercian Studies 209 (Kalamazoo, Michigan: Cistercian Studies, 2003), 56–59.

9. Athanasius, *Life of Saint Anthony* 2.5, 134; Vivian and Athanassakis, 58–59.

10. Athanasius, *Life of Saint Anthony* 3.6, 138; Vivian and Athanassakis, 62–63; *Apophthegmata Patrum,* Anthony 1, PG 65: 76 AB.

11. Evagrius of Pontus, *Antirrhêtikos* 1.63 and 64, *Talking Back: A Monastic Handbook for Combating Demons,* trans. David Brakke, Cistercian studies series, no. 229 (Collegeville, Minn.: Liturgical Press, 2009), 67.

12. David Brakke, *Athanasius and the Politics of Asceticism* (Oxford: Clarendon, 1995), 201–65.

13. Dennis Trout, *Paulinus of Nola: Life, Letters, and Poems* (Berkeley: University of California Press, 1999), 2–10.

14. On *ponos* as "drudgery," see M. I. Finley, *The Ancient Economy* (Berkeley: University of California Press, 1973), 44–41; and Aldo Schiavone, *The End of the Past: Ancient Rome and the Modern West* (Cambridge, MA: Harvard University Press, 2000), 37: work was "a kind of dead zone for civilization…a 'dark hole' of community life." For the life of Adam without *'amla'* see *Liber Graduum* 21.7, ed. M. Kmosko, *Patrologia Syriaca* 1: 3 (Paris: Firmin Didot, 1926), 600. *The Book of Steps: The Syriac Liber Graduum,* trans. Robert Kitchen and M.F.G. Parmentier, Cistercian Studies 196 (Kalamazoo, MI: Cistercian Publications, 2004), 238.

15. *Papyri Kellis Coptici* 32.1–13, in *Coptic Documentary Texts from Kellis I,* ed. Iain Gardner, Anthony Alcock, and Wolf-Peter Funk (Oxford: Oxbow, 1999), 214.

16. *Papyri Kellis Coptici* 31. 17f, 210–11.

17. *Apostolic Constitutions* 8.40, ed. M. Metzger, *Les Constitutions Apostoliques 3,* Sources Chrétiennes 336 (Paris: Le Cerf 1987), 254. See now E. Magnani, "Alms-giving, *Donatio pro Anima,* and Eucharistic Offering in the Early Middle Ages of Western Europe," in *Charity and Giving in Monotheistic Religions,* ed. Miriam Frenkel and Yaacov Lev, Studien zur Geschichte und Kultur des islamischen Orients, N.F., Bd. 22 (Berlin: De Gruyter, 2009), 111–21. Many types of food and drink other than bread and wine were used in differing early Christian Eucharists. They were vivid condensations for each group of widely differing views of society and of the natural world. See esp. Andrew McGough, *Ascetic Eucharists: Food and Drink in Early Christian Ritual Meals* (Oxford: Clarendon, 1999), 89–142.

18. Augustine, *de haeresibus* 46.3.

19. Jason Be Duhn, *The Manichaean Body: In Discipline and Ritual* (Baltimore: Johns Hopkins University Press, 2000), 163–208.

20. Ibid., 209–33.

21. Augustine, *de moribus manichaeorum* 2.13.20–18.66.

22. *The Cologne Mani Codex: "Concerning the Origin of His Body,"* 97.1–99.1, ed. and trans. Ron Cameron and Arthur J. Dewey (Missoula, MT: Scholars Press, 1979), 78; Augustine, *Enarratio in Psalmos* 140.12.

23. Kephalaion 150, *Kephalaia I: Zweite Hälfte, Lieferung 13/14,* ed. Wolf-Peter Funk, Manichäische Handschriften der Staatlichen Museen Berlin (Stuttgart: Kohlhammer, 1999), 365.11–17.

24. *Cologne Mani Codex: "Concerning the Origin of His Body"* 9.1, 12.

25. George Tate, *Les campagnes de la Syrie du Nord du IIe au VIIe siècle* (Paris: de Boccard, 1992); P. L. Gatier, "Les villages du Proche-Orient protobyzantin (4ème–7ème siècles). Étude régionale," *The Byzantine and Early Islamic Near East 2: Land Use and Settlement,* ed. G.R.D. King and Averil Cameron (Princeton, NJ: Princeton University Press, 1994), 17–48; Clive Foss, "The Near Eastern Countryside in Late Antiquity," *Journal of Roman Archaeology,* Supplement 14 (Providence: Journal of Roman Archaeology 1995): 213–34.

26. Bodo Gatz, *Weltalter, goldene Zeit und sinnverwandte Vorstellungen,* Spudasmata 16 (Hildesheim: G. Olms 1967); M. L. West, *The East Face of Helicon. West Asiatic Elements in Greek Poetry and Myth* (Oxford: Clarendon Press. 1997), 276–333.

27. "Atrahasis 190," in B. R. Foster, *Before the Muses: An Anthology of Akkadian Literature* (Bethesda, MD: CDL Press, 2005), 165.

28. Jacques Cauvin, *The Birth of the Gods and the Origins of Agriculture* (Cambridge: Cambridge University Press, 2000), 67–72.

29. *Liber Graduum* 25.3, Kmosko, 737; Kitchen and Parmentier, 293. See D. Juhl, *Die Askese im Liber Graduum und bei Afrahat. Eine vergleichende Studie zur frühsyrischen Frömmigkeit,* Orientalia Biblica et Christiana 9 (Wiesbaden: Harassowitz, 1996), 71–76 and Kitchen and Parmentier, xlix–lxxxiii.

30. *Liber Graduum* 21.2–7, 592–601; Kitchen and Parmentier, 232–38.

31. *Liber Graduum* 15.13, 365–66; Kitchen and Parmentier, 150–51.

32. Philippe Escolan, *Monachisme et Église. Le monachisme syrien du ive au viie siècle. Un ministère charismatique,* Théologie historique 109 (Paris: Beauchesne 1999): 183–225.

33. D. Caner, *Wandering, Begging Monks: Spiritual Authority and the Promotion of Monasticism* (Berkeley: University of California Press, 2002), 158–205.

34. P. Brown, "Alms and the Afterlife: A Manichaean View of an Early Christian Practice," *East and West: Papers in Ancient History presented to Glen W. Bowersock,* ed. T. C. Brennan and H. I. Flower (Cambridge: Department of Classics, Harvard University, 2009), 145–58.

35. The classic statement of this view, which became widely available to later, Western readers is John Cassian, *Institutes* 10. 22, ed. J.-C. Guy, *Sources Chrétiennes* 109 (Paris: Le Cerf 1965): 420–22; see also *Historia Monachorum in Aegypto* 18.2–3; Palladius, *Historia Lausiaca* 32.9. All these are accounts by visitors to Egypt, not by Egyptians themselves.

36. *Apophthegmata Patrum,* Sisoes 16: PG 65: 397B; for an English translation see Benedicta Ward, *The Sayings of the Desert Fathers,* Cistercian Studies 59 (Kalamazoo, MI: Cistercian Studies 1975), 212–22; here 215. See esp. Hermann Dörries, "Mönchtum und Arbeit," *Wort und Stunde* (Göttingen: Vandenhoeck and Ruprecht 1966), 1: 277–301.

37. H. Bacht, *Der Vermächtnis des Ursprungs* (Würzburg: Echter 1971), 1: 229.

38. *Apophthegmata Patrum* John Kolobos (the Dwarf): PG 65: 203D-204A; Ward, *Sayings,* 73.

39. Augustine, *de moribus ecclesiae catholicae* 1. 31.65–67; see A. de Vogüé, *Histoire littéraire du mouvement monastique dans l'antiquité: Première partie: Le monachisme latin* (Paris: Le Cerf 1993), 2: 129.

40. Augustine, *de moribus ecclesiae catholicae* 1.31.65.

41. G. Schopen, *Buddhist Monks and Business Matters* (Honolulu, HI: University of Hawaii Press, 2004), 15. See esp. Ewa Wipszycka, "Le monachisme égyptien et les villes," *Travaux et Mémoires* 12 (1994): 1–44, at 35; Wipszycka, "Les aspects économiques de la vie de la communauté de Kellia," *Le site monastique de Kellia,* now in *Études sur le christianisme dans l'Égypte,* Studia Ephemeridis Augustinianum 52 (Rome: Institutum Patristicum Augustinianum 1996), 337–62; Wipszycka, "Contribution à l'étude de l'économie de la congrégation pachômienne," *Journal of Juristic Papyrology* 26 (1996): 167–210; Wipszycka, "Les formes institutionnelles et les formes d'activité économique du monastère égyptien," *Foundations of Power and Conflicts of Authority in Late Antique Monasticism,* ed. A. Camplani and S. Filoramo, Orientalia Lovaniensia Analecta 157 (Louvain: Peeters 2007), 109–54, at 149–50; R. Bagnall,

"Monks and Property: Rhetoric, Law and Patronage in the *Apophthegmata Patrum* and the Papyri*," Greek, Roman, and Byzantine Studies* 42 (2001): 7–24; A. Laniado, "The Early Byzantine State and the Christian Ideal of Poverty," *Charity and Giving in Monotheistic Religions,* 15–43.

42. I. Silber, *Virtuosity, Charisma, and Social Order: A Comparative Sociological Study of Monasticism in Theravada Buddhism and Medieval Catholicism* (Cambridge: Cambridge University Press, 1995), 213–16.

43. Fa-hsien, *A Record of the Buddhistic Kingdoms* 16, trans. J. Legge (Oxford: Clarendon, 1886), 42, cited in Xinru Liu, *Ancient India and Ancient China: Trade and Religious Exchanges* (Delhi: Oxford University Press, 1988). See also J. Kieschnick, *The Impact of Buddhism on Chinese Material Culture* (Princeton, NJ: Princeton University Press, 2003), 107.

44. *Discourse on the Compassion of God and of the Archangel Michael,* trans. E.A.W. Budge, Coptic Texts in the Dialect of Upper Egypt (London: British Museum 1915), 757–58.

Chapter 3

1. Georges Duby, *La société aux XIe et XIIe siècle dans la région mâconnaise* (Paris: Armand Colin, 1953) and *Les trois ordres: ou, L'imaginaire du féodalisme* (Paris: Gallimard, 1978), the latter translated into English in 1980.

2. Lewis Mumford, *Technics and Civilization* (New York: Harper, 1934); Lynn White, Jr., *Medieval Religion and Technology* (Berkeley: University of California Press, 1978); Jacques Le Goff, *Time, Work, and Culture in the Middle Ages* (Chicago: University of Chicago Press, 1980); George Ovitt Jr., *The Restoration of Perfection: Labor and Technology in Medieval Culture* (New Brunswick, NJ: Rutgers University Press, 1987); Patricia Ranft, *The Theology of Work: Peter Damian and the Medieval Religious Renewal Movement* (New York: Palgrave Macmillan, 2006); Sabine MacCormack, "The Virtue of Work: an Augustinian Transformation," *Antiquité tardive* 9 (2001): 219–37; *Le travail au moyen âge: une approche interdisciplinaire,* ed. Jacqueline Hamesse and Colette Muraille-Samaran (Louvain-la-Neuve: Institut d'études médiévales de l'Université catholique de Louvain, 1990). There J. Le Goff, "Le travail dans les systems de valeur de l'occident médiéval" (7–21) speaks of a valorization or positive turn from the twelfth century, but linked this to the mechanical arts, not monks. A more recent summing up is by Klaus Schreiner, "'Brot der Mühsal': Körperliche Arbeit im Mönchtum des hohen und späten Mittelalters: Theologisch motivierte Einstellungen, regelgebundene Normen, geschichtliche Praxis," in *Arbeit im Mittelalter: Vorstellungen und Wirklichkeiten,* ed. Verena Postel (Berlin: Akademie Verlag, 2006), 133–70. Both Ovitt, *Restoration of Perfection,* 19–52, and Ranft, *Theology of Work,* 5–8, offer further bibliographies.

3. *Polycraticus* VI.20, ed. C. Webb (Oxford: Clarendon, 1909) II, 58–59. To expose this working peasant multitude to injury was as it were, he says, to un-shoe (*discalciata*) the commonwealth (*res publica*). To afflict these people was to give the prince gout (*principis podagram*).

4. *Biblia Latina cum glossa ordinaria* (1480/81, reprint Turnhout: Brepols, 1992), 29 (ad Gen. 3:17/18).

5. Nicholaus de Lyra, *Postilla super totam bibliam* (Strassburg, 1492; reprint 1971) I *ad* Gen. 3:17–19.

6. Nicholas, *Postilla ad* Gen 2:2–3 and Ex. 20:8–11.

7. Rupert, *De sancta trinitate et operibus eius* II.17, ed. Hrabanus Haacke (Corpus Christianorum Continuatio Mediaevalis 21; Turnhout: Brepols, 1971), 202.

8. Ibid., XII.32, ed. Haacke, 725.

9. Rather, *Praeloquia* I.2: ed. Peter Reid (Corpus Christianorum Continuatio mediaevalis 46A; Turnhout: Brepols, 1984), 5.

10. Honorius Augustodunensis, *Elucidarium* II.17–18: *Patrologiae cursus completus: series latina* [= PL], ed. J-P Migne (Paris, 1844–64), 172.1147–49.

11. Rupert, *De sancta trinitate* XII.45, ed. Haacke, 742. Cp. XXXIII.15, 1795.

12. *Glossa ordinaria ad* II Thess. 3:10 (IV, p. 403); Nicholas, *Postilla ad* II Thess. 3:10.

13. An enormous literature; see most conveniently and importantly, Giles Constable, *Three Studies in Medieval Religious and Social Thought* (Cambridge: Cambridge University Press, 1995).

14. Rupert, *De sancta trinitate* XXXVIII.20, ed. Haacke, 2000.

15. A massive subject, though with no definitive study; for the early rules, see J. Dubois, "Le travail des moines au moyen âge," in Hamesse and Muraille-Samaran, eds., *Le Travail,* 61–80.

16. Pierre Hadot, *Exercices spirituels et philosophie antique* (Paris: Bibliothèque de l'évolution de l'humanité, 1981).

17. John Cassian, *Collationes* IX.2, ed. Michael Petschenig (Corpus scriptorum ecclesiasticorum latinorum 13; Vienna: Austrian Academy of Sciences, 2004), 250–51.

18. Cassian, *De institutis coenobiorum* X.8–15, ed. Michael Petschenig (CSEL 17, Vienna: Austrian Academy of Sciences, 2004), 181–86.

19. Ibid., X.23, 192.

20. The best orientation remains Jean-Marie André, *L'Otium dans la vie morale et intellectuelle romaine, des origines à l'époque augustéenne* (Paris: Presses universitaires de France, 1966).

21. The first to set out the complex monastic usages of *otium* was Jean Leclercq, *Otia monastica: études sur le vocabulaire de la contemplation au moyen âge* (Rome: Herder, 1963).

22. The word appears to be of Christian making. Its first sustained usage is that by Cassian in n. 18.

23. Augustine, *De opere monachorum* XVII.20, XXV.33, ed. Joseph Zycha (CSEL 41; Vienna: Austrian Academy of Sciences, 1900), 564–65, 580.

24. See MacCormack, "The Virtue of Work," and Martin Meiser, "Muss ein Mönch arbeiten? Augustin, *De opere monachorum* im Horizont der altkirchlichen Diskussion," in: *Arbeit in der Antike, in Judentum und Christentum,* ed. Detlev Dormeyer, Folker Siegert, J. Cornelis de Vos (Münster: LIT Verlag, 2006), 114–40 (with a rich comparative discussion of the Thessalonian texts).

25. Benedict, *Regula Benedicti* 48.

26. Jerome, *Epistola* 125.11 (ad Rusticum), ed. Isidorus Hilberg (CSEL 56, Vienna: Austrian Academy of Sciences, 1918), 131. As Benedict would more than a century later, he expected "constant prayer" (*oratio sine intermissione*) and encouraged hand labor (here, fishing) together with reading/writing to supply sustenance and avoid *otium*.

27. See Augustine's *Praeceptum,* most approachable through George Lawless, *Augustine of Hippo and his Monastic Rule* (Oxford: Clarendon, 1987), here 80–84, a text written at virtually the same time (391/93) as his *De opere monachorum* cited above.

28. Dubois (n. 15 above), 98 said bluntly "l'agriculture cessa d'être l'occupation ordinaire des moines, quand ils devinrent prêtres."

29. Honorius (n. 10 above) alludes to this motif, actually common in monastic commentary traditions; see the opening of my "'God is No Respecter of Persons': Sacred Texts and Social Realities," in *Intellectual Life in the Middle Ages: Essays Presented to Margaret Gibson,* ed. Leslie Smith and Benedicta Ward (London: Continuum, 1992), 243–64.

30. Rodulphus Glaber, *Historiarum libri quinque* 5.1, ed. John France (Oxford: Clarendon, 1989), 217.

31. See representatively Lester K. Little, *Religious Poverty and the Profit Economy in Medieval Europe* (Ithaca: Cornell University Press, 1983), and Giles Constable, *The Reformation of the Twelfth Century* (Cambridge: Cambridge University Press, 1996).

32. For orientation to a large literature, see Martha Newman, *The Boundaries of Charity* (Stanford: Stanford University Press, 1996); Constance Bouchard, *Holy Entrepreneurs: Cistercians, Knights, and Economic Exchange in Twelfth-Century Burgundy* (Ithaca: Cornell University Press, 1991); Brian Noell, "Expectation and Unrest among Cistercian Lay Brothers in the Twelfth and Thirteenth Centuries," *Journal of Medieval History* 32 (2006): 253–74, with a clearheaded sense of the larger literature and issues; Lisa M. Sullivan, "Workers, Policy-makers, and Labor Ideals in Cistercian Legislation, 1134–1237," *Cîteaux* 3 (1989): 175–98. I have not been able to consult James France, *Separate but Equal: Cistercian Lay Brothers, 1120-1350* (Collegeville: Cistercian Publications, 2012).

33. Bernard, *Sermones super Cantica canticorum* I.12, ed. J. Leclercq (Sources Chrétiennes 414, Paris: Éditions du Cerf, 1996), 78.

34. Christopher Holdsworth, "The Blessings of Work: The Cistercian View," in *Sanctity and Secularity,* ed. Derek Baker (Oxford: Blackwell, 1973), 59–76.

35. *Cistercian Lay Brothers: Twelfth-century Usages with Related Texts,* ed. Chrysogonus Waddell (Brecht: Citeaux, 2000), 56, 164–65.

36. Rupert, *Super capitula regulae Benedicti* III.1–2: PL 170, 511–12. For background, see my *Rupert of Deutz* (Berkeley: University of California Press, 1983), 310–23.

37. Rupert, *Super capitula* III.3–5: PL 170, 512–13.

38. Ibid., III.8: PL 170.513.

39. Ibid., III.9–10: PL 170.516–17.

40. See my "Theophilus Presbyter and Rupert of Deutz: The Manual Arts and Benedictine Theology in the Early Twelfth Century," *Viator* 11 (1980): 147–63.

41. See Peter Sterngael, *Die "artes mechanicae" im Mittelalter: Begriffs- und Bedeutungsgeschichte bis zum Ende des 13. Jahrhunderts* (Kallmünz: Verlag Michael Lassleben, 1966) and *Artes mechanicae en Europe médiévale,* ed. R. Jansen-Sieben (Brussels: Archives et bibliothèques de Belgique, 1989). Ovitt, *Restoration of Perfection,* 107–36, took a stern view of the earlier literature as too forward-looking in its valuation of work; too stern in my view.

42. See now Jonathan Riley-Smith, *Templars and Hospitallers as Professed Religious in the Holy Land* (Notre Dame, IN: University of Notre Dame Press, 2010).

43. See still Gaines Post, "Masters' Salaries and Student-Fees in the Mediaeval Universities," *Speculum* 7 (1932): 181–98. The issue entered canon law under the larger rubric of possible "crimes": *Decretales* 5.5, ed. E. Friedberg, *Corpus iuris canonici* (Leipzig: Bernhard Tauchnitz, 1879) II, 767–71.

44. A recent orientation: Gregory M. Sadlek, *Idleness Working: The Discourse of Love's Labor from Ovid through Chaucer and Gower* (Washington, DC: Catholic University of America Press, 2004).

45. Ailred of Rievaulx, *De speculo caritatis* II.4–16, ed. A. Hoste and C.H. Talbot (Corpus Christianorum Continuatio Mediaevalis 1; Turnhout: Brepols, 1971), 67–74 (with explicit reference to Paul on laboring for one's bread, here applied to internal work).

46. I have dealt with this earlier in *Rupert of Deutz,* for instance, 276, and more recently in "Wrestling with the Word: Rupert's Quest for Exegetical Understanding," in: *Rupert von Deutz—Ein Denker zwischen den Zeiten,* ed. Heinz Finger, Harold Horst, and Rainer Klotz (Libelli rhenani 31, Cologne: Erzbischöfliche Diözesan- und Dombibliothek, 2009), 185–99.

47. Rupert, *Commentaria in euangelium sancti Johannis,* ed. Haacke (Corpus Christianorum 9, Turnhout: Brepols, 1969), 1; Rupert, *De glorificatione trinitatis:* PL 169.11.

48. See for instance Rupert, *In Apocalypsim:* PL 169.825–28.

49. Giles Constable, *The Letters of Peter the Venerable* (Cambridge 1967), no. 20, 38–39.

50. Petrus Damiani, *Die Briefe* 62, ed. Kurt Reindel (Die Briefe der deutschen Kaiserzeit IV, Hannover: Monumenta Germaniae Historica, 1988) II, 219. My translation is deliberately slightly more literal than that of Owen Blum, *Letters 61–90* (Washington, DC: Catholic University of America Press, 1992), 14.

51. Petrus Damiani, *Letter* 54, ed. Reindel II, 145.

52. Ibid., 96, ed. Reindel III, 47.

53. Ibid., 49, ed. Reindel II, 77.

54. Ibid., 77, ed. Reindel II, 385.

55. Ibid., 100, ed. Reindel III, 105, 102–3.

56. Joachim, *Tractatus in expositionem vite et regule beati Benedicti* III.6, ed. Alexander Patschovsky (Rome: Istituto storico italiano per il Medio Evo, 2008), 254–58.

57. Ibid., III.5, ed. Patschovsky, 243.

58. Joachim, *Psalterium decem cordarum* II (IV.4), ed. Kurt-Victor Selge (Quellen zur Geschichte des Geistesgeschichte des Mittelalters 20, Hannover: MGH, 2009), 285.

59. Joachim, *Tractatus* IV.4, II.3, ed. Patschovsky, 189–90, 193, 304–5.

60. Ibid. III.6, 274.

61. Ibid. II.2B, IV.4, ed. Patschovsky, 170, 304–5.

62. Joachim, *Psalterium* II[II.2], ed. Selge, 123–29. Joachim says people might find the analogy to coins more apt (*congruentius*).

63. Ibid. II[II.4], ed. Selge, 137–39.

Chapter 4

1. Cited in Richard Bulliet, *The Case for Islamo-Christian Civilization* (New York: Columbia University Press, 2004), 99–100. Emphasis added.

2. Samuel Huntington, "The Clash of Civilizations?" *Foreign Affairs* 72, no. 3 (summer 1993): 35. For "bloody borders" see Huntington, *The Clash of Civilizations and the Remaking of World Order* (New York: Touchstone, 1997), 258.

3. Bulliet, *Case for Islamo-Christian Civilization,* 9–13.

4. *The Joint Declaration of the Paris Summit of the Mediterranean* can be accessed at the Union for the Mediterranean's website: http://www.ufmsecretariat.org/en/institutional-documents.

5. Cf. Benjamin, "Theses on the Philosophy of History," VII: "There is no document of civilization which is not at the same time a document of barbarism." Walter Benjamin, *Illuminations,* trans. Harry Zohn (New York: Schocken, 1977).

6. The official translation of Benedict XVI's speech is available on the Vatican's website, at http://www.vatican.va/holy_father/benedict_xvi/speeches/2006/september/documents/hf_ben-xvi_spe_20060912_university-regensburg_en.html. For a much more extended version of the arguments I am presenting in this section of this paper, see my "Judentum und Islam in der europäischen Dialektik von Glaube und Vernunft: Anmerkungen zur Geschichtstheologie Papst Benedikts XVI," in *Religionskontroversen im Verfassungsstaat,* ed. Hans G. Kippenberg and Astrid Reuter (Göttingen: Verlag Vandenhoeck & Ruprecht, 2010), 181–207.

7. http://avalon.law.yale.edu/20th_century/hamas.asp. For a slightly different translation, see http://www.thejerusalemfund.org/www.thejerusalemfund.org/carryover/documents/charter.html.

8. All quotes in this and the following paragraph were provided to me by Media Matters for America.

9. See the introduction to Rauf's *What's Right with Islam: A New Vision for Muslims and the West* (New York: HarperCollins, 2004), 2.

10. Ibid., 275.

11. See Joel Kraemer, *Maimonides: the Life and World of One of Civilization's Greatest Minds* (New York: Doubleday, 2008), 37–41, and Sarah Stroumsa, *Maimonides in His World: Portrait of a Mediterranean Thinker* (Princeton, NJ: Princeton University Press, 2009), 8–10, 59–61.

12. Throughout his *Persian Wars,* trans. A. D. Godley (Cambridge, MA: Harvard University Press, 1920–25), Herodotus switches freely between "barbarians" and "Persians" when naming the enemy of the Greeks. This does not mean, of course, that Herodotus cannot also use comparisons with the Persians to criticize the Greeks.

13. Johann Gottfried Herder, *Briefe zu Beförderung der Humanität,* in Herder, *Werke,* edited by Martin Bollacher et al., Bd. 7 (Frankfurt am Main: Deutscher Klassiker, 1991), 475, 483.

14. All NT translations quoted here are from the Revised Standard Version. Hebrew Bible quotations are from the JPS translation.

15. Some modern New Testament commentators argue that these words should not be attributed to Christ. *The New Oxford Annotated Bible,* 3rd ed., ed. Michael Coogan (Oxford: Oxford University Press, 2001), for example, suggests that Luke 19:11–27 be read as a parable alluding to the uneasy succession from Herod to Archelaus in 4 BCE. The "voice" commanding execution would then be that of Archelaus, not Jesus. Nevertheless many early Christian thinkers, ignorant of modern scholarship and apologetics, read these passages as authentic quotations of Jesus.

See, e.g., John Chrysostom's use of the "slay them before me" passage in *Against the Jews,* I.2 (PG 48.846).

16. See Jonathan Riley-Smith, "Crusading as an Act of Love," *History* 65, no. 214 (June 1980): 177–92.

17. Michael Gaddis, *There Is No Crime for Those Who Have Christ: Religious Violence in the Christian Roman Empire* (Berkeley: University of California Press, 2005); Brent D. Shaw, *Sacred Violence: African Christians and Sectarian Hatred in the Age of Augustine* (Cambridge: Cambridge University Press, 2011). On the relationship between Christian imperial Holy War and early Islamic ideas about sacred violence, see Tom Sizgorich, *Violence and Belief in Late Antiquity: Militant Devotion in Christianity and Islam* (Philadelphia: University of Pennsylvania Press, 2009).

18. The tradition is discussed in Uri Rubin, *Between Bible and Qur'an: the Children of Israel and the Islamic Self-Image* (Princeton: Darwin, 1999), 137. Cf. 117–46.

19. Deuteronomy 27–28.

20. Galatians 3:15–17 (on what the "seed of Abraham" means) and 4:29–31 (on the difference between children born to a slave as opposed to a free woman), or Romans 4:2–4 (where Paul's interpretation of Genesis 15:6 undergirds the entire doctrine of justification by faith).

21. My use of the term *sectarian community* owes a great deal to the observations of John Wansbrough *The Sectarian Milieu: Content and Composition of Islamic Salvation History* (Oxford: Oxford University Press, 1978).

22. On the many prophetic traditions within the Qur'an, see Brannon Wheeler, *Prophets in the Qur'an: An Introduction to the Qur'an and Muslim Exegesis* (London: Continuum, 2002). For Judaeo-Christians, see S. Pines, "Notes on Islam and on Arabic Christianity and Judaeo-Christianity," *Jerusalem Studies in Arabic and Islam* 4 (1984): 135–52. On the Samaritans see the article by John Bowman, *"Banū Isrā'īl* in the Qur'ān," *Islamic Studies* 2 (1963): 447–55, who argues that many Samaritans greeted Muhammad as the "prophet like unto Moses" promised in Deuteronomy 18:18. See also P. Crone and M. Cook, *Hagarism: The Making of the Islamic World* (Cambridge: Cambridge University Press, 1977), 14–15, 21–28. On the importance of Syriac Christian gospel commentaries and traditions in the Qur'anic community, see Joseph Witztum, "The Foundations of the House (Q 2:127)," *Bulletin of the School of Oriental and African Studies,* 72 (2009): 25–40, as well as the same author's forthcoming Ph.D. dissertation (Princeton University). For some new methodological approaches to the study of intertexts, see Dirk Hartwig, Walter Homolka, Michael Marx, and Angelika Neuwirth, eds., *"In Vollen Licht der Geschichte:" Die Wissenschaft des Judentums und die Anfänge der kritischen Koranforschung,* Ex Oriente Lux 8 (Würzburg: Ergon, 2008).

23. Unless otherwise indicated, all translations from the Qur'an (henceforth Q) are from *The Meaning of the Holy Qur'ān,* trans. 'Abdullah Yusuf 'Ali, 11th ed. (Amana Publications: Beltsville, MD, 2006).

24. On this see, among others: Cornelia Horn, "Syriac and Arabic Perspectives on Structural and Motif Parallels Regarding Jesus' Childhood in Christian Apocrypha and Early Islamic Literature: the 'Book of Mary', the *Arabic Apocryphal Gospel of John* and the Qur'ān," *Apocrypha* 19 (2008): 267–91; Neal Robinson, "Creating Birds from Clay: A Miracle of Jesus in the Qur'an and Classical Muslim Exegesis," *Muslim World* 79, no. 1 (1989): 1–13.

25. Babylonian Talmud, Shabbat 88a. See also BT Avoda Zara. Other Aggadic traditions derive the same story from Cant. 8.5, "Under the Apple tree did I stir thee up:" Midrash shir-ha-shirim (ed. L. Grünhaut, Jerusalem), 47b. and Cant. Rabba 45a col. B (top).

26. The Qur'anic transformation of this phrase, however, was itself deeply influenced by rabbinic Jewish commentaries, as Julian Obermann brilliantly demonstrated in "Koran and Agada: The Events at Mount Sinai," *American Journal of Semitic Languages and Literatures* 58 (1941): 23–48. See also G. D. Newby, "Arabian Jewish history in the Sīrah," *Jerusalem Studies in Arabic and Islam* 7 (1986): 121–38, here 136–38; and I. de Mateo, "Il Tahrīf od alterazione della Bibbia secondo i musulmani," *Bessarione* 38 (1922): 64–111, 223–360.

27. See Friedrich Nietzsche, "On the Uses and Disadvantages of History for Life," in *Untimely Meditations,* trans. R. J. Hollingdale (Cambridge: Cambridge University Press, 1997), 57–124.

28. Italics added. On these terms see L. Kinberg, "*Muḥkamāt* and *mutashābihāt* (Koran 3/7): Implications of a Koranic pair of terms in Medieval Exegesis," *Arabica* 35 (1988): 143–72.

29. John Wansbrough, *Quranic Studies: Sources and Methods of Scriptural Interpretation* (Amherst, NY: Prometheus, 2004), 149.

30. There is an important bibliography on this verse, its variant versions, and its vocabulary. See above all Stefan Wild, "The Self-Referentiality of the Qur'ān: Sura 3:7 as an Exegetical Challenge," in *With Reverence for the Word: Medieval Scriptural Exegesis in Judaism, Christianity, and Islam,* ed. Jane Dammen McAuliffe et al. (Oxford: Oxford University Press, 2010), 421–36.

31. See Friedrich Niewöhner, "Zum Ursprung von der Lehre von der doppelten Wahrheit: Eine Koran-Interpretation des Averroes," in *Averroismus im Mittelalter und in der Renaissance,* ed. F. Niewöhner and Loris Sturlese (Zurich: Spur, 1994), 23–41. The translation is by George F. Hourani, *Averroes on the Harmony of Religion and Philosophy* (London: Luzac, 1961), 66. The Arabic is in Ibn Rushd, *Kitāb faṣl al-maqāl wa-taqrīr mā bayna sharī'a wa-l-ḥikma mina l-ittiṣāl,* ed. Albert N. Nader (Beirut: n.p., 1961), 53. Cf. *Kitāb faṣl al-maqāl,* 38–39. I say "seemed" in order to avoid opining on the question—contentious long before Leo Strauss and his followers highlighted its relevance for modern thought—of whether or not Ibn Rushd believed that the two truths did indeed contradict each other.

32. The most important work of Taha's that has been translated into English is *The Second Message of Islam,* trans. Abdullahi Ahmed An-Na'im (Syracuse: Syracuse University Press, 1987). On the life of Ustadh Mahmoud see An-Na'im's introduction to *The Second Message,* as well as his article "The Islamic Law of Apostasy and its Modern Applicability: a Case from the Sudan," *Religion* 16, no. 3 (1986): 197–224 (written in response to Taha's 1985 execution by the regime of President Numeiri). Taha was first known as a leader in the Sudanese independence movement, and later as a major figure in that country's Republican Party. Numeiri banned Taha from lecturing publicly (in 1973), then imprisoned him (1983–84), and finally had him condemned and executed him. For fuller treatment, see Mohamed A. Mahmoud, *Quest for Divinity: A Critical Examination of the Thought of Mahmud Muhammad Taha* (Syracuse: Syracuse University Press, 2007), esp. 12–40.

33. Jews might think here of parallels with the "Doctrine of Accommodation" developed by Maimonides, a doctrine he himself described with a word adapted from the Qur'an: *talaṭṭuf*, God's "shrewdness in the service of loving kindness." The theme runs throughout the *Guide for the Perplexed,* trans. M. Friedlander (New York: Dover, 1956), but see 3.29–50. Christians might think of parallels with I Corinthians 3:1–2: "I fed you with milk and not solid food, for you were not able to take it."

34. On Taha's flexible and contextual style of Qur'anic hermeneutics, see Mahmoud, *Quest for Divinity,* 97–99 ("The Qur'an as Open Text") and 100–104 ("Interpretive Strategies"). On Taha's philosophy of history, see ibid., 132–38. Taha's point is summarized nicely in ibid., 177: "Islam is historical, and by virtue of this historicity it assumes a changeable and mutable nature that allows it not only to respond to the needs of past societies but also to the more complex needs of present-day global societies."

35. Taha, *Second Message,* 165: "God wishes us to have more of His knowledge every moment. He says: 'Everyday He [reveals Himself] in a fresh state'" (55.29).

36. *"Ha-peshtot ha-methadshim be-khol yom"* Rashbam, *Commentary on the Pentateuch (Perush ha-Torah)* (Jerusalem: Hotsa'at Sefarim Horev, 2009), 37, 2. The passage was brought to my attention by Israel Yuval.

37. Taha, *Second Message,* 149: "For this reason it is false to assert that the Qur'an may be finally and conclusively explained."

38. Ibid., 169.

39. Cf. ibid., 166, for his citations of 9:5, 3:159, and 88:21–22, though he cites those same verses throughout his work.

40. For more on Numeiri's imposition of Shari'a law to the detriment of women and non-Muslim Sudanese, see Ann M. Lesch, "The Fall of Numeiri," *University Field Staff International Reports* 9 (1985): 1–14, esp. 9–10 on "Islamization." See also ibid., 11, on the hanging of Taha and the humiliation of the Republicans.

41. The 2003 document is available at http://archive.org/details/nationalstrategy 29185gut. The 2006 update can be found at http://www.cfr.org/terrorism/national-strategy-combating-terrorism-2006/p11389. Cheryl Benard, *Civil and Democratic Islam: Partners, Resources, Strategies* (Pittsburgh: Rand Corporation, 2003).

42. Saba Mahmood, "Secularism, Hermeneutics, and Empire: The Politics of Islamic Reformation," *Public Culture* 18, no. 2 (2006): 323–47. The figure of $1.3 billion is provided by Mahmood, 330.

43. On the reappropriation of Ibn Taymiyya, see *Ibn Taymiyya and His Times,* ed. Yossef Rapoport and Shahab Ahmed (Karachi: Oxford University Press, 2010), especially the essay by Mona Hassan, "Modern Interpretations and Misinterpretations of a Medieval Scholar: Apprehending the Political Thought of Ibn Taymiyya," 338–66. An argument against the categorization of Ibn Taymiyya as a fundamentalist or "extremist" can be found in Yahya Michot, *Muslims under Non-Muslim Rule: Ibn Taymiyya,* trans. Jamil Qureshi (Oxford: Interface, 2006). See also Jon Hoover's *Ibn Taymiyya's Theodicy of Perpetual Optimism* (Leiden: Brill, 2007), which even suggests the presence of "rationalistic" and "egalitarian" possibilities in his writings.

44. See Jean-Luc Nancy, *Dis-Enclosure: The Deconstruction of Christianity,* trans. Bettina Bergo, Gabriel Malenfant, and Michael B. Smith (New York: Fordham University Press, 2008).

Chapter 5

1. This chapter is based on my oral presentation at the University of Florida on December 1, 2008. These remarks are now considerably expanded in *Early Modern Jewry: A New Cultural History* (Princeton: Princeton University Press, 2010).

2. See, for example, Sanjay Subrahmanyam, "Connected Histories: Notes towards a Reconfiguration of Early Modern Eurasia," *Modern Asian Studies* 31 (1997): 735–62 (reprinted in Victor Liebermann, ed. *Beyond Binary Histories: Re-Imagining Eurasia to c. 1800* [Ann Arbor: University of Michigan Press, 1999], 289–316); *Explorations in Connected History: From the Tagus to the Ganges* (New Delhi: Oxford University Press, 2004); and the companion volume, *Explorations in Connected History: Mughals and Franks* (New Delhi: Oxford University Press, 2004).

3. For what follows, I rely heavily on the essays of Elhanan Reiner, including his "The Ashkenazic Elite at the Beginning of the Modern Era: Manuscript versus Printed Text," in *Jews in Early Modern Poland,* ed. Gershon Hundert, Polin vol. 10 (London: Littman Library, 1997), 85–98; Reiner, "Transformations in the Polish and Ashkenazic *Yeshivot* during the Sixteenth and Seventeenth Centuries and the Dispute over *Pilpul,* (Hebrew)" *Ke-Minhag Ashkenaz ve-Polin: Sefer Yovel le-Chone Shmeruk* (Jerusalem: Merkaz Zalman Shazar le-Toldot Yisrael, 1989), 9–80; Reiner, "The Attitude of Ashkenazi Society to the New Science in the Sixteenth Century," *Science in Context* 10 (1997): 589–603; Reiner, "A Biography of an Agent of Culture: Eleazar Altschul of Prague and his Literary Activity," in *Schöpferische Momente des europäischen Judentums in der frühen Neuzeit,* ed. M. Graetz (Heidelberg: Winter, 2000), 229–47; Reiner, "The Rise of the Large Community: On the Roots of the Urban Jewish Community in Poland in the Early Modern Period (Hebrew)," *Gal-Ed* 20 (2006): 13–36 (This essay appears in English in a shorted version entitled: "The Rise of an Urban Community: Some Insights on the Transition from the Medieval Ashkenazi to the 16th Century Jewish Community in Poland," *Kwartalnik Historii Żydów Jewish Historical Quarterly* 3 [2003]: 364–72). Reiner is presently completing a monograph on this topic. I wish to thank him for allowing me to read part of this work before publication. On the *Shulhan Arukh* in general, see Isadore Twersky, "The *Shulhan Aruk:* Enduring Code of Jewish Law," *Judaism* 16, no. 2 (1967): 141–58; Joseph Davis, "The Reception of the "Shulhan Arukh" and the Formation of Ashkenazic Jewish Identity," *Association for Jewish Studies Review* 26 (2002): 251–76.

4. Reiner, "Ashkenazic Elite," 97–98.

5. On the controversies over the invasion of the Sephardic library in Eastern Europe, including the debate over the study of Maimonides's philosophical works in Isserles's *yeshivah,* see Reiner's essays in note 3 above. On the printing and circulation of exegetical, homiletical, philosophical, and kabbalistic works in Eastern Europe, see Jacob Elbaum, *Petihut ve-Histagrut: Ha-Yezirah ha-Ruhanit-Ha-Sifrutit be-Folin u-be-Arzot Ashkenaz be-Shalhei Ha-Me'ah Ha-Sheh-Esrei* (Jerusalem: Magnus, 1990), 67–248. On scientific works, see ibid., 248–79; and David Ruderman, *Jewish Thought and Scientific Discovery in Early Modern Europe,* 2nd ed. (Detroit: Wayne State University Press, 2001), 54–99. On Tobias Cohen's medical encyclopedia, see Ruderman, *Jewish Thought,* 229–55. See also Shifra Baruchson, *Sefarim ve-Korim: Tarbut Ha-Keriyah shel Yehudei Italia be-Shalhei Ha-Renasans* (Ramat Gan: Bar Ilan University Press, 1993); Baruchson, "Diffusion of Books: Sacred

Writing and Classical Literature in the Libraries of Renaissance Jews," (Hebrew) *Italia* 8 (1989): 87–99; Robert Bonfil, "The Libraries of Jews," (Hebrew) *Pe'amim* 52 (1992): 4–15; Ze'ev Gries, "Printing as a Means of Communication among Jewish Communities," 5–17; Gries, *Sifrut Ha-Hanhagot: Toldedoteha u-Mekoma be-Hayyai Hasidov shel ha-Besht* (Jerusalem: Mosad Byalik 1989); Gries, *Sefer Sofer ve-Sippur be-Reshit Ha-Hasidut* (Tel Aviv: Kibbutz ha-Me'uhad, 1992); Gries, *The Book in the Jewish* World (Oxford: Littman Library, 2007); Joseph Hacker, "The Hebrew Press in Constantinople in the Sixteenth Century (Hebrew)," *Areshet* 5 (1972): 457–93; and Meir Benayahu, "The Shift of the Center of Hebrew Printing from Venice to Amsterdam and the Competition with the Jewish Printing in Constantinople (Hebrew)," *Mehkaram al Toledot Yahadut Holland,* ed. Jozeph Michman, vol. 1 (Jerusalem: Magnus, 1975), 41–68.

6. See Lester Segal, *Historical Consciousness and Religious Tradition in Azariah de' Rossi's Me'or Einayim* (Philadelphia: JPS, 1989), 153–61; and Robert Bonfil, "Some Reflections on the Place of Azariah de Rossi's *Meor Eynayim* in the Cultural Milieu of Italian Renaissance Jewry," in *Jewish Thought in the Sixteenth Century,* ed. Bernard Cooperman (Cambridge, MA: Harvard University Press, 1983), 23–48. Modena's reference is in Marc Saperstein, *Jewish Preaching, 1200–1800: An Anthology* (New Haven: Yale University Press, 1989), 412.

7. See Reiner, "A Biography of an Agent of Culture"; the works of Ze'ev Gries mentioned in note 5; Chone Shmeruk, *Sifrut Yidish be-Polin* (Jerusalem: Magnus, 1991); Elbaum, *Petihut ve-Histagrut;* Moshe Rosman, "Culture in the Book (Hebrew)," *Zion* 56 (1991): 321–44; Rosman, "On Being a Jewish Woman in Poland-Lithuania at the Beginning of the Modern Era," in *Kiyum ve-Shever,* ed. by Israel Bartal and Israel Gutman (Jerusalem, Machon Shazar, 2001), 415–34; Israel Halperin, "The Council of Four Lands and the Hebrew Book," in *Yehudim ve-Yahadut be-Mizrah Eropah* (Jerusalem: Magnus, 1968), 78–107.

8. See Gershom Scholem, *Major Trends in Jewish Mysticism* (New York: Schocken Books, 1960), 244–324; Scholem, *Sabbatai Sevi: The Mystical Messiah 1626–1676* (Princeton: Princeton University Press, 1973); Moshe Idel, *Kabbalah: New Perspectives* (New Haven and London: Yale University Press, 1988); Yehudah Liebes, *Sod ha-Emunah ha-Shabta'it* (Jerusalem: Mosad Byalik, 1995).

9. See Isaiah Tishby, "The Controversy about the *Zohar* in the Sixteenth Century in Italy (Hebrew)," in his *Hekrei Kabbalah u-Sheluhoteha* (Jerusalem: Magnus, 1982), 79–130; Moshe Idel, "From Hiding to Printing an Esoteric Law: Between R. Isaac Sagi Nahor and Rabbi Isaac Luria," typescript.

10. See Gries, *Sifrut Ha-Hanhagot;* Jacob Barnay, *Shabta'ut: Hebetim Hevrati'im* (Jerusalem: Merkaz Zalman Shazar le-toldot Yisrael, 2000), 69–90; Barnay, "The Spread of the Sabbatean Movement in the Seventeenth and Eighteenth Centuries," in *Communication in the Jewish Diaspora: The Pre-Modern World,* ed. Sophia Menache (Leiden: Brill, 1996), 313–37.

11. On Yiddish books, see Shlomo Berger, "Yiddish and Jewish Modernization in the 18th Century," (Hebrew) *Braun Lectures in the History of the Jews in Prussia* 12 (Ramat Gan: Bar Ilan University Press, 2006); Berger, "An Invitation to Buy and Read: Paratexts of Yiddish Books in Amsterdam 1650–1800," *Book History* 7 (2004): 31–61; Chava Turiansky and Erika Timm, *Yiddish in Italia* (Milano: Associazione italiana amici dell'Università di Gerusalemme, 2003); Miriam Gutchow, *Inventory of*

Printed Books in the Netherlands (Leiden: Brill, 2006); and Jerold Frakes, *Early Yiddish Texts 1100–1750* (Oxford: Oxford University Press, 2004). See also the interesting essay of Avriel Bar-Levav, "Between Library Awareness and the Jewish Republic of Letters (Hebrew)," in *Sifriyot ve-Osfei Sefarim,* ed. Yosef Kaplan and Moshe Sluhovsky (Jerusalem: Merkaz Zalman Shazar le-toldot Yisrael, 2006), 201–24.

12. On Ladino, see Yitshak Molcho, "La Littérature judéo-espanole en Turquie au premier siècle après les expulsions d'Espagne et du Portugal," *Tesor de los Judios Sefardies* 1 (1959): 15–53; Abraham Yaari, *Catalogue of Books in Judeo-Spanish* (Hebrew) (Jerusalem: Kiriyat Sepher, 1934); Aron Rodrigue, *Guide to the Ladino Materials in the Harvard College Library* (Cambridge, MA: Harvard College Library, 1992); Elena Romero, "Literary Creation of the Sephardi Diaspora," in *Moreshet Sepharad: The Sephardic Legacy,* 2 vol. (Jerusalem: Magnus, 1992), 1:438–60; and Matthias B. Lehmann, *Ladino Rabbinic Literature and Ottoman Sephardic Culture* (Bloomington: University of Indiana, 2005).

13. On Leone Ebreo's work, see, for example, Arthur Lesley, "The Place of the *Dialoghi d'amore* in Contemporaneous Jewish Thought," in *Essential Papers on Jewish Culture in Renaissance and Baroque Italy,* ed. David Ruderman (New York: NYU Press, 1992), 170–88; Barbara Garvin, "The Language of Leone Ebreo's *Dialoghi d'amore,*" *Italia* 13–15 (2001): 181–210; On Usque's work, see *Samuel Usque's Consolation for the Tribulations of Israel,* trans. Martin Cohen (Philadelphia: JPS, 1965). On Delmedigo's work, see M. David Geffen, "Insights into the Life and Thought of Elijah Delmedigo Based on his Published and Unpublished Works," *Proceedings of the American Academy for Jewish Research* 41–42 (1973–74): 69–86. On Mantino, see David Kaufmann, "Jacob Mantino: une page de l'histoire de la Renaissance," *Revue des études juives* 27 (1893): 30–60, 207–38.

14. See Robert Bonfil, *Rabbis and Jewish Communities in Renaissance Italy* (Oxford: Littman Library, 1990), 298–316; *Preachers of the Italian Ghetto,* ed. David Ruderman (Berkeley: University of California Press, 1992); Saperstein, *Jewish Preaching,* 1–63.

15. See Mark Cohen, "Leone da Modena's Riti: A Seventeenth Century Plea for Social Toleration of Jews," in *Essential Papers on Jewish Culture,* ed. David Ruderman (New York: NYU Press, 1992), 429–73; Benjamin Ravid, *Economics and Toleration in Seventeenth Century Venice* (Jerusalem: American Academy for Jewish Research, 1978); *Menasseh ben Israel and his World,* ed. Yosef Kaplan, Henry Méchoulan, and Richard Popkin (Leiden: Brill, 1989); Yosef Kaplan, *From Christianity to Judaism: The Story of Isaac Orobio de Castro* (Oxford: Oxford University Press, 1989).

16. Simone Luzzatto, *Discorso circa il stato de gl'hebrei et in particular dimoranti nell'inclita città de Venetia* (Venice: Appresso Gioanne Calleoni, 1638), 73–85. For a discussion of this work, see Ravid, *Economics and Toleration.* See also Profiat Duran, *Ma'aseh Efod* (Vienna: J. Holzwarth, 1865), introduction. On Reuchlin, see note 20 below. For a different interpretation of this chapter, see Robert Bonfil, "A Cultural Profile," in *The Jews of Early Modern Venice,* ed. Robert Davis and Benjamin Ravid (Baltimore: Johns Hopkins University Press, 2001), 170–73.

17. On the use of English manuals on Judaism written simultaneously for internal and external usage, see David Ruderman, *Jewish Enlightenment in an English Key: Anglo-Jewry's Construction of Modern Jewish Thought* (Princeton: Princeton University Press, 2000), 240–68. On the illustration of *Minhag* books, see Diane Wolfthal, "Imagining

the Self: Representations of Jewish Ritual in Yiddish Books of Customs," in *Imagining the Self, Imagining the Other: Visual Representation and Jewish-Christian Dynamics in the Middle Ages and Early Modern Period,* ed. Eva Frojmovic (Leiden: Brill, 2002), 189–211. On Picart and representations of Jews in the early modern period, see Richard Cohen, *Jewish Icons: Art and Society in Modern Europe* (Berkeley: University of California Press, 1998), 10–67; Samantha Baskind, "Bernard Picart's Etchings of Amsterdam's Jews," *Jewish Social Studies* 13 no. 1 (2007): 40–64; and Lynn Hunt, Margaret C. Jacob, and Winjhand Mijnhardt, *The Book that Changed Europe: Picart's and Bernard's Religious Ceremonies of the World* (Cambridge, MA: Belknap Press of Harvard University Press, 2010).

18. Scholarship on medieval Christian attitudes towards Judaism and Jewish texts is vast. A sampling might include Beryl Smalley, *The Study of the Bible in the Middle Ages* (Oxford: Blackwell, 1983); Harry Halperin, *Rashi and the Christian Scholars* (Pittsburgh: University of Pittsburgh Press, 1963); Jeremy Cohen, *The Friars and the Jews: The Evolution of Medieval Anti-Judaism* (Ithaca: Cornell University Press, 1982); Cohen, *Living Letters of the Law: Ideas of the Jews in Medieval Christianity* (Berkeley: University of California Press, 1999); and more recently, Deeana Copeland Klepper, *The Insight of Unbelievers: Nicholas of Lyra and Christian Reading of Jewish Text in the Later Middle Ages* (Philadelphia: University of Pennsylvania Press, 2007).

19. For a more detailed discussion of Pico and the Christian kabbalah, see David Ruderman, "The Italian Renaissance and Jewish Thought," in *Renaissance Humanism: Foundations, Forms and Legacy,* 3 vols., ed. Albert Rabil Jr. (Philadelphia: University of Pennsylvania Press, 1987), 1:382–433. See also Umberto Cassuto, *Ha-Yehudim Be-Firenzi bi-Tekufat ha-Renasans* (Jerusalem: Makhon Ben Tzvi, 1967); Fabrizio Lelli, "Yohanan Alemanno, Giovanni Pico della Mirandola e la cultura ebraica italiana del xv secolo," in *Giovanni Pico della Mirandola, convegno internazionale di studi nel cinquecentesimo anniversario della morte, 1494–1994,* ed. Gian Carlo Garfagnini (Firenze: Mirandola, 1994); Bernard McGinn, "Cabalists and Christians: Reflections on Cabala in Medieval and Renaissance Thought," in *Jewish Christians and Christian Jews: From the Renaissance to the Enlightenment,* eds. Richard Popkin and Gordon Weiner (Dordrecht: Kluwer Academic, 1994), 11–34; Frances Yates, *The Occult Philosophy in the Renaissance* (London: Routledge, 1979); and Chaim Wirszubski, *Pico della Mirandola's Encounter with Jewish Mysticism* (Cambridge, MA: Harvard University Press, 1989).

20. Jerome Friedman, *The Most Ancient Testimony: Sixteenth Century Christian Hebraica in the Age of Renaissance Nostalgia* (Athens, OH: Ohio University Press, 1983); Heiko Obermann, *The Roots of Anti-Semitism in the Age of the Renaissance and Reformation* (Philadelphia: Fortress Press, 1984); Erika Rummel, *The Case Against Johann Reuchlin: Social and Religious Controversy in Sixteenth-Century Germany* (Toronto: University of Toronto Press, 2002).

21. See especially Friedman, *The Most Ancient Testimony;* and more recently, Dean Phillip Bell and Stephen Burnett, eds., *Jews, Judaism, and the Reformation in Sixteenth-Century Germany* (Leiden: Brill, 2006).

22. Frank Manuel, *The Broken Staff: Judaism through Christian Eyes* (Cambridge, MA: Harvard University Press, 1992); *Hebraica Veritas? Christian Hebraists, Jews, and the Study of Judaism in Early Modern Europe,* ed. Allison Coudert and Jeffrey Shoulson

(Philadelphia: University of Pennsylvania Press, 2004); Allison Coudert, *The Impact of the Kabbalah in the Seventeenth Century: The Life and Thought of Francis Mercury van Helmont (1614–1698)* (Leiden: Brill, 1999); *Christliche Kabbala,* ed. Wilhelm Schmidt-Biggeman (Ostfildern: Thorbecke, 2003); Steven Burnett, *From Christian Hebraism to Jewish Studies: Johannes Buxtorf (1564–1629) and Hebrew Learning in the Seventeenth Century* (Leiden: Brill, 1996), and see the review of the latter by Amnon Raz-Krakotzkin in *Tarbiz* 68 (1999–2000): 449–55. See most recently, Jason Rosenblatt, *Renaissance England's Chief Rabbi: John Selden* (Oxford: Oxford University Press, 2006) David Ruderman, *Connecting the Covenants: Judaism and the Search for Christian Identity in Eighteenth-Century England* (Philadelphia: University of Pennsylvania, 2007); and Eric Nelson, *The Hebrew Republic: Jewish Sources and the Transformation of European Political Thought* (Cambridge, MA: Harvard University Press, 2010).

23. See Yaakov Deutsch, "A View of the Jewish Religion: Conceptions of Jewish Practice and Ritual in Early Modern Europe," *Archiv für Religionsgeschichte,* 3, Band, 2001: 273–95; Steven Burnett, "Distorted Mirrors: Antonius Margaritha, Johann Buxtorf and Christian Ethnographies of the Jews," *Sixteenth Century Journal* 25 (1994): 275–87; Ronnie Po-chia Hsia, "Christian Ethnographies of Jews in Early Modern Germany," in *The Expulsion of the Jews: 1492 and After,* eds. Raymond Waddington and Arthur Williamson (New York: Garland, 1994), 223–35.

24. In addition to the references in the previous notes, see especially Stephen G. Burnett, "Christian Hebrew Printing in the Sixteenth Century: Printers, Humanism, and the Impact of the Reformation," *Helmantica* 51 (2000): 13–42.

25. See, for example, the testimony of Elijah Halfan, cited in Moshe Idel, "The Magical and Neoplatonic Interpretations of the Kabbalah in the Renaissance," in *Essential Papers on Jewish Culture in Renaissance and Baroque Italy,* ed. David Ruderman (New York: NYU Press, 1992), 107–8.

26. On Kennicott and Lowth, see Ruderman, *Jewish Enlightenment,* chapters 1–2. On Michaelis and Christian critiques of the Massoretic text, see Edward Breuer, *The Limits of Enlightenment: Jews, Germans, and the Eighteenth-Century Study of Scripture* (Cambridge, MA: Harvard University Press, 1995).

27. On Jewish converts, see Elisheva Carlebach, *Divided Souls: Converts from Judaism in Germany 1500–1750* (New Haven: Yale University Press, 2001); and Ruderman, *Connecting the Covenants.*

Chapter 6

1. Guy G. Stroumsa, *A New Science? The Discovery of Religion in the Age of Reason* (Cambridge, MA: Harvard University Press, 2010).

2. Joseph Juste Scaliger, *Scaligerana, ou Bons mots, rencontres agreables, et remarques judicieuses & sçavantes de J. Scaliger* (Amsterdam: Chez les Huguetans, 1695), 184, 218–19.

3. See *"All my books in foreign tongues": Scaliger's Oriental legacy in Leiden, 1609–2009: Catalogue of an Exhibition on the Quatercentenary of Scaliger's Death, 21 January 2009,* ed. Arnoud Vrolijk et al. (Leiden: Leiden University Library, 2009).

4. *Scaligerana,* 383.

5. Ibid., 219, 332.

6. Ibid., 173, 184. The Hebrew text in question was the Josippon, the medieval Hebrew translation of Josephus.

7. Scaliger's draft is preserved in Leiden University Library MS Or. 6882.

8. See, e.g., *Printing the Talmud: From Bomberg To Schottenstein,* ed. Sharon Liberman Mintz and Gabriel Goldstein (New York: Yeshiva University Museum, 2005); Albert von der Heide, *Hebraica veritas: Christopher Plantin and the Christian Hebraists* (Antwerp: Plantin-Moretus Museum/Printroom, 2008); Theodor Dunkelgrün, "Radical Philology: The Confluence of Textual Traditions in the Making of the Antwerp Polyglot Bible (1568–1573)," Ph.D. diss., University of Chicago, 2012.

9. R. Po-chia Hsia, *The Myth of Ritual Murder: Jews and Magic in Reformation Germany* (New Haven: Yale University Press, 1988); Hsia, *Trent 1475: Stories of a Ritual Murder Trial* (New Haven: Yale University Press, 1992).

10. See Hans-Martin Kirn, *Das Bild vom Juden im Deutschland des frühen 16. Jahrhunderts: dargestellt an den Schriften Johannes Pfefferkorns* (Tübingen: Mohr, 1989); Ellen Martin, *Die deutschen Schriften des Johannes Pfefferkorn: zum Problem des Judenhasses und der Intoleranz in der Zeit der Vorreformation* (Göppingen: Kümmerle, 1994); Johannes Pfefferkorn, *The Jews' Mirror,* trans. Ruth Cape, ed. Maria Diemling (Tempe: Arizona Center for Medieval and Renaissance Studies, 2011).

11. There were medieval precedents for the arguments that Mithridates used, though the scale at which he worked may have been novel. For the case of Petrus Alfonsi, also a convert, see John Tolan, *Petrus Alfonsi and his Medieval Readers* (Gainesville: University of Florida Press, 1993), 12–27.

12. See Flavius Guillelmus Ramundus Mithridates, *Flavius Mithridates Sermo de passione Domini,* ed. Chaim Wirszubski (Jerusalem: Israel Academy of Sciences and Humanities, 1963); Chaim Wirszubski, *Pico della Mirandola's Encounter with Jewish Mysticism* (Cambridge, MA: Harvard University Press, 1989); and *Guglielmo Raimondo Moncada alias Flavio Mitridate: un ebreo converso siciliano,* ed. Mauro Perani and Luciana Pepi (Palermo: Officina di Studi Medievali, 2008).

13. Johann Amerbach, *Correspondence,* ed. and trans. Barbara Halporn (Ann Arbor: University of Michigan Press, 2000), 360–61; Basel, Öffentliche Bibliothek, MS A VII 2, fol. 273 recto-verso.

14. Basel, Öffentliche Bibliothek, MS A VII 2, note on Psalm 22:16 (17).

15. The extent to which early modern Hebraists depended on tools forged by medieval Christian scholars remains to be explored: for a rich presentation of the evidence see *Crossing Borders: Hebrew Manuscripts as a Meeting-place of Cultures,* ed. Piet von Boxel and Sabine Arndt (Oxford: The Bodleian Library, 2010).

16. See François Secret, *Les kabbalistes chrétiens de la Renaissance* (Paris: Dunod, 1964); David Price, *Johannes Reuchlin and the Campaign to Destroy Jewish Books* (Oxford: Oxford University Press, 2011); Stephen Burnett, *Christian Hebraism in the Reformation Era (1500–1660): Authors, Books, and the Transmission of Jewish Learning* (Leiden: Brill, 2012).

17. Münster's edition of Jonah is *Ionas propheta in quatuor orbis principalioribus linguis: Graeca, Latina, Hebraea atque Chaldaica, pulchre sibi correspondentibus columnellis* (Basel, 1524). Conrad Gesner's copy of Abraham ibn Ezra, *Decalogus praeceptorum divinorum,* ed. and trans. Sebastian Münster, is in Zurich, Zentralbibliothek, 27.651,4, with some notes by Gesner on the forms of Hebrew letters. This forms part of

a Sammelband that also includes Hebrew grammars by Wolfgang Capito, Moses Kimhi (translated by Münster), and Münster himself.

18. Erasmus Oswald Schreckenfuchs, *Māamar Ḳinah...al mot rabi he-ḥakham Sebasstiyan Munster* (Basel, 1553).

19. Moses Maimonides, *Symbolum Fidei Iudæorum,* ed. Gilbert Génébrard (Paris, 1569).

20. Milton Gatch and Bruce Nielsen, "The Wittenberg Copy of the Bomberg Talmud," *Gutenberg-Jahrbuch* 78 (2003): 296–326; Kenneth Stow, "The Burning of the Talmud in 1553, in Light of Sixteenth-Century Catholic Attitudes toward the Talmud," *Bibliothèque d'Humanisme et Renaissance* 34 (1972): 435–49; Stow, *Catholic Thought and Papal Jewry Policy, 1555–1593* (New York: Jewish Theological Seminary of America, 1977); Fausto Parente, "The Index, the Holy Office, the Condemnation of the Talmud and Publication of Clement VIII's Index," in *Church, Censorship and Culture in Early Modern Italy,* ed. Gigliola Fragnito (Cambridge: Cambridge University Press, 2001), 163–93; and Piet van Boxel, "Robert Bellarmine Reads Rashi: Rabbinic Bible Commentaries and the Burning of the Talmud," in *The Hebrew Book in Early Modern Italy,* ed. Joseph Hacker and Adam Shear (Philadelphia: University of Pennsylvania Press, 2011), 121–32.

21. See Dunkelgrün, "Radical Philology."

22. Stephen Burnett, *From Christian Hebraism to Jewish Studies: Johannes Buxtorf (1564–1629) and Hebrew Learning in the Seventeenth Century* (Leiden: Brill, 1996).

23. There is no full study of Scaliger's Judaic scholarship. For some indications, see *"All my books in foreign tongues."*

24. For Casaubon and his Hebrew scholarship see Anthony Grafton and Joanna Weinberg, *"I have always loved the holy tongue": Isaac Casaubon, the Jews, and a Forgotten Chapter in Renaissance Scholarship* (Cambridge, MA: Belknap Press of Harvard University Press, 2011).

25. Ibid., 105.

26. Paris, Bibliothèque Nationale, MS lat. 690; see Henk Jan de Jonge, *De bestudering van het Nieuwe Testament aan de Noordnederlandse universiteiten en het Remonstrants Seminarie van 1575 tot 1700* (Amsterdam: Noord-Hollandse uitgevers maatschappij 1980), 79.

27. Oxford, Bodleian Library, MS Casaubon 30, 82 recto.

28. Basel, Öffentliche Bibliothek, MS A XII 20.

29. *Scaligerana,* 241.

30. Isaac Casaubon, *Epistolae,* ed. Th. Janson van Almeloveen (Rotterdam, 1709), 569.

31. *Scaligerana,* 73–74.

32. On Crusius and his passion for late and popular Greek see Panagiotis Toufexis, *Das Alphabetum vulgaris linguae graecae des deutschen Humanisten Martin Crusius (1526–1607): Ein Beitrag zur Erforschung der gesprochenen griechischen Sprache im 16. Jh.* (Cologne: Romiosini, 2005). For his manuscripts—including his translations of sermons—see Thomas Wilhelmi, *Die griechischen Handschriften der Universitätsbibliothek Tübingen: Sonderband Marin Crusius. Handschriftenverzeichnis und Bibliographie* (Wiesbaden: O. Harassowitz, 2002).

33. Basel, Öffentliche Bibliothek, MS A XII 20, 49–121.

34. For Casaubon's correspondence in Hebrew with a converted Jew, see Grafton and Weinberg, "*I have always loved,*" 231–90.

35. Karlsruhe, Badische Landesbibliothek, MS Reuchlin 2, fol. 96 verso.

36. *Scaligerana,* 332.

37. Johann Buxtorf to Caspar Waser, December, 23, 1593; Zurich, Zentralbibliothek, MS S-149, 124, 1.

38. Ibid., May 1, 1594; Zurich, Zentralbibliothek, MS S-150, 32 recto.

39. Johnn Buxtorf to Jacob Zwinger, August 4, 1593; Basel, Öffentliche Bibliothek, MS Fr Gr II 9, 89.

40. Johann Buxtorf to Caspar Waser, October 1595; Zurich, Zentralbibliothek, MS S-149, 124, 2.

41. Jacob Buxtorf, *Bibliotheca rabbinica,* published with *De abbreviaturis Hebraicis* (Basel, 1640), 289–90.

42. Conrad Gesner, *Bibliotheca universalis* (Zurich, 1545), Zurich, Zentralbibliothek, Dr M 3, 146 recto.

43. Ibid., 514 recto.

44. Josias Simler, *Epitome bibliothecae Conradi Gesneri* (Zurich, 1555), 133 verso.

45. Buxtorf, *Bibliotheca rabbinica,* 367–68.

46. For Casaubon's responses to Jewish prayer-books see Grafton and Weinberg, "*I have always loved*" 42–52. For Buxtorf see Basel, Öffentliche Bibliothek, MS A XII 20, 254–64.

47. Ibid., 173–74.

48. Ibid., 1–49.

49. A well-annotated translation of Buxtorf's work by Alan Corré is available in digital form at https://pantherfile.uwm.edu/corre/www/buxdorf/, accessed July 30, 2012.

50. Buxtorf to Matthias Martinius, September 4, 1606; quoted by Burnett, *From Christian Hebraism,* 152 n. 50.

51. Basel, Öffentliche Bibliothek, MS A XII 20, 282.

52. London, British Library, 848.b.19.

53. See Milton McC Gatch and Bruce E. Nielsen, *The Wittenberg Copy of the Bomberg Talmud* (Mainz: Gutenberg-Gesellschaft, 2003).

54. Robert Wilkinson, *Orientalism, Aramaic, and Kabbalah in the Catholic Reformation* (Leiden: Brill, 2007), 46–47 n. 60. By contrast, the Jewish convert Johannes Isaac Levita recalled exchanging anti-Jewish exegeses with Bomberg; see Anthony Grafton, *The Culture of Correction in Renaissance Europe* (London: British Library, 2011).

55. See Burnett, *Buxtorf,* 50–51, and Burnett, "Johannes Buxtorf I and the Circumcision Incident of 1619," *Basler Zeitschrift für Geschichte und Altertumskunde* 89 (1989): 135–44.

56. J. Derembourg, "L'Édition de la Bible Rabbinique de Jean Buxtorf," *Revue des études juives* 30 (1895): 70–78.

57. Johann Buxtorf to Caspar Waser, June 15, 1619; Zurich, Zentralbibliothek, MS F 167, 47.

58. Ibid., February 3, 1619; Zurich, Zentralbibliothek, MS F 167, 46; noted by Buxtorf, "Circumcision Incident," whose interpretation I follow.

59. Buxtorf to Cappel, January 1, 1623 (copy); Zurich, Zentralbibliothek, MS F 45, 246 verso–247 verso.

60. Basel, Öffentliche Bibliothek, MS A XII 20, 287, 314.

61. Grafton and Weinberg, *"I have always loved,"* 231–90.

62. *Scaligerana,* 384.

63. *"All my books in foreign tongues,"* 12.

64. *Scaligerana,* 220–21.

65. Joanna Weinberg, "The Quest for Philo in Sixteenth-Century Jewish Historiography," in *Jewish History: Essays in Honor of Chimen Abramsky,* ed. Ada Rapoport-Albert and Steven Zipperstein (London: P. Halban, 1988), 163–87.

66. For a brief treatment see Anthony Grafton, "Ingestion: Table Matter," *Cabinet* 38 (2010), available at http://cabinetmagazine.org/issues/38/grafton.php (consulted July 30, 2012).

67. London, British Library, 1934.f.13.

68. Ibid., 94 verso. For a more detailed study of this book and episode see Grafton and Weinberg, *"I have always loved,"* 55–59.

69. Isaac Casaubon, *Ephemerides,* ed. John Russell, 2 vols. (Oxford: E Typographeo Academico, 1850), II:838.

70. Joseph Scaliger, *Epistolae omnes quae reperiri potuerunt,* ed. Daniel Heinsius (Leiden, 1627), 298.

71. Johann Buxtorf, *Bibliotheca Rabbinica,* printed with his *De abbreviaturis Hebraicis* (Herborn, 1708), 80. This article could not have been written without the generous help, advice, and criticism of Joanna Weinberg, with whom I studied the Hebrew scholarship of Isaac Casaubon.

Chapter 7

1. Maurice Merleau-Ponty wrote that "the world is not what I think, but what I live through." *Phenomenology of Perception* (1945; reprint London: Palgrave, 2002), xviii. Thanks to J. Michelle Molina for steering me to his work.

2. Diego de Córdoba y Salinas, *Vida, Virtudes, y Milagros del Apostol del Peru el B. P. Fr. Francisco Solano de la seráfica Orden de los Menores de la Regular, Obseruancia, patron de la ciudad de Lima* (Madrid: En la Imprenta Real, 1676), fol. 148.

3. Jerónimo Pallas, *Missión a las Indias por el P.e Gerónymo Pallas* [1619], ed. José Jesús Hernández Palomo (Madrid: Consejo Superior de Investigaciones Científicas; La Escuela de Estudios Hispanoamericanos; El Colegio de México, Università degli Studi di Torino, 2006). Also, Acts 9: 15. On early missionization and Christianization in Europe and the circum-Mediterranean, see Ian N. Wood, *The Missionary Life: Saints and the Evangelisation of Europe, 400–1050* (New York: Longman, 2001), and the masterful account by Peter Brown, *The Rise of Western Christendom: Triumph and Diversity, A.D. 200–1000* (Malden, MA: Blackwell, 2003).

4. See my discussion of the manuscript in Kenneth Mills, "Diego de Ocaña (ca. 1570–1608)," in the *Guide to Documentary Sources for Andean Studies, 1530–1900,* ed. Joanne Pillsbury (Norman: University of Oklahoma Press in collaboration with the Center for Advanced Study in the Visual Arts, National Gallery of Art, Washington, DC, 2008), Vol. 3, 457–64.

5. Ocaña, "Relación del viaje," Biblioteca de la Universidad de Oviedo, España, M-215, designated as "de Fray Diego de Ocaña por el Nuevo Mundo (1599–1605)." Internal evidence suggests that Ocaña produced his final copy in a fragmentary

fashion between 1599 and 1608. A new and serviceable scholarly edition is *Viaje por el Nuevo Mundo de Guadalupe a Potosí, 1599–1605,* ed. Blanca López de Mariscal et al. (Monterrey: Instituto Tecnológico de Estudios Superiores de Monterrey, 2010).

6. Wood, *Missionary Life,* 25, 25–52.

7. Reginaldo de Lizárraga, *Descripción breve de toda la tierra del Perú, Tucumán, Río de la Plata y Chile* [c. 1595–1609], Biblioteca de Autores Españoles (Madrid: Atlas Ediciones, 1968); Pedro del Puerto, "Relación del viaje que Fr. Pedro del Puerto profeso de San Jerónimo de Sevilla hizo a las Indias desde 1612 hasta 1623 para tratar asuntos del monasterio de Guadalupe" [1624], Archivo del Real Monasterio de Guadalupe (AMG), Leg. 60. The account is transcribed (with a few errors) and introduced in Pedro del Puerto, "Viaje de un monje gerónimo al virreinato del Perú en el siglos xvi" [1624], ed. J. Francisco V. Silva, *Boletín de la Real Academia de la Historia* 81 (1922): 433–60 and 82 (1923): 132–64 and 201–14.

8. For instance, Psalm 90.

9. Iñigo López de Loyola, *The Autobiography of Ignatius de Loyola,* ed. and trans. Joseph O'Callaghan (New York: Harper and Row, 1974), 65.

10. Jerónimo Nadal, 13ª Exhortatio Complutensis (Alcalá, 1561), § 256, *Monumenta Historica Societatis Iesu,* 90, 469–70. Also, John W. O'Malley, S.J., "To Travel to Any Part of the World: Jerónimo Nadal and the Jesuit Vocation," *Studies in the Spirituality of Jesuits* 16, no. 2 (1984): 1–20; and Simon Ditchfield, "Of Missions and Models: The Jesuit Enterprise (1540–1773) Reassessed in Recent Literature," *Catholic Historical Review* 93 no. 2 (2007) 325–43. Suggestive on purposeful Jesuit pilgrimage, holy vagabondage, and interior journeys in Europe and the Americas, Karin A. Vélez, "Resolved to Fly: The Virgin of Loreto, The Jesuits, and the Miracle of Portable Catholicism, 1650–1750," Ph. D. diss., Princeton University, 2008.

11. Pallas, *Missión,* 280–83.

12. Ibid., 280–82; also 286–88.

13. "I remember—and I really believe this is true—that when I left my father's house my distress was so great that I do not think it will be greater when I die," wrote Santa Teresa. "It seemed to me as if every bone in my body were being wrenched asunder." Teresa De Jesús, *Vida de la Santa Madre Teresa de Jesús escrita por ella misma,* in *Obras de Santa Teresa de Jesús* [1587], tomo I (Madrid: Administración del Apostolado de la Prensa, 1916), Cap. 4, 32, my translation; also Teresa De Jesús, *Life of Teresa de Jesús: The Autobiography of Teresa of Ávila* [1587], ed. and trans. E. Allison Peers (New York: Doubleday, [1960] 2004), chap. 4, 15. For an outstanding study of *recogimiento* based in Peru, Nancy E Van Deusen, *Between the Sacred and the Worldly: The Institutional and Cultural Practice of Recogimiento in Colonial Lima* (Stanford, CA: Stanford University Press, 2001).

14. Francis Xavier, "Xavier to his companions residing in Rome. From Cochin, January 20, 1548" (EX I 375–396; FX III 335–337), in *The Letters and Instructions of Francis Xavier,* ed. and trans. M. Joseph Costelloe, S. J. (St. Louis, MO: Institute of Jesuit Sources, 1992), 179; Francis Xavier, *Epistolae S. Francisci Xaverii aliaque eius scripta (1535–1552),* ed. Georgius Schurhammer, S.J. and Josephus Wicki, S. J., 2 vols. (1944; reprint Rome: Monumenta Historica Societatis Iesu, 1996), vol. 1, 375–96. Also, Ines G. Županov, *Missionary Tropics: The Catholic Frontier in India (16th–17th Centuries)* (Ann Arbor: University of Michigan Press, 2005), 35–110.

15. Marjorie O'Rourke Boyle, *Loyola's Acts: The Rhetoric of the Self* (Berkeley: University of California Press, 1997), 3, 1.

16. Scott F. Johnson, "Late Antique Narrative Fiction: Apocryphal Acta and the Greek Novel in the Fifth-Century *Life and Miracles of Thekla,*" in *Greek Literature in Late Antiquity: Dynamism, Didacticism, Classicism,* ed. Scott Fitzgerald Johnson (Aldershot, UK: Ashgate, 2006), 204.

17. Scott F. Johnson, *The Life and Miracles of Thekla: A Literary Study* (Washington, DC: Center for Hellenic Studies, Harvard University Press, 2006), 10, 6–10; on "elasticity," also Averil Cameron, *Christianity and the Rhetoric of Empire: The Development of Christian Discourse* (Berkeley: University of California Press, 1991), 89–119.

18. The nine *códices* preserved in the Archivo del Real Monasterio de Guadalupe (AMG) record miracles between 1407 and 1722; edited miracle selections appeared first in the 1597 history of the image and shrine which Ocaña carried to the Indies: Gabriel de Talavera, *Historia de Nuestra Señora de Guadalupe consagrada la soberana Magestad de la reyna de los angeles, milagrosa patrona de este sanctuario. por Fray Gabriel de Talavera prior de la misma casa* (Toledo: en casa de Thomas de Guzman, 1597), Libro 5. On the sixteenth-century context, see especially Françoise Crémoux, *Pèlerinages et Miracles: À Guadalupe au Xvie Siècle* (Madrid: Casa de Velázquez, 2001). Surveying the volumes: Antonio Ramiro Chico, "Nueve códices." Other extant Guadalupan miracle collections include Biblioteca Nacional de España (BNE) Ms. 1176 and Biblioteca del Escorial (BE), cód. IV-a.

19. AMG, Cód. 3, Milagros de Nuestra Señora de Guadalupe desde 1490 hasta 1503," prologo, fols. 1r–1v; 1r–2r.

20. The literature on the desert in the early and medieval Christian imagination is massive. See especially Bernard McGinn, "Ocean and Desert as Symbols of Mystical Absorption in the Christian Tradition," *Journal of Religion* 74, no. 2 (1994): 156–64; "Exode," *Dictionnaire de spiritualité* (Paris: Beauchesne, 1937–), IV, 1957–95; Jean Leclercq, *Chances de la spiritualité occidentale* (Paris: Cerf, 1966), 247–77; Benedicta Ward, "The Desert Myth: Reflections on the Desert Ideal in Early Cistercian Monasticism," in *One Yet Two: Monastic Tradition, East and West,* ed. M. Basil Pennington (Kalamazoo, MI.: Cistercian Publications, 1976), 183–99; Belden C. Lane, ed., *The Solace of Fierce Landscapes: Exploring Desert and Mountain Spirituality* (Oxford: Oxford University Press, 1998).

21. Giles Constable, *Monks, Hermits, and Crusaders in Medieval Europe* (London: Variorum Reprints, 1988), 242–49; Maribel Dietz, *Wandering Monks, Virgins, and Pilgrims: Ascetic Travel in the Mediterranean World, A.D. 300–800* (University Park: Pennsylvania State University Press, 2005), 73–78.

22. On contemporary perceptions of "depopulated" zones and itineraries through them, see Sylvia Sellers-García, *Distance and Documents at the Spanish Empire's Periphery* (Stanford, CA: Stanford University Press, 2013).

23. On Pariacaca's prominence as divine forefather of the Yauyos people and remembered position as one of the greatest native Andean divinities in the early seventeenth century, see Felipe Guaman Poma De Ayala, *El Primer Nueva Corónica Y Buen Gobierno,* ed. John V. Murra, Rolena Adorno, and Jorge Urioste (México:

Siglo Veintiuno, 1980), vol. 1, 241[fols. 268–269]. The collected sacred histories of Pariacaca are the principal motors within the "Huarochirí manuscript." See Anonymous, *Huarochirí: Manuscrito Quechua del siglo XVII,* 3 vols, ed. Gérald Taylor (Lima: Lluvia Editores y el Instituto Francés de Estudios Andinos, 2001); and an excellent English translation and edition, *The Huarochirí Manuscript: A Testament of Ancient and Colonial Andean Religion,* ed. and trans. Frank Salomon and Jorge Urioste (Austin: University of Texas Press, 1991). The classic contextualizing study of the region in English is Spalding, *Huarochirí.* For a broader sense of *huacas,* see Kenneth Mills, "The Naturalization of Andean Christianities," in *The Cambridge History of Christianity,* vol. 6, *Reform and Expansion, 1500–1660,* ed. R. Po-Chia Hsia (Cambridge: Cambridge University Press, 2007), 508–39; and Kenneth Mills, *Idolatry and Its Enemies: Colonial Andean Religion and Extirpation, 1640–1750* (Princeton: Princeton University Press, 1997), 39–74, 211–66.

24. For a fresh investigation of the fitful process by which Spaniards puzzled over and adapted to an Andean landscape, Jeremy Ravi Mumford, *Vertical Empire: The General Resettlement of Indians in the Colonial Andes* (Durham, NC: Duke University Press, 2012).

25. John Hyslop, *The Inka Road System* (New York: Academic Press, 1984), 224; Donald E. Thompson and John V. Murra, "The Inca Bridges in the Huánuco Region," *American Antiquity* 31 (1966): 632–39; Craig Morris and Donald E. Thompson, *Huánuco Pampa: An Inca City and Its Hinterland* (London: Thames and Hudson, 1985); Terence N. D'altroy, *The Incas* (Oxford: Blackwell, 2002), 242, 251.

26. Pedro de Cieza De León, *Crónica Del Perú, Segunda parte,* ed. Francesca Cantú (Lima: Pontificía Universidad Católica del Perú Fondo Editorial, Academia Nacional de la Historia, 1984), 40–41.

27. Heidi V. Scott is brilliant on this theme and utilizes a few key sources treating the peak of Pariacaca, movement, and space in Huarochirí in *Contested Territory: Mapping Peru in the Sixteenth and Seventeenth Centuries* (Notre Dame, Indiana: Notre Dame University Press, 2009), 75-107.

28. José de Acosta, *Historia natural y moral de las Indias: en que se tratan de las cosas notables del cielo, elementos, metales, plantas y animales dellas, y los ritos y ceremonias, leyes y gobierno de los indios* [1590], 2d ed. (1940; reprint Fondo de Cultura Económica, 1962), Libro III, Cap. 9, pp. 104–5; 103–7. Following up the "scientifically" descriptive angle of the story, Daniel L. Gilbert, "The First Documented Description of Mountain Sickness: the Andean or Pariacaca Story," *Respiration Physiology* 52, no. 3 (1983): 327–47.

29. Acosta had noted the relative advantage afforded a traveler who was, like Ocaña, acclimatized to significant altitude and moved toward the sea as opposed to ascending from sea level toward the interior; Acosta, *Historia natural y moral,* Libro III, Cap. 9, 105.

30. Acosta, *Historia natural y moral,* Libro III, Cap. 9, 106–7.

31. Diego Dávila Brizeño, "Descripción y relación de la provincia de los Yauyos toda, Anan Yauyos y Lorin Yauyos, "in *Relaciones geográficas de las Indias,* ed. Marco Jiménez de la Espada, Biblioteca de Autores Españoles, Perú (1881–97; reprint, Madrid: Atlas Ediciones, 1965), vol. 1 [Biblioteca tomo 183], 61–78.

32. Ocaña, "Relación," fol. 343v.

33. Ibid., fol. 344v.

34. Alain Saint-Saëns, *La nostalgie du désert. L'idéal érémitique en Castille au Siècle d'Or* (San Francisco: Mellen Research University Press, 1993); also Trevor Johnson, "Gardening for God: Carmelite Deserts and the Sacralisation of Natural Space in Counter-Reformation Spain," in *Sacred Space in Early Modern Europe,* ed. Will Coster and Andrew Spicer (Cambridge: Cambridge University Press, 2005), 193–210.

35. Ocaña, "Relación," fol. 345r.

36. Ibid., fol. 345r.

37. Ibid., fol. 345v.

38. Dietz, *Wandering Monks,* 21.

39. Ocaña, "Relación," fol. 345v.

40. On this feature in the Bible's narratives, see Robert Alter, *The Art of Biblical Narrative* (New York: Basic Books, 1981), 35–36.

41. Ocaña, "Relación," fols. 345v–346r.

42. Ibid., fols. 346r–v.

43. Ibid., fol. 346v.

44. Fernando R. de la Flor, "Sacrificial Politics in the Spanish Colonies," in *Reason and its Others: Italy, Spain and the New World,* ed. David R. Castillo and Massimo Lollini (Nashville: Vanderbilt University Press, 2006): 250, 250–55. Illuminating the theme, also Beatriz Pastor Bodmer, *El jardín y el peregino: el pensamiento utópico en América Latina (1492–1695)* (Mexico City: Universidad Nacional Autónoma de México, 1999); and Ramón Mujica Pinilla, "Identidades alegóricas: Lecturas iconográficas del barroco al neoclasicismo," in *Barroco Peruano,* vol. 2 (Lima: Banco de Crédito, 2004), 251–335.

45. Ocaña, "Relación," fols. 346r–346v. Ocaña adds that when he left Peru for good (in early 1606), he gave this mule to someone as a special gift.

46. Douglas Burton-Christie, *The Word in the Desert: Scripture and the Quest for Holiness in Early Christian Monasticism* (Oxford: Oxford University Press, 1992), 6.

47. Ocaña, "Relación," fols. 346v–347r.

48. McGinn, "Ocean and Desert."

49. Ocaña, "Relación," fol. 347r.

Chapter 8

1. See *The Protestant Ethic Turns 100: Essays on the Centenary of the Weber Thesis,* ed. William H. Swatos Jr. and Lutz Kaelber (Boulder, CO: Paradigm, 2005).

2. Weber looms large (thirty citations in the index) over Charles Taylor's Templeton Prize-winning *A Secular Age* (Cambridge, MA: Belknap/Harvard University Press, 2007).

3. See Robert Scribner's essay, "Incombustible Luther: The Image of the Reformer in Early Modern Germany," *Past and Present* 110 (February 1986): 38–68.

4. First expressed in his essay, "Wissenschaft als Beruf" (Science as a Vocation), published in 1918, Weber borrowed this catch-phrase from Friedrich Schiller. See H. H. Gerth and C. Wright Mills, "Bureaucracy and Charisma: A Philosophy of History" in R. Glassman and W. Swatos, *Charisma, History, and Social Structure* (Westport, CT: Greenwood Press, 1986), 11–15.

5. Taylor, *A Secular Age,* 26–159.

6. Heinz Schilling, *Konfessionskonflikt und Staatsbildung* (Gütersloh: Mohn, 1981); Wolfgang Reinhard. "Zwang zur Konfessionalisierung? *"Zeitschrift für historische Forschung* 10 (1983): 257–77; Erika Rummel, *The Confessionalization of Humanism in Reformation Germany* (Oxford: Oxford University Press, 2000).

7. *Social Discipline in the Reformation,* ed. R. Po-chia Hsia (New York: Routledge, 1989); Philip S. Gorski, *Disciplinary Revolution: Calvinism and the Rise of the State in Early Modern Europe* (Chicago: University of Chicago Press, 2003).

8. Wolfgang Reinhard, "Gegenreformation als Modernisierung?" *Archiv für Reformationsgeschichte* 68 (1977): 226–52; Susan R. Boetcher, "Confessionalization: Reformation, Religion, Absolutism, and Modernity," *History Compass* 2, no. 1 (January 2004).

9. For example, Steven Pincus, *1688: The First Modern Revolution* (New Haven: Yale University Press, 2009).

10. On consecrated behavior, see Clifford Geertz, "Religion as a Cultural System," in *Anthropological Approaches to the Study of Religion,* ed. Michael Banton (New York: Praeger, 1966), 3, 28–29; on symbolic behavior, see Victor Turner, *Dramas, Fields, and Metaphors* (Ithaca: Cornell University Press, 1974), 55–56; on social glue, see Emile Durkheim, *The Elementary Forms of the Religious Life,* trans. Karen E. Fields (New York: Free Press, 1995); and also the critique by John Bossy, "Some Elementary Forms of Durkheim," *Past and Present* 95 (May 1982): 3–18.

11. Among the most extreme examples of this approach one can cite Michael Walzer's *Revolution of the Saints* (Cambridge: Harvard University Press, 1965), which argues that Calvin "was not primarily a theologian" (27) and that Calvinism must be viewed as a political rather than religious phenomenon, a mere "response to disorder and fear" (77).

12. Social scientists such as Victor Turner and Clifford Geertz do not deny the effect that myths, symbols, and rituals have on culture or society, but tend to approach these immaterial factors more as responses than causes. See Geertz, "Religion as a Cultural System," 28; and Victor Turner, *From Ritual to Theatre* (New York: Performing Arts Journal Publications, 1982), 82ff.

13. Max Weber, "Science as a Vocation," *Essays in Sociology,* ed. H. H. Gerth and C. Wright Mills (New York: Oxford University Press, 1946), 155.

14. Weber's "disenchantment" thesis is an essential component of one of the most influential books on early modern religion: Keith Thomas, *Religion and the Decline of Magic* (Oxford University Press, 1971). Unlike Scribner, Thomas does not challenge Weber, but rather elaborates on his "disenchantment" thesis. See also *Weber's "Protestant Ethic": Origins, Evidence, Contexts,* ed. Hartmut Lehmann and Guenther Roth (Cambridge: Cambridge University Press, 1993).

15. "The Reformation, Popular Magic, and the 'Disenchantment of the World," *Journal of Interdisciplinary History* 23, no. 3 (1993): 475–94.

16. Ibid., 491.

17. See Michael D. Bailey, "The Disenchantment of Magic: Spells, Charms, and Superstition in Early European Witchcraft Literature," *American Historical Review* 111, no. 2 (April 2006): 383–404. See also Bailey's *Magic and Superstition in Europe. A Concise History* (New York: Rowman and Littlefield, 2007), 76–106.

18. In Catholic Spain exposing superstition became a learned task. See Fabián Alejandro Campagne, *Homo Catholicus, Homo Superstitiosus: El discurso antisupersticioso en la España de los siglos XVI al XVIII* (Madrid: Miño y Dávila, 2002).

19. "Dieux blancs": Antoine Fromment, *Les Actes et Gestes Merveilleux de la Cité de Genève* (1544), reissued by J. G. Fick (Geneva, 1954), 144–45. The witches' brew in William Shakespeare, *Macbeth* IV, i, 14–15: "Eye of newt, and toe of frog, wool of bat, and tongue of dog..."

20. See Randall Styers, *Making Magic* (Oxford: Oxford University Press, 2004).

21. Scribner, "The Reformation," 475.

22. Louis Richeome, S.J., *Trois discours pour la religion catholique* (Bordeaux, 1597).

23. Charles Taylor has coined the awkward term "social imaginary" to describe this complex relation between conceptual structures and social realities (*Secular Age,* 146). He has also argued that "modern secularization can be seen from one angle as the rejection of higher times, and the positing of time as purely profane" (196).

24. For a social-scientific take on religion that seems unaware of Protestantism and its take on this basic dialectic, see Mircea Eliade, *The Sacred and the Profane* (New York: Harcourt, Brace, 1959).

25. The most eloquent and succinct summary of this worldview can be found in Peter Brown, *The Cult of the Saints* (Chicago: University of Chicago Press, 1981).

26. In a literal sense, an "iconoclast" (Greek. *eikon* = image + *klastes* = breaker) is someone who destroys images or simply rejects them, especially those that carry special meaning. In a figurative sense, an iconoclast is someone who identifies certain objects, institutions, or ideas as "false" and calls for their removal.

27. "Commentary on the True and False Religion" (1525), *The Latin Works and the Correspondence of Huldreich Zwingli,* ed. S. M. Jackson, 3 vols. (London: G. P. Putnams's Sons, 1912–29), vol. 2, 92.

28. *Ioannis Calvini opera* [*CO*], 59 vols. (Braunschweig: Schwetschke, 1863–1900), vol. 24, 387.

29. *Huldreich Zwinglis Sämtliche Werke,* [*ZW*] (Berlin: Schwetschke, 1905–90), vol. 8, 194–95.

30. *CO* 6. 55–59.

31. Martin Bucer was among the earliest Reformers to stress these points. See *Martin Bucers Deutsche Schriften,* ed. R. Stupperich (Gütersloh: G. Mohn, 1960–2007), 17 vols. Hereafter cited as DS, with volume and page number: "Summary," DS 1.108–113; "Grund und Ursach," DS 1, 210; 218–19; 273.

32. Fromment, *Actes et Gestes,* 144–45.

33. "Whiggish" historians hail the Protestant Reformation as the beginning of modernity and of the upward march of science, progress, and freedom. See Herbert Butterfield, *The Whig Interpretation of History* (London: Bell, 1931), 5–20. Butterfield used the terms *protestant history* and *whiggish history* interchangeably.

34. An assumption brilliantly questioned by Fabián Alejandro Campagne in "Witchcraft and the Sense-of-the-Impossible in Early Modern Spain," *Harvard Theological Review* 96, no.1 (January 2003): 25–62.

35. See Anthony Cascardi, *The Subject of Modernity* (New York: Cambridge University Press, 1992); Stanley Jeyaraja Tambiah, *Magic, Science, Religion, and the Scope of Rationality* (Cambridge: Cambridge University Press, 1990).

36. Campagne, "Witchcraft"; Andrew Keitt, *Inventing the Sacred* (Leiden: Brill, 2005); Julie Crawford, *Marvelous Protestantism* (Baltimore: Johns Hopkins University Press, 2005); Lorraine Daston, "Marvelous Facts and Miraculous Evidence in Early Modern Europe," in *Questions of Evidence,* ed. James Chandler et al. (Chicago: University of Chicago Press, 1994), 243–74; and Lorraine Daston and Katharine Park, *Wonders and the Order of Nature* (New York: Zone Books, 1998).

37. See D. P. Walker, "The Cessation of Miracles." In *Hermeticism and the Renaissance,* ed. Ingrid Merkel and Allen Debus (Washington: Folger Shakespeare Library, 1988), 110–24.

38. For a detailed analysis of Luther's complex attitude toward the miraculous, see Philip Soergel, *Miracles and the Protestant Imagination* (Oxford: Oxford University Press, 2011), 33–66.

39. Commentary on the Gospel of Matthew 7:24, *Luther's Works,* vol. 21, 276.

40. Erlangen edition, xii, 236, quoted by Wilhelm Herrmann, *The Communion of the Christian with God, Described on the Basis of Luther's Statements,* trans. J. Sandys Stanyon, 2nd ed. (New York: G. P. Putnam's Sons, 1906), 231.

41. *D. Martin Luthers Werke: Kritische Gesamtausgabe, Tischreden* [Table Talk], 6 vols. (Weimar, 1912–1921). Hereafter cited as WAT by volume and passage number: WAT 6. 6811.

42. WAT 3. seeing and hearing 3601; hare 4040; ape 6814; dog on bed 5358b.

43. "Martin Butzers an ein christlichen Rath un Gemeyn der statt Weissenburg Summary einer Predig dselbst gehon" (1523), in DS 1.101.

44. DS 1. 107–12.

45. Jane Shaw, *Miracles in Enlightenment England* (New Haven: Yale University Press, 2006), 24–26.

46. *Institutes of the Christian Religion* I.8. 5–6, ed. by J. T. McNeill, 2 vols. (Philadelphia: Westminster, 1960); also *Commentary on Acts* 5:15 (CO 48.104).

47. "Prefatory Address," *Institutes,* ed. McNeill, 1:16–17.

48. For an exhaustive account of medieval and early modern demonology, see Stuart Clarke, *Thinking with Demons* (Oxford: Clarendon Press, 1997).

49. *Commentary on Acts, CO* 48.104.

50. For a more detailed analysis of Reformed Protestant attitudes toward miracles, see Moshe Sluhovsky, "Calvinist Miracles and the Concept of the Miraculous in Sixteenth-Century Huguenot Thought," *Renaissance and Reformation* 19, no. 2 (1995): 5, 6–24; Bernard Vogler, "La Reforme et le Miracle," *Revue d'Histoire de la Spiritualite.* 48 (1972): 145–49.

51. On this aspect of Lutheranism, see Soergel, *Miracles and the Protestant Imagination.*

52. André Vauchez, *Saints, prophètes et visionnaires* (Paris: Albin Michel, 1999).

53. Steven Ozment, *Mysticism and Dissent* (New Haven: Yale University Press, 1973).

54. Heiko A. Oberman, "Simul gemitus et raptus: Luther and Mysticism," and Steven Ozment, "Homo Viator: Luther and Late Medieval Theology," both in *The Reformation in Medieval Perspective,* ed. Steven Ozment (Chicago: Quadrangle Books, 1971), 219–52.

55. *Commentary on John's Gospel,* CO 47.90.

56. For an ecumenically minded take on mystical influences on Calvin, see Dennis Tamburello, *Union with Christ: John Calvin and the Mysticism of St. Bernard of Clairvaux* (Louisville: Westminster John Knox Press, 1994).

57. *Institutes of the Christian Religion,* II.3.2, vol. 1, 292.

58. Montague Summers, *The Physical Phenomena of Mysticism* (New York: Barnes and Noble, 1950); and Herbert Thurston, *The Physical Phenomena of Mysticism* (Chicago: Regnery, 1952).

59. Carlos Eire, "The Good, the Bad, and the Airborne" in *Ideas and Cultural Margins in Early Modern Germany,* ed. Robin Barnes and Elizabeth Plummer (Burlington, VT: Ashgate, 2009), 307–24. Also Angelo Pastrovicchi, *St. Joseph of Copertino,* trans. Francis S. Laing (St. Louis: Herder, 1918).

60. Sor María de Jesús de Agreda, *La mística ciudad de Dios* (1670), ed. Augustine Esposito (Potomac: Scripta Humanistica, 1990). Abridged English translation: *The Mystical City of God* (Rockford, IL: Tan Books, 2009).

61. See Clark A. Colahan, *The Visions of Sor Maria de Agreda* (Tucson: University of Arizona Press, 1994); Marilyn H. Fedewa, *Maria of Agreda* (Albuquerque: University of New Mexico Press, 2009).

62. Martin Gonzalez de Cellorigo, *Memorial de la política necesaria* (Valladolid, 1600). Translated by J. H. Elliott, in *Spain and its World* (New Haven: Yale University Press, 1989), 262–86.

63. Craig M. Koslofsky, *The Reformation of the Dead* (New York, 2000); *The Place of the Dead: Death and Remembrance in Late Medieval and Early Modern Europe,* ed. Bruce Gordon and Peter Marshall (Cambridge: Cambridge University Press, 2000); Susan C. Karant-Nunn, *The Reformation of Ritual* (New York: Routledge, 1997).

64. Martin Luther, "On the Misuse of the Mass" (1521): *Luther's Works* [LW] (St. Louis: Concordia, 1955–), vol. 36, 191.

65. "First Invocavit Sermon," LW 51:70.

66. Nicholas Manuel, *Die Totenfresser* (1523), translated by Steven Ozment, *The Reformation in the Cities* (New Haven: Yale University Press, 1975), 112–13.

67. The model for all such research was established by French historians, especially Michel Vovelle, in *Piété baroque et déchristianisation en Provence au XVIIIe siècle* (Paris: Plon, 1973).

68. Simon Fish, "A Supplication for the Beggars," cited by Stephen Greenblatt, *Hamlet in Purgatory* (Princeton: Princeton University Press, 2002), 11.

69. *CO* 5. 304–5.

70. Cardinal William Allen, *A Defense and Declaration of the Catholike Churches Doctrine, touching Purgatory* (Antwerp, 1566), fol. 215v. Cited by Stephen Greenblatt, *Hamlet in Purgatory,* 33.

71. For a detailed account see Eamon Duffy, *The Voices of Morebath* (New Haven: Yale University Press, 2001).

72. *Canons and Decrees of the Council of Trent,* trans. T. A. Buckley (London: George Rutledge, 1851): Decree Concerning Purgatory, 212–13.

73. Ibid., 213–15.

74. Carlos Eire, *From Madrid to Purgatory* (Cambridge: Cambridge University Press, 1995), 168–231.

75. Sara Nalle, *God in La Mancha* (Baltimore, MD: Johns Hopkins University Press, 1992), 175, 188, 202–5.

76. See Eire, *Madrid to Purgatory,* 371–510.

77. William Shakespeare, *Hamlet,* I. v. 9–13.

78. See Greenblatt, *Hamlet in Purgatory,* esp. 1–101. Also Bruce Gordon, "Malevolent Ghosts and Ministering Angels" in Marshall and Gordon, *The Place of the Dead,* 87–109.

79. Wenceslaus Link, in Ozment, *Reformation in the Cities,* 87.

80. Wolfgang Capito, in Ozment, *Reformation in the Cities,* 87.

81. See Peter Marshall's observations on the idioms of memory, *The Place of the Dead,* 18.

82. Philipe Aries, *The Hour of Our Death* (New York: Knopf, 1981), 605–8; John Bossy, *Christianity in the West, 1400–1700* (Oxford: Oxford University Press, 1985).

83. Max Weber, *The Protestant Ethic and the Spirit of Capitalism* (1924), trans. Talcott Parsons (New York: Scribner, 1958), 120, 105.

84. H. C. Eric Midelfort, *Exorcism and Enlightenment* (New Haven: Yale University Press, 2005), 6.

Chapter 9

1. Rachel Labouchere, *Abiah Darby of Coalbrookdale, Wife of Abraham Darby II, 1716–1793* (York, UK: William Sessions, 1988).

2. T. S. Ashton, *Iron and Steel in the Industrial Revolution* (Manchester: Manchester University Press, 1924), appendix, 249–52.

3. Labouchere, *Abiah Darby,* 129.

4. Abiah Darby to John Fletcher, 22/6th month/1784, John Rylands Library, MSS. MAM Fl 2.7/1.

5. Until the death of John Wesley in 1792, Methodism was officially a branch of the Anglican church, and members were encouraged to attend both Anglican and Methodist services and to receive communion from Anglican ministers.

6. Henry Moore, *The Life of Mrs. Mary Fletcher, Consort and Relict of Rev. John Fletcher, Vicar of Madeley, Salop* (New York: Nelson & Phillips, 1872–79).

7. John Fletcher died in 1785, she died in 1815. Abraham Darby died in 1763, Abiah died in 1793.

8. Abiah Darby to Mary Fletcher n.d. John Rylands Library, MAM Fl 2.7/3.

9. Labouchere, *Abiah Darby,* 242.

10. Abiah Darby, "An Expostulatory Address to All who Frequent Places of Diversion and Gaming, etc." (Shrewsbury, 1765), 14. Emphasis added.

11. Moore, *Mary Fletcher,* 321–22.

12. Abiah Darby, *Useful Instruction for Children, by way of Question and Answer* (London: by Luke Hinde, 1763), 40–41.

13. On companionate marriage in the eighteenth-century, Ruth Perry, *Novel Relations: The Transformation of Kinship in English Literature and Culture 1748–1818* (New York: Cambridge University Press, 2004).

14. Voltaire, *Letters on England,* trans. Leonard Tancock (London: Penguin, 1980, orig. 1734), 23.

15. Friends House Library, London, MSS. Port 38 No. 2.

16. Phyllis Mack, *Visionary Women: Ecstatic Prophecy in Seventeenth-Century England* (Berkeley: University of California Press, 1992).

17. On Quakers in business, Arthur Raistrick, *Quakers in Science and Industry: Being an Account of the Quaker Contributions to Science and Industry during the 17th and 18th Centuries* (London: Bannisdale Press, 1950); James Walvin, *The Quakers: Money and Morals* (London, 1997).

18. James Jenkins, *The Records and Recollections of James Jenkins,* ed. J. William Frost Edwin Mellen Press (1776; reprint New York, 1984), 85.

19. On traveling women ministers, see Rebecca Larson, *Daughters of Light: Quaker Women Preaching and Prophesying in the Colonies and Abroad, 1700–1775* (New York: Knopf, 1999).

20. Darby, "An Expostulatory Address," 14, 15, 16. Emphasis added.

21. Journal of Abiah Darby, 1744–69, Friends House London, fol. 70–71. Emphasis added.

22. Ibid., fol. 49.

23. Ibid., fol. 17.

24. Ibid., fol. 17.

25. Abiah Darby, "An Exhortation in Christian Love, to All Who Frequent Horse-racing, Cock-fighting, Throwing at Cocks, Gaming, Plays, Dancing, Musical Entertainments, or Any Other Vain Diversions," 3rd ed. (Newcastle: by I. Thompson, Esq. 1770), 18, 19, 26, 38.

26. David Hempton, *Methodism: Empire of the Spirit* (New Haven: Yale University Press, 2005).

27. Henry D. Rack, *Reasonable Enthusiast: John Wesley and the Rise of Methodism* (1989; reprint Nashville, TN: Abingdon Press, 1992), 546.

28. Mary Bosanquet to Mrs. Ryan, n.d. Fletcher/Tooth Collection MAM Fl 37/7.

29. Sarah Ryan to Mary Bosanquet, n.d., Fletcher/Tooth Collection MAM Fl 6/9/17.

30. Mary Bosanquet Fletcher, "Watchwords," Fletcher/Tooth Collection MAM F1 /27/4/18.

31. Madeley Society Business Fletcher/Tooth Collection MAM Fl 38.4.

32. Moore, *Mary Fletcher,* 147–48.

33. Zachariah Taft, *Biographical Sketches of the Lives and Public Ministry of Various Holy Women,* 2 vols. (Leeds: H. Cullingworth, 1828), 1:26–27.

34. Moore, *Mary Fletcher,* 252.

35. Journal of Abiah Darby, fol. 127.

36. Moore, *Mary Fletcher,* 285.

37. Ibid., 323–24.

38. Ibid., 116 or 270–71.

Chapter 10

1. Marcel Mauss, *The Gift: The Form and Reason for Exchange in Archaic Societies,* trans. W. D. Halls (New York: Norton, 1990).

2. Michael Pregill, "Isra'iliyyat, Myth, and Pseudepigraphy: Wahb b. Munabbih and the Early Islamic Versions of the Fall of Adam and Eve," *Jerusalem Studies in Arabic and Islam* 34 (2008): 215–84.

3. Angelika Neuwirth, "Two Views of History and Human Future: Qur'anic and Biblical Renderings of Divine Promises," *Journal of Qur'anic Studies* 10 (April 2008): 1–20.

4. Susannah Heschel, *Abraham Geiger and the Jewish Jesus* (Chicago: University of Chicago Press, 1998).

5. Susanne Zantop, *Colonial Fantasies: Conquest, Family, and Nation in Pre-Colonial Germany, 1770–1870* (Durham, NC: Duke University Press, 1997).

6. Suzanne Marchand, *German Orientalism in an Age of Empire: Religion, Race, and Scholarship* (New York: Cambridge University Press, 2009), xxiv.

7. Amy Newman, "The Death of Judaism in German Protestant Thought from Luther to Hegel," *Journal of the American Academy of Religion* 61 (fall 1993): 455–84.

8. Lee Edelman: *No Future: Queer Theory and the Death Drive* (Durham, NC: Duke University Press, 2004).

9. Susannah Heschel, "Revolt of the Colonized: Abraham Geiger's Wissenschaft des Judentums as a Challenge to Christian Hegemony in the Academy," *New German Critique* 77 (spring/summer 1999): 61–86. See also Jonathan Hess, *Germans, Jews, and the Claims of Modernity* (New Haven: Yale University Press, 2002).

10. Joseph von Hammer-Purgstall, *Gemäldesaal der Lebensbeschreibungen grosser moslimischer Herrscher der ersten sieben Jahrhunderte der Hidschret,* 2 vols. (Leipzig: C. W. Leske, 1837); cited by Tav Pfanmüller, *Handbuch der Islam-Literatur* (Berlin: Walter de Gruyter, 1923), 176. See also Paula Fichtner, *Terror and Toleration: The Habsburg Empire Confronts Islam, 1526–1850* (London: Reaktion, 2008), 130–61.

11. Monika Richarz, "Juden, Wissenschaft und Universitäten. Zur Sozialgeschichte der jüdischen Intelligenz und der akademischen Judenfeindschaft, 1780–1848," *Jahrbuch des Instituts für deutsche Geschichte,* Beiheft 4 (1982): 55–72.

12. Ludwig Geiger, "Introduction," Abraham Geigers Briefe an J. Derenbourg, *Allgemeine Zeitung des Judentums* (1896): 52. For a discussion of the relationship between the two men, see Michael Graetz, "The History of an Estrangement between Two Jewish Communities: Germany and France during the 19th Century," in *Toward Modernity: The European Jewish Model,* ed. Jacob Katz (New Brunswick, NJ: Transaction Books, 1987), 159–69.

13. On Freytag's career at the University of Bonn, see Christian Renger, *Die Gründung und Einrichtung der Universität Bonn und die Berufungspolitik des Kultusministers Altenstein* (Bonn: Ludwig Röhrscheid Verlag, 1982), 237–39. Due to loss of university records, it is no longer possible to determine in which seminars and lectures Geiger enrolled.

14. University of Bonn archives, Matriculation Records: Album Academiae Borussicae Rhenanae, D. XVIII October 1829 Album der Universität Bonn 1827–1829, 1 IMB 1827/2.1839.

15. Abraham Geiger, *Was hat Mohammed aus dem Judenthume aufgenommen? Eine von der Königl. Preussischen Rheinuniversität gekrönte Preisschrift* (Bonn, 1833; reprinted Leipzig: M. W. Kaufmann, 1902; Osnabruck: Biblio Verlag, 1971).

16. On Fleischer, see Sabine Mangold, *Eine "weltbürgerliche Wissenschaft": Die deutsche Orientalistik im 19 Jahrhundert* (Stuttgart, 2004); Johann J. Fueck, *Die arabischen Studien in Europa bis in den Anfang des 20. Jahrhunderts* (Leipzig, 1955); Martin Kramer, ed., *The Jewish Discovery of Islam* (Tel Aviv, 1999); Holger Preissler, "Heinrich Lebrecht Fleischer: Ein Orientalist, seine jüdischen Studenten, Promovenden und Kollegen," *Leipziger Beiträge zur Jüdischen Geschichte und Kultur,* ed. Dan Diner IV (2006), 245–68; on Jena, Stefan Heidemann, "Zwischen Theologie und Philologie: Paradigmenwechsel in der Jenaer Orientalistik, 1770 bis 1850," *Der Islam* 84 (2007) 140–84.

17. Universitätsarchiv Leipzig, Philosophische Fakultät, Promotionen. Consulted July 2009. See also Holger Preissler, "Heinrich Lebrecht Fleischer: Ein Leipziger Orientalist, seine juedischen Studenten, Promovenden, und Kollegen," *Leipziger Beitraege zur Juedischen Geschichte und Kultur* 4 (2006): 245–68; Ismar Schorsch, "Converging Cognates: The Intersection of Jewish and Islamic Studies in Nineteenth Century Germany," *Leo Baeck Institute Yearbook* 55 (2010): 3–36.

18. Geiger, *Was hat Mohammed,* 25.

19. Geiger, *Judaism and Islam* (New York: Ktav, 1970), 21.

20. Ibid., 12–16.

21. Ibid., 14.

22. Ibid., 17.

23. Ibid., 75–82; Sura 5:32: "Because of that, We have prescribed for the Children of Israel that whoever kills a soul, other than in retaliation for [another] soul or for corruption in the land, will be as if he had killed all the people; and whoever saves one will be as if he had saved the life of all the people." The Qur'an, trans. Alan Jones (Cambridge: Gibb Memorial Trust, 2007), 115. Mishnah Sanhedrin 4:5: "We find it said in the case of Cain who murdered his brother, "The voice of your brother's blood cries out" (Gen. 4:10). It is not said here blood in the singular, but bloods in the plural, that is, his own blood and the blood of his seed. Man was created single in order to show that to him who kills a single individual it shall be reckoned that he has slain the whole race, but to him who preserves the life of a single individual it is counted that he hath preserved the whole race."

24. This account also appears in less complete form in six other passages. Geiger, *Judaism and Islam,* 75–77.

25. Ibid., 77; see T. B. Sanhedrin 29a–b; Midrash Rabbah on Genesis, paragraph 8; Leopold Zunz, *Die gottesdienstlichen Vorträge der Juden* 291, footnote.

26. Abraham Geiger, *Das Judentum und seine Geschichte. In zwölf Vorlesungen. Nebst einem Anhange: Ein Blick auf die neuesten Bearbeitungen des Lebens Jesu* (Breslau: Schlettersche Buchhandlung, 1864), 156.

27. Hartwig Hirschfeld, Preface, *Composition and Exegesis of the Qur'an* (London: Royal Asiatic Society, 1902), ii.

28. Heinrich Graetz, *Geschichte der Juden,* 9 vols. (Berlin, 1820–28), 5:101.

29. Heinrich Heine, "Almansor," *Saemmtliche Werke,* ed. Hans Kaufmann (Munich: Kindler Verlag, 1964), vol. 4.

30. Hermann Cohen, *Religion der Vernunft,* 107–8: "Die jüdische Philosophie des Mittelalters erwächst nicht sowohl aus dem Monotheismus des Islam, als vielmehr aus dem ursprünglichen Monotheismus, und höchstens kann die Verwandtschaft, die zwischen dieser Tochterreligion und der der Mutter besteht, die innige Beziehung

verständlich machen, welche intimer als sonstwo zwischen Judentum und Islam sich anbahnt."

31. S. D. Goitein, "Muhammad's Inspiration by Judaism," *Journal of Jewish Studies* (1958), 144–62, 162.

32. Josef van Ess, "Goldziher as a Contemporary of Islamic Reform," in *Goldziher Memorial Conference,* ed. Eva Apor and Istvan Ormos (Budapest: Hungarian Academy of Sciences, 2005), 37–50.

33. Ibid., 38.

34. See G.H.A. Juynboll, *The Authenticity of the Tradition Literature: Discussions in Modern Egypt* (Leiden: Brill, 1969).

35. Gottfried Heuer, "Jung's Twin Brother: Otto Gross and Carl Gustav Jung," *Journal of Analytical Psychology* 46, no. 4 (October 2001), 655–88; Martin Stanton, "The Case of Otto Gross: Jung, Stekel, and the Pathologization of the Protestant," in *Psychoanalysis in its Cultural Context,* ed. Edward Timms and Ritchie Robertson (Edinburgh: Edinburgh University Press, 1992), 49–56.

36. Eran J. Rolnik, *Freud in Zion: Psychoanalysis and the Making of Modern Jewish Identity,* trans. Haim Watzman (London: Karnac, 2012), 45.

37. Gerald Windhager, *Leopold Weiss alias Muhammad Asad: Von Galizien nach Arabien 1900–1927* (Vienna: Boehlau, 2002), 125.

38. Muhammad Asad, *The Road to Mecca* (New York: Simon and Schuster, 1954), 70f.

39. Yossef Schwartz, "On Two Sides of the Judeo-Christian Anti-Muslim Front: Franz Rosenzweig and Muhammad Asad," *Tel Aviv Yearbook of German History* 37 (2009): 77.

40. Sidra Ezrahi, *Booking Passage: Exile and Homecoming in the Modern Jewish Imagination* (Berkeley: University of California Press, 2000), 4.

41. Ibid., 9.

42. Gil Eyal, *The Disenchantment of the Orient: Expertise in Arab Affairs and the Israeli State* (Stanford, CA: Stanford University Press, 2006), 2.

43. Cited by Liora R. Halperin, "Orienting Language: Reflections on the Study of Arabic in the Yishuv," *Jewish Quarterly Review* 96, no. 4 (2006): 481.

44. Joseph Klausner, "Fear," *HaShiloah* (1905); cited by Yaron Peleg, *Orientalism and the Hebrew Imagination* (Ithaca, NY: Cornell University Press, 2005).

45. Amnon Raz-Krakotzkin, "The Zionist Return to the West and the Mizrahi Jewish Perspective," in *Orientalism and the Jews,* ed. Ivan Davidson Kalmar and Derek J. Penslar (Waltham, MA: Brandeis University Press 2005), 162–81, 164.

46. Ibid., 164

47. Menahem Milson, "The Beginnings of Arabic and Islamic Studies at the Hebrew University in Jerusalem," *Judaism* 45, no.2 (spring 1996): 169–83.

48. Klaus Hermann, "Das Bild des Islam im Reformjudentum des 19. und fruehen 20. Jahrhunderts," *Orient als Grenzbereich? Rabbinisches und Ausserrabbinisches Judentum,* ed. Annelies Kuyt und Gerold Necker (Wiesbaden: Harrassowitz, 2007), 217–47.

49. Leora Batnitzky, "Leo Strauss's Disenchantment with Secular Society," *New German Critique* 94 (2005): 106–26.

50. Suzanne Marchand, *German Orientalism in an Age of Empire* (New York: Cambridge University Press, 2008).

51. Patricia Crone, *Roman, Provincial, and Islamic Law: The Origins of the Islamic Patronate* (Cambridge: Cambridge University Press, 1987), appendix 2.

Chapter 11

1. For more details see, L. Sanneh, *Disciples of All Nations: Pillars of World Christianity* (New York: Oxford University Press, 2008).

2. Elliott R. Kendall, *End of an Era: Africa and the Missionary* (London: SPCK, 1978).

3. Fernand Braudel, *Mediterranean and the Mediterranean World in the Age of Philip II,* trans. Sian Reynolds (New York: Harper and Row, 1972).

4. Aylward Shorter, *Cross and Flag in Africa: The "White Fathers" during the Colonial Scramble (1892–1914)* (Maryknoll, NY: Orbis Books, 2006), 2–3.

5. A. W. Lawrence, *Trade Castles and Forts of West Africa* (London: Jonathan Cape, 1963).

6. Ibid., 63–64.

7. Jean Comaroff and John L. Comaroff, *Of Revelation and Revolution,* vol. 1, *Christianity, Colonialism, and Consciousness in South Africa* (Chicago: University of Chicago Press, 1991), 309–10.

8. Alan Cowell, "Christians Are Torn in the Land of Dr. Livingstone," *New York Times,* December 28, 1982, A2.

9. See John Michael Wallace-Hadrill, *The Frankish Church* (Oxford: Clarendon Press, 1983), 386.

10. Rhodes and Liana Lupas, eds., *The Translators to the Reader: The Original Preface to the King James Version of 1611 Revisited* (New York: American Bible Society, 1997), 42.

11. Peter Brown, *The Rise of Western Christendom: Triumph and Diversity, A.D. 200–1000,* 2nd ed. (Oxford: Blackwell, 2003), 14.

12. The translators noted that the Roman Catholic Church had never denied the translatability of Christianity and was not in principle opposed to Bible translation: they only required a written license for it. Actually, Catholics are best fitted to translate the Bible into English. "They have learning, and they know when a thing is well, they can *manum de tabula* ("hands off the tablet," quoting Cicero)." Rhodes and Lupas, *Translators to the Reader,* 44.

13. Ibid., 33–34.

14. Ibid., 54.

15. Ibid., 35.

16. A. L. Rowse, *William Shakespeare: A Biography* (New York: Harper and Row, 1963), 111, 374–75.

17. Rev. G. E. Igwe and M. M. Green, *Igbo Language Course,* book 3, *Dialogue, Sayings, Translation* (Ibadan, Nigeria: Oxford University Press, 1970), 68–70.

18. David Livingstone, *Missionary Researches and Travels in South Africa* (London: John Murray, 1857), 114.

19. Cited in J.F.A. Ajayi, *Christian Missions in Nigeria, 1841–1891: The Making of a New Elite* (Evanston, IL: Northwestern University Press, 1969), 127–28.

20. Ibid., 72.

21. Ibid., 184.

22. 1 Peter 1: 4.

23. Ajayi, *Christian Missions in Nigeria,* 224.

24. Rhodes and Lupas, *Translators to the Reader,* 32.

25. Ajayi, *Christian Missions in Nigeria,* 222.

26. Rev. Mojola Agbebi, *Inaugural Sermon* (New York, 1903), extract in J. Ayo Langley, ed., *Ideologies of Liberation in Black Africa, 1856–1970* (London: Rex Collings, 1979), 72–77. Also S.I.J. Schereschewsky, *The Bible, Prayer Book, and Terms in Our China Missions* (Geneva, NY: W. F. Humphrey, 1888), 6–8. Stephen Neill estimated that the *Book of Common Prayer* has been translated into more than two hundred languages. Stephen Neill, *The Christian Society* (London: Collins, Fontana Library of Theology and Philosophy, 1952), 135.

27. Modupe Oduyoye, "The Planting of Christianity in Yorubaland: 1842– 1888," in Ogbu Kalu, ed., *Christianity in West Africa: The Nigerian Story* (Ibadan: Daystar Press, 1978), 251–52.

28. On the political uses of the Bible in Africa and elsewhere see Philip Jenkins, *New Faces of Christianity: Believing the Bible in the Global South* (New York: Oxford University Press, 2006).

29. Edwin W. Smith, *The Shrine of a People's Soul* (London: Edinburgh House Press, 1929), 195.

30. Ibid., 195–96.

31. Ibid., 196.

32. Diedrich Westermann, "The Place and Function of the Vernacular in African Education," *International Review of Mission* 14 (January 1925): 26–27, 28. Defending the Bible as an instrument of education in the building of moral character, Thomas Huxley protested against its exclusion in schools in England. "By the study of what other book," he asked, "could children be so humanized?" Cited in Smith, *Shrine,* 198–99.

33. Smith, *Shrine,* 44.

34. Edwin Smith, *The Golden Stool: Some Aspects of the Conflict of Cultures in Modern Africa* (London: Holborn, 1926), 295, 303.

35. Edwin W. Smith, *In the Mother Tongue* (London: British and Foreign Bible Society, 1930), 8. Oliver Wendell Holmes expressed a similar sentiment in pithy words thus: "Language is a solemn thing; it grows out of life, out of its agonies, its wants and its weariness. Every language is a temple in which the soul of those who speak it is enshrined." *Professor of the Breakfast Table* (New York: Dutton, 1906), 40.

36. For a discussion of how language origins might be located in a single universal tongue, see Robert Wright, "Quest for the Mother Tongue: Is the Search for an Ancestor of all Modern Languages Sober Science or Simple Romanticism?" *The Atlantic* (April 1991), 39–68.

37. J. H. Oldham, "Educational Policy of the British Government in Africa," *International Review of Mission* 14 (1925): 421–27.

38. P.N.C. Molokwu, "Vernacular in Ishan Schools," in *Nigerian Teacher* 1, no. 5 (1935): 53.

39. Abubakar Tafawa-Balewa, "The City of Language," *The Nigerian Teacher* 1, no. 4 (1935): 52.

40. Molokwu, "Vernacular I Ishan Schools," 54.

41. Ibid., 53–55, 54.

42. Todd M. Johnson and Kenneth R. Ross, eds., *Atlas of Global Christianity* (Edinburgh: Edinburgh University Press, 2010). See also the statistical summaries at the end of this essay.

43. J.D.Y. Peel, *Aladura: A Religious Movement among the Yoruba* (London: Oxford University Press for the International African Institute, 1968). See also the same author's *Religious Encounter and the Making of the Yoruba* (Bloomington: Indiana University Press, 2000).

44. David B. Barrett, *Schism and Renewal in Africa* (Nairobi: Oxford University Press, 1968).

45. Andrew F. Walls, "From Christendom to World Christianity: Missions and the Demographic Transformation of the Church," *The Cross-Cultural Process in Christian History* (Maryknoll: Orbis Books, 2002), chap. 3, 49–71. Also Todd M. Johnson and Sandra S. Kim, "The Changing Demographics of World Christianity," available at World Christian Database, www.worldchristiandatabase.org. Also see a companion piece, Todd Johnson and Sun Young Chung, "Tracking Global Christianity's Statistical Centre of Gravity AD 33–AD 2100," *International Review of Mission* 93, no. 369 (2004): 166–81.

46. For a report on new African Pentecostal churches in New York, see Andrew Rice, "Mission from Africa," *New York Times Magazine*, April 8, 2009.

47. For a summary of the history of Bible translation see L. Sanneh, *Translating the Message: The Missionary Impact on Culture,* 2nd ed. (Maryknoll: Orbis Books, 2009).

48. Lewis writes, "The truth is that if we are to have translation at all we must have periodical re-translation. There is no such thing as translating a book into another language once and for all, for a language is a changing thing." C. S. Lewis, *God in the Dock: Essays on Theology and Ethics,* chapter 10, "Modern Translations of the Bible" (Grand Rapids, MI: Eerdmans, 1970), 230–31.

49. Fiona Macleod [William Sharp], *Winged Dynasty: Studies in the Spiritual History of the Gael* (London: Chapman and Hall, 1904), 223.

Chapter 12

1. Solomon Schechter, "The Seminary as a Witness" (April 26, 1903), in *Seminary Addresses and Other Papers* (1915; reprint n.p.: Burning Bush Press, 1959), 48.

2. *Church of the Holy Trinity v. United States,* 143 US (226) 1892, 471; David J. Brewer, *The United States a Christian Nation,* Haverford Library Lectures (Philadelphia: John C. Winston, 1905), 39.

3. George Gallup Jr., *The Gallup Poll: Public Opinion 2000* (Wilmington, DE: Scholarly Resources, 2001), 349.

4. *The Gallup Poll Tuesday Briefing* (January 2005), 96.

5. Reported in Cindy Crosby, "Not Your Mother's Bible," *Publishers Weekly,* October 30, 2006, 29.

6. Garry Wills, "Mason Weems, Bibliopolism," *American Heritage* (February–March 1981), 68.

7. Robert Alter, *Pen of Iron: American Prose and the King James Bible* (Princeton: Princeton University Press, 2010).

8. *The Original Feminist Attack on the Bible (The Woman's Bible),* ed. Barbara Welter, 2 vols. (1895, 1898; reprint New York: Arno, 1974), 2:200–201.

9. Benjamin Trumbull, *A Discourse* (New Haven, CT: Thomas & Samuel Green, 1773); David Ramsay quoted in *Princetonians 1748–1768,* ed. James McLachlan (Princeton: Princeton University Press, 1976), 518.

10. *The Presidents Speak: The Inaugural Addresses of the American Presidents from Washington to Nixon,* ed. Davis Newton Lott, rev. ed. (New York: Holt, Rinehart and Winston, 1969), 270, 271, 283.

11. William J. Clinton, "Acceptance Speech to the Democratic National Convention," the American Presidency Project at www.presidency.ucsb.edu/shownomination. php?convid=7, April 5, 2006.

12. Quotations are from "Second Inaugural Address," *The Collected Works of Abraham Lincoln,* ed. Roy P. Basler, 9 vols. (New Brunswick, NJ: Rutgers University Press, 1953), 9:332–33.

13. Quotations are from Martin Luther King Jr., *I Have a Dream: Writings and Speeches that Changed the World,* ed. James Melvin Washington (San Francisco: HarperSanFranciso, 1992), 102–6.

14. The categories are adapted from Joseph R. Fornieri, *Abraham Lincoln's Political Faith* (DeKalb: Northern Illinois University Press, 2003), 38–69.

15. See especially, A. E. Elmore, *Lincoln's Gettysburg Address: Echoes of the Bible and Book of Common Prayer* (Carbondale: Southern Illinois University Press, 2009).

16. William Jennings Bryan, "Speech Concluding Debate on the Chicago Platform," in *The First Battle: The Story of the Campaign of 1896* (Chicago: W. B. Conkey, 1896), 206.

17. David L. Chappell, *A Stone of Hope: Prophetic Religion and the Death of Jim Crow* (Chapel Hill: University of North Carolina Press, 2004).

18. For further treatment of biblical arguments about slavery, see Mark A. Noll, *The Civil War as a Theological Crisis* (Chapel Hill: University of North Carolina Press, 2006), 31–50.

19. Quoted in Stephen Ward Angell, *Bishop Henry McNeal Turner and African-American Religion in the South* (Knoxville: University of Tennessee Press, 1992), 256.

20. See Ray Allen Billington, *The Protestant Crusade: A Study of the Origins of American Nativism* (1938; reprint Chicago: Quadrangle, 1964), 220–37.

21. *The Papers of Woodrow Wilson,* vol. 23, *1911–1912,* ed. Arthur S. Link (Princeton: Princeton University Press, 1977), 11.

22. Ibid., 15–16.

23. *Papers of Wilson,* vol. 36, *January–May 1916,* ed. Arthur S. Link (Princeton: Princeton University Press, 1981), 631.

24. Examples are found in *Religion and State in the American Jewish Experience,* ed. Jonathan D. Sarna and David G. Dalin (Notre Dame: University of Notre Dame Press, 1998).

25. David Gelernter, "Americanism—and Its Enemies," *Commentary* (January 2005): 41–48, 42.

26. Schechter, "Abraham Lincoln" (lecture on February 11, 1909), in *Seminary Addresses,* 156–57.

27. For more details on these efforts, see Mark A. Noll, "The Bible, Minority Faiths, and the Protestant Mainstream," in *Minority Faiths and the Protestant Mainstream,* ed. Jonathan Sarna (Urbana: University of Illinois Press, 1998), 200–204.

28. Quotations in the next paragraphs are from Schechter, "The Seminary as a Witness," 48–50.

29. *New Testament with Psalms and Proverbs, New Revised Standard Version* (Cambridge: Cambridge University Press, 1989), ix.

30. Apologies to H. M. Kuitert, *Everything Is Politics But Politics Is Not Everything* (Grand Rapids, MI: Eerdmans, 1986).

Contributors

Peter Brown, Philip and Beulah Rollins Professor of History emeritus at Princeton University, has played a foundational role in shaping the field referred to as late antiquity (250–800 AD), the period during which Rome fell, the three major monotheistic religions took shape, and Christianity spread across Europe. Professor Brown's primary interests are the transition from antiquity to the Middle Ages and the rise of Christianity. He is the author of a dozen books, including *Augustine of Hippo* (1967, 2000), *The World of Late Antiquity* (1971), *The Cult of the Saints* (1982), *The Body and Society: Men, Women, and Sexual Renunciation in Early Christianity* (1988, 2008), *Power and Persuasion in Late Antiquity: Towards a Christian Empire* (1992), *Authority and the Sacred: Aspects of the Christianization of the Roman World* (1995), *The Rise of Western Christendom* (1996, 2003), *Poverty and Leadership in the Later Roman Empire* (2002), and most recently, *Through the Eye of a Needle: Wealth, the Fall of Rome, and the Making of Christianity in the West, 350–550 AD* (2012).

Nina Caputo, associate professor in the Department of History at the University of Florida, is a scholar of medieval Jewish history and interfaith relations in medieval Europe. Her first book, *Nahmanides in Medieval Catalonia: History, Community, Messianism* (2007), explores the history of encounters between Jewish and Christian interpretations of history and redemption. She is currently working on a book that uses Petrus Alfonsi to explore the figure of the convert and conversion narratives in the Middle Ages. She is also working on a short study of medieval commentaries on Genesis 6:1–4 and the motif of the *nephiliim*.

Carlos Eire, Riggs Professor of History and Religious Studies at Yale University, specializes in the social, intellectual, religious, and cultural history of late medieval and early modern Europe, with a focus on both the Protestant and Catholic Reformations, the history of popular piety, and the history of death. His publications include *War against the Idols: The Reformation of Worship from Erasmus to Calvin* (1986), *From Madrid to Purgatory: The Art and Craft of Dying in Sixteenth Century Spain* (1995), and *A Very Brief History of Eternity* (2010). His autobiographical work, *Waiting for Snow in Havana* (2003), won the National Book Award in Nonfiction, and his latest memoir, *Learning to Die in Miami* (2010), explores the exile experience. He is currently researching attitudes toward miracles in the sixteenth and seventeenth centuries.

Susanna Elm is professor of history and classics at the University of California, Berkeley. Elm's primary research interests are the Later Roman Empire and its transformation into a Christian Empire. She has also published on the relation between religion and contemporary and ancient medicine. In addition to numerous articles and edited volumes, she is the author of *"Virgins of God": The Making of Asceticism in*

Late Antiquity (1994, 1996, 1999, 2003) and, most recently, *Sons of Hellenism, Fathers of the Church: Emperor Julian, Gregory of Nazianzus, and the Vision of Rome* (2012). Her next major project will be on the role of slavery in the formation of Christianity.

Anthony Grafton is Henry Putnam University Professor of History at Princeton University. His special interests lie in the cultural history of Renaissance Europe, the history of books and readers, scholarship and education in the West from Antiquity to the nineteenth century, and the history of science from Antiquity to the Renaissance. His books include *Joseph Scaliger: A Study in the History of Classical Scholarship,* 2 vols. (1983–93), *Christianity and the Transformation of the Book: Origen, Eusebius, and the Library of Caesarea,* with Megan Williams (2006), *Worlds Made by Words: Scholarship and Community in the Modern West* (2009), *Cartographies of Time: A History of the Timeline* (2010), with Daniel Rosenberg. *"I have always loved the holy tongue": Isaac Casaubon, the Jews, and a Forgotten Chapter in Renaissance Scholarship* (2011), with Joanna Weinberg, and *The Culture of Correction in Renaissance Europe* (2011). He is currently studying early modern efforts to reconstruct the Passover Seder that Jesus and his disciplines were widely thought to have celebrated on the night of the Last Supper.

Susannah Heschel is the Eli Black Professor of Jewish Studies at Dartmouth College. Her scholarship focuses on Jewish-Christian relations in Germany during the nineteenth and twentieth centuries, the history of biblical scholarship, and the history of anti-Semitism. Her numerous publications include *Abraham Geiger and the Jewish Jesus* (1998), which won a National Jewish Book Award; *The Aryan Jesus: Christians, Nazis, and the Bible in Nazi Germany* (2008); and the edited volumes, *Moral Grandeur and Spiritual Audacity: Essays of Abraham Joshua Heschel* (1997) and *Insider/Outsider: American Jews and Multiculturalism* (1998). She has received four honorary doctorates and numerous awards and fellowships, including a Carnegie Scholar's Grant in Islamic Studies, grants from the Ford Foundation, and a Rockfeller Fellowship at the National Humanities Center. In 2011–12 she was a fellow at the Wissenschaftskolleg zu Berlin. She is currently writing a book on the history of Jewish scholarship on Islam.

Phyllis Mack is professor of history at Rutgers University and a member of the core faculty of the Department of Women's and Gender Studies. Her research focuses on European and women's history and history of religion, and she is interested in seventeenth- and eighteenth-century popular religion and gender in England and America. Her publications include *Visionary Women: Ecstatic Prophecy in Seventeenth-Century England* (1992), which won the Berkshire Conference of Women Historians Book Prize in 1993; the coedited volume, *In God's Name: Genocide and Religion in the 20th Century* (2001); and most recently, *Heart Religion in the British Enlightenment: Gender and Emotion in Early Methodism* (2008).

Kenneth Mills is professor of history at the University of Toronto. A historian of colonial Latin America and the early modern Spanish world, his work focuses on religious change and the emergence of local Christianities in Spanish South America. His publications include *Idolatry and Its Enemies: Extirpation and Colonial Andean Religion, 1640–1750* (1997, 2012), and *Colonial Latin America: A Documentary History* (2002), edited with William B. Taylor and Sandra Lauderdale Graham. With Anthony Grafton he has coedited the collections *Conversion: Old Worlds and*

New and *Conversion in Late Antiquity and the Early Middle Ages: Seeing and Believing* (both 2003). His multidisciplinary, multiauthor *Lexikon of the Hispanic Baroque: Transatlantic Exchange and Transformation,* edited with Evonne Levy, was published by the University of Texas Press in 2014. He is currently writing a book about and around the transatlantic journey of a Castilian image maker and alms gatherer, Diego de Ocaña (ca. 1570–1608).

David Nirenberg is Deborah R. and Edgar D. Jannotta Professor of Medieval History and Social Thought at the University of Chicago, and the director of the university's Neubauer Family Collegium for Culture and Society. His most recent book, *Anti-Judaism: The Western Tradition,* was published by W. W. Norton in 2013, and traces the uses of Judaism as a figure of thought from Ancient Egypt to the 1950s. His earlier *Communities of Violence: Persecution of Minorities in the Middle Ages* (1996) examines the complex interfaith relations between Jews, Christians, and Muslims in late medieval Spain and southern France. He has also coedited a number of books, including *Judaism and Christian Art: Aesthetic Anxieties from the Catacombs to Colonialism* (2011) with Herbert L. Kessler. He is currently working on a study of the collapse of religious pluralism and the emergence of genealogical models of religious identity in Iberia from 1300 to 1500.

Mark A. Noll is Francis A. McAnaney Professor of History at University of Notre Dame. His research concerns mostly the history of Christianity in the United States and Canada, especially race, religion, and politics as intersecting and at times intertwined modes of discourse. His publications include *The Scandal of the Evangelical Mind* (1994), *America's God: From Jonathan Edwards to Abraham Lincoln* (2002), *The Civil War as a Theological Crisis* (2006), and most recently *God and Race in American Politics: A Short History* (2009). He is currently working on a history of the Bible in American public life.

David B. Ruderman is Joseph Meyerhoff Professor of Modern Jewish History and the Ella Darivoff Director of the Center for Advanced Judaic Studies at the University of Pennsylvania. His many publications include *Kabbalah, Magic, and Science: The Cultural Universe of a Sixteenth-Century Jewish Physician* (1988), *Jewish Thought and Scientific Discovery in Early Modern Europe* (1995, 2001), and *Jewish Enlightenment in an English Key: Anglo-Jewry's Construction of Modern Jewish Thought* (2000). His most recent books are *Connecting the Covenant: Judaism and the Search for Christian Identity in Eighteenth-Century England* (2007), and *Early Modern Jewry: A New Cultural History* (2010), which also received the National Jewish Book Award in history in 2011.

Lamin Sanneh, D. Willis James Professor of Missions and World Christianity and professor of history at the Yale University School of Divinity, has published broadly in such diverse fields as the study of race, interfaith relations, and secularism. His many publications include *Piety and Power: Muslims and Christians in West Africa* (1996); *Faith and Power: Christianity and Islam in "Secular" Britain,* with Lesslie Newbigin and Jenny Taylor (1998); *Abolitionists Abroad: American Blacks and the Making of Modern West Africa* (2000); *Whose Religion Is Christianity? The Gospel beyond the West* (2003); *Disciples of All Nations: Pillars of World Christianity* (2008); *Translating the Message: The Missionary Impact on Culture* (2009); and his memoir, *Summoned from the Margin: Homecoming of an African* (2012). With Joel A. Carpenter he coedited the volume *The Changing Face of Christianity: Africa, the West, and the World* (2005). He has just finished writing a new book, *Beyond Jihad: Islam and Society in West Africa.*

Andrea Sterk is associate professor of history at the University of Florida. A historian of ancient and medieval Christianity, her primary research has focused on monks, bishops, and processes of Christianization in late antiquity. Her publications include *Renouncing the World Yet Leading the Church: The Monk-Bishop in Late Antiquity* (2004), and the sourcebook *Readings in World Christian History: Earliest Christianity to 1453,* with John Coakley (2004). She has also published *John Comenius: The Labyrinth of the World,* with Howard Louthan (1998), and edited the volume *Religion, Scholarship, and Higher Education: Perspectives, Models, and Future Prospects* (2002). She is currently writing a book on eastern Christian mission after Constantine, focusing on mission from below.

John Van Engen, Andrew V. Tackes Professor of History at the University of Notre Dame and former director of Notre Dame's Medieval Institute (1986–98), is a historian of religious and intellectual life in the European Middle Ages. He has focused on twelfth-century church reform movements and on late medieval mysticism and devotional practices. His books and essays have dealt with monasticism, women's writing, schools and universities, inquisition, canon law, notions of reform, and medieval religious culture generally. Many of his articles have been republished in *Religion in the History of the Medieval West* (2004). His most recent book is *Sisters and Brothers of the Common Life: The Devotio Moderna and the World of the Later Middle Age* (2008).

INDEX

abolitionism, 153, 200, 211, 212
Abrahamic Religions, 5, 65, 71, 74
Acosta, Jose de, 123–25, 128, 129
Acts, 73, 116, 117, 119, 154, 166, 189
Adam and Eve. *See* Fall
Africa: colonialism in, 171; growth of
    Christianity in, 185–87, 188, 198–200;
    Islam in, 177, 185, 186, 199, 200;
    North Africa, 177, 185, 186; religion
    in, 1, 6–8, 45, 185; sub-Saharan Africa,
    186, 199; translation of Bible in,
    191–97, 201; and vernacular
    education, 198
African-Americans, 207, 212–15
agency, 76, 138, 170, 194; female agency,
    153–55, 167; and study of religion,
    4, 5, 7, 9
agnosticism, 2, 3
Alexander II (pope), 59
Alexandria, 24, 35, 36
alms: alms collection, 117, 121, 128, 129,
    131, 152; almsgiving, 32–40, 42, 43,
    45, 46
Ambrose of Milan, 17, 23, 24, 70
American Bible Society, 206, 214
American Revolution, 6, 200; and the
    Bible, 208
Amsterdam, 83, 86, 88, 89, 93, 97
Andes, 117, 121–23, 125, 127
Angels, 41, 43–44, 46, 175
Anglican Church, 152, 162
Anselm of Canterbury, 57
Anthony of Egypt, 35–37, 51, 120
anthropomorphism, 169, 172, 176, 184
antipaganism, 176
antisemitism, 171, 181
apocalypticism, 5, 59, 184
apocryphal literature, 73, 236n24,
    249n16
apostasy, 15–17, 21–25, 29, 30, 92. *See also*
    conversion
Apostolic Ideal: and labor, 52, 55, 56,
    61; and miracles, 138, 139; narrative
    tradition of, 9, 117, 119, 121, 130, 131;

and translation, 189, 190; and wandering,
    34–36, 116
Arabic: Bible translation into, 188; Christian
    study of, 92, 103, 111; and Hebrew
    language in the Qur'an, 73, 74; Jewish
    literature in, 172; Jewish study of, 111,
    172, 173, 177, 178, 181, 182
Arabs, 72, 180, 181, 182
Aramaic, 73, 94, 97, 99, 100, 104
Aristotle, 18, 22, 30, 117
Arminianism, 162
Asad, Muhammad (né Leopold Weiss),
    178–81; conversion of, 180
asceticism, 7; and early modern missionar-
    ies, 120, 126, 131; and labor, 57; mendi-
    cant, 35; and monasticism, 36, 37, 42–45;
    and Protestantism, 147, 157, 166; and
    wandering, 35, 36, 37
Asia, religion in, 1, 35, 45, 46, 200
Athanasius of Alexandria, 36
atheism, 1, 3, 63
Augustine, of Hippo, 17, 23, 24, 70; and
    labor, 48, 49, 51, 52–54, 58, 60; on
    Manichaeanism, 43, 44

Bedouin culture: Jewish adoption of,
    181, 182
begging: monks and, 41, 45, 46, 51,
    61–62
Benedictine monasticism, 48, 50, 51, 53–57
Benedict of Nursia, 48, 53–57, 59–61
Benedict XVI (pope), 23, 66–68, 70, 79
Bernard of Clairvaux, 54, 55, 57, 60, 142
Bible: and American culture, 204–8; and
    American political life, 203, 205, 208–19;
    contested readings of, 8; partisan use of
    in America, 214–19; Polyglot Bible, 101;
    The Woman's Bible, 207. *See also* scriptures
Bible, Christian: and early Christian
    exegesis, 30; and early modern
    missionaries, 117, 119, 128; and female
    preaching, 154, 156, 159, 164, 166; and
    Hebrew Bible, 92, 97; KJV, 188–91, 193,
    204, 206, 212–14; and labor, 49, 54,